A PERFECT PINT'S
BEER GUIDE
TO THE HEARTLAND

MICHAEL AGNEW

University of Illinois Press
Urbana, Chicago, and Springfield

© 2014 by the Board of Trustees
of the University of Illinois
All rights reserved
Manufactured in the United States of America
P 5 4 3 2 1
∞ This book is printed on acid-free paper.

Library of Congress Cataloging-in-Publication Data

Agnew, Michael.
A Perfect Pint's beer guide to the Heartland / Michael Agnew.
    pages cm. — (Heartland foodways)
        ISBN 978-0-252-07827-9 (paperback : alkaline paper) —
        ISBN 978-0-252-09358-6 (e-book)
1. Beer—Midwest—Guidebooks.
2. Breweries—Midwest—Guidebooks.
3. Microbreweries—Midwest—Guidebooks.
I. Title. II. Title: Beer guide to the Heartland.

TP577.A36   2014
663.'420977—dc23   2013045040

CONTENTS

ACKNOWLEDGMENTS

I want to thank the brewers who gave me their time and shared their beer. If there is one thing that I love to do, it's talk about beer. One of the best parts of this process was the opportunity to do so with so many of the passionate individuals who make it.

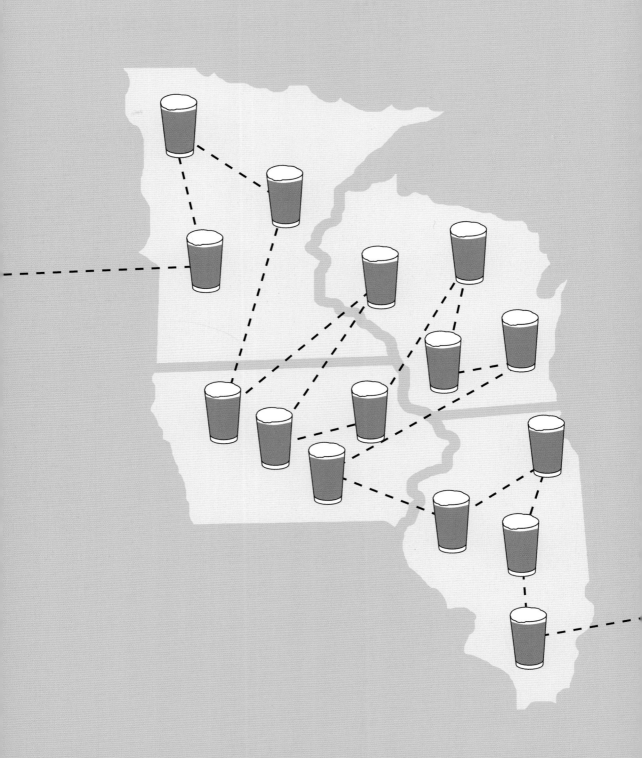

A PERFECT PINT'S BEER GUIDE TO THE HEARTLAND

INTRODUCTION

About four years ago, while savoring a pint with a friend at my favorite local establishment, I first expressed my interest in writing this book. Exciting things were happening in the Minnesota beer scene: New breweries were opening in the Twin Cities and beyond. Restaurants that had not previously given beer a second thought were suddenly adding multiple taps of decent brews, many of them local. As I looked beyond my home state, I realized that the same thing was happening throughout the region. Wisconsin already had a well-developed craft-beer scene that was continuing to evolve. In Chicago, an industry that had barely existed when I moved from there in 2002 was now exploding. And Iowa? What was happening in Iowa? I had no idea, but my curiosity was aroused.

Grandiose as it may now seem, I began to envision the Midwest as the next great beer region—the obvious successor to the Colorado Front Range as the microbrew revolution continued its march from the coasts into the heart of macrobrew territory. I wanted to be a soldier for the cause. I wanted to let everyone in on the excitement that was building around beer in the heartland. That was the impulse that led me to write this book.

Within two weeks after signing a contract with the University of Illinois Press, I hit the road. Starting with the low-hanging fruit, I took short day-trips to nearby breweries in Minnesota and western Wisconsin. I was psyched. I have long loved visiting breweries; I stop at brewpubs everywhere I go. But now my visits had a purpose. Talking with brewers at new and long-established firms, I learned more about the industry in those first few weeks than I had in all my previous years of studying beer. While driving home from one of these early trips, I gushed to my traveling companion, that same friend to whom I had first disclosed my idea, "This is going to be a great year."

Writing a book takes more than evangelical fervor, however. After about six months, the real scope of the project sunk in. I had chosen to write this book during one of the biggest boom times in the history of American brewing. I was committed to visiting, or at least attempting to visit, every brewery in four states in one of the fastest-growing regions of the country.

As the brewery list grew, the pressure I put on myself mounted. The word count and the miles ratcheted up. The deadline loomed. Rather than gushing, I found myself fretting, "What have I gotten myself into?"

As I write these words, I breathe a sigh of relief. Browsing through the hundreds of pictures I took on my journeys has afforded me an opportunity to reflect. After two and a half years, over ten thousand miles, twenty-five hotel rooms, scores of road meals, and countless gallons of beer and gas, the job is done. I have personally visited over two hundred breweries in the region—a reasonable survey, I think. Those that I couldn't visit I interviewed on the phone. The result is the most comprehensive compendium of brewing in the heartland that has been compiled to date. It's an exciting time to be involved with beer.

REGIONAL TRENDS

It is difficult to ascribe an overarching character to the region. It is a mish-mash of people and places, encompassing diverse landscapes from the rural small towns of Iowa, to the lake-studded forests of northern Minnesota and Wisconsin, to bustling urban centers like Chicago. Newcomers from all over the world layer their cultural influences on top of the deep imprint left by earlier German and Scandinavian settlement and even earlier Native American occupation.

If one were to draw generalizations, I think it would be fair to talk about balance. The region is the physical center of the United States, acting like a fulcrum between the East and West Coasts. When trends arrive here from the coasts, they are combined and tempered by our more moderate sensibilities. Midwesterners are a no-frills folk. There's a lack of pretense here. What you see is what you get. We're simple meat and potatoes. Our up-front friendliness is balanced by an underlying reserve. We'll greet you warmly at the door, but we won't necessarily let you into our homes. Our stoic nature is carried over from our Germanic ancestors. But these are only generalizations, an overall pattern discerned when the mosaic is viewed from afar.

So what is the character of midwestern beer? That is almost as difficult to pin down as the region's culture. Each state does things slightly differently. Drawing inspiration from its famous past, Wisconsin is still the land of lagers, with more of the crisp, clean, German-style beers brewed there than in the other three states. But Wisconsin brewers are making plenty of top-notch ales as well. In Minnesota, especially the Twin Cities, it's all about the hops. Bitter is better for beer fans in the Land of Lakes. Iowa takes the opposite approach, tending toward slightly sweeter versions of traditional styles. With its beer industry centered heavily in Chicago, Illinois brewers show a more cosmopolitan influence. Here you find a greater willingness to play and to push at the boundaries. But the straightforward midwestern attitude keeps things grounded even as the flavors of the city's multiple ethnicities infiltrate the beers.

Despite these local differences, the more general regional character can be discerned. Like the people, the region's beers aren't flashy or pretentious. They still reflect that nineteenth-century Germanic heritage. Traditional classic styles are the norm, and balance is key. The majority of beers in the heartland are brewed to appeal to a broad palate. High alcohol, heaps of hops, and experiments with exotic ingredients are more the exception than the rule. Even those breweries with reputations for the extreme, like Surly in Minnesota or Ale Asylum in Wisconsin, have lineups that prove to be more mainstream on closer inspection. As Ale Asylum co-owner Otto Dilba puts it, "Our extremity lies in our aggressive refusal to follow the trends. We believe in making boldly flavored beers brewed according to traditional styles and using only four ingredients: malt, hops, water, and yeast." That statement pretty well sums up the region.

If any one of those traditional ingredients rises above the others across the region, it is malt. The midwestern palate prefers sweet beers over bitter. As markets demand, so brewers produce. Beers across the region generally lean a bit sweeter than their coastal compatriots. Malty Vienna lagers and amber ales abound. Rich and chocolaty porters and stouts are popular picks in all four states. Even traditionally hoppy styles like pale ale and IPA have a more substantial and sweeter malt backbone in the Midwest than in other parts of the country.

This character is best expressed in what I have dubbed the Midwestern IPA, the signature style of the heartland. I encountered it everywhere I went, at breweries and brewpubs large and small. When I mentioned it to brewers, they knew exactly what I meant. The Midwestern IPA has bitterness and hop flavor that are assertive enough for it to be called an IPA, but it remains modest compared to those brewed on the coasts. Lower attenuation leaves behind ample residual sugars, giving it an elevated sweetness that lingers into the finish. This sweetness is balanced by a light bitterness that hangs on with it. Residual sugar also gives the Midwestern IPA a thicker mouthfeel that is markedly distinct from the dryer versions found in other regions. It is an IPA tailored to the temperament and tastes of the region.

But moderate and malty beers aren't all that the region has to offer. From Surly's Abrasive Ale double IPA to the hopped-up Belgian IPAs at the Haymarket in Chicago, there is plenty of the brash and the bitter to be had. And upper Midwest brewers aren't afraid to experiment with unique ingredients. At CIB Brewery in western Iowa, Alex Carlton has crafted a remarkably easy-drinking beer with oranges and Trinidad Scorpion peppers, the world's hottest chilies. At the Whistle Stop in tiny Woodman, Wisconsin, surprisingly tasty creations like mint IPA or red ale with rosewater and rose hips have led brewer Dennis Erb to call his place the "Dogfish Head of Wisconsin," albeit on a small scale.

Barrel aging is common in the region. Everything from beefy barleywine to delicate saison is being put into barrels. All over Iowa you'll find beer aged in Templeton Rye whisky barrels. Elsewhere, brewers are using barrels from Heaven Hill, Koval, and other distilleries. The Goose Island Fulton Street Brewery has one of the largest barrel programs in the country, with entire warehouses full from floor to ceiling with whisky and wine barrels. Sour beers are part of the mix. Goose Island brewmaster Brett Porter and his crew are conducting extensive research into Brettanomyces and bacterial fermentation to aim for more consistent results. Several other breweries in the region also have sour beers in their lineups on a regular or occasional basis.

TIPS FOR BEER TRAVELERS

Two years of intensive beer travel has given me valuable insight into the planning and execution of a successful tour. I humbly offer some of the lessons learned on the road.

Perhaps the most important thing to keep in mind is that beer travel is really all about managing urination. Beer is a diuretic. Copious sampling tests the limits of your bladder. Take the opportunity to relieve the situation whenever it presents itself. Even if you feel it isn't necessary, make one more stop before moving on to your next destination. You'll be glad you did.

Intrepid beer travelers should know that ardent brewery touring can be exhausting. You must learn pacing. On most of my travel days I visited three to four breweries, tasting every beer available. I became quite adept at pacing, seldom finishing all of the samples offered. But with sampling beginning at nine or ten in the morning and going until six or seven at night, by the end of the day I was done. There were times when it would have been nice to sit at the bar to savor a pint and relax at the last stop of the day. Instead, I frequently wound up back in my room contemplating sleep by 9:00.

There will be days when your efforts at pacing fall short. It's helpful to book a hotel room near your last stop. For instance, the Rock Bottom Brewery in Des Moines was my fourth stop on a four-brewery day. Head brewer Eric Sorensen had fifteen beers on tap. Having just finished a weeklong celebration of strong beers, at least seven of them were 9 percent alcohol or above. My notes from that night become less legible with every beer sampled. About two-thirds of the way through, I scribbled the desperate words, "I will get through this." By a lucky coincidence, one that I was not aware of when I reserved the room, my hotel was a mere half-mile away.

If you're making multiple stops in a day, plan your visits around meals. Visit breweries in the morning and afternoon. Stop at brewpubs during meal times—you'll kill two birds with one stone, visiting a brewery and keeping yourself fueled up. Plus, you won't have to take time for a separate stop at some less satisfying fast-food joint.

Be wary of going to the brewer's home for a tasting of cellared beers at the end of your visit. It will likely lead to a rough morning. And that is all that I will say about that.

Chat people up. Bartenders can offer a wealth of knowledge about a brewery and its beers. Regular patrons will give you a deeper sense of what makes each place unique, one that can't be gleaned from a couple hours sitting by yourself at the bar. Brewers love to talk about beer. In the rare moments when they aren't too busy making it, they are usually more than willing to discuss it. When brewers ask for your opinion about their beer, they generally really want to hear it. But if they don't ask for it, don't offer it—unless, of course, it's positive.

Finally, make an effort to get off of the interstate. As seen from the interstate, the Midwest is as boring as its reputation. The only way to truly experience the region is to take the back roads. One of my greatest pleasures in researching the book was moving from brewery to brewery along the two-lane state and county roads that wind casually through the beautiful birch and pine forests of the far north and carry you up and down the undulating hills of the Driftless Region in southwestern Wisconsin. Even the relentless flatness of central Illinois is tolerable on the small roads. The back roads offer a chance to relax, slow down, and let your thoughts expand. There's no need to rush; you're traveling for beer. Back roads are the only way to reach many of the breweries in this book, so you have a good excuse to take them. Follow the beer.

A FINAL THOUGHT

I'm told that in the 1990s, the famed beer writer Michael Jackson set out to create a guide to the breweries and brewpubs of the midwestern United States. He reportedly abandoned the project when the pace of new brewery openings became too much for him to track. I know exactly how he felt. When I began this journey in November 2010, I compiled the most up-to-the-minute list I could manage, consulting multiple resources to unearth every last brewery that had beer in a bottle or a glass in the four states I was to cover. There were just over 160 entries on that list. When I submitted the first version of the manuscript in June 2012, there were more like 185, with at least ten more set to open by the end of the year. Over that eighteen-month period, some twenty-seven new breweries opened. Only two closed.

Because I wanted this to be the most up-to-date and complete survey of the region's breweries that was possible, I felt obligated to include all of them that were actually making beer. That meant trying to visit them all. As soon as I would check one part of a state off the list, a quick survey of my sources would reveal that a return was already required. I found myself wishing that the words would flow faster and that real life would quit interfering so that I could complete the thing before any more opened. And if it wasn't new breweries opening, it was brewers moving from place to place. I interviewed four different brewers at one brewpub, requiring four rewrites of the profile. Many times I expressed my wish that everyone would just sit tight for a couple of months to let me finish. They would be free to do as they wished after I turned in my manuscript. As that moment approached, I had a discussion with Bill Regier, the director of the University of Illinois Press, about a list of breweries that was to accompany the manuscript. He told me, "Don't number the list, in case you want to add more while the manuscript is with our readers." My brain seized. I knew the flood that was about to occur.

I did add more. By March 2013 the list was up to 236. But if there was to ever actually be a book, the process had to end at some point. A line had to be drawn. It's a line that demarcates an arbitrary date more than any concrete development in the industry. Therefore, this book should be viewed as a snapshot in time. Many of the breweries listed as "in planning" will have opened by the time you read this; some may have been only weeks away when the line was drawn. Other upstarts as yet unknown to me have likely taken their place in line. It is at once frustrating and exhilarating to accept that the book is already out of date. I guess I'll just have to hit the road again.

THE RISE OF THE MEGABREWERIES
AFTER PROHIBITION

The middle part of the twentieth century was a diffi-cult time for the American beer industry. The period saw the number of companies making beer in the United States fall from 1,345 in 1915 to only forty-four in 1980. Industry experts at the time predicted that by the end of the century there would be only five. Closings and consolidation led to increasing concen-tration of market share to just a few large firms. By 1980, the top ten breweries controlled 94 percent of the U.S. beer market; 75 percent of the market was controlled by the top five.

The root causes of this concentration are com-plex. By the end of the nineteenth century, a few of the larger regional breweries had begun using the railroad lines to expand their distribution areas. They took advantage of economies of scale to produce beer at lower cost than their smaller, local competitors. When the Volstead Act outlawed the production of alcoholic beverages in 1919, it dealt a devastating blow to those smaller producers. Only 331 breweries reopened when Prohibition was repealed in 1933. Fac-ing a vastly diminished competition, the large brew-eries emerged strong, but regulatory pressures and the continued threat of prohibition restrained them from pursuing aggressive competitive practices. They turned instead to capacity building and investments in greater efficiency to further lower costs. When regulatory threats were lifted during and after World War II, they expanded their market areas to take ad-vantage of excess capacity. Continued low demand after the war left vast amounts of unused capacity, which in turn led to the resumption of aggressive marketing practices that the smaller breweries were unable to counter. Most of them either succumbed to the pressure or were swallowed up by their bigger counterparts.

THE BREWING INDUSTRY
BEFORE PROHIBITION

To understand how this came about, it is helpful to know a bit about the beer industry before Prohibition. By the 1860s, beer in the United States was big busi-ness, and it was experiencing unprecedented growth. An influx of immigrants from beer-drinking nations like Germany, Ireland, and Britain, along with increas-ing urbanization and industrialization and the higher wages that accompanied it, led to a rapid rise in beer consumption. Between 1865 and 1915, per capita con-sumption increased from just over three gallons to nearly nineteen gallons annually. During the same period, the industry saw annual production rise from 3.7 million barrels to nearly sixty million barrels. By 1910, brewing had become one of the leading manu-facturing industries in the country.

The industry was split into small geographic re-gions that were dominated by a few larger regional players. The consolidation that would accelerate after Prohibition was already under way. Despite the increase in consumption, the number of breweries declined from 3,286 in 1870 to 1,345 in 1915. As tech-nological advances in brewing allowed for greater efficiency, a smaller number of brewers were able to produce ever greater volumes of beer. Those brewer-ies that could afford to invest in equipment upgrades were able to achieve economies of scale to lower costs, making them significantly more competitive. This forced many smaller producers to exit the industry.

Beer consumption at the time was primarily cen-tered in saloons. The "tied-house" system, in which breweries owned or controlled the saloons, allowed breweries with sufficient capital to invest in large sa-loon holdings, thereby insuring control of the market in particular areas. Some smaller breweries consoli-dated and combined their saloon holdings in an effort to remain competitive.

The expansion of the railroads facilitated the rise of regional "shipping breweries," which invested in massive expansions of production scale and distribu-tion area to control ever larger percentages of the re-gional market. These companies, among them Pabst in Milwaukee and Anheuser-Busch in St. Louis, be-came the first nationally oriented breweries. Although this development exerted pressure on smaller produc-ers, all was not lost for them. Despite the big brewers' lower production costs, the expense of shipping led to price equilibrium for delivered goods, which allowed many of the local brewers to remain competitive and profitable.

THE PROHIBITION YEARS

The start of Prohibition in 1919 brought this vibrant industry to a screeching halt. For many brewers, the only option was to sell off equipment, often at a loss, and get out. Others were able to remain open by converting their businesses to other purposes. Some turned to dairy processing or the production of soft drinks, malt syrup, and "near beer." Miller Brewing Company in Milwaukee went into real estate and leased out its massive refrigerated warehouses for use as cold-storage facilities. Anheuser-Busch even began building trucks.

Many of these alternative industries left the larger breweries well positioned for what was to come after Prohibition's repeal. Some were granted a special license from the federal government to produce alcohol for medicinal purposes. Others turned to the production of malt syrups used in baking and home-brewing or "near beer," often simply a dealcoholized version of their pre-Prohibition product. This allowed them to keep their equipment operational and their brewing staff employed and made it easier for them to get up and running after repeal. Anheuser-Busch's investment in trucks prepared them for the regional expansion that would occur in the 1930s and 1940s. Further, while 85 percent of beer had been kegged for sale in saloons, 80 percent of "near beer" and soft drinks were bottled for consumption at home. This meant a significant investment in high-speed bottling lines—an investment that would pay off as patterns of beer consumption shifted away from saloons following Prohibition.

THE 1930S

On April 7, 1933, President Roosevelt signed a law revising the Volstead Act to allow the sale of beer. In December of that year, the Twenty-first Amendment was ratified, officially ending Prohibition. Beer was flowing once again. But the fourteen-year experiment had taken a toll; only 331 breweries reopened after Prohibition. Those that did survive faced a new set of realities governing the industry. The breweries that were strong before Prohibition were well positioned to come back strong after repeal, and they faced significantly diminished competition. The tied-house system had been replaced by the "three-tier" system

that outlawed direct ownership of retail outlets by producers. Lower personal income during the Depression caused a dramatic decrease in beer consumption from pre-Prohibition levels. What consumption did occur was moving from the saloon to the home. And while Prohibition was no longer the law, pro-temperance sentiment and the threat of government regulation continued to loom large, forcing the industry as a whole to adopt a position of restraint that slowed its growth but also allowed many local breweries to stay afloat.

For the first two years after repeal, the price equilibrium that had existed prior to Prohibition continued. The larger brewers could produce their beer at lower cost—on average, $7.61 per barrel versus $9.65 per barrel for those making less than one hundred thousand barrels annually—but the cost of shipping increased the average per-barrel price of delivered goods to $10.87. This premium price at retail initially allowed local breweries to thrive. By 1935 the number of breweries had risen to 766. But that number would never go any higher and would in fact begin a steady decline as new technologies enabled the shippers to close that price gap through the remainder of the 1930s.

On the production side, the shipping breweries invested in mechanization and larger vessels to increase efficiency and achieve greater economies of scale, boosting their cost advantage vis-à-vis the local producers. On the delivery side, the availability of inexpensive refrigerated trucks enabled them to expand their distribution range beyond the railroad lines. Between 1933 and 1939, for instance, Pabst established six hundred new distribution relationships. With each new wholesale relationship, they reached an average of thirteen new retailers. The introduction of cans in 1935 further reduced shipping costs. They were lighter, easier to stack, and better protected the beer from spoilage. Canning lines were too costly an investment for small breweries to afford, leaving them at a competitive disadvantage.

In 1936, St. Louis–based Falstaff overcame a final technological barrier when it opened a second facility for the production of its flagship brand. The brewing process is finicky, and differences in equipment and water can have a dramatic effect on the flavor of the beer. Prior to 1936, breweries would not attach their brand name to beers brewed at other facilities for fear of damaging the brand reputation. When Falstaff proved the technology, others followed suit. By producing beer in multiple locations, they could reduce the distance it had to be transported and thereby lower the cost of shipping.

Social and economic development during the 1930s further advantaged the large brewers. The Depression left Americans with less money in their pockets. While demand for beer spiked immediately after repeal, it followed a steady decline thereafter. Many small producers were simply unable to sell enough beer to stay afloat. Further, the smaller breweries packaged most of their beer in kegs for sale in saloons. But consumption of beer in saloons was decreasing. The negative reputation of saloons prior to Prohibition and the dangers of speakeasy culture during it had driven drinking into the home. This sentiment coincided with the wider availability of refrigerators, making it more convenient to keep beer at home. Unable to afford costly bottling lines, small brewers were faced with the erosion of their primary sales outlet.

That local breweries weren't driven out of the market entirely during the 1930s is due in no small part to moderation exercised by the large firms. The public remembered industry abuses that led to Prohibition and were in no mood to see a return to the aggressive practices of the past. The Twenty-first Amendment gave states the option to remain dry. Twenty-eight states chose to continue Prohibition or to heavily regulate alcohol. The brewers' fear of a return to Prohibition was very real; they also faced the possibility of increased government regulation. Repeal was sold largely as a Depression-relieving jobs program. Large brewers wanted to avoid being seen as eliminating industry jobs by driving smaller competitors out of business.

To head off these dual threats, the industry regulated itself, creating a Brewers Code that specified restrictions on conduct. Aggressive advertising was discouraged, to avoid raising the ire of a suspicious public. Though production and shipping costs had fallen to a point that the price of delivered goods was competitive, the large breweries kept their prices artificially high to relieve pressure on smaller ones.

By the start of World War II, the smaller breweries were in a tenuous position. Unable to match economies of scale of the large breweries, they incurred higher production costs. Meanwhile, their price advantage at the retail level had evaporated even as those bigger competitors lowered shipping costs and expanded their distribution into formerly safe territory away from rail lines. They were being artificially propped up by the reticence of large brewers to aggressively compete.

WORLD WAR II

During the war years, the smaller breweries were granted a reprieve. As the Depression waned, restraints on the public's personal income were eased. Demand for beer rose dramatically as per capita consumption climbed nearly 50 percent from 1939 to 1945. But the larger shipping breweries were unable to capitalize on this increase. Fear of regulation continued as pro-Prohibition factions sought to restrict alcohol from military bases. A rise of anti-German sentiment in the leadup to the war reminded this German-dominated industry of similar attitudes during World War I that had helped tilt the public in favor of Prohibition. Wartime shortages of raw materials like steel, cork, and ingredients kept them from expanding capacity. The large brewers' market share fell 3 percent during this period, while their smaller competitors thrived.

But as the war went on, many of the restraints that had held the shippers back were lifted. To help pay for the war effort, the federal government placed a heavy tax on beer. The industry's importance as a revenue source began to outweigh its stigma as a social ill. The brewers' concerns about a return to Prohibition ended in 1945 when the federal government ordered an end to a Minneapolis teamsters strike against brewers on the grounds that the strike hindered the war effort. While the reason given publicly for ending the strike was troop morale, behind the scenes the strike was interfering with a much-needed revenue stream.

THE POSTWAR YEARS

As the war drew to a close, the brewing industry projected a large increase in beer consumption. With wartime shortages and concerns about regulation behind them, the big breweries were looking forward to capitalizing on that growth, and they had the wherewithal to do it. Recent advances in brewing chemistry had allowed for the doubling of capacity without significant investment. But they did invest, building capacity all along the line of the brewing process, from brewhouse to bottling line. They committed to operating breweries of unprecedented size, achieving levels of efficiency and economies of scale that lowered costs significantly.

But the expected expansion of the market failed to materialize. In fact, between 1947 and 1958, per capita beer consumption actually declined by 18 percent. Those optimistic projections had been based on pre-Prohibition models that no longer fit the realities of the marketplace. The old model of growth had been based on sale in saloons. After the war, consumers continued to substitute packaged beer for beer sold on draft. The large breweries were slow to pick up on the shift. Increased consumption of soft drinks was also cutting into beer sales, and higher levels of taxation meant that beer prices rose at a more dramatic rate relative to wine and spirits, causing consumers to switch.

The big brewers were caught by surprise, and they found themselves sitting on huge amounts of excess capacity. Failure to operate at capacity lessened economies of scale and increased production costs. To make matters worse, those chemical-process advances that allowed them to increase production also made it possible for smaller breweries to produce higher-quality, more consistent goods at lower cost, creating unexpected competition. The large breweries responded by expanding distribution areas, ramping up price competition, and launching intensive advertising campaigns.

Brewers sought new consumers in expanded markets in order to raise production to fill capacity. Breweries like Pabst, Miller, and Anheuser-Busch became the first truly national breweries by expanding rapidly outward one region at a time. The tactic backfired at first, as expansion required the purchase or construction of breweries in the new regions, further increasing unexploited capacity. Additionally, they faced stiff competition not only from each other but also from midsized breweries with greater brand recognition in the new regions.

To rectify this situation, these newly national players launched massive advertising campaigns to build their brands. While advertising had accounted for a negligible portion of brewery outlays in the 1930s, it increased steadily in the postwar years. Between 1946 and 1951, advertising costs nearly doubled from an industry average of 2.6 percent to 5.1 percent. And they continued to rise through the 1950s, as the large producers engaged in advertising wars against each other. Unable to compete on this scale, the smaller players gradually lost ground. This, combined with stiff price competition, created a one-two punch that put many of them out of business or forced consolidation. The number of breweries dropped 46 percent, from 465 in 1947 to 252 in 1958, and the combined market share of the top five increased from 21.1 percent in 1947 to 30.6 percent in 1958.

This process of closure and consolidation continued unabated until the early 1980s, when a new breed of small breweries began to emerge. In the three decades since then, the rise of the craft-beer movement has brought about a revitalization of the American beer industry. There are currently more breweries operating in the United States than at any time since the late nineteenth century.

MINNESOTA'S BEER:
THE HISTORY OF GRAIN BELT

In 1850, a German immigrant named John Orth established a small brewery at the corner of Marshall Avenue and Twelfth Street in the town of St. Anthony, now the "Nordeast" neighborhood of Minneapolis. His was only the second brewery in the state. But with its opening, he set in motion a chain of events that would weave together the histories of six regional breweries and produce what many consider to be the quintessential Minnesota beer, Grain Belt Premium.

The story of the Grain Belt brand traces the development of the brewing industry in Minnesota and encapsulates the growth, decline, and rebirth of the American beer industry as a whole. Grain Belt was born of the 1890 merger of four of Minnesota's pioneer breweries. It became a national player through the first half of the twentieth century, only to see its fortunes change as competition from bigger brands forced a wave of brewery closures and consolidations beginning in the 1960s. After multiple changes of ownership through the 1970s, the once-mighty brand was relegated to the discount shelves before finally disappearing altogether in 1990, almost a century after it was introduced. The growth of the craft-beer movement in the following decade brought a revival of the American brewing industry, and along with it a revival of the Grain Belt brand.

Ironically, it was competition and consolidation that originally brought Grain Belt into being. In the late nineteenth century, competition from larger breweries and foreign syndicates motivated the merger of four early Minneapolis breweries, John Orth Brewing Company, Heinrich Brewing Association, Germania Brewing Association, and Noerenberg Brewing Company, creating the Minneapolis Brewing Company, the original producers of Grain Belt.

EARLY BEGINNINGS

After brief sojourns in other parts of the country, John Orth settled in St. Anthony and opened Minnesota's second brewery in 1850. He chose a location near the Mississippi River, giving him easy access to likely markets downstream in Minneapolis and St. Paul. Orth's venture was a success. From small beginnings in an eighteen-by-thirty-foot wooden building with a two-and-a-half-barrel brewhouse, it became one of the largest breweries in the state, boasting a 120-barrel brewhouse and producing over seven thousand barrels of beer annually by 1880.

In 1866, John Kranzlein and John Mueller built a brewery at the steamboat landing in Minneapolis. Their riverside location made for easy shipping, allowing them to quickly become one of the city's largest breweries. During the following years, the brewery underwent a series of ownership changes. Mueller left in 1871 to found another brewery, leaving Kranzlein to carry on alone. In 1874 Kranzlein sold the brewery back to Mueller, who had taken on a new partner, Adolph Heinrich. By 1877, Mueller and Heinrich were shipping beer to cities throughout the state. When Mueller sold out in 1884, Heinrich was joined by his three sons, and the business became the Heinrich Brewing Association.

When John Mueller ended his partnership with Kranzlein in 1871, he joined Herman Westphal to build a brewery near Keegan's Lake, west of Minneapolis. Westphal had been a successful ice dealer, and the new brewery was built near his icehouse on a property that reportedly also contained a bowling alley and a dance hall. The partnership of an ice dealer and a brewer made perfect sense, as the cold conditioning of lager beers required large amounts of ice in the days before the advent of mechanical refrigeration. After Mueller's departure in 1874, Westphal ran the brewery himself until 1888, when he sold out to the Germania Brewing Association, a collection of saloon owners who had joined together to gain market leverage against large brewers that controlled a significant number of the state's drinking establishments.

The final core piece of the Grain Belt puzzle began with Anton Zahler, a foreman at St. Paul's Stahlmann Brewery. In 1874 Zahler crossed the river to start a brewery in Minneapolis, just up the Mississippi from the Heinrich plant. An experienced brewery manager, Zahler increased his production fivefold in the first year of operation. In 1877 he was joined by Friederich Noerenberg. The pair built their brewery into the city's fourth largest beer producer. When Zahler died suddenly in 1878, Noerenberg took over and re-organized the company as the Noerenberg Brewing Company.

Two other early breweries that would later play a role in the Grain Belt story were the Jacob Schmidt Brewing Company and the August Schell Brewing Company. The story of the Schmidt brewery began in 1855, when Christopher Stahlmann opened a brewery on Seventh Street in St. Paul—the same Stahlmann Brewery where Anton Zahler gained his expertise prior to opening the Noerenberg Brewery. Stahl-mann's brewery rapidly became the state's largest, producing 1,200 barrels by 1860 and exporting beer to as far away as Memphis. In 1879 he became the first Minnesota brewer to produce more than ten thou-sand barrels in a year, and by 1887 it had reached a capacity of almost twenty-five thousand barrels. Stahlmann's death from tuberculosis in 1883 precip-itated a long series of management changes and buy-outs. The Stahlmann family sold the brewery to the St. Paul Brewing Company in 1897. It was sold again three years later to Jacob Schmidt.

August Schell arrived in the southwestern Minne-sota town of New Ulm in 1856, helping to settle the town with a group of German immigrants called the Turner Society, who practiced a philosophy of "sound mind and sound body." By 1860 Schell had opened his brewery in the Cottonwood River Valley, a site chosen for its access to a strong spring that provided water for brewing. Production in that first year was only two hundred barrels, making it one of the smallest in the state. The brewery survived early hardships such as the 1862 Dakota War, in which more than one hundred buildings in the town were destroyed, in-cluding competing breweries. Increasing settlement in southwestern Minnesota was good for business. By 1870 Schell was producing 1,300 barrels annually.

MINNEAPOLIS BREWING COMPANY

By the late 1880s, Orth, Heinrich, Germania, and No-erenberg were among the largest breweries in the state. But in the face of increasing market incursions from much larger concerns in Milwaukee and St. Louis and brewing syndicates from overseas, none of them was strong enough to compete on its own, so in 1890 these pioneering brewers joined together to form the Minneapolis Brewing and Malting Company. The move consolidated their individual saloon holdings, affording them control of a substantial share of the Minnesota beer market. They continued to operate out of the four original breweries until 1893, when an impressive, castle-like, 150,000-barrel brewery was completed on the site of the old John Orth brewery. The stately brewhouse structure was built in four dis-tinctly different architectural styles, representing the four breweries that made up the company. It was one of the largest breweries in the country at the time. In the same year, the company reorganized as the Min-neapolis Brewing Company and launched its flagship brand, Grain Belt Golden Lager.

The thirty-year period from merger to Prohibition saw the venture grow in leaps and bounds. By the turn of the twentieth century, the brewery was producing over five hundred thousand barrels of Grain Belt an-nually and controlled a third of the saloons in Minne-apolis. To enhance their competitive position vis-à-vis the larger breweries, they sought expanded markets, opening depots throughout Minnesota and in states as far away as Michigan, Montana, and Colorado. The Minneapolis Brewing Company was taking the first steps toward making Grain Belt a national brand.

While Prohibition rang the death knell for many of the old regional breweries, this was not so for the Minneapolis Brewing Company. As Prohibition ap-proached, company assets were transferred to a new entity, the Golden Grain Juice Company. When the Volstead Act outlawed the production of "intoxicating liquors" in 1919, brewery operations were switched to the production of "near beer" and soft drinks.

After the repeal of Prohibition in 1933, the brewery undertook a massive modernization effort and was able to resume production of Grain Belt within a few months. The brand quickly regained market share and during the next two decades experienced a pe-riod of rapid expansion. This included an expansion of the product line. In 1947 Grain Belt Golden Lager was joined by Grain Belt Premium, a lighter-flavored beer created in response to changing consumer tastes following World War II.

By the mid 1950s the brand was at its peak. Annual production of Grain Belt had reached nearly nine hun-dred thousand barrels. It was one of the best-selling brands in Minnesota. The Minneapolis Brewing Com-pany was establishing itself as a major benefactor in the local community. The Grain Belt Bandstand was the site of frequent summer concerts, and Grain Belt Park was a popular gathering place for local families. Located next to the brewery, the park featured lively fountains and tame deer.

Even as it worked to cement its reputation at home, the company never lost sight of its national ambitions. In 1967 it was renamed Grain Belt Breweries Inc. As explained by then-president Frank Kiewel, a scion of another old Minnesota brewing family, "We believe that the old name is too suggestive of a long-ago local business. It does not identify with the name of our product, nor does it suggest the widening area of our marketing opportunities." Distribution of Grain Belt was expanded to include areas as far away as the West Coast and Alaska. Minnesota's beer had gone national.

But trouble was already brewing for the brand. The industry had entered an era of consolidation. Small, local breweries were being bought up by larger regional operations, and these regional breweries were in turn being swallowed up by even larger national concerns. Despite increased distribution, Grain Belt's sales had plateaued and were beginning to slide. Competition from Anheuser-Busch, Miller, and Coors continued to erode market share. In an effort to attract more consumers and compete with new product offerings by these bigger brewers, Grain Belt Breweries lightened the Golden Lager recipe and introduced Grain Belt Light into its product line. But the new brand and lighter flavor failed to catch on. With sales continuing to fall, Grain Belt Breweries Inc. was sold in 1975 to a local investor, who closed the once-mighty Minneapolis brewery and sold the Grain Belt brand to the G. Heileman Brewing Company of Lacrosse, Wisconsin. Production of Grain Belt moved from Minneapolis to the old Schmidt brewery in St. Paul.

THE G. HEILEMAN YEARS

In the years following Prohibition, the Jacob Schmidt Brewing Company became a major regional player. Its flagship brand, City Club, was one of the best-selling beers in the upper Midwest and a serious rival to Grain Belt. Schmidt continued to thrive into the 1950s, when it became an early victim of consolidation. In a story that was repeated many times throughout the country, the Jacob Schmidt Brewing Company was bought out in 1954 by the larger, Detroit-based Pfeiffer Brewing, which was in turn purchased by the even larger Associated Brewing Company in 1962. Finally, in 1972 the brewery and all of its assets ended up in the possession of the G. Heileman Brewing Company.

By 1981, G. Heileman's strategy of buying up smaller regional breweries had made it the nation's fourth largest brewer. But under Heileman's ownership the Grain Belt brand suffered. It became just another brand among the many produced by the conglomerate. Neglect and continued loss of market share, even to other Heileman brands, ultimately landed the once-dominant brand on the supermarket discount shelves. When a series of disastrous management decisions led to Heileman's collapse in 1990, the St. Paul brewery was closed, and any beer remaining in the tanks was poured down the drain. An auction of the company's assets, including its extensive brand portfolio, found no buyers. After nearly a hundred years, the Grain Belt brand had flashed out of existence.

THE MINNESOTA BREWING COMPANY

But change was in the air. While the 1970s saw the number of breweries nationwide fall until it reached an all-time low of eighty in 1983, the 1990s brought the first flood of new breweries in the craft-beer revolution that had begun as a trickle during the 1980s. In Minnesota this rebirth of the small brewery also meant the rebirth of Grain Belt.

In 1991, a group of Twin Cities investors formed the Minnesota Brewing Company. They purchased the Schmidt Brewery and along with it the Grain Belt brands. The new owners set upon a major effort to revitalize the brand. They met with some success. In 1994, Grain Belt Premium won the gold medal for American-style lager beer at the Great American Beer Festival in Denver. The brand was also gaining a following among a new crowd of younger beer drinkers, for whom it had a retro-chic appeal. Grain Belt was making a comeback, but its troubles weren't yet over.

The Minnesota Brewing Company had a rocky existence. Sales of its flagship brands weren't sufficient for the brewery to make efficient use of the two-million-barrel capacity it had purchased from G. Heileman. Contract-brewing beers for other breweries helped take up the slack, but contractors proved fickle, often pulling out of contracts or simply going out of business, leaving the company with tanks full of beer that it couldn't sell. After nine years, financial troubles forced the company into bankruptcy. The Minnesota Brewing Company ceased operations in 2000, and the old Schmidt brewery was shut down for good. Once again, Grain Belt had ceased to exist.

THE AUGUST SCHELL BREWING COMPANY

But the brand proved resilient. As with its previous deaths, this time down did not mean out. Grain Belt was revived again in 2002 by the August Schell Brewing Company.

The August Schell Brewing Company was itself as tenacious as the brand it had bought. It had survived Prohibition by making soft drinks and "near beer." During the 1970s it generated revenue by selling beer packaged in commemorative cans for special events, expanding the scope of the operation to include a hydroponic tomato farm, and even selling for lumber a stand of old-growth walnut trees that grew on brewery property. It emerged from that period of consolidations intact, independent, and still family-owned. When the craft-beer revolution began in the 1980s, Schell's management quickly recognized it as the future of the industry. They began production of more full-flavored beers catering to discerning drinkers in styles that stayed true to their German heritage.

Schell's celebrated the purchase of Grain Belt with a "moving ceremony" at the old Grain Belt brewery building in Nordeast Minneapolis. The original Grain Belt recipe was sealed into a keg and brought from the old brewery to its new home at Schell's. The ceremonial keg is now on display in the Brewing Museum at the Schell brewery.

Schell's immediately set out to revitalize the brand. Because of its battered reputation as a discount beverage, Grain Belt Golden Lager was retired, and the focus went instead to Grain Belt Premium. The brewery launched an ad campaign called "Here's to Local Heroes" that played up the brand's Minnesota heritage by connecting it with local iconic celebrities. Within two years, Grain Belt sales had brought about a doubling of Schell's annual production. The brand that Schell's saved also ultimately saved Schell's. Today, Grain Belt Premium makes up a significant portion of the brewery's output.

The Grain Belt story continues to evolve. In 2010 Schell's launched Grain Belt Nordeast, a nod to the brand's origins in that Minneapolis neighborhood. This darker version of the beer proved so successful that the company was forced to significantly expand capacity to keep up with demand.

AN AFTERWORD ON THE GRAIN BELT BREWERY BUILDING

When Grain Belt Breweries Inc. folded in 1976, the monolithic brewery building in Minneapolis was shuttered. In 1977 it was declared an architectural landmark by the Minneapolis Heritage Preservation Committee. Repeated plans for development on the block were submitted, but they were all rejected by the City of Minneapolis to prevent the building's demolition. The once-proud structure had fallen into serious disrepair when it was finally purchased by the city in 1987. With no one willing to renovate it, the building stood derelict and abandoned for a quarter century.

In 2000 the Ryan Companies, a Minneapolis-based architectural and construction firm, partnered with the Minneapolis Community Development Agency and RSP Architects to restore the historic brewery and convert it into office space. The twenty-two-million-dollar project included thirteen million dollars in public funding to support pollution abatement and historic-element conservation. The building is once again a vital part of the Nordeast neighborhood, housing offices, small businesses, artist studios, cafes, and apartments. The old wagon house and millwright became the Pierre Bottineau branch of the Minneapolis Public Library.

The old brewery office building, located across the street from the brewhouse, was not part of the redevelopment. It remained under city ownership. Repeated attempts to sell the building and an adjacent vacant lot for development found no buyers. The building stood vacant and deteriorating until late 2013 when a bid by Kaas Wilson Architects and Everwood Development was accepted by the city. Work began in November 2013 on the Grain Belt Terrace development project. The renovated office building is to become the headquarters of Kaas Wilson Architects. A 151-unit apartment complex will be built on the vacant lot. The complex will include a small park that will feature the preserved foundation ruins of the original John Orth Brewery.

BREWERY CAVES THEN AND NOW

Every so often, sinkholes appear in the streets and parking lots of Iowa City's old downtown district. While he can't say for certain what's causing them, Marlin Ingalls, an archeological historian at the State Archeologist's Office, has a strong suspicion: networks of vaults and tunnels built in the nineteenth century for the cellaring of lager beer. From the 1850s, the area near the intersection of Linn Street and East Market was home to three breweries, each producing about one thousand barrels of beer annually. In the days before mechanical refrigeration, they needed a way to keep the beer cold as it conditioned. The common practice of the day was to dig caves that kept a constant temperature tens of degrees cooler than at the surface. It is reasonable to assume that each of these historic Iowa City brewers would have had such caves beneath their breweries.

Two of the former breweries are gone—the aboveground structures were demolished in the 1960s—but the subterranean cellars may still exist. The Union Brewery building, the only one still extant, is now a collection of shops called Brewery Square. It has three levels of cellars beneath it, with blinded entries suggesting additional tunnels that run under the streets. Using ground-penetrating radar, Ingalls has discovered a large, rectangular cavity under a nearby parking lot where another of the breweries was located. "It very much affects things today," he says. "For one thing, they haven't been able to build on those lots since those buildings went down because nobody knows what's down there. People know that there are connecting tunnels and things because they do collapse. There has been one collapse in the last decade, I know. You can see where the streets are collapsing around there."

Collapsing streets in Iowa City are not the only way that nineteenth-century brewery caves are having an effect today. These remnants of a bygone era in beer making are being rediscovered and repurposed all over the country and the Midwest. They are being given new utility, serving as everything from meeting rooms to living rooms.

THE HISTORY OF BREWERY CAVES

Lager is one of the two large categories that come under the overarching family of grain-based, fermented beverages that we call "beer." The other one is ale. The main difference between lager and ale is the yeast that is used to ferment them. While ale yeasts ferment at relatively high temperatures, in the sixties to low seventies Fahrenheit, lager yeasts prefer much colder conditions, closer to fifty degrees. The name "lager" comes from the German word "lagern," which means "to store." Lager beers are usually allowed to mature after fermentation at temperatures near freezing for a period of weeks to months. For the brewing of lagers, the ability to maintain the beer at cold temperatures is essential. Before the advent of artificial refrigeration, the easiest way to accomplish this was to keep it in caves where the ambient temperature remained constant and cool.

Lager brewing, and with it beer caves, developed during the Middle Ages in the German-speaking countries of central Europe. It happened almost by accident. At that time, the agent that caused beer to ferment was a mystery. Brewers didn't choose their yeast as they do today. During the warmer months, faster-working ale yeast would dominate, and so brewers produced ale. In the colder winter months, ale yeast went dormant, giving lager yeast the upper hand. The colder temperatures also hindered the growth of beer-spoiling bacteria, meaning that winter-brewed beer tended to last longer. Because of this, Duke Albrecht V of Bavaria decreed that in his realm all brewing had to cease between April 23 and September 29. By default, all beer brewing in Bavaria became lager brewing. Beers brewed near the end of the brewing season had to be preserved through the summer. The common method of achieving this was to "lager," or store them in caves filled with ice harvested from nearby lakes and rivers.

As lager beer gained popularity, the practice of cold fermentation and cold conditioning gradually spread throughout central Europe. By the early 1800s, lager brewing dominated beer production in the region. The clean, crisp profile of lagers made them the beers of choice for drinkers throughout the German-speaking lands.

BREWERY CAVES COME TO THE UNITED STATES

Social upheaval and revolution in the Germanic states of Europe in the mid-nineteenth century brought a wave of German-speaking immigrants to the United States. Between 1830 and 1840, fifteen thousand Germans arrived on American shores annually. The following decade saw that number rise to forty-three thousand. Large numbers of these new arrivals settled in the midwestern states of Iowa, Wisconsin, Minnesota, Ohio, Indiana, Illinois, and Missouri. By 1900, the populations of cities like Cleveland, Milwaukee, and Cincinnati were more than 40 percent German American. Dubuque and Davenport, Iowa, had even larger proportions.

These immigrants represented all strata of German society, from intellectuals and entrepreneurs to skilled tradesmen, farmers, and laborers. Many of them had been forced to emigrate for their participation in revolutionary activities. They were politically adept and good community organizers who quickly assumed prominence in the cities where they settled. German workers came to dominate many of the crafts, while German businessmen built thriving industries.

Once here, the Germans strove to maintain their culture and language. They clustered together in neighborhoods that were frequently referred to as "Germania." Church sermons and school lessons were given in German. They established Turner Societies to promote athletics and healthy living, as well as "Vereine," or clubs dedicated to literature, singing, humor, gymnastics, and other cultural endeavors. German-language newspapers were common and enjoyed large circulation.

One important bit of German culture that the immigrants brought with them was the enjoyment of lager beer. Prior to 1840, there were few if any breweries in the United States making German-style lagers. As the numbers of German immigrants increased, so did the demand for lager beer. Small breweries popped up in towns and cities throughout the Midwest to supply them with it. Cities like Milwaukee, St. Louis, and Dubuque became major centers of lager production. German entrepreneurs like Frederick Pabst, Valentin Blatz, and August Busch created la-

ger-brewing enterprises that would come to dominate the national beer industry. Brewery beer gardens, reminiscent of those in the old country, were popular destinations for family weekend outings.

In the upper Midwest especially, brewers found a hospitable climate for the production of lager. Barley and hops could be locally grown. The winters were cold. Frozen rivers and lakes provided an abundant source of ice to keep the beer cold through the summer. Finally, the regional geography, with a layer of soft sandstone bedrock near the surface, facilitated one of the first tasks these brewers faced: excavating caves in which to cellar their beer.

BREWERY-CAVE CONSTRUCTION

Four hundred and fifty million years ago, a layer of sand was deposited on the bottom of a shallow sea that covered much of what is now the United States. It was brought there by wind and water from older sandstone formations further north. Over millions of years, the action of waves and currents rounded the grains and washed away the softer clays, leaving behind a bed of well-sorted and highly resistant quartz, now known as the St. Peter Sandstone. Geologic uplifting and subsequent erosion caused by glaciers, rivers, and weathering have left this soft rock at or near the surface across much of the upper Midwest.

St. Peter sandstone gave midwestern brewers the perfect medium for digging caves. It is soft and remarkably easy to carve. At the same time, the well-packed, rounded sand grains make it stable and resistant to roof collapse. Because it was relatively near the surface, they didn't have to dig deep.

Brewers built two types of lagering chambers: caves and cellars. Caves are technically defined as any excavated hollow and can refer to both natural and manmade openings. In places where the sandstone layer is exposed, such as the bluffs along the Mississippi River in southern Minnesota, breweries were often built against the cliff face. Brewers could simply excavate caves into the wall behind the buildings. No additional structures or brickwork were needed. Sometimes brewers were able to take advantage of existing, natural caves, expanding and adapting them to suit their needs.

An example of this kind of cliff-wall beer cave can be found in the Bruce Vento Nature Sanctuary along Dayton's Bluff in St. Paul, Minnesota. The North Star Brewery was built against the bluff in 1855, and a natural cave was expanded for storing beer. The cave is now flooded and the entrance gated, but a look inside reveals a perfectly arched, excavated beer cave. Remnants of the brewery's stone walls can still be seen on the bluff next to it.

When no exposed sandstone cliffs were available, brewers dug cellars beneath their breweries. Frequently multileveled, cellars were typically barrel-vaulted structures, the arched ceilings serving to safely distribute the weight of the buildings above through the walls and into the ground below. Most employ a dry-laid voussior arch, a variation in which umortared masonry units of either stone or brick are cut as wedges, with the joined edges defining the radii of the arch's center. The vaulting is a surviving testament to the craftsmanship of German masons of the day. The Union Brewery cellars in Iowa City are a perfect example of this type of construction.

BREWING CAVES TODAY

In 1870, S. Liebmann's Sons Brewing Company in Brooklyn, New York, became the first brewery to install mechanical refrigeration. It was the first commercial use of this new technology, and it marked the beginning of the end for traditional lagering caves. While some smaller breweries continued to use caves for many years—some were still in use as late as the 1970s—their numbers gradually dwindled. By 1891, nearly every brewery in the United States was equipped with refrigeration machines. Many of the disused tunnels were filled in or, like those in Iowa City, simply forgotten. But a few continue to serve useful purposes today.

Some continue to serve as aging cellars, though not always for aging beer. At the Caves of Faribault in Faribault, Minnesota, an old brewery cave is being used to age blue cheese. The cave was built in 1854 by the Fleckenstein Brewing Company and served as a lagering cellar until the brewery was forced to close at the start of Prohibition. In 1936, Felix Frederiksen purchased the cave and began making blue cheese there under the name Treasure Cave. It was the first blue cheese to be manufactured in the United States. Today, Caves of Faribault is the only U.S. cheese maker still curing and aging blue cheese exclusively in caves.

Brewing history is important at the Potosi Brewing Company in Potosi, Wisconsin. It was founded to save an old brewery building and is home to the National Brewing Museum, a vast collection of breweriana and historic brewery artifacts. Its lagering cellar is a classic example of a brewery cave. The buildings sit against a sandstone bluff, and the cave is excavated into the rock behind it. While it currently houses antique brewing machinery, plans have been made to restore it to its original function as the brewery expands its barrel-aging program.

Brewery caves have become popular tourist attractions in Stillwater, Minnesota, and Milwaukee, Wisconsin. Ironically, it's wine that you'll taste in the Joseph Wolf Brewing Company caves on Main Street in Stillwater. The caves and brewery buildings dating to the 1860s now house the Luna Rossa Trattoria and Wine Bar. Thirty-minute tours of the extensive cave system are offered on weekends or can be added to your dining experience by appointment. The restaurant also conducts hosted wine tastings in the caves.

For many, the visit to the cellars is the highlight of the Miller Brewery tour in Milwaukee (aside from tasting beer, of course). In them, the ghost of Frederick Miller emerges from a mural on the wall to explain the history and construction of the caves and their use in the brewing process. The caves at the Miller brewery can also be rented for private functions.

In Galena, Illinois, the cellars of the old City Brewery now serve as a space for private functions and an artist's studio. Pottery artist Charles Fach and his wife Sandy live and work in buildings that once belonged to the brewery. The main structure houses the Stone House Pottery and Gallery—a space for Fach to display and sell his work. The multi-use Artists' Annex occupies the former fermentation and grain-storage areas. A few times a year, the couple offers a two-night pottery class called Glaze and Graze in the cellars beneath the building. On the first night, participants make and glaze a set of ceramic dinnerware. On the second night they are treated to a multicourse dinner in the candle-lit vaults.

The Casanova Beverage Company began making beer in Hudson, Wisconsin, in 1896. The brewery is long gone, but the 150-foot-deep beer cave still exists. Every year it plays host to the Casanova Beer Cave Festival held by the Historic Casanova Liquor store, the site's current owner. Thirty to forty breweries set up shop inside the cave, pouring samples to eager beer fans. The setting makes it one of the most unique, and coolest, summer beer fests in the region. The visceral connection to the history of beer and brewing in the Midwest cannot be overstated. For those interested in beer history, it is an oddly moving experience.

Until 1969, the Bub's Brewery in Winona, Minnesota, made beer at the foot of a limestone pinnacle called Sugerloaf. Bub's beer was lagered in hand-dug caves to the very end. Today the brewery building is occupied by Sugarloaf Antiques and Crafts. Two of the five cave chambers are now used as retail space for the display and sale of antiques. The other three are too damp to use, but current owner Mark Zimmerman, who worked at the brewery in the 1950s, will gladly show them to interested customers.

Retail use could also be in the future for the troublesome cellars under the streets of Iowa City. The Brewery Square building is owned by developer Marc Moen, who has expressed an interest in using them for wine tastings or even turning them into a nightclub. As he told the *Iowa City Gazette* in 2011, "It's too valuable of an asset, to interesting to just say, 'It's down there,' and let it go. We've got to find the right people to make it work."

HOW TO USE THIS GUIDE

Creating a guide to breweries in the heartland is a challenge. The region's beer industry is in the midst of a growth spurt. My master list of breweries was constantly in flux as rumors of new arrivals would surface and upstart breweries would announce their launch. I have been diligent in my attempts to keep up with this rapidly changing landscape. It is possible, however, that some new entries to the region's brewing scene were missed, including those that may have started up after the manuscript was submitted. I apologize for any omissions.

This book is intended as a travel guide. As such, I have only included breweries and brewpubs that have an actual physical facility where brewing occurs. Contract brewers whose beer is produced by another brewery are not profiled. This has meant leaving out some interesting brewers, including some personal favorites. Again, I offer my apologies to those brewers.

For each state there is a section titled "Fermenteries." I define "fermentery" as a place where wort is fermented that is brewed at another facility. The best example is the Granite City brewpub chain that produces all of its wort at a central brewery in Iowa and ships it via tanker truck to the various stores where it is fermented. Because some part of the brewing process occurs at a fermentery, I have included them in the guide. However, since they have no brewery and no actual brewing occurs, they have not been given full profiles.

The guide is divided first by state and then by region. I have attempted to group breweries together in regions that will facilitate easy trip planning. Each brewery profile includes basic information such as brewery name, address, and contact information, the names of the owners and brewers, the year in which the business was established, and the size and make of the brewing system. Breweries and brewpubs frequently change their beer selections, so the beers listed in this guide may not be what you find on your visit. While I do discuss beer quality on occasion, my intent was not to publish a region-wide beer review. I leave that to the reader. Instead, I have attempted to communicate what made each brewery unique to me, whether that was history, the brewer's story, or some other bit of fact or fancy related to the place.

MICHAEL'S PICK: This is not intended as a "best beer" selection. Taste is subjective, and every beer drinker will have their own view on what is a brewer's best. My pick is simply the beer that I enjoyed the most of those available on the day of my visit. It is totally subject to my taste, mood, what I was eating, and any number of other variables. Your own results may vary.

TYPE: Brewery or Brewpub. Breweries produce beer primarily for off-sale, in the retail, bar, and restaurant trade. Brewpubs are typically restaurants that brew beer primarily for sale on the premises.

FLAGSHIP BEER: The brewery's lead product. It could be the beer that the brewery wishes to be identified by, or it may sometimes be the best seller.

YEAR-ROUND BEERS: Those beers that make up the brewery's core production and that are available all year.

SEASONAL BEERS: Limited-release beers that are produced every year in a seasonal rotation.

SPECIAL RELEASES: Occasional releases and one-off products. These are constantly changing, and a particular beer listed may or may not be available during your visit.

TOURS: Some breweries have regularly scheduled times for tours, while many do not. Most brewers are happy to show you around with advanced notice. Be sure to call ahead if you are interested in touring a brewery.

BEER TO GO: Whether or not a brewery or brewpub sells beer for consumption off-site. Laws regulating the off-sale of beer by breweries vary by state and municipality.

FOOD: A simple description of the food offerings at brewpubs or brewery taprooms.

AMENITIES: Extras such as availability of parking, existence of a tasting or taproom, whether or not an establishment has a full bar or food and drink specials.

NEARBY ATTRACTIONS: Things to do when visiting a location, whether beer-related or of tourist interest.

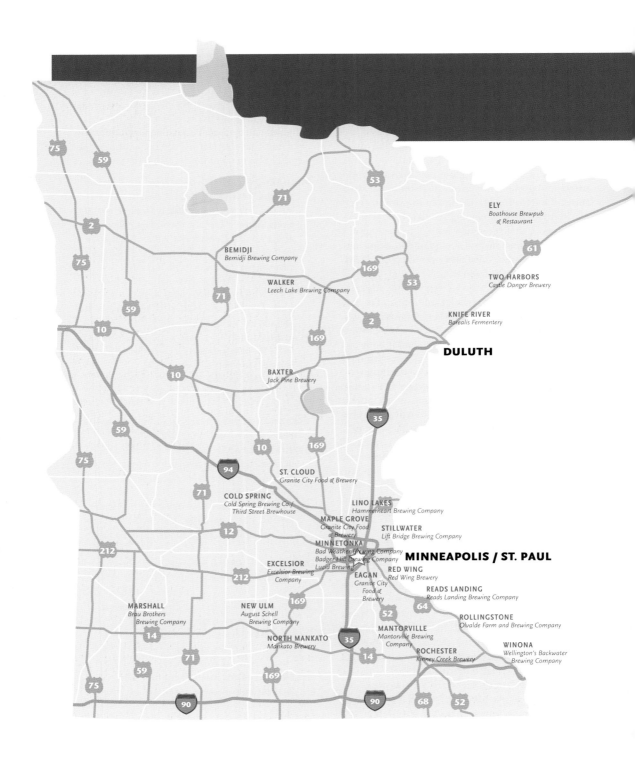

ELY
Boathouse Brewpub & Restaurant

BEMIDJI
Bemidji Brewing Company

WALKER
Leech Lake Brewing Company

TWO HARBORS
Castle Danger Brewery

KNIFE RIVER
Borealis Fermentery

DULUTH

BAXTER
Jack Pine Brewery

ST. CLOUD
Granite City Food & Brewery

COLD SPRING
Cold Spring Brewing Co. / Third Street Brewhouse

LINO LAKES
Hammerheart Brewing Company

MAPLE GROVE
Granite City Food & Brewery

STILLWATER
Lift Bridge Brewing Company

MINNETONKA
Bad Weather Brewing Company
Badger Hill Brewing Company
Lucid Brewing

MINNEAPOLIS / ST. PAUL

EXCELSIOR
Excelsior Brewing Company

RED WING
Red Wing Brewery

EAGAN
Granite City Food & Brewery

READS LANDING
Reads Landing Brewing Company

MARSHALL
Brau Brothers Brewing Company

NEW ULM
August Schell Brewing Company

MANTORVILLE
Mantorville Brewing Company

ROLLINGSTONE
Olvalde Farm and Brewing Company

NORTH MANKATO
Mankato Brewery

ROCHESTER
Kinney Creek Brewery

WINONA
Wellington's Backwater Brewing Company

One of the biggest challenges while creating this book has been keeping the list of breweries up to date as new ones come online, and Minnesota has been one of the biggest problem children in that regard. The state is in the midst of a massive brewery boom. Seven breweries put beer on the street in 2011; 2012 saw the addition of eight more; and 2013 brought another fourteen. As the breweries-in-planning list shows, there are many more waiting in the wings, some of which have likely already opened as you are reading this. It's a great time to be a beer drinker or beer traveler in Minnesota.

The long, slow fuse was lit in 1986, when Mark Stutrud founded Summit Brewing Company in St. Paul. The few years following saw a number of small breweries come and go. In the late 1990s, a wave of brewpubs like Minneapolis Town Hall Brewery and Great Waters Brewing Company in St. Paul piqued the craft-beer appetite of the Twin Cities' drinkers. But the explosion began in 2006, when Surly Brewing Company opened its doors in the Minneapolis suburb of Brooklyn Center. Surly quickly gained an almost fanatical following and introduced a whole new generation to full-flavored beer. Surly was quickly followed by Flat Earth Brewing Company in St. Paul. The movement has steadily picked up steam ever since.

The defining character of Minnesota beer, in contrast to the rest of the region, is hops. Minnesotans love the bitter brews. But the scene offers a wide range of styles and attitudes from breweries large and small, old and new. From Summit's well-crafted versions of classic, English-influenced styles to the German lager beers of August Schell Brewing Company or the authentic Belgian ales from Boom Island Brewing Company, there is a flavor for everyone. Whether you desire

Surly's in-your-face aggressiveness or the quiet, down-home feel of Barley John's Brewpub, you're sure to find something in Minnesota to suit your taste or mood.

The majority of Minnesota breweries are located in and around Minneapolis and St. Paul—twenty-seven at the time of writing—making the Twin Cities a great starting point for any beer tour of Minnesota. From the Twin Cities, it's a quick trip out to Stillwater or Cold Spring to visit Lift Bridge Brewing Company or the Third Street Brewhouse at Cold Spring Brewing Company. Just one hundred miles south of the Twin Cities in the quaint, German town of New Ulm is the historic August Schell brewery, a must-see for any beer tourist in Minnesota. You can make a day of it with stops at Mankato Brewing Company and Brau Brothers.

While you could spend your whole trip in and around the Twin Cities, you would do yourself a disservice not to head "up north," as Minnesotans like to say. Duluth is a beautiful city nestled on the shore of Lake Superior. There are four breweries downtown, all within easy walking distance from one another, including Fitger's Brewhouse, one of the best in the state. Lake Superior Brewing Company, Canal Park Brewing Company, Bent Paddle Brewing Company, and the Thirsty Pagan in Superior, Wisconsin, are only a short drive away. While you're there, be sure to take a stroll on the Duluth lake walk.

The further north you go, the more beautiful the scenery gets. The solace and solitude of the North Woods and the lake country are worth a visit all by themselves. Spend a relaxing week in a cabin on a lake, do some swimming, boating, and fishing, and stop into the Boathouse Brewpub in Ely for a bite and a beer. You'll be glad you did.

Minnesota Contract Breweries:

Bank Beer Company, Hendricks
Bard's Tale Beer Company, Edina
Big Wood Brewery, White Bear Lake
Blacklist Brewing, Duluth
Blue Diamond Brewing Company, St. Paul
Brainerd Lakes Beer, Brainerd
Finnegan's, Minneapolis
Founding Fathers Brewing Company, Orono
Hauenstein Beer, Sleepy Eye
Lakemaid Beer Company, Minneapolis
Lake Monster Brewing, Minneapolis
Pig's Eye Brewing Company, Woodbury
St. Croix Beer Company, St. Paul
Theodore Fyten Brewing Company, St. Paul
Tonka Beer Company, Minnetonka

Minnesota Breweries in Planning (as of March 2013):

Big Wood Brewery, White Bear Lake
Blue Wolf Brewing Company, Anoka
Brewpocalypse, St. Louis Park
Burning Brothers Brewery, St. Paul
Clyde Ironworks Restaurant and Brewing, Duluth
Enki Brewing, Victoria
Fort Road Brewing Company, St. Paul
Four Elements Brewing, St. Paul
Hayes' Public House, Big Lake
Insight Brewing Company, Minneapolis
Jordan Brewery, Jordan
Junkyard Brewing Company, Moorhead

Last City Brewing, St. Paul
Longfellow Brewing, Minneapolis
Minnesota Valley Brewing Company, Chaska
Nosh Restaurant and Bar, Lake City
Pryes Brewing Company, Minneapolis
Rocky Coast Brewing, Silver Bay
Steiner Brewing Company, St. Paul
Third Joker Brewing Company, St. Louis Park
Tin Whiskers, Roseville
Two Carbon Brewing Company, Minneapolis
Urban Growler Brewing Company, St. Paul

Minnesota Beer Festivals:

Mankato Craft Beer Expo, Mankato, January (www.mankatocraftbeerexpo.com)
St. Cloud Craft Beer Expo, St. Cloud, January (www.stcloudcraftbeerexpo.com)
Beer Dabbler Winter Carnival, St. Paul, January (www.thebeerdabbler.com)
Winterfest, St. Paul, February (www.mncraftbrew.org/festivals/winterfest)
Twin Ports Brew Fest, Carlton, February (www.twinportsbrewfest.com)
St. Cloud Craft Beer Tour, St. Cloud, March (www.stcloudcraftbeertour.com)
Firkin Fest, St. Paul, March (www.thehappygnome.com)
Brewers Bazaar, Stillwater, May (www.stillwatersunriserotary.org)
Rochester Craft Beer Expo, Rochester, May (www.rochestercraftbeerexpo.com)
City Pages Beer Festival, Minneapolis, May (www.citypages.com)
St. Paul Summer Beer Fest, St. Paul, June (www.stpaulsummerbeerfest.com)
All Pints North Summer Brew Fest, Duluth, July (www.mncraftbrew.org/festivals/allpintsnorth)
Hopped Up Caribou Beer Festival, Lutsen, July (www.caribouhighlands.com/hoppedupcaribou)
Caledonia Bluff Country Brewfest, Caledonia, July (www.caledoniarotaryclub.org)
Beer Dabbler Highland Fest, St. Paul, July (www.thebeerdabbler.com)
Twin Cities Beer Fest, Minneapolis, August (www.mplsbeerfest.com)
Autumn Brew Review, Minneapolis, September (www.mncraftbrew.org/events/abr)
Nordeast Big River Brewfest, Minneapolis, October (www.esns.org/events)

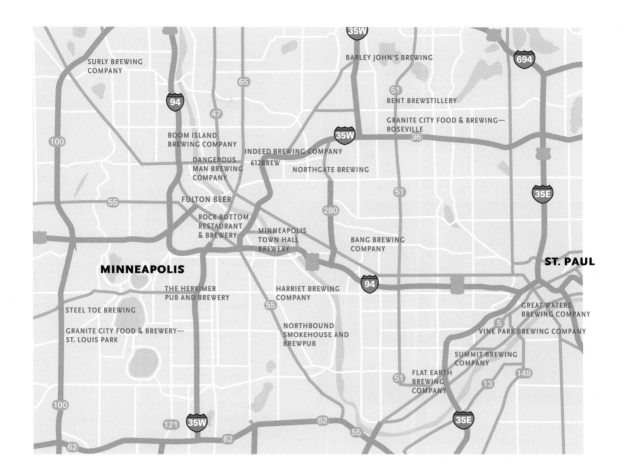

TWIN CITIES/CENTRAL

612Brew

ADDRESS: 45 Broadway St.,
Minneapolis, MN 55413
TELEPHONE: 612–217–0437
EMAIL: info@612brew.com
WEB SITE: www.612brew.com
MICHAEL'S PICK: Rated R: Rye
is an afterthought in this West Coast–style rye IPA,
appearing mostly as a spicy bite in the finish. The main
focus is hops. Bitterness is high but not aggressive,
leaving citrusy hop flavors to take the lead. An ample
cushion of grainy-sweet and vaguely biscuit malt
provides support and balance.
TYPE: Brewery
DATE ESTABLISHED: 2013
OWNERS: Ryan Libby, Robert Kasak, Jamey Rossbach,
and Adit Kalra
BREWMASTER: Adam Schil

BREWING SYSTEM: Fifteen-barrel Zhongde
Equipment Co. brewhouse
FLAGSHIP BEERS: Six, Rated R
YEAR-ROUND BEERS: Six, Rated R, Zero Hour
SEASONAL BEERS: Mary Ann, Maibock, Oktoberfest,
Pilsner, and others
SPECIAL RELEASES: SMaSH (single malt/single hop)
IPAs, and others
TOURS: See Web site for times
BEER TO GO: Growlers
FOOD: A selection of Indian street-food dishes
AMENITIES: Parking lot, taproom, seasonal outdoor
seating, live music on the patio during the summer
PUB HOURS: Wednesday–Saturday, 4:00 to 10:00 P.M.
NEARBY ATTRACTIONS: Boom Island Brewing
Company, Fulton Brewing Company, Indeed Brewing
Company, Dangerous Man Brewing Company, Historic
Grain Belt Brewery building, Nordeast Minneapolis
nightlife, galleries of the Arts District, Guthrie Theatre,
Mill City Museum, performances at the Ritz Theatre,
Twins games at Target Field

NOTES: When I first met the guys from 612Brew, they were working in a South Minneapolis garage, tweaking recipes on a cobbled-together homebrew system and dreaming of bigger things. Two years later, their "garage" is a five-thousand-square-foot warehouse space in a multimillion-dollar commercial redevelopment. The five-gallon glass fermenters have been replaced by thirty-barrel tanks of mirror-polished stainless steel. The steps in between included three business-plan revisions and two canceled leases.

The taproom at 612Brew.

The taproom at 612Brew retains the retro-industrial ambiance of the 1924 factory building that it occupies. Thick maple timbers rise up two stories from the polished concrete floor. The bar top is made from repurposed bowling-alley lanes, while the bottom is faced with boards salvaged from an 1850s vintage home. The gleaming brewery is separated from the public space by wooden standup bars. A tall, glass overhead door looks out onto a patio and rain garden, which is anchored by a stone amphitheater, where live music happens in the warmer months.

612Brew's focus is on hop-centered session beers. They aim to satisfy that craving for bitterness with lower-alcohol brews that allow for more than one pint after work. This may be the only brewery in the country to offer a menu of exclusively Indian food. Co-owner Adit Kalra's family are pioneers of Indian cuisine in the state. They've been in the business for over thirty years and will be handling the catering for the taproom.

The taproom is available for private events, from business meetings to wedding receptions. Brewer Adam Schil is an ordained minister, so hardcore beer fans can hold a beer-themed wedding at the brewery.

Badger Hill Brewing Company

ADDRESS: 6020 Culligan Way Minnetonka, MN 55345
TELEPHONE: 952-303-2739
EMAIL: info@badgerhillbrewing.com
WEB SITE: www.badgerhillbrewing.com
MICHAEL'S PICK: Minnesota Special Bitter: Caramel and toffee lead the way in this take on the English ESB style. Moderate bitterness comes at the start and finish, allowing the malt to shine in the middle. Resiny, orange-marmalade notes combine with yeast-derived fruits and a hint of butterscotch to complete the picture.
TYPE: Brewery
DATE ESTABLISHED: 2012
OWNERS: Broc Krekelberg, Brent Krekelberg, and Britt Krekelberg
BREWMASTER: Broc Krekelberg
BREWING SYSTEM: Fifteen-barrel CGET brewhouse
FLAGSHIP BEER: Minnesota Special Bitter
YEAR-ROUND BEERS: Minnesota Special Bitter (MSB), Three Tree American Rye, Foundation Stout, Porch Pounder Kölsch
SEASONAL BEERS: Imperial Dunkelweizen with Cherries, others planned
SPECIAL RELEASES: Planned
TOURS: Fridays at 4:30 and 5:45 P.M. Call for reservations.
BEER TO GO: Growlers planned
FOOD: None
AMENITIES: Parking lot
PUB HOURS: None
NEARBY ATTRACTIONS: Twin Cities breweries and brewpubs, water activities on Lake Minnetonka, Stages Theatre Company, Old Log Theatre, golf, Valleyfair Amusement Park, twenty minutes from downtown Minneapolis

NOTES: Badger Hill Brewing Company shares facilities with Lucid Brewing in what the federal government calls an "alternating proprietor" arrangement. There is a popular misconception that they are contract brewing, or paying Lucid to produce their beer, but Badger Hill is a fully licensed brewery. Under this arrangement, they lease time on Lucid's brewhouse to produce their own beer. They have also purchased and installed their own fermenting tanks.

The relationship has been mutually beneficial. Badger Hill was able to jump into production without the huge investment in real estate and equipment. The rent allows Lucid to recoup some of their startup costs and to utilize excess capacity. The two companies shared the cost of a bottling line. While the financial advantages are significant, what is even more valuable to brewer Broc Krekelberg is the honest feedback and sharing of ideas that comes with multiple breweries occupying the same space.

Krekelberg describes the Badger Hill approach to brewing as "staying close to the style . . . mostly." His aim is to produce balanced and drinkable ales that veer to a German and Belgian influence but that also add a slight twist to the classics. His beers offer flavors that are new and unexpected in a wrapper that won't offend drinkers less familiar with craft beer. This is especially apparent in his take on the traditional German rye ale or "roggen bier." He coaxes strong, peppery notes from a German wheat-beer yeast that combine with a hopped-up profile and dry finish to create a brew that most closely resembles a Belgian saison.

Bad Weather Brewing Company

ADDRESS: 6020 Culligan Way
Minnetonka, MN 55345
TELEPHONE: None
EMAIL: info@badweatherbrewery.com
WEB SITE: www.badweatherbrewery.com
MICHAEL'S PICK: Windvane: The brewers call this a
Minnesota Red Ale. It's basically a West Coast–style red ale with a slightly maltier profile. Citrus and tropical-fruit hop aromas float over a bed of caramel and toasted malt. The flavors follow the smells, with malt and hops riding a knife edge of balance. Caramel malt almost wins, but a touch of roast gives a grainy dryness to the finish that allows the bitterness to come through and linger.
TYPE: Brewery
DATE ESTABLISHED: 2013
OWNERS: Joe Giambruno and Zac Carpenter
BREWMASTER: Zac Carpenter
BREWING SYSTEM: Fifteen-barrel CGET brewhouse
FLAGSHIP BEER: Windvane Minnesota Red Ale
YEAR-ROUND BEER: Windvane Minnesota Red Ale
SEASONAL BEERS: Ominous Midwest Warmer,
Migration Ale, Firefly Rye, Scarecrow's Friend
SPECIAL RELEASES: Planned
TOURS: See Web site for times
BEER TO GO: Planned
FOOD: None
AMENITIES: Parking lot
PUB HOURS: None
NEARBY ATTRACTIONS: Twin Cities breweries and
brewpubs, water activities on Lake Minnetonka, Stages Theatre Company, Old Log Theatre, golf, Valleyfair Amusement Park, twenty minutes from downtown Minneapolis

NOTES: The first thing that caught my eye about Bad Weather Brewing Company was their branding. The artwork is brooding and dark. It evokes the image and

Label art for Windvane Minnesota Red Ale.

verse of English romanticism and German Sturm und Drang. Beer names talk around the weather, not about it; there is no Thunderstorm IPA. They point your imagination at an impending event or its aftermath, not the thing itself. Words and pictures stand on their own. They rise above their connection to the beer or beer style to give each viewer a personal experience. The art conveys the kind of personal engagement that Joe Giambruno and Zac Carpenter want drinkers to have with their beer. For them, it's about the experience each beer brings, not about adherence to any particular style.

The Bad Weather boys call their style "midwestern edgy." They aren't trying to make the in-your-face styles of the coasts, but they also don't want their beers to be pedestrian. They know the classic styles but don't necessarily brew beers that conform to them. A touch of rye here or a bit of rose hips there create subtle and interesting divergences from the rules. Following the regional trend, Bad Weather beers emphasize malt, but that doesn't mean that they're sweet. And don't assume that there is any shortage of hops. An emphasis on seasonals and specialties gives drinkers a palette of experiences that shifts through the year and leaves them anticipating what comes next—like the weather.

Bad Weather is the second brewery in the region to take advantage of the Tax and Trade Bureau's little-known alternating-proprietorship program that allows multiple fully licensed breweries to operate out of the same physical space. They joined Badger Hill Brewing Company at the Lucid Brewing facility.

Bang Brewing Company

ADDRESS: 2320 Capp Rd.
St. Paul, MN 55114
TELEPHONE: See Web site
EMAIL: jay@bangbrewing.com
WEB SITE: www.bangbrewing.com
MICHAEL'S PICK: Minn Mild: Hops drive the aroma of
this easy-drinker, but the flavor is all about malt. Nutty

and toffee flavors lead the way. Gentle sweetness is tempered by a dry, grainy roastiness that comes in at the finish. Hops aren't completely forgotten. Moderate bitterness and low earthy flavors provide a nice contrast to the malt. Light orangey esters fill in the cracks.

TYPE: Brewery
DATE ESTABLISHED: 2013
OWNERS: Sandy Febbo and Jay Boss Febbo
BREWMASTER: Jay Boss Febbo
BREWING SYSTEM: Ten-barrel JV Northwest brewhouse
FLAGSHIP BEER: Neat
YEAR-ROUND BEER: Neat, Minn Mild
SEASONAL BEERS: Planned
SPECIAL RELEASES: Planned
TOURS: By request
BEER TO GO: Growlers
FOOD: None
AMENITIES: Parking lot, free street parking, taproom
PUB HOURS: Friday: 5:00 to 10:00 P.M.; Saturday: noon to 5:00 P.M.
NEARBY ATTRACTIONS: Harriet Brewing Company, 612Brew, St. Paul Saints games at Midway Stadium, Minnesota State Fairgrounds, University of Minnesota campus

NOTES: How do you know when homebrewers are really serious? They redesign their kitchen around improvements to their brewery. That's exactly what Sandy and Jay Boss Febbo did. The plan included tubes running through the floor to carry hot wort from the stovetop to stainless steel, conical fermenters in the basement. "The contractor had a good laugh about it," says Sandy. That was in 2005. By 2007, the couple was planning to go pro and had already named their brewery.

The Boss Febbos are longtime supporters of the local- and slow-food movement. For them, the brewery is a way to be participants in it rather than just adherents. The slow-food ethos strongly influences how they operate. Bang Brewing Company is the only brewery in the Midwest committed to brewing all organic beers. The brewery landscaping includes barley to illustrate the cycle from ingredients to finished product, and the Boss Febbos are working with local organic farmers to reclaim the soil that has been compacted and contaminated from years of industrial use.

Even the building is an expression of the Boss Febbos' commitment to sustainability. The prefab, grain-bin design bespeaks their respect for the ingredients and their striving for efficiency. Ample natural light makes it both pleasant and energy-efficient. They made extensive use of reclaimed materials in its construction: The driveway timbers were salvaged from a section of the River Parkway near the Mill City Museum in downtown Minneapolis. Other sources of building material included an old backyard deck, a neighbor's fence, and the shipping crates that shielded their grain mill.

The building's design allows for effective use of the limited space. The brewery occupies one side, with the taproom and cooler on the other. In between is a multi-use space that serves the brewery on brew days. When brewing is done, the equipment is rolled aside and replaced with stools to service the taproom. When guests are seated at the bar, they are quite literally in the brewery.

Barley John's Brewpub

ADDRESS: 781 Old Hwy 8 SW
New Brighton, MN 55112
TELEPHONE: 651–636–4670
EMAIL: info@barleyjohns.com
WEB SITE: www.barleyjohns.com
MICHAEL'S PICK: Wild Brunette: Wild Brunette brings a Minnesota twist to a classic brown ale with the addition of wild rice. It's moderately hopped with flavor notes of caramel, brown sugar, and chocolate. The defining character of the beer is the nutty and earthy flavor brought by the rice. I fell in love with this beer the first time I tried it, and it remains my go-to beer on every visit.
TYPE: Brewpub
DATE ESTABLISHED: 2000
OWNERS: John Moore and Laura Subak
BREWMASTER: John Moore
BREWING SYSTEM: Four-barrel Specific Mechanical Brewhouse
FLAGSHIP BEERS: Wild Brunette and Stockyard IPA
YEAR-ROUND BEERS: Little Barley Bitter, Stockyard IPA, Wild Brunette Wild Rice Brown Ale, Old 8 Porter
SEASONAL BEERS: Oktoberfest, Maibock, Dark Knight, Dark Knight Returns, Rosie's Old Ale
SPECIAL RELEASES: Kaffir Pale Ale, Winter Ale, Oatmeal Brown Ale, Zombie Ale, Tropical Stout, Neighborly IIPA, and others
TOURS: No
BEER TO GO: Growlers
FOOD: Upscale pub food: grilled pizza, entrées ranging from beef tenderloin to beer-battered catfish, hot and cold sandwiches, and salads
AMENITIES: Parking lot, full bar with a selection of fine whiskies and rotating guest taps, happy-hour specials, seasonal outdoor seating with a firepit
PUB HOURS: Monday–Saturday: 11:00 A.M. to 1:00 A.M.

NEARBY ATTRACTIONS: Twin Cities breweries and brewpubs, minutes from downtown Minneapolis or St. Paul, Long Lake Regional Park beaches, winter ice fishing on nearby lakes

NOTES: Located just north of Minneapolis in New Brighton, Barley John's Brewpub is a bit off the beaten track, but the easy drive up I-35W is worth the trip. Unique brews, tasty food, and a cozy atmosphere have earned Barley John's the title of Best Brewpub and Best Suburban Bar in the Twin Cities Guide published by the *City Pages* weekly newspaper.

According to John Moore, Barley John's four-barrel brewhouse is the smallest decoction-capable brewhouse in the country. The brewery is not the only thing that is small at Barley John's. The cozy dining room seats only about thirty, with room for maybe ten more in the bar. But there is ample seating on the spacious patio, which is garlanded with hop vines in the summer and warmed by a blazing firepit on the cool evenings of spring and fall.

Barley John's tends its own vegetable garden to supply the kitchen with fresh produce during the summer. It was the first brewery in Minnesota to install solar arrays for energy production. A constantly rotating selection of seasonal and specialty brews means that there is always something good on tap. Must-try beers, if you happen to visit during the colder months, are Dark Knight, a rich and roasty, 13 percent ABV, barrel-aged imperial porter, and Rosie's Old Ale, a super-high-octane, barrel-aged English-style old ale.

Bent Brewstillery

ADDRESS: 1744 Terrace Dr.
Roseville, MN 55113
TELEPHONE: 651-233-3843
EMAIL: Bartley@BentBrewstillery.com
WEB SITE: www.BentBrewstillery.com
MICHAEL'S PICK: Nordic Blonde: Hoppier than the average blond ale, but less so than most pales, this beer is a bit of a hybrid. High attenuation gives it a crisp, dry profile that belies its nearly 6 percent ABV. Czech Saaz hops give it a sharp, spicy edge.
TYPE: Brewery
DATE ESTABLISHED: 2013
OWNER: Bartley Blume
BREWMASTER: Kristen England
BREWING SYSTEM: 20-barrel custom made brewhouse
FLAGSHIP BEER: Nordic Blonde
YEAR ROUND BEERS: Nordic Blonde, Uber Lupin
SEASONAL BEERS: Dark Fatha American Emperial Stout; Maroon & Bold Double Infuriatingly Passive Aggressive Ale

SPECIAL RELEASES: Sour beers, barrel-aged beers, and others planned. Regular taproom-only releases.
TOURS: Check Web site for times
BEER TO GO: Growlers and 750 ml bottles
FOOD: None
AMENITIES: Parking lot, taproom
PUB HOURS: Check Web site for times
OTHER ATTRACTIONS NEARBY: Minnesota State Fair Grounds, several golf courses, Rosedale Center Mall, Gibbs Museum of Pioneer and Dakotah Life, 15 minutes from Minneapolis and St. Paul downtowns

NOTES: Bent Brewstillery founder Bartley Blume doesn't like to be pigeonholed. His motto for the combination brewery/distillery is "breaking the norm." Brewer Kristen England, on the other hand, is rooted in tradition. Much of his influence comes from historical research he has done with British blogger Ron Pattinson, pulling recipes from the historical brewer's logs of England's most revered breweries going back to the 1700s. The tension between these two opposing philosophies results in a lineup of beers that are always just a step off from expectations.

On the one side are hybrid beers, beers that seem to fall somewhere between the classic styles. Nordic Blonde, for instance, has characteristics of both blond ale and pale ale, but isn't quite either one. Dark Fatha has the strength, color, and rich aroma of an imperial stout, but in your mouth its light body and sharp bitterness make it seem to lean toward black IPA.

On the other hand are historical beers with flavors that are familiar and yet unlike anything you know. Maroon & Bold is a big, imperial IPA that showcases hops, but gives almost equal attention to toffee, biscuit, and toasted malt flavors. An award-winning Berliner Weiss is spot-on for the style, but wine-barrel aging gives it vinous and vanilla notes that set it apart from other examples.

In addition to beer, Bent Brewstillery produces a line of distilled spirits. UnPure is an un-aged, all-malt whiskey that is filtered through charred oak and apple wood. A measure of cherry and oak smoked malts give it a smoky inflection. Their gin is made with more than twelve botanicals, including lavender, vanilla, citrus peel, and ginger, in addition to the usual juniper.

Boom Island Brewing Company

ADDRESS: 2014 Washington Ave. N.
Minneapolis, MN 55411
TELEPHONE: 612-227-9635
EMAIL: info@boomislandbrewing.com
WEB SITE: www.boomislandbrewing.com

MICHAEL'S PICK: Silvius Pale Ale: Based on the pale ales of Antwerp, Silvius rides a fine-line balance between biscuity malt and spicy hops. Stone-fruit notes fill in the background. Moderate bitterness and a dry finish make it drinkable for the long haul.

TYPE: Brewery

DATE ESTABLISHED: 2012

OWNER: Kevin Welch

BREWMASTER: Kevin Welch

BREWING SYSTEM: Fifteen-barrel Portland Kettleworks brewhouse

FLAGSHIP BEERS: Silvius Pale Ale, Thoprock IPA

YEAR-ROUND BEERS: Silvius Pale Ale, Thoprock IPA, Hoodoo Dubbel, Brimstone Tripel

SEASONAL BEERS: Can I Get a Witness Witbier, Quadruple, Sours, Saison, Abbey Blond, Witbier, Yule Ale

SPECIAL RELEASES: Thoprock Wet, LoMoMopalooza

TOURS: Planned. Check Web site for days and times.

BEER TO GO: Growlers

FOOD: None

AMENITIES: Free street parking

PUB HOURS: Wednesday–Friday: 4:00 to 9:00 P.M.; Saturday: noon to 9:00 P.M.

NEARBY ATTRACTIONS: Twin Cities breweries and brewpubs, Old Grain Belt Brewery, Minnesota Opera, restaurants and nightlife of the Warehouse District, Hennepin Ave. Theatre District, 1st Avenue music club, Twins Games at Target Field, concerts and sporting events at the Target Center

NOTES: When French-horn playing homebrewer Kevin Welch first got into beer, he went for the big, hoppy ones. But when he tasted the Tripel from the Trappist brewery Westmalle, everything changed. He became enamored of the Belgian brews. On a first trip to Belgium he sampled everything he could get his hands on, filling grocery carts with bottles. By the time of his second trek, he was planning his brewery. This time he visited breweries, talking and brewing with Belgian brewmasters in order to learn the secrets of making great Belgian-style beers.

Welch is putting what he learned to use at Boom Island. He brews only Belgian styles, from a sessionable pale ale to a luxurious quadruple. He maintains a private yeast bank made up of strains that he procured from well-know and obscure Belgian breweries. The fermentation protocols that he follows were picked up from his Belgian mentors. True to the Belgian tradition, all of his beers are bottle-conditioned and cork-finished.

Cold Spring Brewing Co./Third Street Brewhouse

ADDRESS: 219 Red River Ave. Cold Spring, MN 56320

TELEPHONE: 320–685–8686

EMAIL: thirdstreetbrewhouse@gmail.com

WEB SITE: www.thirdstreetbrewhouse.com

MICHAEL'S PICK: Bitter Neighbor Black IPA: Huge citrus and pine aromas hit your nose as you raise the glass. The flavor is balanced, with moderate bitterness and loads of orange and tangerine hop flavor. Chocolate notes fill in the bottom, with a bit of bitter roast supporting the hops. The finish is dry and crisp.

TYPE: Brewery

DATE ESTABLISHED: 1874

OWNER: John Lenore

BREWMASTERS: Mike Kneip and Horace Cunningham

BREWING SYSTEM: Thirty-five-barrel Hauptman brewhouse

FLAGSHIP BEERS: Lost Trout Brown Ale, Rise to the Top Cream Ale, Bitter Neighbor Black IPA

YEAR-ROUND BEERS: Lost Trout Brown Ale, Rise to the Top Cream Ale, Bitter Neighbor Black IPA, Cold Spring Honey Almond Weiss, Cold Spring IPA, Cold Spring Moonlight Ale, John Henry 3 Lick Spiker Ale, Northern Golden Lager, Northern Honey Brown Lager, Northern Reserve Special Light, Olde Johnnie Ale

SEASONAL BEERS: Third Street Sugar Shack Maple Stout, Third Street Jack'd Up Pumpkin Ale, and others

SPECIAL RELEASES: Planned

TOURS: Thursdays 4:00 and 5:00 P.M.; Saturdays 11:00 A.M., 12:00, 1:00, 2:00, and 3:00 P.M.

BEER TO GO: None

FOOD: None

AMENITIES: Free street parking, taproom

PUB HOURS: Fridays 4:00 to 8:00 P.M.

NEARBY ATTRACTIONS: Camping and water activities on nearby lakes, golf, twenty minutes to downtown St. Cloud, 1.25 hours to the Twin Cities

NOTES: The second oldest brewery in the state, Cold Spring Brewing Company is reinventing itself. It has brought on new brewing staff, built a new state-of-the-art brewery, and introduced new brands under the Third Street Brewhouse label that are well suited to today's craft-beer market. The rebranding is bringing renewed vitality and credibility to this brewery that in recent years had garnered a less-than-stellar reputation among Minnesota craft-beer drinkers.

The brewing team is a mix of old and new. Mike Kneip began working on the bottling line while he was still in college and never left. He has worked every job in the brewery on the way to becoming brewmaster.

He is intimately familiar with the ins and outs and idiosyncrasies of the old brewhouse. Horace Cunningham started at Cold Spring in 2011, after thirty years in the industry. He has brewed beer in Germany, England, at Summit Brewing Company in St. Paul, and at Red Stripe in Jamaica. He brings the expertise to make the most of the new facility.

The new Third Street Brewhouse is a beautiful facility, custom built from the ground up. The taproom offers a modern yet intimate space to enjoy a sample. The modern brewhouse and expanded cellaring capacity will allow Cold Spring to increase their production by up to fifty thousand barrels annually. The facility was built with expansion in mind. As production grows, additional fermentation tanks can be added relatively easily.

Cold Spring also does a large volume of contract brewing and nonalcoholic-beverage production, including energy drinks and sparkling juice products.

Dangerous Man Brewing Company

ADDRESS: 1300 2nd St. NE
Minneapolis, MN 55413
TELEPHONE: 612–209–2626
EMAIL: rob@dangerousmanbrewing.com
WEB SITE: www.dangerousmanbrewing.com
MICHAEL'S PICK: Chocolate Milk Stout: "Wow" is all I could say when I first tasted this beer. It's a silky-smooth, chocolate bon bon of a beer with a moderate dose of roast. Nutty notes of grainy, toasted malt send it over the top.
TYPE: Brewery
DATE ESTABLISHED: 2013
OWNERS: Rob Miller and Sarah Bonvallet
BREWMASTER: Rob Miller
BREWING SYSTEM: Ten-barrel Specific Mechanical brewhouse
FLAGSHIP BEERS: None
YEAR-ROUND BEERS: None
SEASONAL BEERS: Chocolate Milk Stout and others
SPECIAL RELEASES: Belgian Strong Golden Ale, Double IPA, Cream Ale, Coffee Porter, Rye Pale Ale, and others
TOURS: By request
BEER TO GO: Growlers
FOOD: None
AMENITIES: Parking lot, free street parking, taproom, seasonal outdoor seating
PUB HOURS: Tuesday–Thursday: 4:00 to 10:00 P.M.; Friday: 4:00 P.M. to midnight; Saturday: noon to midnight
NEARBY ATTRACTIONS: Indeed Brewing Company, 612Brew, Boom Island Brewing Company, Northeast

Arts District, historic Grain Belt Brewery building, Nordeast Minneapolis nightlife, Guthrie Theatre, Mill City Museum, performances at the Ritz Theatre, Twins games at Target Field

NOTES: The development of Dangerous Man happened in fits and starts that parallel recent changes in state and municipal liquor laws. Homebrewing had instilled in Rob Miller a love of the beer-making art. After attending college and sampling craft beers in Montana, he returned home to Minneapolis with the dream of opening a taproom-only brewery. He began working on his business plan only to discover that brewery taprooms weren't legal. He set the plan aside and went to work in the corporate world.

In 2011 a change to state law made it legal for breweries to sell pints on-site. Miller dusted off the business plan and went back to work. He found the ideal space—a space with which he was loath to part. The only problem was that it sat across the street from a church, something city statutes didn't allow. Cue the sound of screeching brakes.

Dangerous Man owner/head brewer Rob Miller.

But Miller didn't give up. He held multiple discussions with the church to build understanding and worked with the city council to change the Prohibition-era law. With Dangerous Man's opening in early January 2013, he finally saw his dream come to fruition.

Dangerous Man's location is a beauty. The turn-of-the-twentieth-century bank building sits in one of the centers of Nordeast nightlife, with great restaurants and neighborhood taverns within easy walking distance. The taproom is dominated by rows of octagonal wooden columns supporting the two-story-high ceiling. The décor has a look that I have dubbed "industrial arts." Shop stools and a bolted-steel bar topped with massive timbers salvaged from a downtown building give the space a feel that falls somewhere between an early 1900s factory and a junior-high shop class.

You won't find Dangerous Man beers anywhere but the taproom. Look for an ever-changing rotation, with very few year-round picks.

Excelsior Brewing Company

ADDRESS: 421 3rd St.
Excelsior, MN 55331
TELEPHONE: 952–474–7837
EMAIL: contact@excelsiorbrew.com
WEB SITE: www.excelsiorbrew.com
MICHAEL'S PICK: Big Island Blond: Big Island Blond sports a fuller-than-expected body while still retaining the light, refreshing character that defines the style. The sweet, graham-cracker-like malt is balanced by gentle bitterness and delicate citrus hop aroma. It's a nice beer for a day on the lake.
TYPE: Brewery
DATE ESTABLISHED: 2012
OWNERS: John Klick, Jon Lewin, and Patrick Foss
BREWMASTER: Bob DuVernois
BREWING SYSTEM: Twenty-barrel JV Northwest brewhouse
FLAGSHIP BEERS: XLCR Pale Ale, Big Island Blonde, Bridge Jumper SPA, Bitteschlappe Brown Ale
YEAR-ROUND BEERS: XLCR Pale Ale, Big Island Blonde, Bridge Jumper SPA, Bitteschlappe Brown Ale
SEASONAL BEERS: Oktoberfest, Summer Ale, Witbier, others planned
SPECIAL RELEASES: Hutmaker, Holiday Ale, planned barrel-aged beers
TOURS: Saturdays noon to 2:00 P.M.
BEER TO GO: Growlers
FOOD: None
AMENITIES: Parking lot, taproom
PUB HOURS: Thursday and Friday: 4:00 to 10:00 P.M.; Saturday: 2:00 to 10:00 P.M.
NEARBY ATTRACTIONS: Lake Minnetonka, Museum of Lake Minnetonka, *Minnehaha* steamboat, Old Log Theatre, shops in historic downtown Excelsior, Minnesota Streetcar Museum and Excelsior Trolley, twenty miles from the Twin Cities

NOTES: Recreating on Lake Minnetonka has always been the center of life in Excelsior. The town was founded in the 1850s as a summer vacation destination, offering relaxation and water activities to residents of Minneapolis and St. Paul, who arrived there by trolley. From 1923 to 1975 it was home to the Excelsior Amusement Park, with its famous Cyclone roller coaster. Steamboats made from trolley cars provided transportation to lake islands and nearby towns.

The amusement park is now gone, but the lake is still Excelsior's main draw, and the town still captures the laid-back essence of its history as a summer getaway. Marinas share the shore with restaurants boasting large lakefront decks. The restored *Minnehaha* steamboat offers daily lake cruises. Water Street features interesting shops, antique stores, art galleries, and several fine and casual dining options in a historic Main Street setting.

Excelsior Brewing Company has adopted the history and the relaxed, lake-life feel into its brand. Beer names and labels invoke local places and favorite activities, such as jumping off of the old Minneapolis and St. Louis railroad bridge that crosses the lake. They make mostly sessionable ales that will enhance a summer day on and around the water.

The brewery sits just off Water Street at the southwestern edge of downtown. The taproom is currently in the brewery, but a planned expansion into an adjacent storefront will allow for the building of a proper public area in the next couple of years. Take-out food is available from several nearby restaurants, some of which have added Excelsior beer to their recipes or developed special menu items just for brewery patrons.

Flat Earth Brewing Company

ADDRESS: 2035 Benson Ave.
St. Paul, MN 55116
TELEPHONE: 651–698–1945
EMAIL: info@flatearthbrewing.com
WEB SITE: www.flatearthbrewing.com
MICHAEL'S PICK: Cygnus X-1 Porter: Cygnus X-1 is named after a song by the Canadian progressive-rock band Rush. They call it a "Canadian porter." Canadian rye adds a subtle spicy bite to this chocolaty brew. Cygnus X-1 serves as the base for several of the brewery's unique infused beers.
TYPE: Brewery
DATE ESTABLISHED: 2007
OWNER: John Warner
BREWMASTER: Bob Roepke
BREWING SYSTEM: Fifteen-barrel JV Northwestern brewhouse
FLAGSHIP BEER: Belgian Pale Ale
YEAR-ROUND BEERS: Angry Planet Pale Ale, Belgian Pale Ale, Cygnus X-1 Porter, Northwest Passage IPA
SEASONAL BEERS: Bermuda Triangle Tripel, Black Helicopter Coffee Stout, Element 115 Lager, Ovni Ale Biére de Garde, Winter Warlock Barleywine, Hep Cat Blond Ale
SPECIAL RELEASES: Red Cape Ale, Rode Haring Flanders Red Ale, Extra Medium American Sour Ale,

infused versions of Cygnus X-1 Porter, Belgian Pale Ale, Hep Cat Blond Ale, 2 Fingers Imperial IPA

TOURS: Second and fourth Saturday of every month at 4:00 P.M. Reservations required.

BEER TO GO: Growlers

FOOD: None

AMENITIES: Limited parking in the lot (be careful not to block the neighboring businesses), free street parking, tasting room

PUB HOURS: Tuesday–Friday: 3:30 P.M. to 6:30 P.M.; Saturday: noon to 6:30 P.M.

NEARBY ATTRACTIONS: Twin Cities breweries and brewpubs, Summit Brewing Company and Vine Park Brewing Company are both located within a mile, Minnehaha Falls, Cathedral of St. Paul, James Hill House, Fort Snelling, Science Museum of Minnesota, Minnesota Children's Museum, sporting events and concerts at the Excel Energy Center, Fitzgerald Theatre, Minnesota History Center

NOTES: Does the government keep aliens locked up at Area 51? Is it suppressing information about Element 115, the fuel that makes interstellar travel possible? Maybe. Maybe not. These are the questions raised by the evocative names of Flat Earth beers. What began as a simple search for quirky monikers gradually evolved into a little universe centered on conspiracy theories and urban legends. The brewery itself was named for the Flat Earth Society, the organization formed in the nineteenth century to promote the theory that the earth is flat. Brands like Cygnus X-1 Porter, Northwest Passage IPA, and Mummy Train Pumpkin Ale are drawn from the same well as UFOs and the Loch Ness Monster.

Flat Earth was the second entry into Minnesota's new brewery boom, opening only a few months after Surly Brewing Company. The brewery's mission is to deliver fresh versions of hard-to-find styles. They have extended that mission to include infused versions of their regular beers, creating unique flavors like an apricot-infused Belgian pale ale called Sunburst and the award-winning S'more version of their Cygnus X-1 Porter. They offer nearly forty different infusions on an irregularly rotating schedule. The brewery's Porterfest, which occurs every November and December, provides a great time to sample a number of these flavorful concoctions.

At the time of writing the brewery was planning a move to the old Hamm's brewery in St. Paul's Eastside neighborhood.

Fulton Beer

ADDRESS: 414 6th Ave. N
Minneapolis, MN 55401

TELEPHONE: 612-333-3208

EMAIL: Form on Web site

WEB SITE: www.fultonbeer.com

MICHAEL'S PICK: The Libertine: I'd call this beer a midwestern version of a West Coast imperial red ale. It's a sneaky 8 percenter that drinks much lighter. Malt is front and center, with spicy rye playing counterpoint to the dominant caramel flavors. But hops haven't been ignored. It has a bitter kick to balance and spicy/citrus hop flavors to add depth.

TYPE: Brewery

DATE ESTABLISHED: 2009

OWNERS: Ryan Petz, Brian Hoffman, Peter Grande, and Jim Diley

BREWMASTER: Peter Grande

BREWING SYSTEM: Twenty-barrel DME brewhouse

FLAGSHIP BEER: Sweet Child of Vine

YEAR-ROUND BEERS: Sweet Child of Vine, Lonely Blond, The Ringer Pale Ale

SEASONAL BEERS: The Libertine, Worthy Adversary

SPECIAL RELEASES: War and Peace Coffee Infused Imperial Stout, The Tart Grapefruit Infused Blond Ale, The Ambassador American Barleywine

TOURS: During pub hours

BEER TO GO: Growlers

FOOD: None

AMENITIES: Free parking in lot and on street, taproom

PUB HOURS: Friday: 3:00 to 10:00 P.M.; Saturday: noon to 10:00 P.M., during Twins home games

NEARBY ATTRACTIONS: Minneapolis breweries and brewpubs, Target Field, restaurants and nightclubs of the Warehouse District, Hennepin Ave. Theater District, Walker Art Center, Loring Park, Minnesota Orchestra, 1st Avenue music club

NOTES: In the late fall of 2009, few in the Twin Cities beer scene even knew about these four guys working in a garage in the Fulton neighborhood of South Minneapolis. Then, suddenly, there was beer. Sweet Child of Vine began appearing on tap at local watering holes, setting Fulton's trajectory into motion.

Fulton Beer's catchphrase is "ordinary guys making extraordinary beer." Indeed, the Fulton foursome began as homebrewing buddies, brewing their first batch together in 2006 on a frigid February afternoon. Gradually the idea hit them to go pro. Fulton began producing beer under contract at the Sand Creek Brewery in Black River Falls, Wisconsin. They took a lot of heat from the local beer community for billing themselves as a Minneapolis brewery while producing their product in another state. That's all behind them now. In mid-November 2011, the guys sold the first growlers of beer from their own Minneapolis facility.

Fulton beers fit comfortably in the midwestern mold. They display a balanced moderation that leaves them flavorful and easy to drink. Nothing is over the top. Sweet Child of Vine IPA, for example, is neither excessively bitter nor too malty sweet. It exists in a gray area somewhere between a hop-centric American IPA and a more balanced and malty English version. At the brewery, be sure to try one of their "randallized" versions. They offer a number of variations filtered through wood chips, spices, coffee beans, and other things.

At the time of writing Fulton was planning to build a second, larger brewery in Minneapolis' Northeast neighborhood. The current location and taproom will remain open.

Great Waters Brewing Company

ADDRESS: 426 St. Peter St.
St. Paul, MN 55102
TELEPHONE: 651–224–2739
EMAIL: brewer@greatwatersbc.com
WEB SITE: www.greatwatersbc.com
MICHAEL'S PICK: New Centurion Mild: Mild is the ultimate English session beer, a low-alcohol, light-bodied brown ale with plenty of flavor. New Centurion is true to form. It pours dark brown with very little head. Nutty, biscuity flavors from English base malts are balanced by low levels of roasted malt and East Kent Goldings hop bitterness. Light chocolate malt and the faintest hint of earthy Goldings hop flavor add depth. Hand-pulled cask service and the use of oats and wheat give this light-bodied beer a smooth, creamy mouthfeel.
DATE ESTABLISHED: 1997
TYPE: Brewpub
OWNER: Sean O'Byrne
BREWMASTER: Tony Digatono
BREWING SYSTEM: Fifteen-hectoliter Price-Schonstrom brewhouse
FLAGSHIP BEER: St. Peter Pale Ale
YEAR-ROUND BEERS: St. Peter Pale Ale, Golden Prairie Blond, Brown Trout Brown Ale, House Ale, New Centurion Mild Ale, Blackwatch Oat Stout
SEASONAL BEERS: Yuletide Ale, King Boreas Imperial Wit, O'Byrnes Irish Red, Tightey Whitey Wit, Kaizerweizer Hefeweizen, Pflugenpflagen Munich Celebration Ale
SPECIAL RELEASES: Frequent special releases
TOURS: By appointment

BEER TO GO: Growlers
FOOD: An eclectic mix of typical pub fare, with some more upscale items and Minnesota specialties scattered in
AMENITIES: Metered street parking or paid parking in nearby structures, cask-conditioned ales, full bar, seasonal outdoor seating, winter patio with ice bar during St. Paul Winter Carnival
PUB HOURS: Daily 11:00 A.M. to 2:00 A.M.
NEARBY ATTRACTIONS: River Center, Xcel Energy Center, Roy Wilkins Auditorium, Minnesota Science Museum, the Landmark Center, the Ordway Theatre, the St. Paul Children's Museum, the Fitzgerald Theatre

NOTES: Great Waters is St. Paul's only brewpub. It is housed in the lobby level of the ornate Hamm Building, which is listed on the National Register of Historic Places. Once home to the Capital Theatre, the largest movie palace in the upper Midwest, the Hamm building also housed the largest illegal gambling operation in the city. Prior to 1915, the site was occupied by the St. Paul Cathedral. A 550-foot-deep well was dug for the cathedral into the underlying aquifer. Great Waters Brewing Company gets its brewing water from this very well.

Great Waters is the place to go for cask-conditioned ales in the Twin Cities. Cask-conditioned beers make up 50 percent of the brewpub's beer sales. There are always four CAMRA-compliant cask selections available, more than any other brewpub in the state. But it's not all about cask ales. They keep six year-round beers on tap, along with a constantly changing selection of seasonal and special releases.

The atmosphere at Great Waters suggests a European bistro, with high ceilings and an open floor crowded with tables. Outdoor seating is available in the summer months. The menu is varied and delicious, with entrées ranging from Minnesota standards like broiled Walleye to more upscale and unique items, such as grilled duck breast glazed in maple sauce and Pollo Caracas, a Venezuelan-influenced chicken dish. Watch out for those Rasta Wings—they are hot, hot, hot!

Hammerheart Brewing Company

ADDRESS: 7785 Lake Dr.
Lino Lakes, MN 55014
TELEPHONE: 651–964–2160
EMAIL:
beer@hammerheartbrewing.com
WEB SITE: www.hammerheartbrewing.com
MICHAEL'S PICK: Surtr's Flame Smoked IPA: On first sip, you might not realize that this beer is smoked.

Only the haziest hints of it break through the bright, citrusy hops and light residual sweetness. But wait a while. Long after you swallow, the fruity, char-pit sensation of cherrywood-smoked malt comes in strong. I wasn't sure what to expect from a smoked IPA, but this one delivers the goods.

TYPE: Brewery
DATE ESTABLISHED: 2013
OWNERS: Austin Lunn and Nathaniel Chapman
BREWMASTER: Austin Lunn
BREWING SYSTEM: Fifteen-barrel ABS brewhouse
FLAGSHIP BEERS: None
YEAR-ROUND BEERS: Surtr's Flame Smoked IPA, Olaf the Stout Oaked Rye Stout, Dublin Raid Norse Red Ale, Hokan's Brown Ale, Thor's Porter Smoked Habanero Imperial Porter, and Loki's Treachery Sour IPA
SEASONAL BEERS: Høst Øl Smoked Harvest Ale, British Invasion English Pale Ale, Fimbulvetr Smoked Winter White Ale, Ginnungagap Oatmeal Coffee Stout, Jul Ale, and others
SPECIAL RELEASES: Aptrgangr Smoked Ghost Chili Imperial Porter, and others
TOURS: See Web site for times
BEER TO GO: Growlers
FOOD: None
AMENITIES: Parking lot, taproom
PUB HOURS: Thursday–Saturday: 2:00 to 10:00 P.M.
NEARBY ATTRACTIONS: Rice Lake Chain of Lakes Reserve, apple picking at Pine Tree Apple Orchard, twenty miles from the Twin Cities

NOTES: It's late December, just a few days before Christmas. A deep snow pack covers the ground. The temperature hovers in the low twenties. Four guys, one of whom looks like a heavy-metal viking, stand shivering in a circle under a grove of pine trees sampling beer. The moment was exquisitely appropriate for a visit to Hammerheart Brewing Company.

At first glance, the mythic, Nordic theme adopted by Hammerheart may seem like a clever marketing gimmick. When you meet the men behind the beer, you quickly realize that it goes much deeper. What began for head brewer Austin Lunn as a historical search for family roots transformed into a life-centering engagement with Nordic history and mythology. This southern boy from Tennessee sealed his connection to the culture and the place with a brewing internship at the Haandbryggeriet in Drammen, Norway.

Don't let the dark intensity of the Norse gods fool you, though. These boys have a trickster-like mischievous side that makes them a lot of fun to hang out with. They've made many of their most important business decisions over a few beers in that same pine grove where I stood with them in the snow. You're likely to hear heavy-metal music blaring in the brewery.

Although Hammerheart beers are mostly German- and English-inspired, the copious use of smoke, oak, wild yeast, and other nontraditional ingredients lends them a distinctly Nordic feel and flavor. Lunn likes his beers fermented to dryness, but they definitely aren't thin. Even the hoppiest brews retain a substantial, malty backbone. I was struck by their long finishes.

Harriet Brewing Company

ADDRESS: 3036 Minnehaha Ave. Minneapolis, MN 55406
TELEPHONE: 612–225–2184
EMAIL: info@harrietbrewing.com
WEB SITE: www.harrietbrewing.com
MICHAEL'S PICK: West Side Belgian Style IPA: This is definitely an American take on the Belgian IPA style. It eschews the typical spicy, Continental hop varieties in favor of juicy, citrusy American hops. This makes for a brighter and better combination with the fruit and spice of the Belgian yeast strain.
TYPE: Brewery
DATE ESTABLISHED: 2010
OWNER: Jason Sowards
BREWMASTER: Jason Sowards
BREWING SYSTEM: Ten-hectoliter Wachsmann Brautechnik brewhouse
FLAGSHIP BEER: West Side Belgian-Style IPA
YEAR-ROUND BEER: West Side Belgian-Style IPA
SEASONAL BEERS: Wodan Weizen, Saison Nourrice, Dark Abbey, Devine Oculust, Elevator Doppelbock
SPECIAL RELEASES: Harriet's Pils, Wit, Coffee Doppelbock, Rauchfest, Sol Bock, East Side Belgian IPA, various infused versions of the regular beers, and others
TOURS: Wednesdays at 6:00 P.M. Technical tours every first Thursday at 5:30 P.M. Reservations required.
BEER TO GO: Growlers
AMENITIES: Free parking lot next to the brewery, taproom, live music, art gallery featuring the work of Jesse Brodd, who created the brewery's label art, and a featured artist of the month
PUB HOURS: Wednesday–Friday: 4:00 to 10:00 P.M.; Saturday: 1:00 to 10:00 P.M.
NEARBY ATTRACTIONS: Twin Cities breweries and brewpubs, Moto-I sake brewery and restaurant, Frank Theatre, In the Heart of the Beast Theatre, Patrick's Cabaret, Winchell Trail walkway along the Mississippi River, Minnehaha Falls, University of Minnesota West Bank campus

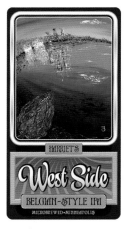

NOTES: Jason Sowards built Harriet Brewing on an idea that is as simple as it is deep—"brew with intention." It is a mindful approach to brewing that emphasizes authenticity and art. The focus is on process, authenticity of style and purpose, and the creative exploration and expression of what beer is and can be. It is this intention that Sowards believes elevates his beer from the mundane.

Art is apparent everywhere at Harriet. The labels and branding materials are the work of local artist Jesse Brodd. The front of the brewery houses a small gallery space that features the work of a different artist every month. Even the taproom has an artsy feel, with a conversation pit composed of old comfy chairs and music from vinyl discs and live musicians. More than just a place to gather, open hours at the taproom are an event.

Harriet's focus is Belgian styles and Old World lagers. The lineup includes a wide range of styles from a Bohemian pilsner, one of my favorites, to a strong Belgian dark ale.

The Herkimer Pub and Brewery

ADDRESS: 2922 Lyndale Ave. S
  Minneapolis, MN 55408
TELEPHONE: 612–821–0101
EMAIL: info@theherkimer.com
WEB SITE: www.theherkimer.com
MICHAEL'S PICK: Eva Cöttbusser: Crisp and oh so light, this one drinks like a table saison. But don't be fooled; it weighs in at nearly 7.5 percent ABV. Honey gives it a light sweetness and dry finish. Oats add a bit of silky texture. Belgian saison yeast brings black pepper spice.
DATE ESTABLISHED: 1999
TYPE: Brewpub
OWNER: Blake Richardson
BREWMASTER: Blake Richardson
BREWING SYSTEM: Ten-hectoliter Beroplan brewhouse
FLAGSHIP BEERS: None
YEAR-ROUND BEERS: A57S Kölsch, A57N Alt
SEASONAL BEERS: Bock, Maibock, Czech Pilsner, Oktoberfest
SPECIAL RELEASES: Tripel Bock, Mummé, EVA Cöttbusser, KLA Kaiser Lichten Alt, Starlight Dunkelweiss, Tomorrow Doppel Pils

TOURS: By appointment
BEER TO GO: None
FOOD: A selection of standard pub favorites
AMENITIES: Small parking lot, metered street parking, happy hour, annual Bockfest and Oktoberfest celebrations, full bar, shuffleboard and beanbags, seasonal outdoor seating
PUB HOURS: Monday–Friday: noon to 2:00 A.M.; Saturday and Sunday: 10:00 A.M. to 2:00 A.M.
NEARBY ATTRACTIONS: Twin Cities breweries and brewpubs, Moto-I sake brewery and restaurant, Jungle Theatre, Bryant Lake Bowl Bowling Alley and Theatre, Intermedia Arts, restaurants and nightlife of the Uptown neighborhood, Minneapolis Chain of Lakes

NOTES: The Herkimer is an example of a brewery changing with the times. For years its focus was on German-style lagers and ales, brewed in strict accordance with the Reinheitsgebot—the German purity law that restricts beer ingredients to barley, hops, water, and yeast. Recently, though, they have broken that mold. While the German influence is still strong, American-style IPAs have entered the mix, along with re-creations of long-lost beer styles like Mummé and Kottbusser. They even brewed a delicious 23 percent ABV Tripel Bock, fermented with sake yeast from Moto-I, their sister establishment down the street.

Staff knowledge has taken on increased importance at the brewpub as well. Servers and bartenders are required to go through an in-house beer school, which includes time in the brewery. Several of the front-of-house staff have passed the Certified Beer Server level of the Cicerone Certification Program, an organization that certifies beer sommeliers.

The Herkimer feels a bit like a modestly upscale sports bar. Television screens above the central bar are tuned to sporting events. A shuffleboard table completes the effect. The décor is a mix of modernist sleek lines and pin-up-girl posters. The brewery is visible behind glass. It can get quite loud on busy nights, but there is patio seating during the summer if you want to escape the noise. Enjoy a game of beanbags while you're out there.

Indeed Brewing Company

ADDRESS: 711 15th Ave. NE
  Minneapolis, MN 55413
TELEPHONE: 612–643–1226
EMAIL: info@indeedbrewing.com
WEB SITE: www.indeedbrewing.com
MICHAEL'S PICK: Shenanigans: American wheat beers have the reputation of being boring. This one is anything but. It's light and quaffable as the style demands, but

has enough hop kick to keep your attention. Honey in the recipe provides supporting sweetness and floral flavor. This summer seasonal is great for those hot and humid Minnesota midsummer afternoons.

TYPE: Brewery

DATE ESTABLISHED: 2012

OWNERS: Thomas Whisenand, Rachel Anderson, and Nathan Berndt

BREWMASTER: Josh Bischoff

BREWING SYSTEM: Thirty-barrel Specific Mechanical brewhouse

FLAGSHIP BEERS: Day Tripper Pale Ale, Midnight Rider American Black Ale

YEAR-ROUND BEERS: Day Tripper Pale Ale, Midnight Rider American Black Ale

SEASONAL BEERS: Sweet Mamma Jamma Sweet Potato Ale, Stir Crazy Winter Ale, Shenanigans Summer Ale, Old Friends

SPECIAL RELEASES: Haywire Double Black IPA, Burr Grinder Coffee Ale, and others

TOURS: Weekdays by appointment, Saturdays during taproom hours

BEER TO GO: 750 ml. bottles

FOOD: None

AMENITIES: Parking lot and free street parking, taproom

PUB HOURS: Thursday–Saturday: 2:00 to 10:00 P.M.

NEARBY ATTRACTIONS: Boom Island Brewing Company, Fulton Brewing Company, 612Brew, Dangerous Man Brewing Company, historic Grain Belt Brewery building, Nordeast Minneapolis bars, restaurants, and art galleries, Guthrie Theatre, Mill City Museum, performances at the Ritz Theatre, Twins games at Target Field

NOTES: Northeast Minneapolis—"Nordeast" to locals—has a lot of history. It's where Minneapolis was founded as the town of St. Anthony. John Orth established the state's second brewery there in 1850. Until 1975, the neighborhood was home to the Grain Belt Brewing Company. The stately old brewery building is still a beloved neighborhood landmark. One of Minnesota's first craft breweries, the James Page Brewing Company, opened there in 1986. Its closure in the mid-1990s put an end to brewing in Northeast—until Indeed Brewing Company came along.

Indeed's ownership trio met while working as staff photographers at *Minnesota Daily* magazine. Nathan Berndt and Thomas Whisenand began homebrewing together and developed an increasing interest in beer. The idea to start a brewery came after Berndt took a tour of Surly Brewing Company. He sent a text to Whisenand saying, "Let's do this." Rachel Anderson was brought on board to do marketing and later became the third partner. They hired brewer Josh Bi-

Indeed Brewing Company in Northeast Minneapolis.

schoff from the Minneapolis Town Hall Brewery to complete the team.

Nordeast is home to a thriving arts scene. The second floor of Indeed's building is given over to artist studios. The Indeed crew is tapping into that energy, using local artists to design their labels and hosting arts-centered soirees in the building's third-floor event space.

The Indeed taproom feels a bit like a nineteenth-century brewery hospitality room. The wood paneling came from Wisconsin oak trees felled and milled for them by a friend. The tables and chairs were once in the club room of a turn-of-the-century milling magazine. Be sure to search the table tops for the carved names of famous figures like Teddy Roosevelt, who visited there.

Lift Bridge Brewing Company

ADDRESS: 1900 Tower Dr. Stillwater, MN 55082

TELEPHONE: 888-430-2337

EMAIL: info@liftbridgebrewery.com

WEB SITE: www.liftbridgebrewery.com

MICHAEL'S PICK: Chestnut Hill: Chestnut brown in color with a creamy off-white head, it has a smooth, lightly toasted, nut and caramel malt profile. The malt is balanced by spicy/herbal hop flavors and enough bitterness to keep it from being sweet without overwhelming the malt. There's cinnamon and allspice in there, too—not enough to notice, but just enough to give it a little something extra. With just a touch of alcohol warmth, it is a good beer for a chilly afternoon.

TYPE: Brewery

DATE ESTABLISHED: 2008

OWNERS: Steve Rinker, Brad Glynn, Dan Schwarz, Jim Pierson, and Trevor Cronk

BREWMASTER: Matt Hall

BREWING SYSTEM: Fifteen-barrel Newlands Systems brewhouse

FLAGSHIP BEERS: Farm Girl Saison, Crosscut Pale Ale

YEAR-ROUND BEERS: Farm Girl Saison, Crosscut Pale Ale, Chestnut Hill

SEASONAL BEERS: Harvestör Fresh Hop Ale, Biscotti, Chestnut Hill, Minnesota Tan

SPECIAL RELEASES: Top Side Oyster Stout, Hop Prop IPA, Commander Barleywine Style Ale, Sillouhet, and others

TOURS: Saturdays at 1:00 and 3:00 P.M. Reservation required.

BEER TO GO: Growlers

AMENITIES: Small parking lot, free street parking, taproom, available for private events

PUB HOURS: Tuesday–Thursday: 5:00 to 8:00 P.M.; Friday: noon to 8:00 P.M.; Saturday: noon to 5:00 P.M.

NEARBY ATTRACTIONS: Near historic downtown Stillwater, antique stores, hiking and cross-country skiing in nearby Minnesota and Wisconsin state parks, St. Croix Vineyards, Afton ski area, thirty minutes from the Twin Cities

NOTES: Steve Rinker once told me, "The day I boiled my first pot of extract in the kitchen, I knew I was going to have a brewery someday." When the former homebrewer confided to his coworker Brad Glynn—another former homebrewer—that he was thinking of resuming the hobby, it started a conversation that led to bigger things. Joined by their friends Dan Schwarz and Jim Pierson, they began brewing pilot batches in the back yard and planning what would become Lift Bridge Brewing Company. The fifth partner, Trevor Cronk, came on board later.

The brewery takes its name from the Stillwater Lift Bridge that spans the St. Croix River from Minnesota to Wisconsin. Choosing this local icon as their namesake fits well with their desire to make the brewery a focal point of the Stillwater community. After a period of contract brewing, they purchased a building in 2010, installed a brewery, and hired a full-time brewmaster. Production at the new facility began in early 2011, making Lift Bridge the first new brewery in Stillwater since Prohibition.

Lift Bridge shies away from extreme beers, preferring instead to craft accessible beers that can appeal to a wide range of people. Their flagship Farmgirl Saison is sort of a "saison-light," with less yeasty funk and peppery bite than a traditional Belgian saison, but still a pleasantly quaffable beer for a summer evening. Chestnut Hill and Biscotti are both full-flavored, complex ales that offer some intrigue while remaining easy to drink.

Lucid Brewing

ADDRESS: 6020 Culligan Way
Minnetonka, MN 55345

TELEPHONE: 612–412–4769

EMAIL: lorenzo@lucidbrewing.com

WEB SITE: www.lucidbrewing.com

MICHAEL'S PICK: Cammo: Be careful with this 9 percent ABV double IPA: it drinks more like 7 percent. It's big and bold with plenty of bitterness and citrusy hops to satisfy even the most dedicated hophead. But the bitterness is kept in check by a good amount of residual sweetness. It's not syrupy, though. The dry finish keeps it crisp and light.

TYPE: Brewery

DATE ESTABLISHED: 2011

OWNERS: Eric Bierman and Jon Messier

BREWMASTER: Eric Bierman

BREWING SYSTEM: Fifteen-barrel CGET brewhouse

FLAGSHIP BEERS: Air, Dyno, Foto, Silo

YEAR-ROUND BEERS: Air, Dyno, Foto, Silo

SEASONAL BEERS: Summertide, Wammo, Project 1, and others

SPECIAL RELEASES: Surfside, Düo, Cammo, Duce, Craig's Ale, BrewRing Homebrewer Collaboration Series

TOURS: Thursdays and Fridays at 4:30 and 5:45 P.M. Reservations required: email tours@lucidbrewing.com.

BEER TO GO: Growlers

FOOD: None

AMENITIES: Free parking in lot

PUB HOURS: None

NEARBY ATTRACTIONS: Twin Cities breweries and brewpubs, water activities on Lake Minnetonka, Stages Theatre Company, Old Log Theatre, golf, Valleyfair Amusement Park, twenty minutes from downtown Minneapolis

NOTES: It is almost a cliché these days when pro brewers speak of their homebrewing roots. Ask nearly any of them how they got started, and the response is likely to be, "I was a homebrewer." But for Eric Beirman and Jon Messier, the dynamic duo behind Lucid, those roots go deep. Before going pro, they both took home numerous medals for their homemade creations. Those same beers are the source for many of the beers they currently craft at Lucid.

The homebrewing community gave them a lot. Now the guys are giving back. The Community Brewing Project allows local homebrewers an opportunity to work with the Lucid team to brew a batch on a commercial scale. As Bierman explained it to me, "A lot of people have the dream of becoming professional brewers but don't have the funding or the know-how to make it happen." As part of the partnership, Bierman and Messier help the fledgling brewer scale his or her recipe to a larger system, arrange for the acquisition of ingredients, and then brew the recipe with them.

They are also giving support to other would-be pros by sharing their brewery in an arrangement called "alternating proprietorship." Sharing a facility allows fully licensed breweries to get up and running without the risk and expense of purchasing equipment before they get established. Badger Hill Brewing Company was the first to take advantage of this arrangement at Lucid.

Lucid crafts beers that will appeal to the palates of nerds and newbies alike. Lucid launched with two beers that fall at opposite ends of the scale. Air is a light, cream-ale-like beer with a good dose of wheat in the grist. Bright citrus hop notes and restrained bitterness make it an easy-drinking session beer. Cammo, however, is a deceptively strong and boldly bitter double IPA.

Minneapolis Town Hall Brewery

ADDRESS: 1430 Washington Ave. S
Minneapolis, MN 55454
TELEPHONE: 612–339–8696
EMAIL: info@townhallbrewery.com
WEB SITE: www.townhallbrewery.com
MICHAEL'S PICK: West Bank Pub Ale: While many would likely choose the Masala Mama IPA as the best that Town Hall has to offer, I prefer the subtler and more sessionable West Bank Pub Ale. Maybe I'm just a sucker for English bitters. This one has a more assertive bitterness than many from England, but the caramel malt and earthy hops are right on target. And at just 4.8 percent ABV, you can enjoy a few.
TYPE: Brewpub
DATE ESTABLISHED: 1997
OWNER: Pete Rifakes
BREWMASTER: Mike Hoops
BREWING SYSTEM: Ten-barrel JV Northwest brewhouse
FLAGSHIP BEER: Masala Mama IPA
YEAR-ROUND BEERS: Dortmunder Local, Masala Mama IPA, Hope and King Scotch Ale, Black H2O Oatmeal Stout, West Bank Pub Ale
SEASONAL BEERS: Czar Jack Barrel Aged Imperial Stout, Maibock, 1800 English IPA, Thunderstorm Honey Ale, Smoked Hefeweizen, Three Hour Tour Coconut Milk Stout, Pumpkin Ale
SPECIAL RELEASES: Special releases weekly, including LSD, Barrel Aged Saison, Potato Stout, Chipotle Scotch Ale, and others

TOURS: First Saturday of every month. Reservation required.
BEER TO GO: Growlers
FOOD: Pub food with a few more upscale items: burgers, pastas, fish tacos.
AMENITIES: Metered street parking and paid parking in ramps. Town Hall runs buses from the pub to and from Target Field for Twins games. Selection of guest taps, full bar with a great selection of scotch, seasonal outdoor seating.
PUB HOURS: Monday–Thursday: 11:00 A.M. to 1:00 A.M.; Friday–Saturday: 11:00 A.M. to 2:00 A.M.; Sunday: 11:00 A.M. to 10:00 P.M.
NEARBY ATTRACTIONS: Twin Cities breweries and brewpubs, Vikings games at the Metrodome, Twins games at Target Field, sporting events and concerts at the Target Center, Theatre in the Round, the Southern Theatre, Mixed Blood Theatre, 1st Avenue music club, music clubs in the Cedar/Riverside area, University of Minnesota campus

NOTES: The atmosphere of a nineteenth-century saloon, solid and reasonably priced pub food, and great beers combine to make Town Hall my favorite Twin Cities brewpub. The year-round beer lineup is excellent, but the real draws for me are the ever-rotating seasonal and specialty brews. Head brewer Mike Hoops and crew brew a dizzying array of styles, ranging from single-hop IPAs to Belgian grand cru and raspberry imperial stout. With new releases happening nearly every week, it can be hard to keep up. There are always two cask-conditioned options. In addition to the Town Hall beers, there is a good selection of guest taps and draft cider.

Town Hall's brewery tours are among the best in town. The seven-dollar admission gets you a pint of Town Hall beer, a tasting glass, and a discount on food at the end. The tour lasts about an hour and takes you into the newly remodeled basement, where another set of taps awaits. They usually put on something special that isn't available at the upstairs bar.

Northbound Smokehouse and Brewpub

ADDRESS: 2716 E. 38th St.
Minneapolis, MN 55406
TELEPHONE: 612–208–1450
EMAIL: info@northboundbrewpub.com
WEB SITE: www.northboundbrewpub.com
MICHAEL'S PICK: Light Rail Pale Ale: Loads of late-addition Cascade hops give this American pale ale an intense citrus aroma that virtually leaps out of the glass. Bitterness is kept to a moderate level, allowing the hop flavor to shine. It's the malt that makes this

beer interesting, with toffee, toast, and biscuit notes providing a tantalizing counterpoint to the hops.

TYPE: Brewpub

DATE ESTABLISHED: 2012

OWNERS: Jamie Robinson, Bryce Strickler, and Amy Johnson

BREWMASTER: Jamie Robinson

BREWING SYSTEM: Seven-barrel DME brewhouse

FLAGSHIP BEER: Big Jim IPA

YEAR-ROUND BEERS: Honey Wheat Ale, Light Rail Pale Ale, Big Jim IPA, Smokehouse Porter

SEASONAL BEERS: Wild Rice Amber, Saison, Autumn Ale, Snowpacolypse, Snowmageddon, and others

SPECIAL RELEASES: Columbus Pale Ale, Single Hop Pacific Jade Double IPA, and others

TOURS: Planned

BEER TO GO: Growlers planned

FOOD: A small selection of appetizers, salads, and sandwiches featuring house-smoked meats, fish, and cheeses

AMENITIES: Free street parking, seasonal outdoor seating, full bar, selection of local guest taps

PUB HOURS: Sunday–Thursday: 11:00 A.M. to 1:00 A.M.; Friday and Saturday: 11:00 A.M. to 2:00 A.M.

NEARBY ATTRACTIONS: Twin Cities breweries and brewpubs, In the Heart of the Beast Theatre, Patrick's Cabaret, Winchell Trail walkway along the Mississippi River, Minnehaha Falls, University of Minnesota West Bank campus

NOTES: The story of Northbound Smokehouse begins with limos. Brewer/co-owner Jamie Robinson was operating a home-based limousine service and homebrewing on the side. Although he was successful, he was dissatisfied. He began considering a career change, and brewing seemed to him to be just the thing. He sold his business, got trained at the Siebel Institute in Chicago, and took a manager position at the Minneapolis Town Hall Brewpub to learn the ropes en route to opening a brewpub of his own.

While at Town Hall, Jamie met Amy Johnson, who was managing a nearby beer bar. Amy just happened to have studied hotel and restaurant management in college. The two became a couple, and the business partnership followed on.

Chef Bryce Strickler entered the picture as a cook at Town Hall. When Jamie one day asked him about his goals, Strickler replied that he was going to open his own restaurant. Conversations ensued, menus were discussed, and the third leg of the ownership stool was set in place.

Unable to find a few high-dollar investors, the trio raised startup capital by soliciting 150 small investors.

In exchange for an investment of one thousand dollars, these "members," as they are called, receive free beer for life at the pub.

Aside from the brewery, the two smokers in the kitchen are the brewpub's driving force. Nearly everything on the menu is smoked, from the cheese to the egg-salad sandwich. The Smokehouse Porter even contains house-smoked malt. The smoked whitefish dip and the porketta sandwich are definite menu must-tries.

Northgate Brewing

ADDRESS: 783 Harding St. NE Minneapolis, MN 55413

TELEPHONE: 612–234–1056

EMAIL: info@northgatebrew.com

WEB SITE: www.northgatebrew.com

MICHAEL'S PICK: Wall's End: A classic North English brown ale, Wall's End delivers Tootsie-Roll chocolate and bitter coffee notes rounded out by toffee sweetness. Moderate bitterness and earthy hop flavors keep things in balance. This would be great with some Heath-bar Crunch ice cream.

TYPE: Brewery

DATE ESTABLISHED: 2013

OWNERS: Todd Slininger, Adam Sjorgen, and Tuck Carruthers

BREWMASTER: Tuck Carruthers

BREWING SYSTEM: Five-barrel converted dairy-tank brewhouse

FLAGSHIP BEER: Wall's End English Brown Ale

YEAR-ROUND BEER: Wall's End English Brown Ale

SEASONAL BEERS: Maggie's Leap Sweet Stout, Parapet ESB, Bliss Pale Ale

SPECIAL RELEASES: Fiddle Smasher Wee Heavy

TOURS: See Web site for times

BEER TO GO: Growlers

FOOD: None

AMENITIES: Parking lot, taproom

PUB HOURS: Thursday: 4:00 P.M. to 10:00 P.M.; Friday: 4:00 P.M. to midnight; Saturday: noon to midnight

NEARBY ATTRACTIONS: 612Brew, Indeed Brewing Company, Dangerous Man Brewing Company, historic Grain Belt Brewery building, Nordeast Minneapolis nightlife, Galleries of the Arts District, Guthrie Theatre, Mill City Museum, performances at the Ritz Theatre, Twins games at Target Field

NOTES: When Adam Sjorgen and Todd Slininger started homebrewing together, Sjorgen's girlfriend thought that she was set as far as buying him gifts. All she had to do was go to the homebrew store and buy whatever was hot. For them, brewing was like an arms race, as each one tried to outdo the other. Batch sizes increased. When one started kegging his beer, the other stepped up from extract brewing to all-grain. But then came Northgate. For the two men, founding the brewery is just the arms race reaching its pinnacle. For Sjorgen's girlfriend, it means having to dream up new gift ideas.

The three Northgate partners—Tuck Carruthers came on board after the business was under way—have been amazed at the level of generosity that others have directed at the brewery. They have found that opening a brewery can open other doors. An army of people suddenly appeared to help move a heavy boiler when it was learned that the thing was destined for a brewery. Need to borrow a forklift? No problem, when it's done in the service of beer.

Northgate brews sessionable ales inspired by the classic British styles—that are best, they say, when consumed close to the source. Their passion for these beers developed on a trip to Ireland. "You always hear that annoying guy who says that Guinness over there is so much better than it is here," says Slininger. "But then you go there and realize that it's really true." To maintain that brewery-fresh flavor, the team is keeping things local. They are serving nearby accounts first and only slowly expanding distribution outward in concentric circles around the brewery. And if a keg doesn't move, they'll take it back rather than let it get stale.

Rock Bottom Restaurant and Brewery

ADDRESS: 800 Lasalle Plaza
Minneapolis, MN 55402
TELEPHONE: 612–332–2739
EMAIL: minneapolis@rockbottom.com
WEB SITE: www.rockbottom.com/Minneapolis
MICHAEL'S PICK: Bastogne Blond: A silver-medal winner at the 2010 Great American Beer Festival, this occasionally recurring, special-release Belgian blond ale is one of those beers that makes you say, "This is what beer should be." It features sweet pilsner malt flavor with bracing bitterness and balancing spicy hop flavors. The banana character of Belgian yeast is subdued, allowing for beautifully layered complexity.
DATE ESTABLISHED: 1993
TYPE: Brewpub
OWNER: CraftWorks Restaurants and Breweries, Inc.
BREWMASTER: Larry Skellenger
BREWING SYSTEM: Ten-barrel JV Northwest brewhouse
FLAGSHIP BEERS: Kölsch, White Ale, Red Ale, IPA
YEAR-ROUND BEERS: Kölsch, White Ale, Red Ale, IPA, rotating dark ale

SEASONAL BEERS: Intoxicator Rauch Doppelbock, Erin Isle Irish Stout, American Dream IPA, Anniversary IPA, Hop Bomb Double IPA, Fire Chief Ale, rotating wheat beers in summer
SPECIAL RELEASES: Black Ale, Hopfen König Inda Pale Lager, St. Paul Pilsner, Czech-It Pilsner, Headlight Hefeweizen, Bastogne Blond, Smoked Porter, occasional barrel-aged offerings, Coconut Chai Stout, Paranoid IPA, New World IPA, Angry Hippie, Cocoamotion Porter, and others
TOURS: By appointment
BEER TO GO: Growlers and 750 ml bottles
FOOD: Standard Rock Bottom Restaurant menu: pub food, sandwiches and burgers, salads, chili, and a range of entrées. Good selection of steaks.
AMENITIES: Metered street parking or paid parking in nearby ramps, happy-hour specials, full bar, pool tables, cask-conditioned offerings
PUB HOURS: Monday–Thursday: 11:00 A.M. to 1:00 A.M.; Friday and Saturday: 11:00 A.M. to 2:00 A.M.; Sunday: 11:00 A.M. to midnight
NEARBY ATTRACTIONS: Hennepin Ave. Theatre District, Block E, the Target Center, Target Field, and Nicolette Mall

NOTES: Larry Skellenger is grateful for the opportunities he has been given as a brewer. He had no previous brewing experience when he started. He has never homebrewed, nor did he attend brewing school. Skellenger came to the career late in life, having spent twenty-five years at a desk job before retiring from the corporate world. And yet he has managed to work his way up to the position of head brewer in what is usually a younger person's game.

Skellenger's brewing journey began at the Rock Bottom in Des Moines, where he was a charter Mug Club member. He had just retired from his corporate job when head brewer Eric Sorensen approached him about becoming assistant brewer. Sorensen had just been named regional brewer for Rock Bottom and knew that an assistant would be needed to man the brewery while he was away at other locations. He was aware of Skellenger's background in biology and engineering, two knowledge areas that are useful to brewers. Sorensen also knew that Skellenger had a true appreciation for good beer and believed that he would be a fast learner. It was enough for Sorensen to take the risk.

After seven years in a part-time position Skellenger was forced to take the reins when Sorensen sustained an injury that took him temporarily out of commission. Seven years of Sorensen's tutelage had prepared him, and he performed well enough that he was offered the head brewer position in Minneapolis when it opened up. "It was the scariest moment in my life," he says of the moment when he accepted the offer. "If anyone had asked me seven years ago if my aspirations were to be a head brewer, I would have said no." Now that he's there, he wouldn't want to be anywhere else.

The ambience and menu at Rock Bottom are fairly standardized across the chain. Look for slightly up-scale pub food with some nicer items tossed in. That said, the food is always delicious. The Minneapolis location draws a big theater crowd for dinner every night and can get quite busy. If you come before a Twins game, expect to find it jam-packed.

Steel Toe Brewing

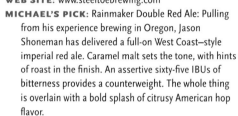

ADDRESS: 4848 W. 35th St.
   St Louis Park, MN 55416
TELEPHONE: 952-955-9965
EMAIL: brewer@steeltoebrewing.com
WEB SITE: www.steeltoebrewing.com
MICHAEL'S PICK: Rainmaker Double Red Ale: Pulling from his experience brewing in Oregon, Jason Shoneman has delivered a full-on West Coast–style imperial red ale. Caramel malt sets the tone, with hints of roast in the finish. An assertive sixty-five IBUs of bitterness provides a counterweight. The whole thing is overlain with a bold splash of citrusy American hop flavor.
TYPE: Brewery
DATE ESTABLISHED: 2011
OWNERS: Jason Schoneman and Hannah Schoneman
BREWMASTER: Jason Schoneman
BREWING SYSTEM: Fourteen-barrel converted dairy-tank brewhouse
FLAGSHIP BEER: Size 7 IPA
YEAR-ROUND BEERS: Provider Ale, Rainmaker Double Red Ale, Size 7 IPA, Dissent Dark Ale
SEASONAL BEERS: Lunker Rye Barrel Aged Barleywine, Bourbon Barrel Aged Imperial Stout, Size 11 Triple IPA, Scotch Ale
SPECIAL RELEASES: Before the Dawn Barrel Aged Black Barleywine
TOURS: Saturdays. Check Web site for times.
BEER TO GO: Growlers
FOOD: None
AMENITIES: Parking lot, taproom
PUB HOURS: Tuesday and Thursday: 3:00 to 5:00 P.M.; Friday: 3:00 to 7:30 P.M.; Saturday: noon to 10:00 P.M.
NEARBY ATTRACTIONS: Twin Cities breweries and brewpubs, Four Firkins Specialty Beer Store, the Baaken Museum, Museum of Broadcasting, Minneapolis

Chain of Lakes, including Lake Harriet, Lake Calhoun, Cedar Lake, and Lake of the Isles, walking and biking trails, summer concerts at the Lake Harriet Bandshell, restaurants and nightlife in the Uptown neighborhood

NOTES: Steel Toe brewer Jason Schoneman isn't just another homebrewer deciding to go pro. He opened Steel Toe with years of professional experience behind him. His career began at Lightning Boy Brewery in Bozeman, Montana, where he started out working fifteen-hour days washing kegs and filling bottles. "That was the test," he says. "If you still love it after that, then it's the right fit for you. For me, it was the greatest thing. It didn't feel like work."

With that experience under his belt, he decided it was time to take brewing seriously. He enrolled in the three-month Diploma Course at the Siebel Institute World Brewing Academy in Chicago. "I did the whole thing. Racked up the credit cards and took a leap of faith. We figured if you're going to do it, do it right."

From there he was hired at the Pelican Pub and Brewery in Pacific City, Oregon, where he once again started out washing kegs and filling bottles. Within four years he had advanced to the position of head brewer. The time at Pelican was formative. He learned there what it takes to make a brewery go, gaining experience in all aspects of brewery operations: wholesale distribution, dealing with customers, tours, brewery logistics, and maintenance.

All that experience is reflected in the beers he is producing. Steel Toe beers are consistently clean and crisp, with well-articulated layers of flavor that invite another pint. Steel Toe started small, and the plan is to keep it local. They foresee limiting distribution to a tight circle around the Twin Cities metro area.

Summit Brewing Company

ADDRESS: 910 Montreal Circle
   St Paul, MN 55102
TELEPHONE: 651-265-7800
EMAIL: info@summitbrewing.com
WEB SITE: www.summitbrewing.com
MICHAEL'S PICK: India Pale Ale: At 6.5 percent ABV and sixty bittering units, this is a beautiful example of the English-style IPA. It pours amber with a tall, off-white head. The crisp bitterness and earthy, lightly citrus Golding hop character is lusciously backed by ample caramel malt.
DATE ESTABLISHED: 1986
TYPE: Brewery
OWNER: Mark Stutrud
BREWMASTER: Mark Stutrud

BREWING SYSTEM: 220-hectoliter Ziemann brewhouse

FLAGSHIP BEER: Extra Pale Ale

YEAR-ROUND BEERS: Extra Pale Ale, Pilsner, India Pale Ale, Great Northern Porter, Horizon Red IPA, Saga IPA

SEASONAL BEERS: Maibock, Summer Ale, Oktoberfest

SPECIAL RELEASES: Oatmeal Stout, Unchained Series Beers, Union Series Beers

TOURS: Tuesdays and Thursdays at 1:00 P.M.; Saturdays at 10:30 A.M. and 1:00 P.M. Reservations required for Saturday tours.

BEER TO GO: None

FOOD: None

AMENITIES: Parking lot, taproom, gift shop

PUB HOURS: Friday and Saturday: 4:00 to 9:00 P.M.

NEARBY ATTRACTIONS: Twin Cities breweries and brewpubs, Flat Earth Brewing Company and Vine Park Brewing Company are both located within a mile, Minnehaha Falls, Cathedral of St. Paul, James Hill House, Fort Snelling, Science Museum of Minnesota, Minnesota Children's Museum, sporting events and concerts at the Excel Energy Center, Fitzgerald Theatre, Minnesota History Center

NOTES: Mark Stutrud was a pioneer. In the early 1980s, the beer selection in Minnesota was limited, to say the least. Most bars had only three taps pouring Schmidt's, Hamm's, and Grain Belt Premium. Nationwide there were only a handful of craft breweries, none of which were located in the Midwest. So when this former substance-abuse counselor decided to open a craft brewery, people thought he was crazy. That crazy idea has turned into one of the most successful small breweries in the region. Since rolling out the first keg of Extra Pale Ale in 1986, Summit has grown into a regional powerhouse, with annual production exceeding one hundred thousand barrels.

Many Minnesota beer fans cite Extra Pale Ale as their gateway into the world of craft beer. Eschewing the trend toward extreme beers, Summit crafts solid examples of classic English and European styles. Their beers are full of flavor and yet accessible. They can satisfy the hardcore beer drinker without offending the novice. They are session beers that enhance conversation rather than demanding to be the center of attention.

Not content to rest on its laurels, Summit continues to innovate. A new small-batch system is allowing them to test new recipes and make unique beers available in the tasting room. The Unchained Series gives Summit's brewers complete control of a limited-release beer from recipe formulation all the way through to packaging. Each individual brewer determines the style, crafts the beer, and decides when it is ready to bottle. This has resulted in some of Summit's most intriguing beers to date.

Surly Brewing Company

ADDRESS: 4811 Dusharme Dr. Brooklyn Center, MN 55429

TELEPHONE: 763-535-3330

EMAIL: beer@surlybrewing.com

WEB SITE: www.surlybrewing.com

MICHAEL'S PICK: Bender: Surly Bender is a stylistic conundrum. If you ask owner Omar Ansari, it's an American brown ale. Brewer Todd Haug has called it an oatmeal brown porter. I just call it good. Layers of English malt character reveal caramel, cocoa, coffee, and comforting roastiness. The malt is balanced and enhanced by crisp but subtle hops. Bender is a soothing session beer that works equally well on a cold winter's night or a sunny summer afternoon.

TYPE: Brewery

DATE ESTABLISHED: 2006

OWNER: Omar Ansari

BREWMASTER: Todd Haug

BREWING SYSTEM: Thirty-barrel Sprinkman brewhouse

FLAGSHIP BEER: Furious

YEAR-ROUND BEERS: Furious, Bender, Coffee Bender, Hell, Cynic Ale

SEASONAL BEERS: Abrasive Ale, Surlyfest, Bitter Brewer, Darkness, Smoke, Mild, Wet, Schadenfreude, Pentagram

SPECIAL RELEASES: One, Two, Three, Four, Five, Six, Bandwagon, Damian Black IPA, specialty casks

TOURS: Most Friday evenings from 6:00 to 8:00. Reservations are required. Sign up on the Web site. Attendees are required to bring a nonperishable food item for donation to a local food shelf.

BEER TO GO: None

FOOD: None

PUB HOURS: Wednesday–Friday: 3:00 P.M. to 9:00 P.M.; Saturday: Noon to 9:00 P.M.

AMENITIES: Parking lot, tasting room opens during tours

NEARBY ATTRACTIONS: Twin Cities breweries and brewpubs, ten minutes from downtown Minneapolis, Walker Arts Center, Loring Park, Hennepin Ave. Theater District, Guthrie Theatre, sporting events and concerts at the Target Center, Twins games at Target Field

NOTES: Releasing its first beer in 2006, Surly was the first of the new wave of breweries in Minnesota. Despite limited distribution range, Surly quickly gained a national reputation and an almost cultlike following. Its reputation continues to grow as high demand spurs rapid expansion. Plans are in the works for a twenty-million-dollar destination brewery in Minneapolis.

Surly's reputation is built on solid brewing and innovative beers. Many Surly brews push the limits of the palate and stretch the boundaries of stylistic convention. Flagship Furious sports a whopping ninety-nine bittering units, and the aptly named Abrasive has even more. Bender falls between styles, causing debate among beer fans whether to call it a porter or a brown ale. As early adopters of cans, even their packaging is unique.

But Surly isn't only about extreme. They also make excellent examples of classic session styles that have been underrepresented in the region. Among their lineup are a Munich helles and dunkel, an English mild, and a convincing Saison.

Surly has been turning up the heat on community involvement as well with the Surly Gives a Damn program. The mission of this project is to harness the energy of the legions of Surly fans to support charitable organizations and community causes. They sponsor regular blood drives, help with cleanup efforts in area parks and bike paths, and donate food to a local food shelf.

At the time of writing, Surly is planning a move to a new "destination brewery" in the Nordeast neighborhood of Minneapolis. The new facility will include a restaurant, beer garden, and meeting space.

Vine Park Brewing Company

ADDRESS: 1254 7th St. W
St Paul, MN 55102
TELEPHONE: 651–228–1355
EMAIL: newsletter@vinepark.com
WEB SITE: www.vinepark.com
MICHAEL'S PICK: Cuvee de Beertrips Belgian Ale: This beer was born from a bus-ride conversation among participants in a Vine Park–sponsored beer trip to Belgium. Cuvee is brewed primarily in the Belgian pale ale style, with a soft, biscuity malt profile balanced by moderate spicy hops and bitterness. The subtle Belgian yeast character finishes this light, easy-to-drink Belgian session beer.
DATE ESTABLISHED: The brew-on-premises opened in 1995, the microbrewery in 2008
TYPE: Brewery
OWNERS: Daniel Justesen and Andy Grage
BREWMASTER: Andy Grage
BREWING SYSTEM: Three-barrel Price Schonstrom brewhouse
FLAGSHIP BEERS: None

YEAR-ROUND BEERS: (Variable availability throughout the year) Mulligan Ale, Capitol Hill Pilsner, Stumpjumper Amber Ale, Tornado Alley Alt, Rabid Penguin Porter, Horny Toad Pale Ale
SEASONAL BEERS: Bavarian Hefeweizen, Belgian Witte, Oktoberfest, Black Magic Imperial Stout, Celebratory Maibock
SPECIAL RELEASES: Belgian Dubbel, Cuvee de Beertrips Belgian Ale, and others
TOURS: No
BEER TO GO: Growlers
FOOD: None
AMENITIES: Free street parking, make your own beer at the brew-on-premises
PUB HOURS: None
NEARBY ATTRACTIONS: Twin Cities breweries and brewpubs, Flat Earth Brewing Company and Summit Brewing Company are both located within a mile, Minnehaha Falls, Cathedral of St. Paul, James Hill House, Fort Snelling, Science Museum of Minnesota, Minnesota Children's Museum, sporting events and concerts at the Excel Energy Center, Fitzgerald Theatre, Minnesota History Center

NOTES: Operating as both a brew-on-premises and a microbrewery, Vine Park Brewing Company occupies a unique space in the American brewing landscape. Federal law prohibits both types of business existing in the same space, so some creative thinking was required to make this dual identity work. The solution was to separate them by time. For twelve hours each day, Vine Park is a microbrewery, producing beer for off-premises sale. For the other half of the day they are a brew-on-premises, allowing customers to brew twelve-gallon batches on the extract brewing system.

While they do make a few semi-year-round beers for off-sale, owners Daniel Justesen and Andy Grage pretty much brew whatever they are in the mood to drink. The offerings vary from week to week and season to season. Many of the brews are all-grain versions of the extract beers from the brew-on-premises recipe list. With over fifty to choose from, they don't have to repeat themselves very often. And if you're in the mood, they make a nice root beer as well.

Operating the two businesses side by side creates some complications that other breweries don't face. Vine Park cannot open a taproom and cannot provide samples when the brew-on-premesis is operating. That doesn't mean you can't taste their beer. They hold frequent beer and cheese events that give customers the opportunity to try their wares. Check the Web site for times and dates. You can always pick up a growler to go.

NORTHERN

Bemidji Brewing Company

ADDRESS: 401 Beltrami Ave. NW
Bemidji, MN 56601

TELEPHONE: 218–444–7011

EMAIL: info@bemidjibeer.com

WEB SITE: www.bemidjibeer.com

MICHAEL'S PICK: Sour Red: Lactic tartness and dark stone-fruit flavors define this Flemish red-style ale. Subtle barnyard notes add some earthy depth. Hints of caramel and toasted malt remain despite a high level of attenuation. It's light, bright, and pretty darn tasty.

TYPE: Brewery

DATE ESTABLISHED: 2012

OWNERS: Justin Kaney, Tom Hill, and Tina Hanke

BREWMASTER: Tom Hill

BREWING SYSTEM: 1.5-barrel Blichmann Engineering brewhouse

FLAGSHIP BEERS: None

YEAR-ROUND BEERS: Dry-Hopped Pale Ale, Robust Porter

SEASONAL BEERS: Planned

SPECIAL RELEASES: Belgian Blonde, Sour Red, Afternoon Ale, Rye Saison, Table Saison, and others

TOURS: By request

BEER TO GO: Growlers

FOOD: None

AMENITIES: Parking lot, taproom, available for private parties

PUB HOURS: Thursday to Saturday 4:00 to 9:00 P.M.

NEARBY ATTRACTIONS: Paul Bunyan and Babe the Blue Ox statues, Paul Bunyan Playhouse, water activities on Lake Bemidji, golf and winter sports at area resorts, year-round outdoor activities in area state parks, headwaters of the Mississippi, Headwaters Science Center

NOTES: One of the greatest hurdles to starting a brewery is securing financing. It's difficult to convince individuals and banks to invest without product and proven success. Many budding brewers choose contract brewing—paying others to make the beer—as a way to build a brand before they build a brewery. But working this way means giving up a certain amount of control over your product.

The folks at Bemidji Brewing took a different route. By starting small, they could begin making beer with a minimal initial investment while maintaining complete control of the process. Brewing small batches on a thirty-gallon system gets beer out to consumers and allows the threesome to tweak old recipes and develop new ones as they work toward bigger things.

Bemidji Brewing began in a shared, community kitchen run by the Harmony Food Coop. The rent was hourly, so they paid only for their actual brewing time, saving them considerable overhead cost. But this arrangement also created problems with federal regulators. The Tax and Trade Bureau that issues brewers' licenses requires "protection of revenue," meaning that fermenters and finished product cannot be accessible to nonbrewery personnel. Dealing with this meant building padlocked cages in the kitchen's walk-in cooler. And the brewers had to move their entire system into and out of the space for every brew day. A move to their own space alleviated these issues and allowed them to open a taproom.

Head Brewer Tom Hill's tendency is to well-attenuated session beers—quenching beers for drinking rather than contemplating. But don't rule out the occasional double IPA or imperial stout. Even before the brewery opened, he was already getting requests for those big beers from Bemidji beer fans.

Bent Paddle Brewing Company

ADDRESS: 1912 W. Michigan St.
Duluth, Minnesota 55806

TELEPHONE: 218–279–2722

EMAIL: info@bentpaddlebrewing.com

WEB SITE: www.bentpaddlebrewing.com

MICHAEL'S PICK: Venture Pils: This well-made pilsner straddles the line between the Bohemian and German styles. It's not quite as malty as a Czech pils, and not quite so dry and bitter as a German pils. Grainy, graham-cracker malt gives a lightly sweet base with subtle hints of toast. It's bracingly bitter, but balanced. Perfumed and spicy hops have undertones of citrus and black current.

TYPE: Brewery

DATE ESTABLISHED: 2013

OWNERS: Bryon Tonnis, Karen Tonnis, Colin Mullen, and Laura Mullen

BREWMASTERS: Colin Mullen and Bryon Tonnis

BREWING SYSTEM: Thirty-barrel DME brewhouse

FLAGSHIP BEERS: Bent Hop Golden IPA, Bent Paddle Black Ale, 14 Degree ESB, Venture Pils

YEAR-ROUND BEERS: Bent Hop Golden IPA, Bent Paddle Black Ale, 14 Degree ESB, Venture Pils

SEASONAL BEERS: Planned

SPECIAL RELEASES: Planned

TOURS: Saturdays. Check Web site for times.

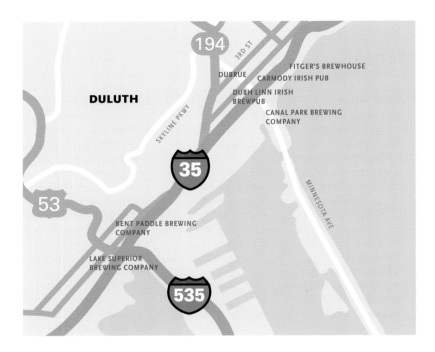

194

3RD ST

DUBRUE

FITGER'S BREWHOUSE

CARMODY IRISH PUB

DUBH LINN IRISH
BREWPUB

CANAL PARK BREWING
COMPANY

DULUTH

SKYLINE PKWY

MINNESOTA AVE

35

53

BENT PADDLE BREWING
COMPANY

LAKE SUPERIOR
BREWING COMPANY

535

BEER TO GO: Growlers

FOOD: None

AMENITIES: Parking lot, taproom

PUB HOURS: Wednesday and Thursday: 3:00 to 10:00 P.M.; Friday: 3:00 to 11:00 P.M.; Saturday: 1:00 to 11:00 P.M.

NEARBY ATTRACTIONS: Duluth-area breweries and brewpubs, Enger Park and Enger Tower, Great Lakes Aquarium, Duluth Entertainment and Convention Center, North Shore Scenic Railroad, Canal Park entertainment district

NOTES: Bryon Tonnis honed his brewing skills during his tenure as head brewer at the Minneapolis Rock Bottom brewpub. Shortly after starting there, his mash paddle broke. An avid canoeist, Tonnis happened to have a bent-shaft canoeing paddle in his truck, which he applied as a replacement. Once he used it, he never went back. When picking a name for the brewery, Bent Paddle just seemed like the right choice. But the name isn't only a tribute to Tonnis's favorite tool; it also expresses the whole crew's love of being outdoors in the lake country of northern Minnesota.

Tonnis and co-brewer Colin Mullen were brought together by their wives. They knew each other from the brewing community and had worked together on the board of the Minnesota Craft Brewers Guild, but neither knew that the other was planning a brewery and finding the process similarly frustrating. At the suggestion of their spouses, the two sat down over beers and discovered that their brewing styles and business plans were remarkably similar. The two families formed a partnership and headed to Duluth.

The family-affair partnership works well for them. Each couple had already run a business together. With those businesses, the families had collaborated on projects. They knew the working relationship was a good one. As Bryon Tonnis told me, "We couldn't ask for a better partnership."

Bent Paddle entered the booming Duluth brewing scene as the city's largest brewery and the first with a taproom. The beer lineup reflects the brewers' shared love of subtlety. While they both enjoy a big, brash beer on occasion, their preference is for more delicate brews that allow for the consumption of more than one pint without wrecking your palate or making it difficult to get home.

Boathouse Brewpub and Restaurant

ADDRESS: 47 E. Sheridan St.
Ely, MN 55731

TELEPHONE: 218–365–4301

EMAIL: boathouse@frontiernet.net

WEB SITE: www.boathousebrewpub.com

MICHAEL'S PICK: Mahnomen Wild Rice Brown Ale: A nutty/toasty malt aroma greets you before you even lift the glass. Malty but not sweet, it's full of biscuit, toast, and light chocolate flavors that are balanced by a dry finish and light, earthy hop flavors. Locally grown, hand-parched wild rice adds a delicious nutty depth.

TYPE: Brewpub

DATE ESTABLISHED: 2008

OWNER: Mark Burzek

BREWMASTER: Ben Storbeck

BREWING SYSTEM: 3.5-barrel ABT brewhouse

FLAGSHIP BEER: Entry Point Golden

YEAR-ROUND BEER: Entry Point Golden

SEASONAL BEERS: Blueberry Blond, Mahnomen Wild Rice Brown, Barleywine

SPECIAL RELEASES: Pilot Pub Ale, Hasselhop Rye Pale Ale, Eelpout Oatmeal Stout, Basswood Brown, Spruce Road Copper Ale, 1160 Porter, Pulaski IPA

TOURS: By request

BEER TO GO: Growlers

FOOD: Classic North Country diner food, from breakfast omelets and pancakes to burgers and battered walleye

AMENITIES: Parking lot behind building, free street parking, occasional live music

PUB HOURS: Daily: 6:00 A.M. to 1:00 A.M.

NEARBY ATTRACTIONS: Boundary Waters Canoe Area, International Wolf Center, North American Bear Center, myriad outdoor activities in all seasons: hunting, kayaking, canoeing, fishing, boating, hiking, skiing, snowmobiling

NOTES: When going to Ely, be sure to take the route that follows U.S. Highways 1 and 2. Located at the northern terminus of fabled Highway 1, Ely is the quintessential North Country tourist town and the gateway to the Boundary Waters Canoe Area. It is surrounded by vast expanses of pine and aspen forest that is dotted with lakes and home to black bears, moose, and other wildlife. It's beautiful country.

Boathouse is located in the heart of downtown Ely. It has the feel of a North Country diner, right down to the menu that features a full array of hearty breakfast items. Knotty-pine paneling on the walls finishes the effect. It's a place that is equally welcoming to tourists and locals alike. I noticed several tables of regulars on the day I visited.

Boat House Brewpub in Ely, Minnesota.

Brewer Ben Storbeck came to Boathouse from Lake Superior Brewing in Duluth, where he was becoming frustrated with the regularity of production brewing. He loves the freedom that brewpub brewing gives him. He keeps Entry Point Golden Ale on tap year-round, but the rest of his beers are a "perpetually rotating" selection that always includes a hoppy beer, a malty beer, and a beer that is balanced between the two.

A small brewhouse and limited fermentation capacity means that Storbeck sometimes has a difficult time keeping up with demand in the busy summer tourist season. During the slower season, the brewpub has started doing monthly beer dinners featuring other Minnesota breweries as well as Storbeck's own beers.

Borealis Fermentery

ADDRESS: PO Box 130
Knife River, MN 55609

TELEPHONE: 218–834–4856

EMAIL: info@borealisfermentery.com

WEB SITE: www.borealisfermentery.com

MICHAEL'S PICK: Raisin Liaison Saison: This farmhouse ale is sharp and dry with pronounced, spicy, phenolic notes. Malt and raisin sweetness is there, but it stays somewhat in the background. Subtle wild, barnyard flavors round out the profile.

TYPE: Brewery

DATE ESTABLISHED: 2012

OWNER: Ken Thiemann

BREWMASTER: Ken Thiemann

BREWING SYSTEM: Twenty-gallon modified Sabco Systems brewhouse

FLAGSHIP BEER: Mon Cherries Cherry Dubbel

YEAR-ROUND BEERS: La Lune Special Ale, Speckled Ghost Abbey Ale, Mon Cherries Cherry Dubbel, Homdinger Belgian Style IPA

SEASONAL BEERS: Planned

SPECIAL RELEASES: Planned

TOURS: No

BEER TO GO: None

FOOD: None

AMENITIES: None

PUB HOURS: None

NEARBY ATTRACTIONS: Castle Danger Brewery, hiking on the Superior Hiking Trail and other nearby trails, boating and fishing on Lake Superior and nearby rivers, Split Rock Lighthouse, North Shore Scenic Railroad from Duluth (check out the fall beer-tasting train), North Shore All-American Scenic Drive, vacation at nearby lakeside resorts, thirty minutes from Duluth.

NOTES: The beer world has a do-it-yourself mentality. Brewers like to fiddle, tinker, and self-engineer solutions to problems. Ken Thiemann has taken this attitude to an extreme. His brewery, which resembles a Belgian monastery, is the only brewery in the country housed in a straw-bale structure, and he built it himself from the ground up.

There are no nails in the building. The frame is all hand-hewn timbers fastened with wooden pegs. It's covered in sixty-seven thousand pounds of stucco; every pound was hauled by Thiemann in five-gallon buckets. A fall from a ladder nearly killed him. During months of construction, Thiemann and his wife lived in an uninsulated shed with sleeping bags and a 1930s-era wood stove. As he told me, "I've got the greatest wife in the world."

Thiemann makes only Belgian-style beers in his monastic-looking brewhouse. Many of them are aged on oak chips and spirals that he sometimes toasts himself—another nod to self-sufficiency. He learned to love the Belgians while working in the Netherlands as a canal engineer. He was impressed by the beer culture in Belgium, which treats beer with as much respect as wine. He also loved the sense of play; Belgian brewers have no rules. Compared to the Germans, with their purity laws, the Belgians could put anything in beer to give it intriguing flavors and aromas. Beer in Belgium is fun. And like good cheese, it has a "funk" that he enjoyed.

He's pleased that his own beers have begun to find their own special funk. He reports that they have taken on pleasing house flavors like grain, straw, and earth. Is it the special yeasts that he brought back from Belgium? Or could it be the straw bales adding their own little touch? Whatever it is, he couldn't be happier with the result.

Canal Park Brewing Company

ADDRESS: 300 Canal Park Dr.
Duluth, MN 55802

CANAL PARK
BREWING COMPANY
DULUTH, MINNESOTA
EST. 2012

TELEPHONE: 218–464–4790
EMAIL: info@canalparkbrewery.com
WEB SITE: www.canalparkbrewery.com
MICHAEL'S PICK: Click Drag Kölsch: You can taste the grain in this lovely, light-bodied beer. Graham-cracker-sweet pilsner malt is given added depth by some tasty, toasty notes. The malt is balanced by moderate bitterness and licorice-like hop flavor. Delicate fruit is layered on top.
TYPE: Brewpub
DATE ESTABLISHED: 2012

OWNER: Rockie Kavajecz
BREWMASTERS: Dan Aagenes and Badger Colish
BREWING SYSTEM: Twenty-barrel DME brewhouse
FLAGSHIP BEER: Stoned Surf IPA
YEAR-ROUND BEERS: Stoned Surf IPA, Wetsuit Malfunction Wit, Pack Sacker Stout, Dawn Treader Tripel, Nut Hatchet Brown, Click Drag Kölsch, Clean Dirt Pub Draft
SEASONAL BEERS: Sinter VMO, Winter Warmer, Scottish Ale, Black IPA
SPECIAL RELEASES: Planned
TOURS: By request
BEER TO GO: Growlers
FOOD: Classic brewpub favorites with a North Country slant: cheese curds, deviled eggs, brats, Lake Superior fish tacos
AMENITIES: Public pay lot next door, full bar, seasonal outdoor seating on patio overlooking Lake Superior
PUB HOURS: Daily: 11:00 A.M. to close
NEARBY ATTRACTIONS: Duluth-area breweries and brewpubs, Canal Park restaurants and shops, Lake Superior Scenic Cruises, four-mile lake walk, Park Point Beach, Omnimax Theatre, Lake Superior Maritime Visitors Center, Great Lakes Aquarium, Duluth Convention Center, S.S. *Meteor* Whaleback Ship Museum

NOTES: In the 1980s, the city of Duluth undertook the revitalization of a dilapidated lakefront warehouse district just across Interstate 35 from downtown. The result is Canal Park, one of the city's premiere tourist and recreation areas. Visitors will find an array of museums, antique and specialty shops, cafes and restaurants, and hotels. Canal Park is connected by the iconic Aerial Lift Bridge to the beaches of the Park Point Sandbar. A four-mile-long lake walk offers stunning views of Lake Superior and downtown Duluth.

The view is the first thing I noticed when I walked into Canal Park Brewing Company. The brewpub is situated just steps from Lake Superior. A full wall of windows allows an unobstructed view of the lake from the dining room and bar. During the warmer months, patio seating brings you even closer. The dining room has a casual, modern feel with a light, industrial edge. Quirky touches like bar lights made from growlers add some fun. Take note of the tap handles: they are made of wood salvaged from the original fermenting tanks at the old Fitger's Brewery.

Brewers Dan Aagenes and Badger Colish avoid what they call "kitchen-sink beers." Rather than adding this, that, and the other thing to their brews, they strive to pull complex flavors from simple ingredients.

The year-round lineup consists of classic brewpub standards: a lighter beer, an IPA, something Belgian, and something dark. But they are all well made and a pleasure to drink. Look for barrel-aged and stronger beers in the seasonal selections.

Carmody Irish Pub

ADDRESS: 308 E. Superior St. Duluth, MN 55802

TELEPHONE: 218-740-4747

EMAIL: carmodyirishpub@yahoo.com

WEB SITE: www.carmodyirishpub.com

MICHAEL'S PICK: Toomy Vara IPA: Orange and melon flavors define this beer. Multiple dry-hop additions give it loads of hop flavor and aroma, but it goes light on bitterness. It's easy on the palate, so you can still enjoy the flavors after the second.

TYPE: Brewpub

DATE ESTABLISHED: 2006, began brewing in 2009

OWNERS: Eddie Gleeson, Liz Gleeson, and Rick Boo

BREWMASTER: Mike Miley

BREWING SYSTEM: 2.5-barrel "Frankenstein" brewhouse

FLAGSHIP BEERS: Agnes Irish Red, Scanlon India Pale Ale

YEAR-ROUND BEERS: Agnes Irish Red, Scanlon India Pale Ale, Tipplers Golden, Famine 47 Irish Stout

SEASONAL BEERS: Bitter Boo ESB, Cinnamon Nut Brown, Roast Mint Stout, Toomy Vara IPA

SPECIAL RELEASES: Tangerine Porter, Raspberry IPA, Pumpkin Beer

TOURS: By request

BEER TO GO: Growlers

FOOD: Small selection of simple sandwiches; pizzas available late night

AMENITIES: Free parking in the Sheraton ramp after 5:00 P.M., live music six nights a week, good selection of guest beers, full bar with a large selection of Irish whiskies

PUB HOURS: Daily: 3:00 P.M. to 2:00 A.M.

NEARBY ATTRACTIONS: Duluth-area breweries, multiple single-track mountain-bike trails nearby, downhill and cross-country ski access, Lake Superior scenic cruises, Canal Park, Park Point, Duluth Convention Center, Omnimax Theatre, Fitger's Brewery Museum

NOTES: Carmody owner Eddie Gleeson has a colorful and varied past. He's been a cop, a traveling salesman, and a playwright with work produced off-Broadway. He's a gregarious fellow who loves to talk about his Irish roots, roots that run deep both in Duluth and Ireland, where he lived for many years. His grandfather owned a saloon in Duluth. Another ancestor once worked for People's Brewing Company, an Irish-owned nineteenth-century Duluth brewery with connections to the old IWW labor organization.

Carmody doesn't feel like most American versions of the Irish pub. Gleeson rejected what he calls the "curvy wood" model in his attempt to re-create the pubs he frequented in Ireland. Carmody is a rough-edged place with a clear working-class vibe. It's dimly lit, with dark-wood paneling and football-club banners covering the walls. Still, it's warm and welcoming. Gleeson himself is likely to greet you from a stool at the bar as you enter. I've never been to Ireland, but this is what I imagine a real Irish pub to be.

Brewer Mike Miley does his work in the basement on a small system cobbled together from odds-and-ends tanks that have been picked up here and there. He started as a homebrewer in college. He brewed briefly at Thirsty Pagan across the bay in Superior, Wisconsin, before landing the job at Carmody. He says that making beer allows him to meld his creative side (he also writes a comic strip) with his love of working with his hands. It's a good feeling when someone asks, "Who made this?" and the answer is, "Mike Miley."

Castle Danger Brewery

ADDRESS: 17 7th St. Two Harbors, MN 55616

TELEPHONE: 218-834-5800

EMAIL: cdbinfo@frontier.com

WEB SITE: www.castledangerbrewery.com

MICHAEL'S PICK: Danger Ale: Full-bodied and full-flavored, this is not your ordinary American Amber Ale. The blend of prominent caramel malt flavors with spicy noble hops is like a mashup of English-style old ale and a German-style bock. It leans to the sweet side, but a solid bitter bite and dry finish keep it from being cloying. This is a nice beer for a northern Minnesota winter.

TYPE: Brewery

DATE ESTABLISHED: 2011

OWNERS: Clint MacFarlane and Jamie MacFarlane

BREWMASTER: Clint MacFarlane

BREWING SYSTEM: Thirty-barrel Marks Design and Metalworks brewhouse

FLAGSHIP BEER: Danger Ale

YEAR-ROUND BEER: Danger Ale

SEASONAL BEERS: Camp Depression Lager, Castle Cream Ale, Nestor Grade Amber Ale, Gale Force Wheat, George Hunter Stout

SPECIAL RELEASES: Rye Juniper Ale and others

TOURS: See Web site for times

BEER TO GO: Growlers

FOOD: None

AMENITIES: Free parking, taproom

PUB HOURS: Wednesday, Friday, and Saturday:
4:00 to 7:00 P.M.

NEARBY ATTRACTIONS: Boundary Waters Canoe Area, myriad outdoor activities in all seasons, Superior Hiking Trail, Gooseberry State Park

NOTES: Jamie MacFarlane's great-grandfather first settled on the rugged shores of Lake Superior in 1902. Over one hundred years and four generations later, the land is still owned by the family. Since the 1930s it has been the site of the Castle Havens Cabin Resort. Clint and Jamie have managed the resort since 2005.

It's a secluded spot perched on the shores of the Great Lake about a mile off Minnesota Highway 61—the kind of place that families return to year after year for recreation and relaxation. The idyllic setting is not the first place one would think to put a brewery, but it is certainly one of the most beautiful.

The view of Lake Superior from the original Castle Danger brewery location.

The idea to start a brewery on the resort was hatched several years ago when Clint started home-brewing during the slower winter season. Like many who fall in love with the hobby, he began dreaming of opening his own brewery. He read books on the subject and discussed the idea until Jamie finally told him, "I'm sick of hearing about it. Either do it or don't." He took the leap. The gamble paid off. Within a year, the brewery had outgrown its tiny lakeside location and moved upshore to a larger facility in Two Harbors.

Clint's brews tend toward the big and the bold. He wants them to represent the rugged nature of Lake Superior's North Shore. He doesn't aim to fit his beers into any particular style categories, preferring instead to play with combinations of ingredients in pursuit of uniquely flavored beers that are their own thing.

ADDRESS: 109 W. Superior St.
Duluth, MN 55802

TELEPHONE: 218–727–1559

EMAIL: dubhlinnduluth@yahoo.com

WEB SITE: www.dubhlinnpub.com

MICHAEL'S PICK: Double Hop IPA: While there are some grapefruit-pith overtones, this one is more about bitterness than hop flavor. A simple, grainy sweetness does provide balance. It finishes fast and dry. All in all, a nondescript but palatable and refreshing IPA.

TYPE: Brewpub

DATE ESTABLISHED: 2006, brewing began in 2011

OWNER: Mike Maxim

BREWMASTER: Erik Larson

BREWING SYSTEM: Three-barrel converted soup-kettle brewhouse

FLAGSHIP BEERS: Double Hop IPA, Maple Ale

YEAR-ROUND BEERS: Double Hop IPA, Maple Ale, Peach Radler, Potato Stout

SEASONAL BEERS: Planned

SPECIAL RELEASES: Planned

TOURS: No

BEER TO GO: None

FOOD: Assortment of made-from-scratch brewpub standards—wings, burgers and sandwiches; small selection of Irish-themed specialties

AMENITIES: Paid parking in nearby ramps, full bar boasting Minnesota's largest selection of Irish whiskey and single-malt scotch, happy-hour specials, live comedy, banquet room available

PUB HOURS: Monday–Friday: 11:00 A.M. to 2:00 A.M.; Saturday: noon to 2:00 A.M.

NEARBY ATTRACTIONS: Duluth-area breweries, multiple single-track mountain-bike trails nearby, downhill and cross-country ski access, Lake Superior scenic cruises, Canal Park, Park Point, Duluth Convention Center, Omnimax Theatre, Fitger's Brewery Museum, and other Duluth attractions

NOTES: When Dubh Linn opened in 2006, it was just an Irish-themed bar. But Mike Maxim wanted something more. Comedy was the answer. Taking advantage of touring acts looking to fill empty road dates, he was able to book national comedians, many of whom had appeared on Letterman and Leno. The Saturday-night comedy shows have become a mainstay for the pub, drawing both locals and out-of-towners.

With the entertainment in place, Maxim found that customers wanted to make a night of it. They wanted food. A kitchen was added and a menu developed. Then Maxim's longtime friend and homebrewer

Erik Larson suggested the addition of hand-crafted beer to accompany the made-from-scratch food. He engineered a system out of old restaurant steam kettles and assumed the role of brewer, establishing the three pillars of the business: national comedy, tasty food, and homemade beer.

It's difficult for me to call Dubh Linn an "Irish pub." Aside from some green paint and a few Irish-themed specialties on the menu, there's very little about it that bespeaks the Emerald Isle. It feels more like a trendy nightspot, but not upscale or fancy. If you are a whiskey fan, the selection of Irish whiskeys and single malt scotches is truly impressive. They've got it all, from the bottom shelf to the extreme high end.

Dubrue

ADDRESS: 211 E. 2nd St.
Duluth, MN 55805
TELEPHONE: 218–341–0988
EMAIL: nicktimcam@gmail.com
WEB SITE: www.dubrue.com
MICHAEL'S PICK: India Black Ale: Most India black ales are little more than dark-colored IPAs. This one is different. A significant roasted-malt component and a touch more sweetness balances the bitterness and citrus flavors of American hops. Chocolate notes add some welcome interest. It's sharp and creamy at the same time. I'm not generally a fan of the style, but I like this beer.
TYPE: Brewery
DATE ESTABLISHED: 2011
OWNERS: Bob Blair and Nick Cameron
BREWMASTER: Bob Blair
BREWING SYSTEM: Fifteen-barrel converted dairy-tank brewhouse
FLAGSHIP BEERS: Pub Ale, India Black Ale
YEAR-ROUND BEERS: Pub Ale, India Black Ale
SEASONAL BEERS: None
SPECIAL RELEASES: Berliner Weiss, Belgian Strong Golden
TOURS: By appointment
BEER TO GO: Growlers
FOOD: None
AMENITIES: Free street parking
PUB HOURS: Thursday and Friday: 4:00 to 5:00 P.M.
NEARBY ATTRACTIONS: Duluth-area breweries, Maritime Museum, Enger Tower, multiple single-track mountain-bike trails nearby, downhill and cross-country ski access, Lake Superior scenic cruises, Canal Park, Park Point, Duluth Convention Center, Omnimax Theatre

NOTES: When talking with the Dubrue duo Nick Cameron and Bob Blair about beer, the conversation can become quite manic. Their excitement and passion is palpable. Sentences get bounced back and forth as each one finishes the other's thoughts or diverts him onto a tangent. I'm glad I had a recording device to keep up.

The two met while working at the nearby Fitger's Brewhouse. Blair came on as a brewer after returning to Minnesota from Oregon, where he had earned a degree in brewing. Cameron started as a bartender and gradually worked his way up to keg washer and eventually to running brew sessions. While both enjoyed working at Fitger's, they felt they would have more freedom, and potentially make more money, doing it themselves. Thus, Dubrue was born.

They describe their respective contributions to the partnership as "how and what" versus "why." Cameron plays the "how and what" role—he helps with brewing, takes charge of sales, and knows the right questions to ask as they work to build the business. Blair is the one with the answers, at least as they pertain to making beer. With his deeper knowledge of brewing, he's the nuts-and-bolts "why" guy, formulating recipes, setting the schedule, and maintaining the brewery.

Blair and Cameron want craft brewing to become a big-tent movement. Their beers are aimed at helping make that happen. In their view, the industry can't grow market share solely on extreme beers. Dubrue's flagships, Pub Ale and India Black Ale, are sharp and full-flavored, yet approachable even to light beer drinkers.

Finding Dubrue is slightly tricky. The address is on 2nd Street, but the brewery entrance is around the corner on 2nd Avenue next to the auto-repair shop.

Fitger's Brewhouse

ADDRESS: 600 E. Superior St.
Duluth, MN 55802
TELEPHONE: 218–279–2739
EMAIL: brew@brewhouse.net
WEB SITE: www.brewhouse.net

MICHAEL'S PICK: Sasquatch Scotch Ale: Rich, toffee-sweet, and slightly warming, this seasonal scotch ale sits nicely when it's ten degrees outside. It would be pleasant sitting by the lake on a cool northern Minnesota summer evening as well. It pours a crystal-clear, hazelnut amber. The creamy texture and malty sweetness are just balanced by earthy hops and light bitterness.
TYPE: Brewpub

DATE ESTABLISHED: 1995

OWNERS: Tim Nelson and Rod Raymond

BREWMASTER: Dave Hoops

BREWING SYSTEM: Ten-barrel Specific Mechanical brewhouse

FLAGSHIP BEERS: Starfire Pale Ale, El Niño IPA, Apricot Wheat, Brewhouse Brown, Big Boat Oatmeal Stout

YEAR-ROUND BEERS: Starfire Pale Ale, El Niño IPA, Chester Creek Pale, Superior Trail IPA, Lighthouse Golden, Apricot Wheat, Brewhouse Brown, Big Boat Oatmeal Stout

SEASONAL BEERS: Rotating selection of 110 beers. Always a wheat beer and at least one lager.

SPECIAL RELEASES: Cherry Batch, Bourbon Barrel Aged Edmund Imperial Stout, Sasquatch Scotch Ale, Blitzen's Blueberry Porter, Apostle Apple, Gale Force Cranberry, Devil's Track Pumpkin, Grand Cru, Timmy's Edelstoff, and others

TOURS: Saturdays at 4:00 P.M.

BEER TO GO: Growlers (they deliver)

FOOD: An eclectic assortment of pub food with some interesting locally sourced and vegetarian options

AMENITIES: Paid parking ramp, metered street parking, full bar, happy-hour specials, unique shops in the Fitger's Brewery complex, spend a night at the elegant Fitger's Inn

PUB HOURS: Monday–Friday 11:00 A.M. to 10:00 P.M.; Saturday and Sunday 11:00 A.M. to 11:00 P.M.

NEARBY ATTRACTIONS: Duluth-area breweries, multiple single-track mountain-bike trails nearby, downhill and cross-country ski access, Lake Superior Scenic Cruises, Canal Park, Park Point, Duluth Convention Center, Omnimax Theatre, Fitger's Brewery Museum, and other Duluth attractions.

NOTES: Fitger's brewmaster Dave Hoops espouses a belief that "you should never go into a brewpub and get a crappy beer. And if you do, you should send it back." This philosophy is demonstrated in his brewing process. He doesn't filter any of his beers, as he believes it strips out flavor. He takes the time to let his beers properly condition, even refusing to release any 10 percent or higher ABV beer before it is a year old. The result is some of the best beer in the state.

Hoops and crew brew eighty to one hundred different recipes every year. You will always find eleven Fitger's beers on tap, including one cask-conditioned ale. Hoops describes himself as "obsessed with German lagers." There is always at least one lager and a wheat beer available. Fitger's also has an active barrel program that produces wood-aged and sour beers.

The Brewhouse has the family-friendly atmo-sphere of a slightly upscale pub. It is a comfortable place to either have a seat at the triangular bar or take a table in the dining room. The brewpub is housed in the brewhouse of the historic Fitger's Brewery complex right on Lake Superior. It's an interesting stroll around the building. Check out the unique shops while you are there.

Jack Pine Brewery

ADDRESS: 7942 College Rd., Suite 115 Baxter, MN 56425

TELEPHONE: 218–270–8072

EMAIL: info@jackpinebrewery.com

WEB SITE: www.jackpinebrewery.com

MICHAEL'S PICK: Duck Pond Brown Ale: This straightforward English brown ale is built on a malty base of toffee and toast, with a bit of coffee-like, grainy roast. The roasted malt gives it a dryness that boosts the moderate hop bitterness. Light, earthy, English hops round out the flavors.

TYPE: Brewery

DATE ESTABLISHED: 2012

OWNER: Patrick Sundberg

BREWMASTER: Patrick Sundberg

BREWING SYSTEM: 1.3-barrel homemade brewhouse

FLAGSHIP BEERS: Duck Pond Nut Brown, Fenceline Pale Ale, Dead Branch Cream Ale

YEAR-ROUND BEERS: Duck Pond Nut Brown, Fenceline Pale Ale, Dead Branch Cream Ale

SEASONAL BEERS: Hornets Nest Honey Lemon Wheat, Harvest Red Ale, Big Buck Barleywine

SPECIAL RELEASES: Barbwire Imperial IPA, Trespass Porter, Red Fox Amber Ale, Rhubarb Ale, Wild Rice Ale, and others

TOURS: See Web site for times

BEER TO GO: Growlers

FOOD: None

AMENITIES: Parking lot, taproom

PUB HOURS: Fridays: 4:00 to 7:00 P.M. Check Web site for additional hours.

NEARBY ATTRACTIONS: Paul Bunyan Bike Trail, Cuyuna Mountain Bike Trail system, all-season outdoor activities at nearby lakes and forests, lake resorts, skiing and snowboarding at Mount Ski Gull, Brainerd International Raceway, North Central Speedway, Northland Arboretum, Paul Bunyan Land

NOTES: The Brainerd Lakes area is located in the middle of the state, about two hours northwest of the Twin Cities. Easy access to over five hundred lakes and numerous hiking and biking trails makes it a popular all-season destination for outdoor enthusiasts. The small towns surrounding Brainerd and Baxter beckon with unique shops and restaurants in an atmosphere that is as close to a "Main Street" shopping experience as you'll ever get.

To Jack Pine founder and brewer Patrick Sundberg, the Brainerd Lakes area is more than just a place; it's a way of life. Situated on the dividing line between civilized southern Minnesota and the wilderness of the north, it engenders a lifestyle of laid-back self-sufficiency. It's a town and country blend in which the conveniences of the city are readily available, but it may take days to dig out after a heavy snow. Easy access to the outdoors is just a part of life. Says Sundberg, "It's fun to be around the lakes. But it's also fun to be able to take them for granted."

Sundberg applied this sense of self-sufficiency in the creation of his brewery. With the occasional help of friends in the trades, he did all of the work himself, from dealing with City Hall to building out the space. He says that brewing speaks to all sides of his personality. He is a self-described "geek" at heart, someone who loves measuring pH levels and calculating hop additions. But he also has an artistic side that is fulfilled by designing recipes and imagining flavor combinations. A self-starter by nature, he has always wanted to build his own business. Opening the brewery has allowed him to do just that.

Sundberg makes American-style ales for the people who live in and visit the region. He aims to be the brewer of the Brainerd Lakes. His is the only brewery in the area, and his small size restricts his distribution to just the local area.

Lake Superior Brewing Company

ADDRESS: 2711 W. Superior St.
Duluth, MN 55805
TELEPHONE: 218–723–4000
EMAIL: info@lakesuperiorbrewing.com
WEB SITE: www.lakesuperiorbrewing.com
MICHAEL'S PICK: Mesabi Red Ale: Mesabi Red could be called a robust American amber. The malt profile includes biscuit notes and slight hints of roast that complement the expected caramel flavors. The malt is balanced by an assertive bitterness and citrus/pine American hop flavors. A bit of fruity yeast character rounds things out.
TYPE: Brewery
DATE ESTABLISHED: 1994
OWNERS: Don Hoag, Jo Hoag, Dale Kleinschmidt, John Judd, and Karen Olesen
BREWMASTER: Dale Kleinschmidt

BREWING SYSTEM: Fifteen-barrel Specific Mechanical and dairy-tank brewhouse
FLAGSHIP BEER: Special Ale
YEAR-ROUND BEERS: Special Ale, Kayak Kolsch, Mesabi Red, Sir Duluth Oatmeal Stout
SEASONAL BEERS: Split Rock Bock, Oktoberfest, Old Man Winter Warmer
SPECIAL RELEASES: None
TOURS: By request
BEER TO GO: Growlers
AMENITIES: Parking lot, handicap accessible
PUB HOURS: None
NEARBY ATTRACTIONS: Multiple single-track mountain-bike trails nearby, downhill and cross-country ski access, Superior Hiking Trail, Lake Superior scenic cruises, Canal Park, Park Point, Duluth Convention Center, Omnimax Theatre, Heritage Hockey Center, Lincoln Park, Enger Tower, Wade Stadium

NOTES: Lake Superior Brewing Company began in 1994 as a homebrew supply store and small brewery housed in the old Fitger's Brewery Complex. It was the first new brewery in northern Minnesota since 1972, when the Fitger's Brewery closed its doors. Special Ale, the first Lake Superior beer and still the flagship, was based on a homebrew recipe of founder Bob Dromeshauser. With a rotating group of homebrewers serving as taste-testers, Dromeshauser took an improvisational approach to recipe formulation. Starting from a simple base recipe, he would brew and rebrew, each time tweaking the mix until he achieved the desired character.

By 1996 the brewery had outgrown its cramped quarters at the Fitger's Complex and moved to its current location in West Duluth. As the brewery continues to grow, another expansion and move may be in the works.

Following Dromeshauser's departure in 2001, Dale Kleinschmidt took over as brewmaster. Kleinschmidt had been one of those original taste-testers. He was asked to join the brewery as an employee shortly after it opened. Kleinschmidt exemplifies the ingenuity and MacGyver-like problem-solving skills common to professional brewers. When I arrived for my visit, he was busy repairing a piece of the bottling machine with what appeared to be a knife and screwdriver. The brewery's dairy-tank mash tun sits on the floor. When it comes time to drain the wort during a brew, the entire vessel is raised with a forklift to let gravity do the work. The creativity of brewers is always amazing.

Leech Lake Brewing Company

ADDRESS: 195 Walker Industries Blvd. Walker, MN 56484

TELEPHONE: 218–547–4746

EMAIL: brewmaster@leechlakebrewing.com

WEB SITE: www.leechlakebrewing.com

MICHAEL'S PICK: Driven Snow Robust Porter: This robust porter drinks lighter than its 6.5 percent alcohol. It goes down smooth and easy, with a great balance of molasses sweetness and coffee roast. Bittersweet chocolate lingers long after swallowing.

TYPE: Brewery

DATE ESTABLISHED: 2010

OWNERS: Greg Smith and Gina Smith

BREWMASTER: Greg Smith

BREWING SYSTEM: 1.5-bbl converted soup-kettle brewhouse

FLAGSHIP BEER: Loch Leech Monster

YEAR-ROUND BEERS: 47° North IPA, Loch Leech Monster, Minobii ESB, Driven Snow Robust Porter, Blindside Pale Ale, Three Sheets Imperial IPA, Loon's Eye Red Ale

SEASONAL BEERS: Brown Ale, Maris the Otter, Burrbutt, Cream Stout IPA, 150' Deep Stout

SPECIAL RELEASES: Wild Pale Ale, Pineapple Pale Summer Ale

TOURS: By request for groups of ten or more

BEER TO GO: Growlers and package

FOOD: None

AMENITIES: Parking lot, taproom

PUB HOURS: Tuesday, Thursday, and Saturday: 4:00 to 6:00 P.M. (subject to change; please check Web site)

NEARBY ATTRACTIONS: Fishing, boating, and other water sports on Leech Lake, outdoor activities in Chippewa National Forest, Paul Bunyan and Heartland Bike Trails, Eelpout Festival in February, Forestedge Winery

NOTES: Leech Lake Brewing Company is nestled in a wooded area at the edge of the small tourist town of Walker. You might think you're lost as you make your way there, but don't fret, the brewery has garnered enough attention that Google Maps and most GPS units know where it is.

Tourism sustains the town and the brewery. Walker is a destination for "up-north" outdoor activities, drawing streams of vacationers from the Twin Cities and beyond. Situated on the shore of Leech Lake, the third-largest lake in the state, the town provides easy access to boating and fishing. Chippewa National Forest offers hiking trails, hunting, and camping year-round. Two major bike trails intersect nearby. If you like to play outside, there's something here for you.

Greg and Gina Smith see Leech Lake as a boutique brewery that fits in well with the nature of the town. The steady stream of tourists from the Twin Cities has been good for Leech Lake Brewing. Within the first two months of operation, they were already straining the capacity of their tiny 1.5-barrel brewhouse. During peak season they have lines out the door during taproom hours, especially on rainy days, when people come off the lake.

The best place to taste Leech Lake beers is at the brewery, where they are at their freshest. The must-try beers are Driven Snow Porter and Three Sheets Imperial IPA. The signature beer-blends are also worth a sample. The South African is a blend of their Porter and IPA that brings out rich chocolate flavors from the porter that aren't as apparent in the beer by itself. Naughty Scotsman is a mix of Loch Leech Monster Scotch Ale with the IPA.

SOUTHEAST

Kinney Creek Brewery

ADDRESS: 1016 7th St. NW Rochester, MN 55901

TELEPHONE: 507–282–2739

EMAIL: kinneycreek@kinneycreekbrewery.com

WEB SITE: www.kinneycreekbrewery.com

MICHAEL'S PICK: Xtra Special Bitter (ESB): A mix of toffee and biscuit from English malts is balanced by sharp but not too aggressive bitterness. Hop flavors offer grassy and earthy contrast to the malt's sweetness. Some buttery diacetyl detracts a bit, but overall this is not a bad beer.

TYPE: Brewery

DATE ESTABLISHED: 2012

OWNER: Donovan O. Seitz

BREWMASTER: Donovan O. Seitz

BREWING SYSTEM: Fifteen-gallon homemade brewhouse

FLAGSHIP BEER: Sunny Days

YEAR-ROUND BEERS: Xtra Special Bitter (ESB), Opener IPA, Sunny Days, Smoked Porter

SEASONAL BEERS: Oktoberfest, Holiday Bourbon Ale, Mega Mocha Stout, Kinney Creek American Ale, Honey Blonde, Old Town Ale, Pepper Passion

SPECIAL RELEASES: None

TOURS: By request

BEER TO GO: Growlers

FOOD: None

AMENITIES: Parking lot, taproom

PUB HOURS: Friday and Saturday: 1:00 to 8:00 P.M.

NEARBY ATTRACTIONS: Mayo Clinic, concerts and performances at the Mayo Civic Center, Rochester Art Center, Rochester Repertory Theatre, Rochester Civic Theatre, Goonies Comedy Club, outdoor activities at Quarry Hill Nature Center and Silver Lake Park, biking on Douglas Trail

NOTES: Being the first brewery in Rochester since the mid-1990s, Donovan Seitz didn't know what to expect on Kinney Creek's opening day. He wanted to have enough beer on hand to get him through the weekend, but not so much that he would be sitting on kegs if traffic was light. But that first day revealed just how eager Rochester residents were for home-town beer. Two of his four initial offerings sold out by closing time. The last keg ran dry just before he shut the doors on day two.

Seitz is a bit of a jack-of-all-trades. He has been a mechanic, worked construction, and spent time in the corporate world. He came to brewing via home winemaking. After accumulating a couple hundred bottles of wine, he figured it was time for a switch to beer. After a few messy stovetop batches, he was banned from the kitchen. Exiled to the more spacious garage, his equipment and batch sizes grew ever larger. He finally decided that if he was going to make that much beer, he might as well start sharing it with others.

The leap from homebrewer to pro came easily to Seitz. He has always owned his own businesses and likes the challenge of a startup. He recognized a need in Rochester, a town that was just coming around to better beer. The time seemed right to make the plunge. He renovated an old pawn shop and moved his homebrew system from the garage. As the brewery grows, a second building out back gives Seitz some room to expand.

Mantorville Brewing Company

ADDRESS: 101 E. 5th St.
Mantorville, MN 55955

TELEPHONE: 651–387–0708

EMAIL: info@mantorvillebeer.com

WEB SITE: www.mantorvillebeer.com

MICHAEL'S PICK: Stagecoach Golden Ale: Tod Fyten says that Golden Ale was brewed to appeal to the palates of his local southern Minnesota customers. Sweet malt is the defining feature of this beer. Low levels of bitterness just barely serve to balance. Spicy continental hops and prominent fruity esters round things out. A touch of honey malt in the grist leaves its mark in the finish.

TYPE: Brewery

DATE ESTABLISHED: 1996

OWNER: Tod Fyten

BREWMASTER: Tod Fyten

BREWING SYSTEM: Ten-barrel converted dairy-tank brewhouse

FLAGSHIP BEER: Stagecoach Amber Ale

YEAR-ROUND BEERS: Stagecoach Amber Ale, Stagecoach Smoked Porter, Stagecoach Golden Ale, St. Croix Cream Stout, St. Croix Cream Ale

SEASONAL BEERS: None

SPECIAL RELEASE: Fytenburg Grand Cru

TOURS: Saturdays: 2:00 to 4:00 P.M., or by appointment

BEER TO GO: Growlers

AMENITIES: Parking lot and free street parking, samples available during tours

PUB HOURS: None

NEARBY ATTRACTIONS: The entire twelve blocks of downtown Mantorville are on the National Registry of Historic Places, classic melodramas at the Mantorville Theatre Company during the summer, Historic Hubbel House Hotel and Restaurant, Stagecoach Bicycle Trail, outdoor activities at nearby state parks

NOTES: To sit down for a conversation with Tod Fyten is to get a lesson in the history of brewing in Minnesota. Fyten has a well-deserved reputation as a talker, but he also has a lot of interesting stories to tell. His entire life has been connected to the beer industry. As a child he listened to stories of his grandparents' Prohibition-era bootlegging exploits. As an adult he has gone from an intern at a malting company to work in beer sales, distribution, publishing, and brewing.

Mantorville Brewing Company was started in 1995 by six Mantorville-area homebrewers. They managed to get their beer into local bars and restaurants but never found wider distribution. By 1999, the stress of holding down full-time jobs while running the brewery was starting to take its toll on the brewers and the beer. That's when Fyten entered the scene, buying out three of the original partners. He bought the remaining shares in 2002 to become the sole owner and brewer.

When visiting the brewery, it is worth taking a stroll around town. The entire downtown is on the National Registry of Historic Places. The well-preserved, limestone buildings evoke a time when the now sleepy burg was a major stagecoach stop.

The tiny Mantorville brewery sits at the edge of town just down the street from the historic Hubbel House. The brewery, constructed from converted dairy tanks, has a rugged, cut-and-paste feel to it that recalls the do-it-yourself early days of craft brewing. As of this writing, brewing is split between two locations. Keg and growler beer are brewed at the Mantorville brewery, while bottled beer is contracted out to Lake Superior Brewing Company in Duluth.

Olvalde Farm and Brewing Company

ADDRESS: 16557 County Rd. 25
  Rollingstone, MN 55969
TELEPHONE: 507–205–4969
EMAIL: info@olvalde.com
WEB SITE: www.olvalde.com
MICHAEL'S PICK: The Auroch's Horn: This 10 percent ABV golden ale is brewed with barley, wheat, and local honey. Herbal and spicy notes blend delicately with nectarlike malt. It's a sweet but rough-hewn beer that manages to be "Belgianesque" without being Belgian. It's a style all its own.
TYPE: Brewery
DATE ESTABLISHED: 2011
OWNER: Joe Pond
BREWMASTER: Joe Pond
BREWING SYSTEM: Fifteen-barrel JV Northwest brewhouse
FLAGSHIP BEER: The Auroch's Horn
YEAR-ROUND BEER: The Auroch's Horn
SEASONAL BEERS: None
SPECIAL RELEASES: Brynhildr's Gift, Ode to a Russian Shipwright, Rhubarb Auroch's Horn
TOURS: No
BEER TO GO: None
FOOD: None
AMENITIES: None
PUB HOURS: None
NEARBY ATTRACTIONS: Wellington's Backwater Brewery, Mantorville Brewing Company, Great River Shakespeare Festival, Winona art galleries and museums, outdoor activities in nearby state parks, National Eagle Center, concerts and cultural events at Winona State University, Mississippi River cruises, Seven Hawks and Garvin Heights Vineyards

NOTES: Joe Pond thinks about beer differently than most brewers: he eschews the industrial model of beer production, desiring instead to bring beer back to its agricultural roots. At his farmstead brewery he is attempting to craft true farmhouse ales that make use as much as possible of the ingredients at hand.

When most people think of farmhouse ales, they think of Belgian styles. To Pond, the idea of "farmhouse" goes beyond particular styles. "To me, a beer style is a little bit restrictive," he says. "If I'm going to brew something I call a 'Belgian beer,' then I'm going to emulate the Belgian water. I'm going to get Belgian malts. But I'm trying to brew good beer with what we have around here, which really, that's how Belgian beer got to be Belgian beer."

Outside the brewery he tends a brewer's garden of native herbs and spices that he uses to bitter and flavor his beers. He sources honey from nearby bee keepers and harvests hop cones from wild vines on the property. He has even tried his hand at growing and malting his own barley. He is seeking heirloom barley varieties to see if they will grow in Minnesota.

Pond is the first to admit that his views on beer making are a bit romanticized, but he is working to make them real. Because fermentation is the one factor that is totally in his control, his beers are yeast- and fermentation-centered. All Olvalde beers are naturally bottle-conditioned and hand-corked.

Reads Landing Brewing Company

ADDRESS: 70555 202nd St.
  Reads Landing, MN 55968
TELEPHONE: 651–560–4777
EMAIL: rlbrewingco@hotmail.com
WEB SITE: www.rlbrewingco.com
MICHAEL'S PICK: Firebox: This California common lager features rich caramel malt flavors with overtones of toast. Sweetness is balanced by moderate bitterness, which, if a bit low for the style, still makes an impression. The woody flavors of Northern Brewer hops complete the picture.
TYPE: Brewpub
DATE ESTABLISHED: 2011, brewing began in 2012
OWNER: Bob Nihart
BREWMASTER: Bob Nihart
BREWING SYSTEM: Three-barrel Brewmation electric brewhouse
FLAGSHIP BEER: Cremona Cream Ale
YEAR-ROUND BEER: Cremona Cream Ale
SEASONAL BEERS: Wagmu Pumpkin Ale, Firebox, Blackleg Porter, and others
SPECIAL RELEASES: Planned
TOURS: By request
BEER TO GO: Growlers
FOOD: Small selection of pub favorites with a focus on fresh, locally sourced ingredients. Changes seasonally.
AMENITIES: Parking lot, seasonal outdoor seating, good selection of guest taps and bottles

NOTES: While you wouldn't think it now, tiny Reads
Landing (pop. 121) was once in the running to become
the capital of Minnesota and was considered a den of
iniquity to residents of nearby towns. An important
hub of commerce on the Mississippi River, the now-
sleepy town was home to thirty saloons, twenty hotels, two breweries, and likely more than one brothel.

Those glory days are done, but at Reads Landing
Brewing Company one can still feel a connection to
that past. Originally built as a dry-goods store in 1870
during the town's heyday, it occupies a riverfront spot
on what was once a bustling Main Street. Bob Nihart's
grandfather purchased it in 1939 and opened a bar
that was operated by various family members until
1957. In that year it became the Anchor Inn Supper
Club, one of the first family-style, all-you-can-eat
restaurants in the state. Old-timers recall always having to wait in line for a seat. For thirty years it was a
private cabin for family getaways until Nihart opened
the restaurant in 2011.

Sitting at the bar or at a table in the dining room,
you get a sense of what it might have been like in one
of the town's many saloons. The room has the look
of a nineteenth-century tavern. You can feel the age
of the building. Old brewery signs and photographs
of the town reinforce that sense of history. The big
picture windows in front offer wonderful views of the
river and the occasional freight train that passes on
the tracks just across the road.

Red Wing Brewery

ADDRESS: 1411 Old West Main St.
Red Wing, MN 55066
TELEPHONE: 651–327–2200
EMAIL: info@redwingbrewing.com
WEB SITE: www.redwingbrewing.com
MICHAEL'S PICK: Remmler's Holiday Special: This
beefed-up version of Remmler's Royal Brew smells
and tastes of grain, exuding luscious caramel and
melanoidin notes. It gives you a strong connection to
the raw materials from which the beer is made. The
malty sweetness is balanced by moderate bitterness and
earthy/spicy hop character. It's a rich and satisfying brew.

NOTES: Red Wing's well-preserved downtown attests
to the city's rich history. Founded in 1857, it bears
the name of the Mdewakanton Dakota chief Hupa-
huduta (meaning "a swan's wing dyed in red"). In
the 1870s, the surrounding Goodhue County was the
largest wheat producer in the country. Fueled by easy
access to shipping on the Mississippi River, the town
became one of the state's major manufacturing centers. Two of its early industries, shoes and pottery,
remain famous today.

Years before the boots and crocks, Red Wing was
known for beer. Red Wing's first brewery was established in the same year as the town. At one time there
were four breweries operating there, but Prohibition
took its toll. The last brewery in Red Wing struggled
along until 1951. With its closing, this once-proud industry was all but forgotten.

The current Red Wing Brewery aims to revive
that past with beers based on early recipes from the
old Remmler's and Red Wing breweries. Co-owners
Scott Kolby and William Norman uncovered corre-
spondence between the Remmler brewmaster and

the American Academy of Brewing in Chicago. The letters, dated to 1869, provided a list of ingredients and a chemical analysis of Remmler's Royal Brew. It was enough information for Kolby and Norman to reconstruct the recipe and re-create the beer.

In addition to the historical re-creations, the pair crafts a full lineup of easy-drinking beers mostly inspired by German and English traditions. You can enjoy a brew and a bite in an atmosphere that feels like a blend of nineteenth-century tavern and twenty-first-century coffee house.

Wellington's Backwater Brewing Company

ADDRESS: 1429 W. Service Dr.
Winona, MN 55987
TELEPHONE: 507–452–2103
EMAIL: cc-gardy@hotmail.com
WEB SITE: None
MICHAEL'S PICK: Winter ESB: Of the beers available in the sampler the night of my visit, the seasonal ESB was the one I came back to. It's a decent ESB, displaying nutty malt character with hints of chocolate roast. Medium-high bitterness was a bit harsh but provided nice balance. It was an enjoyable pint.
TYPE: Brewpub
DATE ESTABLISHED: 1995
OWNER: Chris Gardner
BREWMASTER: Chris Gardner
BREWING SYSTEM: One-barrel converted soup-kettle brewhouse
FLAGSHIP BEERS: Cat Tail Pale Ale, River Town Nut Brown Ale
YEAR-ROUND BEERS: Cat Tail Pale Ale, River Town Nut Brown Ale, Bullhead Red Ale, Wing Dam Wheat, Steamboat Stout
SEASONAL BEERS: Winter ESB, Ol' Mississippa IPA, Porter
SPECIAL RELEASES: None
TOURS: By request if the brewer is there
BEER TO GO: None
FOOD: Selection of sandwiches, salads, burgers, and BBQ
AMENITIES: Parking lot, free freshly popped popcorn, sixteen-lane bowling alley, large game room, full bar, daily drink and food specials
PUB HOURS: Daily: 11:00 A.M. to 1:00 A.M.
NEARBY ATTRACTIONS: Olvalde Farmhouse and Brewery, Mantorville Brewing Company, Great River Shakespeare Festival, several art galleries and museums, outdoor activities in nearby state parks, National Eagle Center, concerts and cultural events at Winona State University, Mississippi River cruises, Seven Hawks and Garvin Heights Vineyards

NOTES: Nanobreweries, sub-microbreweries making miniscule amounts of beer for a limited market, are one of the newest trends in craft beer. Wellington's Backwater Brewing Company may have been the first. Brewer and owner Chris Gardner has been crafting four house beers and the occasional seasonal release in his one-barrel, converted soup-kettle brewery since 1995. While most local customers still drink bottled Bud and Coors Light, Chris says that demand for his hand-crafted ales has increased dramatically in the last few years.

Wellington's is located in the Westgate bowling alley, built by Gardner's father in the 1960s. Sitting at the bar, you can look through plate-glass windows and watch the action on the lanes. The ambience is bowling alley/grill/sports bar. Different sporting events play on each of the televisions behind the bar. Neon beer signs light up the dining room, and a popcorn machine sits to the side, from which guests can help themselves. At the far end of the dining room the cramped, one-room brewery is visible through a large window.

The menu is what you would expect: burgers, sandwiches, and salads. The Smokehouse BBQ section of the menu is the most intriguing, boasting "the area's best ribs." I had the BBQ Sampler Platter. While the brisket was a little tough, the pulled pork was delicious.

Wellington's is worth a visit if you are in Winona.

SOUTHWEST

August Schell Brewing Company

ADDRESS: 1860 Schell Rd.
New Ulm, MN 56073
TELEPHONE: 800–770–5020
EMAIL: schells@schellsbrewery.com
WEB SITE: www.schellsbrewery.com
MICHAEL'S PICK: Pils: It's hard to beat a good pilsner, and Schell's pils is a hard pilsner to beat. Brewed solidly in the German style, it is light, crisp, and dry with a sharply bitter bite. Soft, bready flavors of pils malt provide a balancing sweetness. Spicy European hops bring a touch of licorice that lingers into the finish. Schell's Pils is one beer that is always in my refrigerator.
TYPE: Brewery
DATE ESTABLISHED: 1860
OWNER: Ted Marti
BREWMASTER: Jace Marti

BREWING SYSTEM: 150-barrel Nerb GmbH brewhouse

FLAGSHIP BEERS: Deer Brand, Firebrick, Grain Belt Premium

YEAR-ROUND BEERS: Deer Brand, Schell's Light, Schell's Dark, Firebrick, Pils, Grain Belt Premium, Grain Belt Nordeast, Grain Belt Light, Emerald Rye, Schell Shocked Grapefruit Radler

SEASONAL BEERS: Chimney Sweep, Goosetown Gose, Bock, Maifest, Hefeweizen, Zommerfest, Oktoberfest, Snowstorm (brewed to a different style each year), Schmaltz's Alt

SPECIAL RELEASES: Star of the North Berliner Weisse, Stag Series beers: Barrel-aged Schmaltz's Alt, Wild Rice Farmhouse Ale, Classic Rauchbier, Burton Ale, Czech Black Lager, and others; Anniversary Series beers: 1878 Einbecker Doppelbock, 1867 Munich Dunkel, Bavarian Forest Dampfbier, 1890 Schwarzbier, 1924 Deer Brand, Roggenbier, 1905 Vacuum Tonic

TOURS:

September to May Schedule—Friday: 3:00 P.M.; Saturday: noon, 1:00, 2:00, 3:00, and 4:00 P.M.; Sunday (September to December): 1:00, 2:00, 3:00, and 4:00 P.M., Sunday (January to May): 1:00 P.M.

June to August Schedule—Monday–Friday: 1:00, 2:30, and 4:00 P.M.; Saturday: noon, 1:00, 2:00, 3:00, and 4:00 P.M.; Sunday: 1:00, 2:00, 3:00, and 4:00 P.M. Cost: $3. Children under twelve are free.

BEER TO GO: None

AMENITIES: Parking lot, tasting room, August Schell Museum of Brewing, listed on the National Registry of Historic Places, August Schell House and Gardens, Annual Bockfest celebration in March

PUB HOURS: None

NEARBY ATTRACTIONS: Brau Brothers Brewing Company, Mankato Brewery, outdoor activities at nearby state parks, historic downtown New Ulm, Hermann Monument (Herman the German), Morgan Creek Vineyard, German restaurants, Brown County Historical Society Museum

NOTES: Touring the August Schell Brewery is like traveling back in time. A narrow, winding road leads to the old brewery buildings nestled on a hillside overlooking the Cottonwood River. Crowded into this forested cubbyhole with the 1800s-vintage brewhouse are early Schell family residences as well as the palatial mansion and gardens built by August Schell in 1885.

Schell's celebrated its 150th anniversary in 2010. It is the second oldest continuously operating, family-owned brewery in the country. Current CEO Ted Marti is a fifth-generation descendant of the founder, August Schell.

A major reason for Schell's longevity is the beer itself. The management recognized early that the future of the beer industry lay in full-flavored, craft-brewed beers. In the 1980s Schell's helped pioneer craft beer in Minnesota with a line of specialty beers inspired by their German heritage. Their beers have consistently won awards in national and international competitions. In 2002, Schell's Brewery bought the Grain Belt label and revived this Minnesota original, preserving yet another piece of the state's brewing heritage.

Brau Brothers Brewing Company

ADDRESS: 910 E. Main St.
Marshall, MN 56258

TELEPHONE: 507–747–2337

EMAIL: info@braubeer.com

WEB SITE: www.braubeer.com

MICHAEL'S PICK: Moo Joos: Moo Joos has the mouthfeel of a beer that is much bigger than it is. Oats and unfermentable milk sugars give it a creamy-smooth texture that enhances the flavors of chocolate and coffee. Toffee and a touch of dark fruit from English yeast round out the profile.

DATE ESTABLISHED: 2000

OWNERS: Trevor Brau, Dustin Brau, and Brady Brau

BREWMASTER: Dustin Brau

BREWING SYSTEM: Fifteen-barrel JV Northwest brewhouse

FLAGSHIP BEERS: Sheephead Ale, RingNeck Braun Ale

YEAR-ROUND BEERS: Sheephead Ale, RingNeck Braun Ale, Bàncreagie, Moo Joos, Old 56

SEASONAL BEER: Hundred Yard Dash Fresh Hop Ale

SPECIAL RELEASES: Rainwater Stout, Rubus Black, Cherry Bean Coffee Stout, Hop Session Super Pale Ale, Rye Wyne

TOURS: Drop-in or by appointment

BEER TO GO: None

FOOD: Standard pub favorites

AMENITIES: Parking lot, taproom

PUB HOURS: Monday–Saturday: 11:00 A.M. to 11:00 P.M.; Sunday: 11:00 A.M. to 9:00 P.M.

NEARBY ATTRACTIONS: August Schell Brewing Company, Jackpot Junction Casino, Laura Ingalls Wilder Park and Museum, Ramsey Park, Camden State Park, Upper Sioux Agency State Park, Fort Ridgley State Park, Fieldstone Vineyard

NOTES: Lucan (pop. 220) is a typical southwestern Minnesota prairie town. It's not the type of place you would expect to find a growing craft brewery. But that's exactly where Brau Brothers got its start.

The brewery began as the Brauhaus Brewpub in 2000. Five years later, with demand outpacing capacity, the brothers sold the restaurant and opened a production brewery on a six-acre lot just a couple of blocks to the north. By 2012, Brau Brothers had outgrown Lucan. The brewery's waste water was overwhelming the tiny village's sewers. They picked up and moved twenty-three miles down the road to Marshall, where they opened the current brewery in the spring of 2013.

With only fourteen thousand people, Marshall is still a small town, and that's just fine with brewmaster Dustin Brau. The small-town setting allows the brothers to tend to their brewing without the distractions and pressures of the Twin Cities beer scene, but it's close enough that they can still make regular trips to the cities for festivals and events. The rural location also makes it a popular destination for beer fans seeking an escape from the city.

Brau Brothers has a three-acre hopyard where they grow eleven varieties of hops, most of which end up in their seasonal Hundred Yard Dash Fresh Hop Ale, so named because at the Lucan plant, it was literally a hundred-yard dash from vine to kettle. They are also experimenting with growing and malting their own barley. Small amounts of estate-grown barley end up in nearly all of the Brau Brothers beers. They hope to work with nearby farmers to expand this project in the future.

Brau Brothers recently went through a period of tweaking its lineup and recipes. The result has been an improvement of the product and a remarkable upsurge in popularity. Along with the year-round offerings, special releases like the Rubus Black Blackberry Imperial Porter are definitely worth a try.

Mankato Brewery

ADDRESS: 1119 Center St. North Mankato, MN 56003
TELEPHONE: 507–386–2337
EMAIL: info@mankatobrewery.com
WEB SITE: ww.mankatobrewery.com
MICHAEL'S PICK: Mankato Original: The creamy, white head of foam on this Kölsch-style beer is impressive. The flavor doesn't disappoint, either. Softly sweet malt is balanced by gentle bitterness, as spicy hop flavors float over the top. Delicate fruit in the nose and bready yeast character mark it as an authentic Kölsch. True to an old German saying, the first glass asks for the third.
TYPE: Brewery
DATE ESTABLISHED: 2012
OWNERS: Tim Tupy and Tony Feuchtenberger

BREWMASTER: Bobby Blasey
BREWING SYSTEM: Fifteen-barrel Newlands Systems brewhouse
FLAGSHIP BEER: Mankato Original
YEAR-ROUND BEERS: Mankato Original, Stikum, Organ Grinder Amber Ale, Haymaker IPA
SEASONAL BEERS: Planned
SPECIAL RELEASES: Center Street Series No. 1 Amber Ale, No. 2 American IPA, and others
TOURS: Fridays at 6:00 P.M.; Saturdays at 1:00 P.M. Check Web site for additional times. Reservations can be made online.
BEER TO GO: Growlers
FOOD: None
AMENITIES: Free parking in lot, tasting room, available for private events
PUB HOURS: Friday: 4:00 to 7:00 P.M.; Saturday: noon to 4:00 P.M. Check Web site for additional times.
NEARBY ATTRACTIONS: August Schell Brewing Company, Brau Brothers Brewing Company, Winterhaven Vineyard, Indian Island Winery, Morgan Creek Vineyard, Minneopa State Park, Mt. Kato Ski Area, kayaking and fishing on nearby rivers, road- and mountain-biking trails, Mankato State University campus

NOTES: The original Mankato Brewing Company closed in 1967 after 110 years in operation. The closing left a lasting hole in the community. Kato Beer memorabilia was a common site in the southern Minnesota town. People missed their hometown brew. Entrepreneur and homebrewer Tim Tupy took notice and decided it was time to bring beer back to Mankato.

The town immediately embraced the new Mankato Brewery. When the brewery launched in January 2012, the initial sales far exceeded expectations. Thirty barrels of beer were sold out in three days—the entire contents of one of the brewery's fermentation tanks. It left them scrambling to meet demand and looking to add tanks after only one week in business.

Mankato's brews are centered in German traditions. The first two releases were a Kölsch and an Altbier. They admire the German attitude toward beer—it's just part of life, like food. Drinking beer isn't so much about the beer as it is about the social time spent drinking it. Using the German word for cordiality, they say, "That's Gemütlichkeit."

But they aren't stuck to these styles. The first beers in the limited-release Center Street Series, an American-style amber ale and an IPA, have moved into year-round production. They promise more such creations to come.

FERMENTERIES

GRANITE CITY FOOD AND BREWERY—EAGAN
Address: 3330 Pilot Knob Rd.
Eagan, MN 55121
Telephone: 651–452–4600
Web site: http://www.gcfb.net/location/eagan

GRANITE CITY FOOD AND BREWERY—MAPLE GROVE
Address: 11909 Main St.
Maple Grove, MN 55369
Telephone: 763–416–0010
Web site: http://www.gcfb.net/location/maple-grove

GRANITE CITY FOOD AND BREWERY—ROSEVILLE
Address: 851 Rosedale Center
Roseville, MN 55113
Telephone: 651–209–3500
Web site: http://www.gcfb.net/location/roseville

GRANITE CITY FOOD AND BREWERY—ST. CLOUD
Address: 3945 2nd St. S
St. Cloud, MN 56301
Telephone: 320–203–9000
Web site: http://www.gcfb.net/location/st-cloud

GRANITE CITY FOOD AND BREWERY—ST. LOUIS PARK
Address: 5500 Excelsior Blvd.
St. Louis Park, MN 55416
Telephone: 952–746–9900
Web site: http://www.gcfb.net/location/st-louis-park

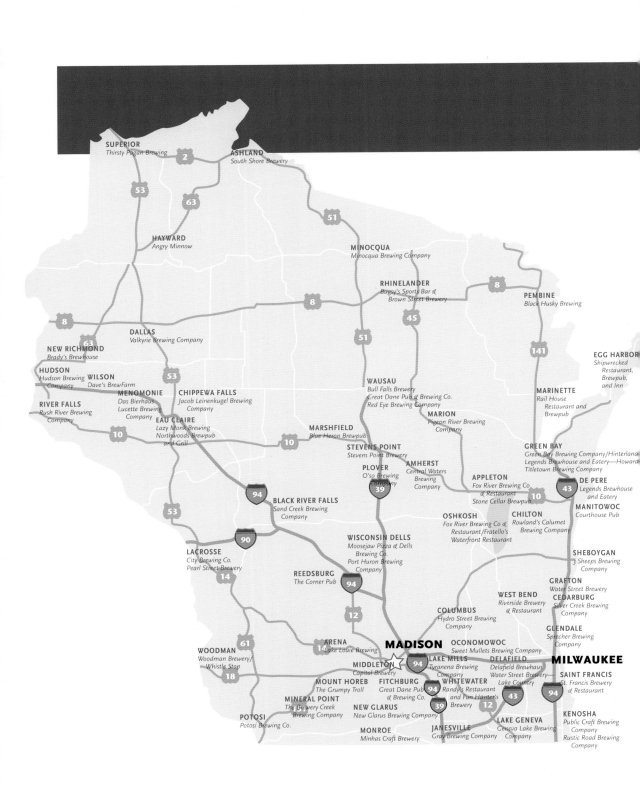

SUPERIOR
Thirsty Pagan Brewing

ASHLAND
South Shore Brewery

HAYWARD
Angry Minnow

MINOCQUA
Minocqua Brewing Company

RHINELANDER
Bugsy's Sports Bar &
Brown Street Brewery

PEMBINE
Black Husky Brewing

DALLAS
Valkyrie Brewing Company

NEW RICHMOND
Brady's Brewhouse

HUDSON
Hudson Brewing
Company

WILSON
Dave's BrewFarm

MENOMONIE
Das Bierhaus
Lucette Brewing
Company

CHIPPEWA FALLS
Jacob Leinenkugel Brewing
Company

RIVER FALLS
Rush River Brewing
Company

EAU CLAIRE
Lazy Monk Brewing
Northwoods Brewpub
and Grill

WAUSAU
Bull Falls Brewery
Great Dane Pub & Brewing Co.
Red Eye Brewing Company

MARION
Pigeon River Brewing
Company

MARINETTE
Rail House
Restaurant and
Brewpub

EGG HARBOR
Shipwrecked
Restaurant,
Brewpub,
and Inn

MARSHFIELD
Blue Heron Brewpub

STEVENS POINT
Stevens Point Brewery

PLOVER
O'so Brewing
Company

AMHERST
Central Waters
Brewing
Company

APPLETON
Fox River Brewing Co
& Restaurant
Stone Cellar Brewpub

GREEN BAY
Green Bay Brewing Company/Hinterland
Legends Brewhouse and Eatery—Howard
Titletown Brewing Company

DE PERE
Legends Brewhouse
and Eatery

MANITOWOC
Courthouse Pub

BLACK RIVER FALLS
Sand Creek Brewing
Company

OSHKOSH
Fox River Brewing Co &
Restaurant/Fratello's
Waterfront Restaurant

CHILTON
Rowland's Calumet
Brewing Company

LACROSSE
City Brewing Co.
Pearl Street Brewery

WISCONSIN DELLS
Moosejaw Pizza & Dells
Brewing Co.
Port Huron Brewing
Company

SHEBOYGAN
3 Sheeps Brewing
Company

REEDSBURG
The Corner Pub

GRAFTON
Water Street Brewery

WEST BEND
Riverside Brewery
& Restaurant

CEDARBURG
Silver Creek Brewing
Company

COLUMBUS
Hydro Street Brewing
Company

GLENDALE
Sprecher Brewing
Company

WOODMAN
Woodman Brewery/
Whistle Stop

ARENA
Lake Louie Brewing

MADISON

OCONOMOWOC
Sweet Mullets Brewing Company

MILWAUKEE

MIDDLETON
Capital Brewery

LAKE MILLS
Tyranena Brewing
Company

DELAFIELD
Delafield Brewhaus
Water Street Brewery—
Lake Country

SAINT FRANCIS
St. Francis Brewery
& Restaurant

MOUNT HOREB
The Grumpy Troll

FITCHBURG
Great Dane Pub
& Brewing Co.

WHITEWATER
Randy's Restaurant
and Fun Hunter's
Brewery

MINERAL POINT
The Brewery Creek
Brewing Company

NEW GLARUS
New Glarus Brewing Company

LAKE GENEVA
Geneva Lake Brewing
Company

KENOSHA
Public Craft Brewing
Company
Rustic Road Brewing
Company

POTOSI
Potosi Brewing Co.

MONROE
Minhas Craft Brewery

JANESVILLE
Gray Brewing Company

Wisconsin is the nation's symbolic "state of beer." An influx of German immigrants in the mid-nineteenth century created an industry that spawned some of the most legendary names in American brewing, past or present: Blatz, Schlitz, Miller, and Pabst, all once among the largest breweries in the world. Milwaukee beer had a reputation for quality that led saloon keepers in other states to advertise its availability in their establishments. By the beginning of the twentieth century, beer from Wisconsin was being sold in nearly every state of the union and in Europe.

Today Wisconsin has the largest number of breweries of the states covered in this book, and the number continues to grow. They range from giants like MillerCoors in Milwaukee and City Brewing in La Crosse to nanobreweries like Black Husky Brewing in tiny Pembine in the northeastern corner of the state. True to Wisconsin's Germanic heritage, lager brewing is still a large part of the scene, but ale brewers also abound, creating everything from tried-and-true classics to more innovative and off-the-wall brews.

The urban centers of Milwaukee and Madison are a good starting point for a Wisconsin brewery trip. Each city offers a large and varied collection of breweries and easy day-trips to places a bit further out. In Milwaukee, it's little more than a ten-minute drive from any one of the city's breweries to another. That leaves plenty of time to take in the town's many cultural and sporting institutions while absorbing its uniquely midwestern blue-collar vibe. And whether it's the recently renovated Pabst complex or the Valentin Blatz building, it's fun to stumble upon the ghosts of Milwaukee's brewing past.

Madison is smaller, with a more cosmopolitan, university-town feel. The breweries in town are a bit more spread out than those in Milwaukee, but it's still an easy drive from one to the other. Madison is a great jumping-off point for day trips to breweries in New Glarus and Lake Mills, or longer trips to visit breweries in the beautiful Driftless Area in the southwestern corner of the state and the Wisconsin Dells to the north.

While visiting Wisconsin, you owe it to yourself to leave the cities behind and explore the wilder parts of the state. With access to two Great Lakes, rolling countryside in the south, and lake-dotted forest land in the north, Wisconsin offers some of the most scenic beer-trip opportunities in the region. The far-northern breweries like Minocqua, Angry Minnow, and South Shore all lie a couple hours apart, but the two-lane highways that connect them meander through state and national forests, making for lovely drives. Break things up by getting out for a hike or a bit of cross-country skiing.

The Door County Peninsula is one of Wisconsin's most popular vacation areas. Jutting seventy-five miles into Lake Michigan, it has over three hundred miles of shoreline and offers five state parks, quaint towns, and historic lighthouses. It is also home to the Shipwreck Brewpub in Egg Harbor. And if you're visiting Door County, it's an easy trip to check out the brewpubs of Green Bay.

The Wisconsin Brewing Industry at a Glance
(Based on 2012 Data)

LARGEST BREWERY: Miller/Coors, Milwaukee—
58,950,000 barrels*

SMALLEST BREWERY: Karben4 Brewery, Madison—
1 barrel*

LARGEST BREWPUB: Great Dane Pub and Brewing
Company (four breweries)—7,300 barrels*

SMALLEST BREWPUB: Pigeon River Brewing, Marion—
22 barrels*

BREWERIES PER CAPITA: .00001 per capita,
or 69,656 persons per brewery**

*Brewers Association Data, *New Brewer* 30.3 (May/June 2013):
86–156.
**Based on 2011 population estimates from the U.S. Census Bureau
(http://quickfacts.census.gov/qfd/states/55000.html) and the
author's brewery list as of December 31, 2012.

Wisconsin Contract Breweries:

3 Dachshunds Beer Company, Cudahy
Barkers Island Inn Resort, Superior
Big Bay Brewing, Shorewood
Blu Creek Brewing, Madison
Buffalo Water Beer Company, Milwaukee
Chameleon Brewing Co., Glenwood
The Coffee Grounds, Eau Claire
Cross Plains Brewing Company, Cross Plains
Fat Boy Brewing, Oak Creek
Fauerbach Brewing Company, Madison
Fountain City Brewing Company, Fountain City
Furthermore Beer, Spring Green
Game On Brewing Company, Glenwood
Gray's Tied House, Verona
Horny Goat Brewing Company, Caledonia
Lead Feather Brewing Company, Jefferson
Milwaukee Ale House, Grafton
Milwaukee Premium Brewing Company, Milwaukee
Old Bavarian Brewing Company, Appleton
Pangaea Beer Company, Wisconsin Rapids
Rhinelander Brewing Company, Rhinelander
Stillmank Beer, Green Bay
Thunder River Beer Co., De Pere
West Bend Lithia Beer Co., West Bend

Wisconsin Breweries in Planning (as of March 2013):

Appleton Beer Factory, Appleton
Balanced Rock Brewery, Fort Atkinson
Barley and Vine Brewery, Franklin
Brenner Brewing Company, Milwaukee
Door County Brewing Company, Sister Bay
Excelsior Brewery, Blue River

Farmers Brewing Co., Shawano
Joseph James Brewing, Franklin
New Wisconsin Brewing Company, Madison
Old Bavarian Brewing Company, Appleton
Oliphant Brewing Company, Somerset
Pangaea Beer Company, Wisconsin Rapids
Pitchfork Brewing Company, Hudson
Re-Public Brewpub, Madison
Rown Brewery, Trevor
Safiri Coffee Pub, Port Washington
Tribute Brewing, Eagle River

Wisconsin Beer Festivals:

Isthmus Beer and Cheese Festival, Madison, January
(www.isthmus.com/beercheese.com)
Fond du Lac Brew Fest, Fond du Lac, February
(https://www.facebook.com/FDLBrewfest)
Milwaukee Public Museum Food and Froth Fest,
Milwaukee, February (www.mpm.edu)
Beer Lover's Brew Fest, Manitowoc, February
(www.manitowocjaycees.org)
Hops and Props, Oshkosh, March
(www.eaa.org/hops%26props)
Flanagan's Beer Fest, Appleton, March
(flanagansbeerfest.com)
Roar on the Shore Brew Fest, Kewaunee, March
(www.kewauneelionsclub.org/brewfest.html)
Gitchee Gumee Brew Fest, Superior, April
(http://www.ggbrewfest.com/)
Dairy State Cheese and Beer Festival, Kenosha, April
(www.kenoshabeerfest.com)
Top of the Hops Beer Festival, Racine, May
(www.topofthehopsbeerfest.com)
Northwest Beer Fest, Chippewa Falls, May
(https://www.facebook.com/northwestbeerfest)
Wisconsin Micro-Brewers Brew Fest, Chilton, May
(www.rowlandsbrewery.com/beerfest.html)
Kohler Festival of Beer, Kohler, June
(www.americanclubresort.com/events/kohler_
festival_of_beer.html)
World of Beer Festival, Menomonee Falls, June
(www.wobfest.com)
Great Northern Beer Festival, Eagle River, June
(www.greatnorthernbeerfestival.com)
Audacious Beer and Cheese Celebration, Heartland, June
(www.audaciousbeers.com)
Chetek Brew and Rib Fest, Chetek, July
(www.chetekbrewfest.com)
Hops on the Hill Beer and Food Tasting, Green Bay, July
(www.heritagehillgb.org/calendar/
hops-on-the-hill-beer-and-food-tasting-/237)

Milwaukee Firkin Craft Beer Festival, Milwaukee, July
(www.milwaukeefirkin.com)

Lac du Flambeau Lions Club Brewfest, Minocqua, July
(www.lacduflambeaubrewfest.com)

Milwaukee Brewfest, Milwaukee, July
(www.milwaukeebrewfest.com)

Great Taste of the Midwest, Madison, August
(www.greattaste.org)

Thirsty Troll Brew Fest, Mt. Horeb, September
(http://www.trollway.com/productlist.asp?cat=85)

Great Lakes Brewfest, Racine, September
(www.greatlakesbrewfest.com)

MADISON

Ale Asylum

ADDRESS: 2002 Pankratz St.
Madison, WI 53704

TELEPHONE: 608-663-3926

EMAIL: bandit@aleasylum.com

WEB SITE: www.aleasylum.com

MICHAEL'S PICK: Bamboozelator Doppelbock: A classic
doppelbock in the mold of Paulaner Celebrator, this
is dark-colored and richly malty with layers of caramel
and dark fruit. Hints of chocolate hide just below the
surface. Hop character is low, but there is the slightest
hint of licorice hop flavor, just enough bitterness to
keep it from being cloying.

TYPE: Brewery

DATE ESTABLISHED: 2006

OWNERS: Dean Coffey and Otto Dilba

BREWMASTER: Dean Coffey

BREWING SYSTEM: Thirty-three-barrel Sprinkman
brewhouse

FLAGSHIP BEER: Hopalicious

YEAR-ROUND BEERS: Hopalicious, Madtown
Nutbrown, Ambergeddon, Contorter Porter

SEASONAL BEERS: Ballistic IPA, Bedlam! IPA,
Satisfaction Jacksin, Sticky McDoogle Scotch Ale, Tripel
Nova, Mercy. Taproom-only seasonals: Bamboozleator
Doppelbock, Big Slick Stout, Hatha-Weizen, Gold
Digger, Happy Ending, Diablo

SPECIAL RELEASES: None

TOURS: Monday–Saturday. Check Web site for times.

BEER TO GO: Growlers and package

FOOD: Limited deli menu featuring pizza and assorted
sandwiches

AMENITIES: Parking lot, taproom, seasonal outdoor
seating on two levels

PUB HOURS: Monday–Wednesday: 11:00 A.M. to
midnight; Thursday–Saturday: 11:00 A.M.to 2:00 A.M.;
Sunday: 2:00 P.M. to midnight

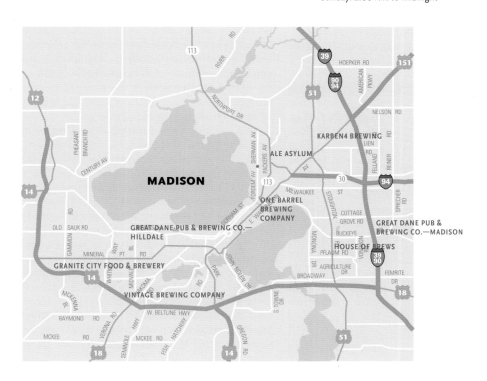

NEARBY ATTRACTIONS: Wisconsin State Capital, Olbrick Botanical Gardens, Capital City State Bike Trail, Monona Terrace Convention Center, Madison Repertory Theatre, Majestic Theatre, Wisconsin Historical Museum, Overture Center for the Arts, Madison Museum of Contemporary Art, University of Wisconsin Badgers sporting events

NOTES: Ale Asylum's branding looks edgy. It suggests the extreme. But extreme is not what Ale Asylum is all about. In a world dominated by bourbon-barrel aging and odd ingredients, this brewery's extremity lies in its aggressive refusal to follow the trends. The folks at Ale Asylum believe in making boldly flavored beers brewed according to traditional styles and using only four ingredients: malt, hops, water, and yeast.

Beer is part of who Dean Coffey is. It is a lifestyle. He has been described as a style-stickler, someone who believes that beer doesn't have to be over the top; it just has to be good. His hardcore adherence to this approach infuses everything that happens at Ale Asylum, from the careful attention to brewing process to the selection of beers on tap.

Ale Asylum has a reputation for big, hoppy beers, but that reputation doesn't really do them justice. The ten beers on tap during my visit ran the gamut from the bitter but balanced Hopalicious to the malty-sweet Sticky McDoogle Scotch Ale. In between was a panoply of consistently well-made beers in a wide range of styles. There is something here for every taste.

I was told that Ale Asylum is a must-visit in the Madison area. I would agree.

Capital Brewery

ADDRESS: 7734 Terrace Ave. Middleton, WI 53562

TELEPHONE: 608–836–7100

EMAIL: capbrew@capital-brewery.com

WEB SITE: www.capital-brewery.com

MICHAEL'S PICK: Autumnal Fire: A strong doppelbock based on an Oktoberfest recipe, this beer pours a beautiful ruddy amber. It features an intense malty sweetness with loads of raisin and dark fruit flavors. A touch of chocolate is barely perceptible in the background. Lightly warming, it's a great seasonal snifter-sipper.

TYPE: Brewery

DATE ESTABLISHED: 1984

OWNER: Private shareholders group

BREWMASTER: Brian Destree

BREWING SYSTEM: Thirty-five-barrel Huppmann brewhouse

FLAGSHIP BEER: Wisconsin Amber

YEAR-ROUND BEERS: Supper Club, Wisconsin Amber, Island Wheat, Pale Ale, Rustic Ale, Capital Pilsner, Capital Dark

SEASONAL BEERS: Maibock, Fest, Oktoberfest, Winter Skal

SPECIAL RELEASES: Blond Doppelbock, Autumnal Fire, Capital Square Series: Imperial Doppelbock, Baltic Porter, Tett Doppelbock, Eisphyre, Eternal Flame

TOURS: Friday at 3:30 P.M. and Saturday at 1:30 and 3:30 P.M. Cost $5. Make reservations online.

BEER TO GO: Growlers and package

FOOD: None

AMENITIES: Small parking lot and free street parking, Bier Stube and Bier Garten, gift shop, seasonal live music in the Bier Garten

PUB HOURS:

Winter hours: Wednesday and Thursday: 4:00 to 9:00 P.M.; Friday: 3:00 to 9:00 P.M., Saturday: noon to 5:00 P.M.;

Summer hours: Tuesday–Thursday: 4:00 to 9:00 P.M.; Friday: 3:00 to 10:00 P.M., Saturday: Noon to 9:00 P.M., Sunday: noon to close

NEARBY ATTRACTIONS: Madison-area breweries and brewpubs, Wollerscheim Winery in Prairie du Sac, National Mustard Museum, University of Wisconsin–Madison campus, UW Badgers sporting events, Blackhawk Ski Area, fifteen minutes from downtown Madison

NOTES: In the mid-1800s, an influx of immigrants from German-speaking, lager-brewing countries built a strong brewing industry in Wisconsin. By the end of that century the state had become the brewing capital of the United States, if not the world. It is this sense of the word "capital" from which the brewery derives its name.

Capital Brewery was founded with the notion of tying into Wisconsin's brewing heritage. Like its Germanic forbearers, Capital concentrates on brewing German-style lager beers. This is rare in the world of craft beer, as lagers take longer and are more expensive to make than ales. Capital's beers spend anywhere from four weeks to two months in cold conditioning before they are packaged.

Capital is well known for its award-winning doppelbocks. The brewery recently embarked upon a unique doppelbock project called Eternal Flame. Each year, a strong doppelbock is brewed. After several months of aging, half of the beer is packaged, and the conditioning tank is topped off with a different doppelbock. This process is repeated every year, yielding a beer that is ever changing, but that always retains some trace of the original.

The Bier Garten at Capital is a great place to wrap up a day of beer touring. Relax over a pint while enjoying live music and a beautiful Wisconsin summer's eve.

Great Dane Pub and Brewing Co–Fitchburg

ADDRESS: 2980 Cahill Main
Fitchburg, WI 53711
TELEPHONE: 608–442–9000
EMAIL: info@greatdanepub.com
WEB SITE: www.greatdanepub.com
MICHAEL'S PICK: Black Earth Porter Cask: A creamy, full-bodied porter with ample caramel, coffee, and chocolate. A mild roasty bite sticks around into the finish. Hop bitterness is low but gets a boost from the coffee-like bitterness of roasted malts. It's a great beer to serve from a cask.
TYPE: Brewpub
DATE ESTABLISHED: 2002
OWNERS: Rob LoBreglio and Eliot Butler
BREWMASTER: Pat Keller
BREWING SYSTEM: Fifteen-barrel Liquid Assets brewhouse
FLAGSHIP BEER: Stone of Scone Scotch Ale
YEAR-ROUND BEERS: Landmark Lite Lager, Crop Circle Wheat, Verruckte Stadt German Pils, Old Glory American Pale Ale, Stone of Scone Scotch Ale, Jon Stoner's Oatmeal Stout
SEASONAL BEERS: Mallard's Cream Ale, Mike's Stout, Fox Tail Red Ale, Maibock, Black Earth Porter, Oktoberfest, Tripel, Foxy Brown Ale, and others
SPECIAL RELEASES: None
TOURS: By request
BEER TO GO: Growlers and kegs
FOOD: Selection of brewpub favorites: burgers, salads, sandwiches, pizzas, and assorted entrées. Interesting specialties include Bacon Mac and Cheese Pizza and Peanut Stew.
AMENITIES: Parking lot, cask-conditioned ales, private dining rooms available, seasonal outdoor seating
PUB HOURS: Monday–Thursday: 11:00 A.M. to 2:00 A.M.; Friday–Saturday: 11:00 A.M. to 2:30 A.M.; Sunday: 10:00 A.M. to 2:00 A.M.
NEARBY ATTRACTIONS: Gunflint Trail Park, Eplegaarden Orchard apple picking, Fitchburg Historical Society, fifteen minutes from downtown Madison

NOTES: The Great Dane Brewpub chain has five locations in Madison and Wausau. While there is an assortment of chainwide recipes, each location (except Eastside in Madison) has a fully functional brewery and its own brewing staff who create a range of specialty beers. Every store is also marked by its own particular ambience.

The Great Dane Fitchburg location is in a suburban shopping center fifteen minutes south of downtown Madison. The nondescript exterior is indistinguishable from the other mall stores except for the large outdoor seating area overlooking the parking lot. Stepping through the doors, you pass the copper-clad brewhouse to enter a nineteenth-century tavern.

The large horseshoe-shaped bar is the central feature of the bright and airy barroom. Beadboard trim and old-fashioned lampposts complete the vintage effect. The dining-room area is a more modern interpretation on the theme. Upstairs is a billiards area with another bar.

Like the other Great Dane locations, the beer at the Fitchburg pub was pleasantly drinkable if not outstanding. The two cask-conditioned offerings on the day of my visit, Fox Tail Red Ale and Black Earth Porter, were noteworthy. It's worth a stop if you find yourself south of the city.

Great Dane Pub and Brewing Co.–Hilldale

ADDRESS: 357 Price Pl.
Madison, WI 53705
TELEPHONE: 608–661–9400
EMAIL: info@greatdanepub.com
WEB SITE: www.greatdanepub.com
MICHAEL'S PICK: Decimation Row: Brewed for Bob Dylan's seventieth birthday, this is a complex and layered imperial red ale. Assertive biscuit and caramel malt is set off by the lightest touch of roast in the finish. Hops explode from the glass, sending whiffs of tangerine, tropical fruit, and grapefruit pith flying in all directions. A dry finish keeps it light and drinkable for its stature.
TYPE: Brewpub
DATE ESTABLISHED: 2006
OWNERS: Rob LoBreglio and Eliot Butler
BREWMASTER: Don Vasa
BREWING SYSTEM: Fifteen-barrel ABT brewhouse
FLAGSHIP BEER: Imperial IPA
YEAR-ROUND BEERS: Landmark Lite Lager, Crop Circle Wheat, Peck's Pilsner, Stone of Scone Scotch Ale, Emerald Isle Stout, Verruckte Stadt German Pils, Old Glory American Pale Ale, Imperial IPA
SEASONAL BEERS: Notoberfest, rotating Belgian styles, Velvet Hammer Bock
SPECIAL RELEASES: Decimation Row, Barleywine, and others

TOURS: No

BEER TO GO: Growlers and kegs

FOOD: Selection of brewpub favorites: burgers, salads, sandwiches, pizzas, and assorted entrées. Interesting specialties include Bacon Mac and Cheese Pizza and Peanut Stew.

AMENITIES: Parking lot and free street parking, live music, full bar, billiards, private rooms available, Sunday brunch

PUB HOURS: Sunday–Thursday: 11:00 A.M. to 2:00 A.M.; Friday and Saturday: 11:00 A.M. to 2:30 A.M.

NEARBY ATTRACTIONS: University of Wisconsin–Madison campus, Hilldale Shopping Center, University of Wisconsin Arboretum, Henry Vilas Zoo, ten minutes from downtown Madison

NOTES: The Great Dane Brewpub chain has five locations in Madison and Wausau. While there is an assortment of chainwide recipes, each location (except Eastside in Madison) has a fully functional brewery and its own brewing staff who create a range of specialty beers. Every store is also marked by its own particular ambience.

The Hilldale location is the flagship brewery of the Great Dane fleet. It is where all the kegged beer is brewed for sale outside the chain and at the Eastside location. It is also where you will find the best beer of the chain. Whether Great Dane standards or unique-to-store specialties, Hilldale brewer Don Vasa is crafting clean and well-made brews. His specialties were among the most layered and interesting I tasted at any Great Dane pub.

The ambience at Hilldale is upscale casual. The main bar and private rooms have wood trim and paned windows that give it the feel of an English country estate. The game room is large and airy with its own central bar. Large round booths line the walls. The colorfully lit brewhouse is visible behind tall windows that reach to the high ceiling.

Great Dane Pub and Brewing Co.–Madison

ADDRESS: 123 E. Doty St.
Madison, WI 53703

TELEPHONE: 608–284–0000

EMAIL: info@greatdanepub.com

WEB SITE: www.greatdanepub.com

MICHAEL'S PICK: Black Earth Porter: A smooth and full-bodied porter that foregrounds caramel sweetness against a backdrop of light coffee and chocolate roast. Smokey wisps add depth. Grassy hops leave only the faintest impression.

TYPE: Brewpub

DATE ESTABLISHED: 1994

OWNERS: Rob LoBreglio and Eliot Butler

BREWMASTER: Eric Brusewitz

BREWING SYSTEM: Ten-barrel PUB brewhouse

FLAGSHIP BEER: Crop Circle Wheat

YEAR-ROUND BEERS: Landmark Lite, Verruckte Stadt German Pils, Peck's Pilsner, Crop Circle Wheat, Old Glory American Pale Ale, Devil's Lake Red Lager, Stone of Scone Scotch Ale, Emerald Isle Stout, Black Earth Porter

SEASONAL BEERS: Maibock, Oktoberfest, Merry Isthmus

SPECIAL RELEASES: Potters Run India Pale Ale, Schwarzbier, Texas Speedway IPA, Mr. Natural Nut Brown Ale, Tri-Pepper Pils, and others

TOURS: First Saturday of the month. Call for availability.

BEER TO GO: Growlers and kegs

FOOD: Selection of brewpub favorites: burgers, salads, sandwiches, pizzas, and assorted entrées. Interesting specialties include Bacon Mac and Cheese Pizza and Peanut Stew.

AMENITIES: Metered street parking, paid parking in nearby garages, full bar, cask ale selections, live music, seasonal outdoor seating, game room with billiards, shuffleboard, and video games

PUB HOURS: Sunday–Thursday: 11:00 A.M. to 2:00 A.M.; Friday and Saturday: 11:00 A.M. to 2:30 A.M.

NEARBY ATTRACTIONS: Within sight of the state capital in the heart of downtown Madison, two blocks from Lake Monona, Monona Terrace Convention Center, Madison Repertory Theatre, Majestic Theatre, Wisconsin Historical Museum, Overture Center for the Arts, Madison Museum of Contemporary Art

NOTES: The Great Dane Brewpub chain has five locations in Madison and Wausau. While there is an assortment of chainwide recipes, each location (except Eastside in Madison) has a fully functional brewery and its own brewing staff who create a range of specialty beers. Every store is also marked by its own particular ambience.

The downtown Madison location is the original. It has a more casual feel than the other locations. Dark wood, high ceilings, and craftsman-style furnishings make the main bar and dining resemble an early twentieth-century tavern. The attached billiard area and downstairs Rathskeller are more like a sports bar.

There were seventeen beers available on the afternoon of my visit, ranging in style from light American lager to full-bodied porter. Most of the beers were quite drinkable, Black Earth Porter and Texas Speedway IPA being standouts. Unfortunately, two beers were clearly past their prime and beginning to go sour. What made this most aggravating is that the condition of these beers was known to the bar staff, and yet they were still being served. If these issues are resolved, the Madison Great Dane is a nice place to stop after seeing the capital sights.

The Grumpy Troll

ADDRESS: 105 S. 2nd St.
Mount Horeb, WI 53572
TELEPHONE: 608–437–2739
EMAIL: info@thegrumpytroll.com
WEB SITE: www.thegrumpytroll.com
MICHAEL'S PICK: Keller Brau: This unfiltered pilsner-style beer is crisp like a lager but creamy from suspended yeast. Gentle pilsner-malt sweetness is rounded out by toasty edges. Moderate bitterness, spicy hop flavors, and hints of lemony citrus make it delightfully easy to drink.
TYPE: Brewpub
DATE ESTABLISHED: 2000
OWNER: Doug Welshinger
BREWMASTER: Mark Knoebl
BREWING SYSTEM: Ten-barrel DME brewhouse
FLAGSHIP BEER: Spetsnaz Stout
YEAR-ROUND BEERS: Captain Fred, Trailside Wheat, Eric the Red, Maggie, Spetsnaz Stout, Norski Nut Brown
SEASONAL BEERS: Sesquicentennial Brew, Sunflower, Norwegian Wit, Old School IPA, Keller Brau, Hop Farm Pale Ale
SPECIAL RELEASES: Rotating IPAs, bourbon-barrel beers, sour beers
TOURS: By appointment
BEER TO GO: Growlers and bottles
FOOD: The downstairs menu includes an eclectic mix of brewpub fare, featuring award-winning burgers. The upstairs pizzeria offers traditional and nontraditional pies as well as soups, salads, and panini.
AMENITIES: Free street parking, seasonal outdoor seating, cask beer selections on weekends, full bar, shuffleboard, English-style darts, family-friendly
PUB HOURS:
Brewpub Hours: Monday–Thursday: 11:00 A.M. to 10:00 P.M.; Friday and Saturday: 11:00 A.M. to 11:00 P.M.; Sunday: 11:00 A.M. to 8:30 P.M.
Pizzeria Hours: Monday–Thursday: 4:00 to 9:00 P.M.; Friday and Saturday: noon to 10:00 P.M.; Sunday: noon to 8:00 P.M.
NEARBY ATTRACTIONS: Troll Capital of the World—take the "Troll Stroll" through downtown, historic Main Street with quaint shops, Mt. Horeb Mustard Museum, bicycle trails including the Military Ridge Trail, mountain biking and cross-country skiing at Blue Mound State Park, downhill skiing at Tyrol Basin Ski Area, Botham Vineyards, thirty minutes from Madison

NOTES: There is something for everyone at the Grumpy Troll. With a menu that includes over fifty-five items and twelve house beers always on tap, you are sure to find something you like. The beers run the gamut from lighter session beers for novices to big and brassy beers for the hardcore hop heads. The lighter beers and lager styles were for me the highlights of an overall solid lineup.

The brewpub is tucked into a former cheese factory on the edge of the quaint, historic downtown. The atmosphere downstairs is very casual. It's the kind of place where strangers talk to each other, which happened to me as I entered the bar. The upstairs pizzeria has more of a sports-bar/game-room feel. Both spaces are small, and I'm told they can get very crowded on weekend nights.

The Grumpy Troll boasts the nation's only "all solar-brewed beer." Indeed, solar panels on the roof provide most of the energy needed to run the brewery.

House of Brews

ADDRESS: 4539 Helgeson Dr.
Madison, WI 53718
TELEPHONE: 608–347–7243
EMAIL: info@houseofbrewsmadison.com
WEB SITE: www.houseofbrewsmadison.com
MICHAEL'S PICK: Full House Pale Ale: At 7 percent ABV, this is more of an IPA than a pale ale. Fitting squarely with the midwestern style, it's got a firm malt backbone that leans a touch to the sweet side. Bitterness is moderate, but just enough to call it an IPA. Big, citrusy hop aroma carries over into the flavor with a burst of grapefruit.
TYPE: Brewery
DATE ESTABLISHED: 2012
OWNER: Page Buchanan
BREWMASTER: Page Buchanan
BREWING SYSTEM: Ten-barrel converted dairy-tank brewhouse
FLAGSHIP BEER: Prairie Rye Ale
YEAR-ROUND BEERS: Prairie Rye Ale, Cellar Dark, A-Frame Amber, Full House Pale Ale, Standing Stones Scotch Ale, Bungalow Rye ESB
SEASONAL BEERS: Snug Oatmeal Stout, others planned
SPECIAL RELEASES: Black IPA, Saison
TOURS: Planned. Check Web site.
BEER TO GO: Growlers
FOOD: None

AMENITIES: Parking lot, taproom, Community Supported Brewery program

PUB HOURS: Planned. Check Web site.

NEARBY ATTRACTIONS: Madison-area breweries and brewpubs, Olbrich Botanical Garden, water activities on Waubesa and Kegonsa Lakes, Ho-Chunk Casino, twenty minutes from downtown Madison

NOTES: House of Brews is Wisconsin's first Community Supported Brewery (CSB), one of only a handful in the nation. For those familiar with community-supported agriculture (CSA), the concept will be familiar: subscribers purchase a share of the brewery's output, which they receive in periodic allotments. At House of Brews, the starting share is one growler a week. In addition, members get limited-release beers that are available only to them. They are also invited to participate in special classes and tasting seminars held at the brewery and to give input as to what beers are produced.

Founder and brewer Page Buchanan hopes that this idea of community participation will permeate the whole brewery operation. He wants tours to be "working tours," with people witnessing the brewery and brewers in action rather than looking at static tanks. He has plans and equipment for a brew-on-premises business, allowing customers to make their own beer at the brewery. He would like to do chef collaborations that put the chefs in the driver's seat, working with them to craft beers that match the food, rather than the more typical model of chefs making food to match the beers.

In terms of beer, Buchanan wants to brew "crowd pleasers." He's aiming for beers that will appeal to novice and nerd alike—full of flavor, but generally low in alcohol and easily approachable. Indeed, his beers fit the popular midwestern mold. They tend to favor malt over hops and sweetness over bitterness. They have rich, solid centers, but lack a certain definition around the edges.

Hydro Street Brewing Company

ADDRESS: 152 W. James St.
Columbus, WI 53925

TELEPHONE: 920-350-0252

EMAIL: aaron@hydrostreetbrew.com

WEB SITE: www.hydrostreetbrew.com

MICHAEL'S PICK: Summer Rescue Amber: This is a simple and straightforward American amber ale. A bit of malty caramel sweetness leads the way to a fairly dry finish. American hops flash low bursts of tangerine and grapefruit over the top. The bitterness is high—perhaps somewhat higher than many examples of the style.

TYPE: Brewpub

DATE ESTABLISHED: 2011

OWNERS: Aaron Adams and Sandye Adams

BREWMASTER: Aaron Adams

BREWING SYSTEM: One-barrel Blichmann Engineering brewhouse

FLAGSHIP BEERS: Seven Sisters Scotch Ale, Campfire Porter

YEAR-ROUND BEERS: Seven Sisters Scotch Ale, Twist and Shout Stout, Columbus Cream Ale, Campfire Porter, Truancy IPA, Throw Back Pale Ale

SEASONAL BEERS: Squashbug Ale, Mary Ann and Ginger Wheat Ale, Summer Rescue Amber, and others

SPECIAL RELEASES: Crawfish IPA, London Pub American Style, Jonalee's We Are Still Alive IPA, Distinguished Citizen, Coffee Stout, London Pub ESB, Aaron's Alt, Belgium Pale Ale, Jonalee's Honey Pot, Double Belgian Big Whale Ale, Not Your Unkel's Dunkel, HSB Hefeweizen, Absent IPA, Vienna, Grinders Island Amber, It's Delightful Hefe, K of P Porter, Old Pappy, Good Neighbor Brown, Newport Red, Dark as the Devil's Eyes, and others

TOURS: By request

BEER TO GO: Growlers and kegs

FOOD: Selection of sandwiches, wraps, burgers, and tapas items featuring ingredients from local organic farms and dairies

AMENITIES: Free municipal parking lot next door, seasonal outdoor seating, live music, Mug Club

PUB HOURS: Sunday–Tuesday: 9:00 A.M. to 10:00 P.M.; Wednesday: 11:00 A.M. to 10:00 P.M.; Thursday–Saturday: 9:00 A.M. to 11:30 P.M.

NEARBY ATTRACTIONS: Tyranena Brewing Company, Wisconsin's largest antique mall, Midwest Horse Fair, thirty miles from Madison, forty-five miles from Wisconsin Dells, seventy-five miles from Milwaukee

NOTES: While many small breweries profess a commitment to the local community, for Aaron and Sandye Adams, the idea of "local" is central to what Hydro Street is all about, from the atmosphere in the dining room to the vendors that supply the meat, cheese, and produce. When they first determined to open their business, the pair believed that small-town Columbus couldn't support a brewpub. After scouting locations elsewhere, as far away as Washington State, they returned home and haven't looked back.

The Adamses describe Hydro Street as a "mom and pop brewpub." They've tried to create a place where locals gather with friends and visitors leave feeling like neighbors. The long, narrow space retains some of its historical feel, with hardwood floors and original woodwork trim. It's a warm and welcoming spot that people say feels like home—in Aaron Adams's words, "a place where you don't have to take off your shoes."

The couple has a strong commitment to buying local. As much as possible, they source their food ingredients from farms located within twenty miles of Columbus. They maintain close, personal relationships with the farmers. This reflects their desire to support local businesses as much as it does their interest in organic farming and sustainability. They see the relationships with their suppliers as mutually beneficial; each one helps the other to succeed.

The annual Hydro Street Brewing Challenge extends this ethos to the homebrew community. The winning entry, judged by members of the pub's Mug Club, is brewed and sold at the brewpub.

Karben4 Brewing

ADDRESS: 3698 Kinsman Blvd.
Madison, WI 53704

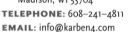

TELEPHONE: 608-241-4811
EMAIL: info@karben4.com
WEB SITE: www.karben4.com
MICHAEL'S PICK: Fantasy Factory IPA: Tangerine and orange hop aromas give a great first impression. This is a beer for sniffing. The flavor profile is aggressively bitter, but well balanced with toffee and biscuit malt sweetness. Pine resin and grapefruit peel hop flavors are the real stars of the show. It goes out crisp, dry, and refreshing.
TYPE: Brewpub
DATE ESTABLISHED: 2012
OWNERS: Ryan Koga, Zak Koga, and Alex Evans
BREWMASTER: Ryan Koga
BREWING SYSTEM: Fifteen-barrel brewhouse, unknown manufacturer
FLAGSHIP BEERS: NightCall Smoked Porter, SamuRyePA American Pale Ale, Block Party Amber Ale, Lady Luck Irish Red, UnderCover, Fantasy Factory IPA
YEAR-ROUND BEERS: NightCall Smoked Porter, SamuRyePA American Pale Ale, Block Party Amber Ale, Lady Luck Irish Red, UnderCover, Fantasy Factory IPA
SEASONAL BEERS: Silk Scorpion Black IPA, other rotating IPAs
SPECIAL RELEASES: Planned
TOURS: By request
BEER TO GO: Growlers
FOOD: A constantly rotating selection of German-, Asian-, and Mediterranean-inspired items emphasizing locally sourced ingredients
AMENITIES: Parking lot, full bar, seasonal outdoor beer garden
PUB HOURS: Monday–Wednesday: 3:00 to 10:00 P.M.;

Thursday: 3:00 P.M. to midnight; Friday: 3:00 P.M. to 2:00 A.M.; Saturday: 11:00 A.M. to 2:00 A.M.
NEARBY ATTRACTIONS: Wisconsin State Capital, Olbrick Botanical Gardens, Capital City State Bike Trail, Manona Terrace Convention Center, Madison Repertory Theatre, Majestic Theatre, Wisconsin Historical Museum, Overture Center for the Arts, Madison Museum of Contemporary Art, University of Wisconsin Badgers sporting events

NOTES: As Ryan Koga explains it, he "tripped and fell into brewing." While pursuing a graduate degree in sports medicine, he found himself in need of rent money. In a clear case of "right place at the right time," he landed a job on the bottling line at Yellowstone Valley Brewing Company in Billings, Montana. He had never homebrewed and had no experience with beer aside from swilling light lagers. One day he pulled a bottle of oatmeal stout off the line and had his mind blown. "I never knew beer could be like that," he says. "I felt like I had been lied to. And that was unacceptable." He never looked back from that experience.

Creating an experience is what brewing is all about for Koga. He has no use for style guidelines. The only important question to him is, "Do you like it?" With every beer that he makes, he is trying to capture a visceral and emotional moment in life. For instance, his Lady Luck Irish Red is an attempt to convey the sense of well-being he gets from drinking Bordeaux wine—not the flavor of the wine, but rather the experience of it. A porter recipe might be an attempt to express the feeling that comes with eating a great steak.

The food at Karben4 also provides guests with a unique experience. It's prepared by the chefs at the Madison Underground Food Collective, a collaborative effort of cooks who believe in serving food that is locally sourced and seasonal. The menu changes regularly and features items from pub favorites like giant pretzels and open-face pulled-pork sandwiches to fantastical takes on the hot dog, as in homemade Frankfurters topped with cole slaw, kimchi, or pesto.

Lake Louie Brewing

ADDRESS: 7556 Pine Rd.
Arena, WI 53503

TELEPHONE: 608-753-2675
EMAIL: tom@lakelouie.com
WEB SITE: www.lakelouie.com
MICHAEL'S PICK: Warped Speed Scotch Ale: Rich and creamy with loads of luscious caramel malt, this Scotch ale exhibits the kind of balance that defines Lake Louie

beers. It is sweet, but slightly amped bitterness and earthy hop flavor keep it from being sticky. It finishes with just the slightest hint of roast.

TYPE: Brewery

DATE ESTABLISHED: 1999

OWNER: Tom Porter

BREWMASTER: Tom Porter

BREWING SYSTEM: Fifteen-barrel JV Northwest brewhouse

FLAGSHIP BEER: Warped Speed Scotch Ale

YEAR-ROUND BEERS: Coon Rock Cream Ale, Warped Speed Scotch Ale, Arena Premium Pale Ale, Tommy's Porter, Kiss the Lips IPA

SEASONAL BEERS: Mosquito Beach, Milk Stout, Dino's Dark

SPECIAL RELEASES: Louie's Reserve, Prairie Moon, Brother Tim's Tripel, Mr. Mephisto's Imperial Stout

TOURS: Sunday at noon and 1:15 P.M.

BEER TO GO: None

FOOD: None

AMENITIES: Parking lot

PUB HOURS: None

NEARBY ATTRACTIONS: Corner Pub brewpub, Grumpy Troll brewpub, New Glarus Brewing Co., Wollersheim Winery, American Players Theatre, House on the Rock, Taliesin Frank Lloyd Wright House, bike trails, water activities on the Wisconsin River, forty minutes from Madison

NOTES: Tom Porter started brewing almost by accident; his background is in engineering. When a friend wanted to upgrade his homebrewing equipment, Porter agreed apply his skills to build the system. They brewed on that system nearly every weekend, but Porter wanted nothing to do with the process. Only interested in enjoying the finished product, he strummed his guitar while his friend made the beer.

When the friend left to attend brewing school, Porter was left without a source of free beer. He had little choice but to learn to make it himself. In the process he found his calling. Within a year of starting to homebrew, he had quit his job to open Lake Louie.

He has come a long way since beginning with a single seven-barrel fermenter and a three-barrel "Frankenstein" brewhouse. Over the years his brewery has seen two major expansions. Porter's engineering roots are evident in his brewing practice. He is a stickler for process. His staff follows strict written protocols regarding maintenance and sanitation. His efforts to increase efficiency go so far as to break down the bottling line in an attempt to eke out additional points above the 95 percent efficiency he was already achieving.

He constantly tweaks his recipes to account for slight variations in raw materials from batch to batch or crop to crop. The result is beer that is consistent, clean, and full-flavored. He shoots right down the middle stylistically, crafting beers that mostly adhere to style guidelines. While he makes the occasional big beer, he tends to avoid extremes. Porter takes great pride in his Coon Rock Cream Ale, believing that you can tell a great brewer by the quality of his or her lighter beers because those beers offer no place to hide flaws. Indeed, the cream ale is a tasty one.

New Glarus Brewing Company

ADDRESS: 2400 State Hwy 69
New Glarus, WI 53574

TELEPHONE: 608–527–5850

EMAIL: Form on Web site

WEB SITE: www.newglarusbrewing.com

MICHAEL'S PICK: Wisconsin Belgian Red: A winner of multiple awards in national and international competitions, Wisconsin Belgian Red is one of the first spontaneously fermented ales produced in the United States. A pound of Door County cherries for each bottle makes this a cherry bomb. The flavor balances delicately between sweet and tart. Hints of malt beneath the fruit provide a pie-crust base. Absolutely stunning.

TYPE: Brewery

DATE ESTABLISHED: 1993

OWNERS: Daniel Carey and Deb Carey

BREWMASTER: Daniel Carey

BREWING SYSTEM:

Riverside Brewery: One-hundred-barrel Huppmann brewhouse

Hilltop Brewery: One-hundred-barrel Steinecker brewhouse

FLAGSHIP BEER: Spotted Cow

YEAR-ROUND BEERS: Moon Man, Spotted Cow, Two Women, Fat Squirrel, Wisconsin Belgian Red, Raspberry Tart

SEASONAL BEERS: Snowshoe Red Ale, Back 40, Coffee Stout, Staghorn Octoberfest, Totally Naked, Dancing Man Wheat, Cabin Fever Honey Bock, Uff-da Bock. Seasonals change yearly.

SPECIAL RELEASES: Unplugged and Thumbprint Series Beers, including IIPA, Imperial Weizen, Smoked Rye Ale, Belgian Quad, Smoke on the Porter, Sour Brown Ale, Enigma, Bohemian Lager, Imperial Stout, and many others

TOURS: Free self-guided tours daily from 10:00 A.M. to 4:00 P.M.

BEER TO GO: Package

FOOD: None

AMENITIES: Parking lot, tasting room, gift shop

PUB HOURS: Monday–Sunday: 10:00 A.M. to 4:00 P.M.

NEARBY ATTRACTIONS: Swiss Historical Village, Sugar River and Badger State Bike Trails, outdoor recreation at New Glarus Woods State Park, Taste of New Glarus and Heidi Festival in June, New Glarus Primrose Winery, thirty miles from Madison

NOTES: The drive from Madison to New Glarus takes you through verdant Wisconsin farmland. You can feel the ghosts of the German immigrants that settled the region. As you enter town from the north you pass the New Glarus Riverside Brewery, its painted stucco making it resemble a Swiss village hall.

Continuing south, it is easy to imagine Highway 69 as the Rhine River. The brewery's Hilltop facility looms like a medieval fortress perched high above. Vineyards running up the hillside are all that is needed to complete the illusion.

From the outside, the Hilltop brewery looks like a German village. Inside it is a testament to order and efficiency. Attention has been paid to every detail, down to the green slate tile that perfectly complements the copper brewing vessels. This attention to detail makes the self-guided walking tours a wondrous journey.

The brewhouse at New Glarus Brewing.

Daniel Carey is one of only a few American brewers who can truly claim the title Brewmaster. In 1992 he passed the Master Brewer Examination of the Institute of Brewing and Distilling in London, becoming the first American to do so since 1978. This experience shows in New Glarus's beers. From light American lagers to imperial IPAs and sour beers, each one is well-crafted, balanced, and extraordinarily drinkable. The brewery has enjoyed tremendous success while keeping it local. They have surpassed one hundred thousand barrels of annual production while limiting distribution to Wisconsin.

One Barrel Brewing Company

ADDRESS: 2001 Atwood Ave.
Madison, WI 53704

TELEPHONE: 608-630-9286

EMAIL: info@onebarrelbrewing.com

WEB SITE: www.onebarrelbrewing.com

Handmade in small batches with love.

MICHAEL'S PICK: Bilbo Baggins Black IPA: "Intense" was a word I used a lot when tasting this beer. Coffee-grounds-like roasted malt character is high for the style. Together with the ample hops and a very dry finish, it yields a brutal bitterness that will satisfy the hop heads. Hop flavors of citrus and pine resin bring some brighter notes to the darkness.

TYPE: Brewery

DATE ESTABLISHED: 2012

OWNER: Peter Gentry

BREWMASTER: Peter Gentry

BREWING SYSTEM: One-barrel Blichmann Engineering brewhouse

FLAGSHIP BEER: Penguin Pale Ale

YEAR-ROUND BEERS: Peguin Pale Ale, Commuter Kölsch, Strong Ale No. 2

SEASONAL BEERS: Bilbo Baggins Black IPA, Breakfast Beer Oatmeal Stout, Emperor Penguin Imperial IPA, Easy Amber, and others

SPECIAL RELEASES: White House Honey Ale, Wisconsin Tripel, 3787 Tripel, Queen Elizabeth IPA, Lemon Saison, and others

TOURS: By request for special events

BEER TO GO: Growlers

FOOD: Small selection of Wisconsin tavern snacks: pickled eggs, meat and cheese board, pizza, pretzels

AMENITIES: Free and metered street parking, limited wine list, selection of guest beers, including several gluten-free beers

PUB HOURS: Monday–Wednesday: 4:00 to 11:00 P.M.; Thursday: 4:00 P.M. to 1:00 A.M.; Friday: 3:30 P.M. to 1:00 A.M.; Saturday: 11:00 A.M. to 1:00 A.M.; Sunday: 11:00 A.M. to 11:00 P.M.

NEARBY ATTRACTIONS: Water activities on Lakes Monona and Mendota, Wisconsin State Capital, Monona Terrace Convention Center, Madison Repertory Theatre, Majestic Theatre, Wisconsin Historical Museum, Overture Center for the Arts, Madison Museum of Contemporary Art, Madison Children's Museum

NOTES: Peter Gentry wants his guests to feel like they are part of the beer. Indeed, when you enter the taproom you are essentially walking into the brewery. The tiny brewhouse is visible behind glass at the back of the room just past the bar. Stainless-steel fermenters fill the space normally claimed by the back bar.

Burbling buckets at the base of each one let patrons know that beer is actually brewing in those tanks.

The room has a minimalist, warehouse aesthetic—a cross between nineteenth-century saloon and modern hipster coffee house. The focal point is the long walnut bar that Gentry built with his father. Exposed brick, hardwood floors, and simple dark-wood furnishings complete the effect.

One Barrel is Madison's first nanobrewery. The impetus to start the brewery came when Gentry, then a homebrewer of fifteen years, entered and won the Grumpy Troll Challenge, a competition sponsored by the Grumpy Troll brewpub in nearby Mt. Horeb. The grand prize was an opportunity to brew his Strong Ale No. 2 at the brewpub. From there it was entered into the U.S. Open Beer Championships, where it received honorable mention. His brewing confidence boosted, he quit his job in newspaper sales, found a space, and started construction. Within a year he was open for business.

Gentry's focus is on the basics. His beers rotate frequently, but he's not brewing anything that is too off-the-wall. He wants to make a few great beers instead of many average beers. To that end, Gentry is constantly honing his recipes based on customer feedback. If guests respond well to a particular beer, they are very likely to see it again.

Tyranena Brewing Company

ADDRESS: 1025 Owen St.
Lake Mills, WI 53551
TELEPHONE: 920–648–8699
EMAIL: info@tyranena.com
WEB SITE: www.tyranena.com
MICHAEL'S PICK: Rocky's Revenge: Half of this American-style brown ale is aged in bourbon barrels, adding smooth bourbon and vanilla layers to the chocolate and caramel malt profile. The whiskey doesn't dominate like it does in some bourbon-barrel beers. Rocky's Revenge is a great beer for a crisp fall evening.
TYPE: Brewery
DATE ESTABLISHED: 1998
OWNER: Rob Larson
BREWMASTER: Rob Larson
BREWING SYSTEM: Thirty-barrel Sprinkman brewhouse
FLAGSHIP BEERS: Bitter Woman IPA, Rocky's Revenge
YEAR-ROUND BEERS: Three Beaches Honey Blond, Headless Man Amber Alt, Stone Tepee Pale Ale, Bitter Woman IPA, Rocky's Revenge, Chief Blackhawk Porter
SEASONAL BEERS: Down and Dirty Stout, Fargo Bros. Hefeweizen, Scurvy IPA, Gemuetlichkeit Oktoberfest,

Painted Ladies Pumpkin Spice, Sheep Shagger Scotch Ale
SPECIAL RELEASES: Dirty Old Man Imperial Rye Porter, HopWhore Imperial IPA, Who's Your Daddy? Bourbon Barrel-Aged Imperial Porter, Bitter Woman from Hell, Bitter Woman in the Rye, Benji's Smoked Chipotle Imperial Porter, and others in the Brewers Gone Wild series
TOURS: Saturdays at 3:30 P.M.
BEER TO GO: Growlers and package
FOOD: None
AMENITIES: Parking lot, taproom, seasonal beer garden, live music, Mug Club program
PUB HOURS: Monday–Thursday: 4:30 to 11:00 P.M.; Friday and Saturday: 3:00 P.M. to midnight; Sunday: noon to 8:00 P.M. Closed Monday and Tuesday from September to May.
NEARBY ATTRACTIONS: Fishing, boating, and swimming on Rock Lake, Azatlan State Park Middle-Mississippian mound-builder cultural site, one hour from Milwaukee, forty minutes from Madison

NOTES: In 1997, Tyranena founder Rob Larson was a shareholder in the nation's third largest manufacturer of inflatable rubber pieces for milking machines. When the shareholders decided to sell, he found himself flush with capital and out of work. What was an avid homebrewer to do? Start a brewery, of course.

In 1998 he broke ground on a new building and purchased equipment from a defunct brewery in the Twin Cities. The next year, the tasting room opened, and Tyranena launched with four beers: Headless Man Amber Alt, Stone Tepee Pale Ale, Chief Blackhawk Porter, and a now-discontinued brown ale.

Lake Mills is a tiny rural town. While Tyranena's main markets are in the bigger urban areas of Madison, Milwaukee, and the Twin Cities, they have maintained firm roots to their home. The Mug Club membership is mostly locals, and all the beers are named after Lake Mills landmarks.

Larson has an affinity for hops. The brewery has built a reputation for bold and bitter beers. In addition to the year-round pale ale and IPA, the Brewers Gone Wild series has allowed him to push the hop envelope even further. He has produced a range of bitter brews, including an orange-peel infused IPA, Double IPAs, Belgian IPAs, and the admittedly unbalanced Hop Whore IPA.

Vintage Brewing Company

ADDRESS: 674 S. Whitney Way
Madison, WI 53711
TELEPHONE: 608–204–2739
EMAIL: vintagemadison@gmail.com
WEB SITE: www.vintagebrewingco.com
MICHAEL'S PICK: Weiss-Blau Weissbier: This beer is everything a classic German weissbier should be. It's light and fresh with a full, wheaty mouthfeel. Banana and clove yeast flavors maintain an equal balance. Light lemony citrus notes float over the top. This is a beer that makes you want one more pint.
TYPE: Brewpub
DATE ESTABLISHED: 2009
OWNERS: Trent Kraemer, Mark Kraemer, Brittany Kraemer, Bryan Manning, Scott Manning, and Mike Bridges
BREWMASTER: Scott Manning
BREWING SYSTEM: Ten-barrel DME brewhouse
FLAGSHIP BEERS: Scaredy Cat Oatmeal Stout, Weiss-Blau Weissbier, Woodshed Oaked India Pale Ale
YEAR-ROUND BEERS: Sister Golden Ale, Scaredy Cat Oatmeal Stout, Weiss-Blau Weissbier, Woodshed Oaked India Pale Ale
SEASONAL BEERS: Better Off Red, Summer Sahti, Joulupukki Winter Sahti
SPECIAL RELEASES: Pint o' Joe Coffee Porter, Palindrome APA, Black Mirror Double Black IPA, Spring Bock, Maximilian Stout, Wee Heavy Scotch Ale, Hibiscus Saison, Wheaty Peaty, Attaboy Amber, Whippoorwill Belgian-style Witbier, and others
TOURS: By appointment
BEER TO GO: Growlers and kegs
FOOD: Selection of brewpub favorites: salads, sandwiches, and entrées, featuring unique signature burgers
AMENITIES: Parking lot, private banquet rooms available, rentable "prison bus" transportation to and from special events, monthly beer dinners, cask ale selections, Wisconsin-brewed guest taps, full bar, family-friendly
PUB HOURS: Sunday–Thursday: 11:00 A.M. to 2:00 A.M.; Friday and Saturday: 11:00 A.M. to 2:30 A.M.
NEARBY ATTRACTIONS: University of Wisconsin–Madison campus, University of Wisconsin Arboretum, Henry Vilas Zoo, Madison Opera, numerous golf courses nearby, ice fishing on area lakes, ten minutes from downtown Madison

NOTES: Scott Manning says that he doesn't like committing to anything but his wife. This attitude guides his "don't get used to it" approach to beer making. He wants his guests to always be trying something new. While a few beers stick around for the long term, a good number of his twelve taps are a constantly changing assortment of classic styles and flights of fancy.

His creative urge was kindled by several years working in a large-production brewery making the same beers day after day. In that corporate setting, making a new beer meant submitting triplicate forms for recipe approval. When he got the call from family members about opening a brewpub in Madison, he leapt at the opportunity. Now the only restriction placed on the beer is to "make it awesome." And that he does. Vintage beers are among the best in the Madison area.

The brewpub prides itself on being a family operation. While you're there, it's quite likely that you'll speak with one of the owners. There are no silent partners.

The ambience is comfortable and casual, a mix of 1950s neighborhood tavern and the bar in your uncle's basement. Vintage beer signs line the walls, providing a kitchy connection to Wisconsin's brewing past. It's a welcoming place where you won't be pushed to clear out when you are finished eating.

MILWAUKEE

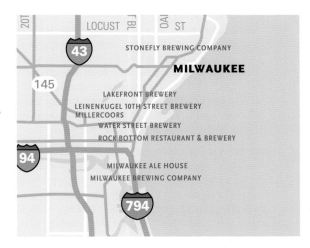

Delafield Brewhaus

ADDRESS: 3832 Hillside Dr.
Delafield, WI 53018
TELEPHONE: 262–646–7821
EMAIL: tknutson@delafield-brewhaus.com
WEB SITE: www.delafield-brewhaus.com
MICHAEL'S PICK: Pewaukee Porter: This is a full-flavored brown porter that features a good blend of

coffee/cocoa roast and caramel sweetness. Bitterness is moderate, and a layer of herbal hop flavors adds interest. It's a solid and sessionable ale.

TYPE: Brewpub

DATE ESTABLISHED: 1999

OWNERS: Eric Knutson and Tricia Knutson

BREWMASTER: John Harrison

BREWING SYSTEM: Twenty-five-barrel Century brewhouse

FLAGSHIP BEER: Delafield Amber

YEAR-ROUND BEERS: Dock Light, Delafield Amber, Pewaukee Porter, Sommerzeit Hefe Weizen

SEASONAL BEERS: Einhorn Bock, Hop Harvest IPA, Oats and Barley Stout, Red Raspberry Lager, Hopfenstange Pils, Millennium Tripel, Leisure Beer, Old No. 27 Barley Wine

SPECIAL RELEASES: Jan Primus, When 7 Matts Aren't Enough, Hometown Honey Blond, Frühlingszeit Maibock, Thames Valley Ale, Bricklayer Pale Ale, Maddy's Mild, Oats and Barley Stout, and others

TOURS: No

BEER TO GO: Growlers and kegs

FOOD: Selection of brewpub favorites: steaks, ribs, pizza

AMENITIES: Parking lot, banquet rooms available, food and drink specials, family friendly, live music on Saturdays, breweriana collection, full bar, seasonal outdoor seating, Mug Club

PUB HOURS: Monday: 3:00 to 11:00 P.M.; Tuesday– Thursday: 11:00 A.M. to 11:00 P.M.; Friday and Saturday: 11:00 A.M. to midnight; Sunday 9:00 A.M. to 10:00 P.M.

NEARBY ATTRACTIONS: Water Street Brewery–Lake Country, outdoor activities at Lapham Peak State Park and Kettle Moraine State Forest, fishing, boating, and swimming on nearby lakes, numerous golf courses, thirty-five minutes from downtown Milwaukee

NOTES: When you come in the front entrance of the Brewhaus, you immediately encounter the brewery, its stainless-steel tanks rising up from the floor and reaching toward the high ceiling like the music-making cylinders of some weird steampunk pipe organ. Stepping further into the main dining room, the space becomes a big box. It seems enormous, with two levels of seating. There is a rough and unfinished feel to it. Breweriana artifacts seem to have been slapped randomly on the walls simply to keep them from being empty.

The beer selection offers good variety. When I visited, there were ten house beers on tap, ranging from the 3.5 percent ABV Dock Light to a 12.5 percent ABV bourbon-barrel aged barleywine. Overall, the beer quality was good, but it was a bit hit or miss. Some beers, like Pewaukee Porter and Hop Harvest

IPA, were quite tasty. Others seemed a bit lackluster or were maybe just a bit past prime. The brewery had a good year in 2011, winning six medals for six beers entered in the World Beer Championships in Chicago.

The food was good and reasonably priced. I had a grilled pork brisket with spätzle and a cheese curd appetizer. The curds were crispy, and the pork was tender and well-seasoned. And how can you miss with spätzle? I left satisfied and very full.

Lakefront Brewery

ADDRESS: 1872 N. Commerce St. Milwaukee, WI 53212

TELEPHONE: 414-372-8800

EMAIL: Form on Web site

WEB SITE: www.lakefrontbrewery.com

MICHAEL'S PICK: Klisch Pilsner: A classic Bohemian pilsner. The beautiful golden color announces the softly sweet pilsner malt that greets your tongue. Sharply bitter to balance, it melds graham cracker malt with perfumed Saaz hop before finishing crisp and dry.

TYPE: Brewery

DATE ESTABLISHED: 1987

OWNER: Russ Klisch

BREWMASTER: Luther Paul

BREWING SYSTEM: Fifty-barrel brewhouse with components from Huppmann, Steinecker, and JV Northwest

FLAGSHIP BEER: Riverwest Stein Beer

YEAR-ROUND BEERS: Wheat Monkey Ale, Cream City Pale Ale, Organic ESB, Fuel Café Stout, IPA, Fixed Gear American Red Ale, Riverwest Stein Beer, Eastside Dark Lager, Klisch Pilsner, New Grist Gluten Free, White Beer

SEASONAL BEERS: Big Easy Imperial Maibock, Snake Chaser Irish Stout, Bock, Cherry Lager, Oktoberfest Lager, Pumpkin Lager, Holiday Spice Lager

SPECIAL RELEASES: Bridge Burner Special Reserve, Local Acre Lager, Rendezvous Biere de Garde, My Turn Series, including BA India-style Black Ale, and others

TOURS: Monday–Thursday: 2:00 and 3:00 P.M. Multiple tours on Friday and Saturday. See Web site for schedule. Cost $7. Advance purchase is recommended.

BEER TO GO: Growlers, package, and kegs

FOOD: Fish fry every Friday evening starting at 5:00

AMENITIES: Small parking lot, free street parking, taproom

PUB HOURS: Open during tour hours

NEARBY ATTRACTIONS: Milwaukee-area breweries and brewpubs, restaurants, galleries, and shops of the Riverwest neighborhood, ten minutes from downtown Milwaukee

NOTES: The fun starts at Lakefront before you even walk in the door. Visitors are greeted by Moe, Larry, and Curly, three whimsical sculptures made from the cut-off ends of the brewery's original fermenters that were painted with the Three Stooges' likenesses while the tanks were still in service. Once inside, you will find the closest thing you will get in the United States to an authentic German beer hall. The Friday-night fish fry even features a two-man oompah band.

Founder and owner Russ Klisch acknowledges that people tour breweries for two things: beer and entertainment. Lakefront strives to provide both. While most breweries only give beer at the end of the tour, Lakefront tours start with beer. There's a quick refill midway through and time for another at the end. Tour guides keep things light and lively. Serious content is interspersed with wisecracks and wit. The experience climaxes with a singalong of the theme from the 1970s TV show *Laverne and Shirley* in front of the actual bottling line that appeared in the show's opening credits.

Aside from frivolity, Lakefront is also known for innovation. According to Russ Klisch, they were the first modern brewery in this lager-loving state to brew an ale, and the first brewery in the country licensed to brew a gluten-free beer. Lakefront's Local Acre Lager was the first beer to be made entirely with Wisconsin-grown barley and hops. The brewery is now experimenting with isolating local yeast strains.

Leinenkugel 10th Street Brewery

ADDRESS: 1515 N. 10th St.
Milwaukee, WI 53205
TELEPHONE: 414–931–3900
EMAIL: leinielodge@leinenkugels.com
WEB SITE: www.leinie.com
MICHAEL'S PICK: Big Eddy Imperial Stout: A complex blend of roasty malt flavors defines this beer: bittersweet chocolate, molasses, and coffee. Dark fruits like figs and prunes swirl underneath. Moderate bitterness keeps the whole thing from becoming too sweet, while hop flavors add dashes of mint, earth, licorice, berries, and citrus.
TYPE: Brewery
DATE ESTABLISHED: 1995
OWNER: MillerCoors
BREWMASTER: Greg Walter
BREWING SYSTEM: Eighty-five-barrel Morton–Briggs brewhouse
FLAGSHIP BEERS: Leinenkugel Original, Honey Weiss
YEAR-ROUND BEERS: Original, Light, Sunset Wheat, Berry Weiss, Red Lager, Creamy Dark, Classic Amber

SEASONAL BEERS: Summer Shandy, Oktoberfest, Fireside Nut Brown, 1888 Bock, Big Eddy Series, including Russian Imperial Stout, Double India Pale Ale, Scotch Ale, and Baltic Porter
SPECIAL RELEASES: Leinenkugel's Limited, small barrel-aging program
TOURS: No
BEER TO GO: None
FOOD: None
AMENITIES: Parking lot, hospitality room for industry functions
PUB HOURS: None
NEARBY ATTRACTIONS: Milwaukee breweries and brewpubs, Pabst Mansion, Milwaukee Public Museum, the Milwaukee Theatre, Milwaukee Repertory Theater, Marcus Center for Performing Arts, Pabst Theatre

NOTES: When MillerCoors bought the Jacob Leinenkugel Brewing Company in 1988, the original Chippewa Falls location was still brewing on an antique system with limited capacity. If distribution was going to be expanded, additional production capacity would be required. The brewery on North 10th Street in Milwaukee, purchased from the failing G. Heileman Brewing Company, met that need.

Since the installation of a bigger brewhouse in Chippewa Falls, the 10th Street Brewery has served mostly as a testing ground for new recipes and as the production facility for Leinenkugel's Big Eddy series of high-gravity ales. The brewery produces about forty-five thousand barrels of beer annually. The small hospitality room is used mostly for private, beer-industry events. The brewery is not open for public tours.

After completing a fermentation-science degree at the University of California–Davis, 10th Street brewmaster Greg Walter intended to go into wine making. An internship at Anheuser-Busch changed his mind. He liked the beer-making process and saw the potential for higher pay in the beer industry. He was recruited by the Miller Brewing Company in 1979. In 1995 he transferred to Leinenkugel's 10th Street Brewery and has been there ever since. Having spent his career at large breweries, he appreciates the greater flexibility and control that the smaller Leinenkugel brewery gives him.

The 10th Street Brewery is the "Tenth" in MillerCoors' Tenth and Blake division, which is devoted to developing more craft-beer-oriented products for the megabrewery.

MillerCoors

ADDRESS: 4251 W. State St.
Milwaukee, WI 53208
TELEPHONE: 414–931–2337
EMAIL: Form on Web site
WEB SITE: www.millercoors.com
MICHAEL'S PICK: Miller High Life: I'll admit that I enjoy a High Life on occasion. Light sweetness is balanced by equally light bitterness. A touch of corniness hangs in the background. It goes down good on a hot summer day or when you're bowling with your buddies.
TYPE: Brewery
DATE ESTABLISHED: 1855
OWNER: MillerCoors
BREWMASTER: Dr. David Ryder
BREWING SYSTEM: Six six-hundred-barrel brewhouses. Manufacturer information unavailable.
FLAGSHIP BEER: Miller Lite
YEAR-ROUND BEERS: Miller Lite, Miller Genuine Draft, Miller High Life, Miller Chill, MGD 64, Keystone Light, Red Dog, Steel Reserve, Southpaw, Sharps, Mickey's Malt Liquor, Olde English 800
SEASONAL BEERS: None
SPECIAL RELEASES: None
TOURS: Daily between 10:30 A.M. and 3:30 P.M. Tours start every twenty minutes. Schedule is subject to change. Call on the day of your visit.
BEER TO GO: None
FOOD: None
AMENITIES: Parking lot, tasting room, gift shop
PUB HOURS: Tasting room only open for tours
NEARBY ATTRACTIONS: Milwaukee-area breweries and brewpubs, Pabst Mansion, Brewers games at Miller Park, ten minutes from downtown Milwaukee

The brewhouse at MillerCoors in Milwaukee.

NOTES: Whatever you think about the big breweries, you can't deny their importance to the history of brewing in the United States, the Midwest, and Milwaukee in particular. It is also good to keep in mind that even these behemoths started small. When Frederick Miller purchased the tiny Plank Road Brewery in 1855, it had an annual capacity of 1,200 barrels. Miller sold only three hundred barrels in his first year.

Of course, things are different now. For those accustomed to visiting smaller breweries, touring the big boys provides some perspective. The scale is mind-blowing. After watching a short promotional video, the actual tour begins in the packaging plant. Bottles whiz by on machines that fill and label 1,400 bottles a minute. The canning line goes even faster, with 1.5 cases completed every second.

Next is the distribution center, where stacked pallets of beer extend as far as one can see. Five hundred thousand cases pass through the two-hundred-thousand-square-foot warehouse every day.

From there you head to the brewhouse. Along the way you walk past bits of Miller history, including the original stables and the 1886 brewhouse. The modern brewhouse holds six 735-barrel lauter tuns and six kettles, each holding 590 barrels.

The highlight of the tour is the caves where Frederick Miller aged his beer. Nooks carved into the sandstone walls held blocks of ice to keep the caves cold. While in the caves you meet the ghost of Frederick Miller, who fills you in on the caves' history and purpose.

The tour ends at the Miller Inn, originally built in the 1880s to house unmarried brewery workers. Here is where you sample the beer, the main reason many people take the tour. You'll be served three beers before being sent on your way. On the way out, stroll past the replica of the original Plank Road Brewery—a reminder of where it all began.

Milwaukee Ale House

ADDRESS: 233 N. Water St.
Milwaukee, WI 53202
TELEPHONE: 414–276–2337
EMAIL: Form on Web site
WEB SITE: www.ale-house.com
MICHAEL'S PICK: Sheepshead Stout: This rich and creamy oatmeal stout is served on nitro at the brewpub. Cookie-dough sweetness is balanced by pleasing roast-malt bitterness and flavors of cocoa, chocolate, and coffee. It's great with the signature blue-cheese potato salad.

TYPE: Brewpub

DATE ESTABLISHED: 1997

OWNER: Jim McCabe

BREWMASTER: Bert Morton

BREWING SYSTEM: Fifteen-barrel Sprinkmann brewhouse

FLAGSHIP BEER: Louie's Demise

YEAR-ROUND BEERS: Downtown Lites, Ulao Wit, Hefeweizen, Solomon Juneau Extra Pale Ale, Pull Chain Pail Ale, Love Rock, Real Blond, Louie's Demise, Blockhead Brown Ale, Sheepshead Stout, Pressing 78 Porter, Polish Moon Milk Stout, Booyah Saison, Hop Happy IPA

SEASONAL BEERS: Orange Blossom Cream Ale, Glen Point, Weizen Bock, India Black Ale, Increase Amber, MBC IPA, Baltic Porter, Dunkel Weizen, and others

SPECIAL RELEASES: Weekend at Louie's, Monkey Paw, Harvest Ale, Cream Ale, Louie's Resurrection, Attitude by Volume (ABV) Series of high-gravity beers, including Godzilla Imperial Wit, Mothra Black Saison, and others

TOURS: By request

BEER TO GO: Bottles

FOOD: A selection of brewpub standards. Late-night menu after 10:00.

AMENITIES: Metered street parking or paid parking ramps, live music, seasonal outdoor seating that overlooks the Milwaukee River, private rooms available, Mug Club, cask-conditioned beers

PUB HOURS: Sunday–Wednesday: 11:00 A.M. to midnight; Thursday–Saturday: 11:00 A.M. to close

NEARBY ATTRACTIONS: Milwaukee breweries and brewpubs, Eisner Museum of Design, Broadway Theatre Center, Historic Third Ward shopping, dining, and nightlife, Milwaukee Art Museum, Marcus Center for the Performing Arts, Milwaukee Institute of Art and Design

NOTES: Ale House founder Jim McCabe was an early admirer of Milwaukee's craft-beer scene. In a city dominated at the time by Pabst and Miller, he gravitated to the products of Milwaukee's craft pioneers, Sprecher and Lakefront. After some time spent enjoying beer in the Pacific Northwest, he returned to Milwaukee ready to get into the business. He saw an opening to bring a West Coast–style brewpub to the city of beer.

Milwaukee Ale House is located in the historic Third Ward. What began in the 1800s as an area of warehousing and manufacturing has become a center of Milwaukee arts and nightlife. A fire in 1892 destroyed most of the buildings. Rapid redevelopment followed, giving the neighborhood a unity of architecture that ties it together.

Fun is the name of the game here. The open industrial space blends Milwaukee history with a casual roadhouse attitude. From live music three nights a week to swing dancing and trivia, there's always something going on.

Every beer I sampled at the Ale House was a winner. There was nothing extreme. Even the high-alcohol selections were restrained and balanced. They were all clean, crisp, and went down easy. I was especially impressed by the lighter beers, which had the delicacy and simple depth that made them both interesting and quaffable.

Milwaukee Brewing Company

ADDRESS: 613 S. Second St. Milwaukee, WI 53204

TELEPHONE: 414–226–2337

EMAIL: Form on Web site

WEB SITE: www.milwaukeebrewingco.com

MICHAEL'S PICK: Booyah Saison: A tasty Belgian saison that finishes dry with sharp, peppery spice. Citrusy fruit notes and a bit of malt sweetness give it body and depth.

TYPE: Brewery

DATE ESTABLISHED: 2007

OWNER: Jim McCabe

BREWMASTER: Bert Morton

BREWING SYSTEM: Fifty-barrel Morton-Briggs brewhouse

FLAGSHIP BEER: Louie's Demise

YEAR-ROUND BEERS: Pull Chain Pail Ale, Love Rock, Louie's Demise, Polish Moon Milk Stout, Booyah Saison, Hop Happy IPA

SEASONAL BEERS: Saison, Hoptoberfest, India Pale Ale

SPECIAL RELEASES: Attitude by Volume (ABV) Series of high-gravity beers, including Godzilla Imperial Wit, Mothra Black Saison, and others

TOURS: Friday: 4:00, 5:00, and 6:00 P.M.; Saturday: 2:00, 3:00, and 4:00 P.M.; Open house from 5:00 to 7:00 P.M. Tour costs $7. Open house costs $10.

BEER TO GO: Growlers and package

FOOD: None

AMENITIES: Free street parking, tasting room

PUB HOURS: During tours

NEARBY ATTRACTIONS: Milwaukee breweries and brewpubs, Eisner Museum of Design, Broadway Theatre Center, Historic Third Ward shopping, dining, and nightlife, Milwaukee Art Museum, Marcus Center for the Performing Arts, Milwaukee Institute of Art and Design

NOTES: Milwaukee Brewing Company is the production arm of the Milwaukee Ale House. The two operate as a single overall brewing operation. When capacity at the Ale House doesn't keep up with demand, some production is shifted to the 2nd Street brewery. When head brewer Bert Morton wants to try out new recipes, they are brewed on the smaller Ale House system and tested on patrons.

Bert Morton came to brewing via cooking. He is a graduate of New York's prestigious Culinary Institute of America and has worked in the kitchens of numerous restaurants, including the Milwaukee Rock Bottom, where he developed an interest in brewing. He started at Milwaukee Ale House as sous chef and later as head chef. By 1998 he had traded his chef's hat for rubber boots, becoming assistant brewer. When the 2nd Street Brewery opened, he took charge of overall brewing operations.

As a former chef, he likes beers that are drinkable the way food is edible. He strives for balance and flavor in his beers, eschewing the overly hopped or hyper-malty profiles of many extreme beers. This emphasis on balance is reflected in the beers that Milwaukee Brewing produces. From session beers to high-alcohol sippers, they all exhibit restraint, getting their impact from the interplay of subtle flavors rather than a heavy-handed emphasis of one flavor over the others.

A sense of fun that permeates the Ale House carries over to the production brewery. As soon as you come in the door you can feel that these folks love what they are doing. This enthusiasm is evident in the beers.

Rock Bottom Restaurant and Brewery

ADDRESS: 740 N. Plankinton Ave.
Milwaukee, WI 53203
TELEPHONE: 414–276–3030
EMAIL: milwaukee@rockbottom.com
WEB SITE: www.rockbottom.com/milwaukee
MICHAEL'S PICK: Naughty Scot Scotch Ale: David Bass has created a classic wee heavy that showcases rich, caramel malt. A touch of chocolate-covered raisin provides some depth. Although he doesn't use smoked malt in this brew, if you pay attention you might catch the subtlest hint of earthy smoke. It finishes sweet, but a light touch of hop bitterness keeps it crisp.
TYPE: Brewpub
DATE ESTABLISHED: 1997
OWNER: CraftWorks Breweries and Restaurants Inc.
BREWMASTER: David Bass
BREWING SYSTEM: Twelve-barrel JV Northwest brewhouse
FLAGSHIP BEERS: Kolsch, White Ale, Red Ale, IPA

YEAR-ROUND BEERS: Kolsch, White Ale, Red Ale, IPA, Naughty Scot Scotch Ale
SEASONAL BEERS: Fallen Angel Dubbel, Blitzen Tripel, St. Nick's Spiced Ale, Still Water Stout, Double Down India Brown Ale, Fire Chief Ale, and others
SPECIAL RELEASES: Summer Blond, Rocktoberfest, Pumpkin Ale, Winter Wheat, Moonshine Porter, Iron Horse Pilsner, Catcher in the Rye, and others
TOURS: By request
BEER TO GO: Growlers and bottles
FOOD: Standard Rock Bottom Restaurant menu: pub food, sandwiches and burgers, salads, chili, and a range of entrées. Good selection of steaks. Some more upscale items.
AMENITIES: Metered street parking or paid parking in nearby ramps and lots, happy-hour specials, full bar, Mug Club, seasonal outdoor seating overlooking the Milwaukee River, private room available, game room downstairs
PUB HOURS: Sunday–Thursday: 11:00 A.M. to midnight; Friday and Saturday: 11:00 A.M. to 2:00 A.M.
NEARBY ATTRACTIONS: Milwaukee-area breweries and brewpubs, Pabst Theatre, Milwaukee Repertory Theater, Marcus Center for the Performing Arts, Milwaukee Public Museum, Milwaukee Art Museum, River Cruises

NOTES: David Bass considers himself a process-oriented brewer; he just likes the act of making beer. Not one to sit at a desk all day, he enjoys the physicality of brewing—always being on the move and actively engaged with raw materials and equipment.

He's also a classic-styles kind of brewer. When approaching new recipes, he looks to history and tradition for inspiration. He wants to understand what was done in the past and why it was done. Armed with this kind of knowledge, he can then put his own stamp on the brew, but he always tries to do so in a way that makes sense historically. This emphasis on the classics doesn't mean he won't venture out every now and again. In the end, he's just trying to make the best beer he can.

The ambience and menu at Rock Bottom are fairly standardized across the chain. Look for slightly upscale pub food with some nicer items tossed in. That said, the food is always delicious. The riverside patio at the Milwaukee location is a big draw during warmer months. It nearly doubles the restaurant's seating capacity. An interesting way to experience Rock Bottom is on a riverboat pub crawl run by River Walk Boat Tours (www.riverwalkboats.com).

Sprecher Brewing Company

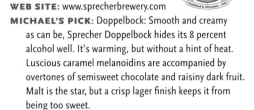

ADDRESS: 701 W. Glendale Ave. Glendale, WI 53209

TELEPHONE: 414–964–7837

EMAIL: beer@sprecherbrewery.com

WEB SITE: www.sprecherbrewery.com

MICHAEL'S PICK: Doppelbock: Smooth and creamy as can be, Sprecher Doppelbock hides its 8 percent alcohol well. It's warming, but without a hint of heat. Luscious caramel melanoidins are accompanied by overtones of semisweet chocolate and raisiny dark fruit. Malt is the star, but a crisp lager finish keeps it from being too sweet.

TYPE: Brewery

DATE ESTABLISHED: 1985

OWNER: Randy Sprecher

BREWMASTERS: Randy Sprecher and Craig Burge

BREWING SYSTEM: Forty-barrel and one-hundred-barrel custom-designed brewhouses

FLAGSHIP BEER: Special Amber

YEAR-ROUND BEERS: Hefe Weiss, Black Bavarian, Pub Ale, Special Amber, Light

SEASONAL BEERS: Mai Bock, Oktoberfest, Winter Brew, Summer Pils

SPECIAL RELEASES: Fresh Hop Amber Lager, Abbey Tripel, Doppel Bock, Russian Imperial Stout, IPA², Pipers Scotch Ale, Generation Porter, Barleywine, Mbege, Shakparo, Bourbon Barrel Scotch Ale, Bourbon Barrel Barleywine, Belgian Dubel, Kriek Lambic

TOURS: Monday–Friday: 3:00 and 4:00 P.M.; Saturday: noon, 1:00, 2:00, and 3:00 P.M. Reservations required. Cost $5 for adults and $3 for minors. Special Reserve Tasting tours available on weekends. Check Web site for schedule. Cost $15.

BEER TO GO: Growlers, kegs, and package

FOOD: None

AMENITIES: Parking lot, gift shop, tasting room, brewery rentals available for private parties, family-friendly tours

PUB HOURS: Gift shop is open daily from 11:00 A.M. to 6:00 P.M.

NEARBY ATTRACTIONS: Milwaukee breweries and brewpubs, Schlitz Audubon Nature Center, Lynden Sculpture Garden, golf, ten minutes from downtown Milwaukee

NOTES: Randy Sprecher's introduction to good beer came in the late 1960s, while he was stationed in Europe with the military. Exposure to the great beers of Germany and Belgium spoiled his taste for the bland brews that he found back home. He started homebrewing in 1971, and by 1974 he was already inquiring with the state of California about becoming a licensed brewer, well before the craft-beer movement began. After completing a program in fermentation science at the University of California–Davis, in 1980 he accepted a position at Pabst, where he learned every aspect of the business, from brewing to bottling. By 1984 the writing was on the wall for Pabst. He terminated his employment and began crafting fine German-style beers on his own.

The brewery still brews primarily German lagers. Their Black Bavarian schwarzbier is one of the best I have tasted, and the doppelbock is to die for. However, they have branched out in other directions, including Belgian styles, barleywines, a kriek, and traditional, gluten-free African beers made from sorghum, millet, and bananas. While these tangents are interesting and often tasty, it is Sprecher's award-winning German-style beers that I always come back to.

Interestingly, 65–70 percent of Sprecher's business comes from their line of sodas. They are all brewed, made-from-scratch recipes using real honey, vanilla, spices, and other natural ingredients.

St. Francis Brewery and Restaurant

ADDRESS: 3825 S. Kinnickinnic Ave. St. Francis, WI 53235

TELEPHONE: 414–744–4448

EMAIL: brewmaster@stfrancisbrewery.com

WEB SITE: www.stfrancisbrewery.com

MICHAEL'S PICK: Double Red Ale: A crisp, dry finish gives this ample imperial red ale an almost lager-like character. That impression is reinforced by the use of spicy continental hops instead of the citrusy American hops typical in beers of this style. The hops maintain an even balance with caramel-sweet and biscuity malt. Subtle chocolate notes fill in the background. Let it warm up a bit to get the full range of flavors.

TYPE: Brewpub

DATE ESTABLISHED: 2009

OWNER: Private ownership group

BREWMASTER: Scott Hettig

BREWING SYSTEM: Seven-barrel Premier Stainless brewhouse

FLAGSHIP BEERS: Kitzinger Kölsch and Archbishop Amber

YEAR-ROUND BEERS: Kitzinger Kölsch, Archbishop Amber, K. K. Weiss, rotating brown and dark beers

SEASONAL BEERS: Bohemian Pilsner, Double Red Ale, Tripel Trouble Belgian Tripel, Chocolate Hazelnut Porter, Oktoberfest, Harvest Strong

SPECIAL RELEASES: Black Sheep Weizenbock, Rey Oh Rye Roggenbier, Pumpkin Pie Spice Ale, Saison, Scotch

Ale, Breakfast Stout, Gose, Toasted Coconut Brown Ale, Cow-Tipper Milk Stout, and others

TOURS: By appointment

BEER TO GO: Growlers

FOOD: Selection of standard brewpub favorites

AMENITIES: Large parking lot, seasonal outdoor seating, private rooms available, cask-conditioned beers, daily food specials, Mug Club, Friday-night fish fry

PUB HOURS: Monday–Friday: 11:00 A.M. to close; Saturday: 10:00 A.M. to close

NEARBY ATTRACTIONS: Milwaukee breweries and brewpubs, close to General Mitchell International Airport, Lakeshore parks, Jack's Charter Fishing Service for Lake Michigan fishing, the Alchemist Theatre, ten minutes from downtown Milwaukee

NOTES: Like many others in the craft-brewing world, head brewer Scott Hettig started out as a homebrewer. At St. Francis he works to celebrate the local homebrewing community from which he came. He maintains membership in the Milwaukee Beer Barons homebrew club to this day. Every year the brewpub sponsors a pale ale competition in which club members submit all manner of pale ales and IPAs to be judged by a panel of Milwaukee's best professional brewers. The winning beer is brewed and served at St. Francis, and the brewer is treated to a party at the pub.

Hettig is a lover of malt. While he does brew the occasional IPA, you're not likely to find many hopped-up ales on tap here. On my visit there were none. Nor will you encounter many exotic concoctions that showcase unusual ingredients. You will find a wide range of balanced beers in a variety of styles, all brewed according to traditional guidelines. The beers are largely solid, with a few standouts like the Double Red Ale and the Tripel Trouble Belgian Tripel.

The menu and décor are classic American brewpub. The open dining room is anchored by a long curved bar and features lots of stone veneer and wood. The specialties of the house include ribs with an oatmeal stout BBQ sauce and a famous Friday-night fish fry.

Stonefly Brewing Company

ADDRESS: 735 E. Center St.
Milwaukee, WI 53212

TELEPHONE: 414–264–3630

EMAIL: info@stoneflybrewing.com

WEB SITE: www.stoneflybrewing.com

MICHAEL'S PICK: Simon Bagley Stout: Simon Bagley Stout is light-bodied and dry as a bone, as a proper Irish stout should be. Bitterness is moderate, but a good dose of roast gives the beer coffee and cocoa-nib flavors.

TYPE: Brewpub

DATE ESTABLISHED: 2006

OWNERS: Julia Laloggia and Rose Billingsly

BREWMASTER: Jacob Sutrick

BREWING SYSTEM: Seven-barrel brewhouse from mixed manufacturers

FLAGSHIP BEER: Mustache Ride Pale Ale

YEAR-ROUND BEERS: Lager Lager, The 53212 Amber Lager, Mustache Ride Pale Ale, Four Wolves English Ale, Brewtown Brown, Pierce Street Porter, Oatmeal Stout, Simon Bagley Stout, Ol' Sealaway Scotch Ale, Brouzard's Special Bitter

SEASONAL BEERS: Imperial Star Destroyer Stout, Oktoberfest, Irish Red Ale

SPECIAL RELEASES: Sixfinger IPA, Brass Knuckle Blond, Flabbergasted Sour Ale, Maibock, Doppelbock

TOURS: By request

BEER TO GO: None

FOOD: Limited selection of brewpub favorites, vegetarian and vegan selections

AMENITIES: Free street parking, seasonal outdoor seating, live music every Friday and Saturday, Saturday and Sunday brunch, daily food specials, happy-hour specials

PUB HOURS: Sunday–Thursday: 4:00 P.M. to 2:00 A.M.; Friday and Saturday: 4:00 P.M. to 2:30 A.M.

NEARBY ATTRACTIONS: Milwaukee-area breweries and brewpubs, University of Wisconsin–Milwaukee campus, Riverwest shops, restaurants, and art galleries, stroll the neighborhood to check out the sidewalk art, ten minutes from downtown Milwaukee

NOTES: Riverwest is one of Milwaukee's more diverse neighborhoods. It has also long been known as an artist community. Comparatively low rents and proximity to the University of Wisconsin campus have lured young bohemians to the area. There are a number of small galleries to peruse. Murals adorn neighborhood buildings, and it's not unusual to see quirky sculptures in front yards.

Stonefly Brewing Company fits right into this milieu. It has a pared-down, casual look that falls somewhere between old-school tavern and bohemian coffee house. The walls are adorned with a mix of breweriana artifacts and contemporary art. A bulletin board near the entrance is covered with notices announcing neighborhood goings-on—appropriate, since the clientele are primarily from the neighborhood.

Jacob Sutrick took over as head brewer in 2004. He worked his way up from the bottom, tending the door and tending the bar before being promoted to assistant brewer. Over the years he has learned pretty much every aspect of the brewpub's operation. The locals, he says, sometimes tell him that he makes strong beer, but falling mostly between 5 and 8 percent ABV, they might seem downright sessionable to the average beer traveler.

The food is satisfying and reasonably priced, with a definite Wisconsin flair—plenty of brats and tots. Those of the vegetarian persuasion will find something for them as well. Many of the dishes come in meatless versions with tofu.

Water Street Brewery–Grafton

ADDRESS: 2615 Washington St.
Grafton, WI 53024
TELEPHONE: 262–375–2222
EMAIL: Form on Web site
WEB SITE: www.waterstreetbrewery.com
MICHAEL'S PICK: Munich Lager: A fresh German-style lager is a thing of beauty. Graham-cracker sweetness of pilsner malt sits in delicate balance with spicy Continental hops and gentle bitterness. It's balanced, crisp, clean, and very well made.
TYPE: Brewpub
DATE ESTABLISHED: 2010
OWNER: R. C. Schmidt
BREWMASTER: George Bluvas III
BREWING SYSTEM: Fifteen-barrel JV Northwest brewhouse
FLAGSHIP BEERS: Honey Lager Light, Old World Oktoberfest, Bavarian Weiss
YEAR-ROUND BEERS: Honey Lager Light, Bavarian Weiss, Water Street Amber, Pale Ale, Old World Oktoberfest, Munich Lager, Raspberry Weiss
SEASONAL BEERS: Irish Stout, Doppelbock, Belgian Wit, Black Lager, Heller Bock, Porter
SPECIAL RELEASES: Peche, Whisky Stout, Shandy, Scottish Ale, Mead, Imperial Stout, and others
TOURS: By appointment
BEER TO GO: Growlers
FOOD: Selection of brewpub favorites
AMENITIES: Parking lot, full bar, weekend brunch, Friday fish fry, catering, breweriana collection
PUB HOURS: Monday–Friday: 11:00 A.M. to close; Saturday and Sunday: 10:00 A.M. to close
NEARBY ATTRACTIONS: Silver Creek Brewing Company, Riverside Restaurant and Brewery, old town of Cedarburg, Milwaukee Ale House–Grafton, outdoor activities at Lion's Den Gorge Nature Preserve and Cedarburg Bog State Natural Area, thirty minutes from downtown Milwaukee

NOTES: The Water Street Brewery in Grafton is the newest and nicest of the chain. It combines Water Street's trademark old-industrial look with the casual feel of a roadhouse. Like the Delafield location, an oval-shaped bar with an ornate, carved-wood backbar is the focal point. It's a casual, family-friendly place where regulars and casual travelers will both feel welcome.

That is exactly what the owners are going for. They describe Water Street as "a pub, but not a bar." It's a place where both food and beer are interesting and well-made, but where "nothing gets too crazy," says brewmaster George Bluvas. "We want things to be reasonably priced and reasonably identifiable. You can come in here and identify most of the things and not worry that you're getting something that you can't pronounce or don't know what it is."

While the beer lists are the same across the three Water Street locations, and beers brewed at one location are often sold at the others, differences in beer flavor due to water sources and equipment are noticeable. In addition to being the showcase facility, Grafton also has the best beer. On my visit, everything tasted beautifully fresh, with excellent definition and layering of flavors. The Bavarian Weiss is a go-to selection. The Munich Lager was just short of perfect.

Water Street Brewery–Lake Country

ADDRESS: 3191 Golf Rd.
Delafield, WI 53018
TELEPHONE: 262–646–7878
EMAIL: Form on Web site
WEB SITE: www.waterstreetbrewery.com
MICHAEL'S PICK: Bavarian Weiss: This one made me say "wow" at the first sip. The pillowy wheat and yeast mouthfeel is right on. It's light but full-bodied. The yeast flavors slightly favor the banana side, but clove is definitely there. Lemony highlights and a crisp, clean finish make this a deliciously refreshing quaff.
TYPE: Brewpub
DATE ESTABLISHED: 1999
OWNER: R. C. Schmidt
BREWMASTER: George Bluvas III
BREWING SYSTEM: Fifteen-barrel JV Northwest brewhouse
FLAGSHIP BEERS: Honey Lager Light, Old World Oktoberfest, Bavarian Weiss
YEAR-ROUND BEERS: Honey Lager Light, Bavarian Weiss, Water Street Amber, Pale Ale, Old World Oktoberfest, Munich Lager, Raspberry Weiss

SEASONAL BEERS: Irish Stout, Doppelbock, Belgian Wit, Black Lager, Heller Bock, Porter

SPECIAL RELEASES: Peche, Whisky Stout, Shandy, Scottish Ale, Mead, Imperial Stout, and others

TOURS: By appointment

BEER TO GO: Growlers

FOOD: Selection of brewpub favorites

AMENITIES: Parking lot, weekend brunch, Friday fish fry, catering, breweriana collection, family-friendly

PUB HOURS: Monday–Friday: 11:00 A.M. to close; Saturday and Sunday: 10:00 A.M. to close

NEARBY ATTRACTIONS: Delafield Brewhaus, outdoor activities at Lapham Peak State Park and Kettle Moraine State Forest, fishing, boating, and swimming on nearby lakes, numerous golf courses, thirty-five minutes from downtown Milwaukee

NOTES: Sitting at the bar at the Water Street Brewery in Delafield, I felt as though I had wandered into a steampunk cathedral built to celebrate the glory of beer. A soaring central vault is topped by an early-industrial-style skylight and supported on wooden posts with riveted metal hardware evoking a nineteenth-century factory or train station. It is flanked on each side by lower sections that resemble the knaves of a gothic church. The towering back-bar rises ceiling-high at one end of the room, reaching for the heavens like an elaborately carved medieval altar.

Despite this exalted architecture, the place is comfortable and casual. Sitting at the bar, it's easy to strike up a conversation with your neighbor. It's also a great place to bring the family for dinner out.

The Delafield location opened the same year that brewmaster George Bluvas took the position. He got his start at Water Street–Milwaukee in the early 1990s, washing dishes and helping in the brewery as "the assistant to the assistant brewer" while simultaneously holding down a shift-brewer position at Lakefront Brewery and brewing at another now-defunct brewpub. After a brief beer-making sojourn in another state, he returned to Water Street in 1999 to oversee brewing operations at all three locations.

While the beer lists are the same across the three Water Street locations, and beers brewed at one location are often sold at the others, differences in beer flavor due to water sources and equipment are noticeable. The Delafield beers were well-made and highly quaffable. The weissbier was fantastic. Also of note were the Pale Ale and Munich Lager.

ADDRESS: 1101 N. Water St. Milwaukee, WI 53202

TELEPHONE: 414–272–1195

EMAIL: Form on Web site

WEB SITE: www.waterstreetbrewery.com

MICHAEL'S PICK: Bavarian Weiss: While this didn't seem quite as fresh and crisp as the weissbiers I tasted at the Lake Country and Grafton locations, it still made for a delicious beer. It retains the slight banana emphasis and citrusy overtones of those other examples, but the fullness, wheaty sweetness, and clarity of flavors were somewhat less defined.

TYPE: Brewpub

DATE ESTABLISHED: 1987

OWNER: R. C. Schmidt

BREWMASTER: George Bluvas III

BREWING SYSTEM: Ten-barrel Price-Schonstrom brewhouse

FLAGSHIP BEERS: Honey Lager Light, Old World Oktoberfest, Bavarian Weiss

YEAR-ROUND BEERS: Honey Lager Light, Bavarian Weiss, Water Street Amber, Pale Ale, Old World Oktoberfest, Munich Lager, Raspberry Weiss

SEASONAL BEERS: Irish Stout, Doppelbock, Belgian Wit, Black Lager, Heller Bock, Porter

SPECIAL RELEASES: Peche, Whisky Stout, Shandy, Scottish Ale, Mead, Imperial Stout, and others

TOURS: By appointment

BEER TO GO: Growlers

FOOD: Selection of brewpub favorites

AMENITIES: Metered street parking, full bar, weekend brunch, Friday fish fry, catering, breweriana collection, family-friendly

PUB HOURS: Monday–Friday: 11:00 A.M. to close; Saturday and Sunday 10:00 A.M. to close

NEARBY ATTRACTIONS: Milwaukee breweries and brewpubs, Pabst Mansion, Pabst Theatre, Milwaukee Public Museum, Milwaukee Art Museum, Grohmann Art Museum, Harley Davidson Museum, Betty Brinn Children's Museum, steps from the Marcus Center for the Performing Arts, Milwaukee Repertory Theater, Milwaukee Theatre

NOTES: The original Water Street Brewery in downtown Milwaukee is the oldest brewpub in the city. When it opened in 1987, good beer was a hard sell. According to Brewmaster George Bluvas, Milwaukee was a lager town, with both Pabst and Miller still brewing millions of barrels locally. A quarter century of pushing palates has paid off. Bluvas reports that local consumers have reached a point where they appreciate the bolder flavors of the traditional European-style beers that Water Street serves up.

While the beer lists are the same across the three Water Street locations, and beers brewed at one location are often sold at the others, differences in beer flavor due to water sources and equipment are noticeable. I found the beers at the Milwaukee location to be the least satisfying of the three locations. The flavors weren't as well-defined, and they lacked the clean crispness that characterized the beers in Delafield and Grafton. Whatever the cause, they seemed like lesser versions of the very good beers tasted at the other locations.

The Milwaukee store has the nineteenth-century industry/rail-station look that defines Water Street's ambience. The low ceilings of the 1800s building in which it is housed give it an intimate and refined feel. It is conveniently located downtown near the river and just steps from the Marcus Center for the Performing Arts. Take a short walk across Water Street along Highland Avenue to discover a piece of Milwaukee brewing history, the old Valentin Blatz Brewery building.

NORTHERN

Angry Minnow

ADDRESS: 10440 Florida Ave. Hayward, WI 54843

TELEPHONE: 715–934–3055

EMAIL: angry.minnow@yahoo.com

WEB SITE: www.angryminnow.com

MICHAEL'S PICK: Redhorse Ale: This seasonal brew is a slightly malt-forward midwestern red ale with toasty biscuit flavors that blend nicely with sweet caramel. Citrus and pine-resin hops offer a bright contrast. Moderate bitterness and a clean, light finish make this a delightful quaff.

TYPE: Brewpub

DATE ESTABLISHED: 2004

OWNERS: Jason Rasmussen and Will Rasmussen

BREWMASTER: Jason Rasmussen

BREWING SYSTEM: Ten-barrel Liquid Assets brewhouse

FLAGSHIP BEER: River Pig American Pale Ale

YEAR-ROUND BEERS: Oaky's Oatmeal Stout, River Pig American Pale Ale, Honey Wheat, Minnow Lite

SEASONAL BEERS: Last Notch Wheat, Tommy A's Oktoberfest, Bitch Hill Belgian, Redhorse Ale

SPECIAL RELEASES: Smoked Porter, occasional barrel-aged offerings, and others

TOURS: By appointment

BEER TO GO: Growlers and backcountry-legal 44-ounce stainless steel growlers

FOOD: Upscale pub fare with an emphasis on locally sourced ingredients and Wisconsin specialties

AMENITIES: Parking lot, free street parking, seasonal outdoor seating, full bar, Friday-night fish fry (featuring fish from Lake Superior)

PUB HOURS: Tuesday–Thursday: 11:00 A.M. to 9:00 P.M.; Friday and Saturday: 11:00 A.M. to 10:00 P.M.

NEARBY ATTRACTIONS: Outdoor activities, including fishing, mountain biking, hiking, snow-shoeing, and cross-country skiing, American Birkebeiner Cross-Country Ski Marathon in February, Fresh Water Fishing Hall of Fame (don't miss the giant Musky), Hook Stone Winery, Fred Scheer's Lumberjack Shows, fall-color drives

NOTES: Will Rasmussen dreamed up the Angry Minnow during a ski trip to Colorado. After visiting several of the state's renowned brewpubs, he thought that the concept might work in Hayward, a center of outdoor activity in summer and winter. He brought his homebrewing brother Jason on board, and in 2004 the Angry Minnow opened.

Jason brews a wide range of beers from "lite" golden ale to imperial IPA. His personal taste is for big, hoppy beers, but he recognizes a need for easier-drinking session beers as well. He also tries to craft beers that will challenge the local patrons and get homebrewers "coming out of the woodwork." During my visit, this meant a very nice smoked porter.

The food has a decidedly Wisconsin bent. Menu items include several varieties of freshwater fish from Lake Superior, wild rice, and locally grown pork fed on spent grains and food waste from the brewpub. Dishes are more upscale than traditional pub food but still reasonably priced.

The atmosphere is decidedly different from the typical brewpub. High ceilings, exposed brick, and dim lighting give an elegant but inviting feel to the dining room. It is an ambience that would serve well for a romantic date or a round of drinks after work. The building itself has a unique and storied past. It has served as the offices of the Northern Wisconsin Lumber Company, an auto-body shop, and just possibly a brothel. Windows in the walkway from the front to the back dining room provide a bird's-eye view of the basement brewhouse.

Black Husky Brewing

ADDRESS: W5951 Steffen Ln.
Pembine, WI 54156

TELEPHONE: 715–324–5152

EMAIL: blackhuskybrewing@wildblue.net

WEB SITE: www.blackhuskybrewing.com

MICHAEL'S PICK: Sproose Joose: On the surface, this seems like a typical imperial IPA—aggressive bitterness, the citrus-peel flavor of American hops, and grainy malt sweetness to hold them both in check. But look deeper and you start to discover subtle blueberry notes from the fresh spruce that is part of the mix. The character of this beer changes through the year as the spruce goes from fresh, young tips to more mature twigs.

TYPE: Brewery

DATE ESTABLISHED: 2009

OWNERS: Tim Eichinger and Toni Eichinger

BREWMASTER: Tim Eichinger

BREWING SYSTEM: 1.5-barrel homemade brewhouse

FLAGSHIP BEERS: Pale Ale, Sproose Joose

YEAR-ROUND BEERS: American White, Harold the Red, Honey Wheat, Pale Ale, Sproose Joose

SEASONAL BEERS: Big Buck Brown, Milk Stout, Cherry Weiss, Hefe Weiss Wheat Ale

SPECIAL RELEASES: Beer-a-Vitae, Pembiner, Beware of the Dog Series, including Three Scrutineers Tripel and Twelve Dog Imperial Stout

TOURS: No

BEER TO GO: Package

FOOD: None

AMENITIES: Parking

PUB HOURS: None

NEARBY ATTRACTIONS: Outdoor activities in numerous parks and natural areas, snowmobiling, fishing and boating on nearby lakes and rivers, Marinette County Waterfalls Tour, Iron Mountain Mine Tour

NOTES: Pembine is located in a remote corner of northeastern Wisconsin, just a stone's throw from Michigan's Upper Peninsula. Black Husky Brewing is even more remote. From the main road, an eight-mile drive takes you to a clearing in the woods and two log cabins that house the brewery and its owners. The nearest permanent neighbor is a quarter mile away. As Tim Eichinger says of the place, "We have a lot of trees, a lot of deer, and a lot of ticks."

The Eichingers built the cabins themselves from a stand of red pine that grew on the property. They cut the trees, prepared the logs, and assembled the buildings by hand. After building their residence, they used the extra logs for a second structure that eventually became what is perhaps the only log-cabin brewery in the country.

The brewery's name comes from the husky kennel that shares the idyllic plot. The dogs are featured prominently on the labels for every Black Husky beer—every beer gets a dog, and every dog gets a beer. This isn't just a gimmick, says Tim Eichinger. These dogs are part of the family. The labels are a legacy to them, keeping them around even after they are gone.

Tim Eichinger takes his brews very seriously. He appreciates the flexibility that small-scale brewing allows. While he tries to keep certain beers available all the time, he has the freedom to respond to the market and his moods in creating what is in reality an ever-rotating selection. His beers can also reflect the seasons. Sproose Joose, his brutally bitter spruce beer, is made year-round. As the character of the spruce tips changes through the year, so does the character of the beer.

Bugsy's Sports Bar and Brown Street Brewery

ADDRESS: 16 N. Brown St.
Rhinelander, WI 54501

TELEPHONE: 715–369–2100

EMAIL: None

WEB SITE: None

MICHAEL'S PICK: Munich Ale: This was the only house beer available on my visit. Think Munich Helles lager, but brewed as an ale. Pilsner malt sweetness is balanced by gentle, spicy hops and moderate bitterness. Fruity notes fill in the background. Some unfortunate fermentation issues in my sample made the beer less pleasing than it might have been.

TYPE: Brewpub

DATE ESTABLISHED: 1998

OWNERS: Bugsy Meinen, Butch Meinen, and Lisa Meinen

BREWMASTER: Bugsy Meinen

BREWING SYSTEM: Four-barrel Micropub International extract brewhouse

FLAGSHIP BEERS: None

YEAR-ROUND BEERS: None

SEASONAL BEERS: None

SPECIAL RELEASES: Amber Light, Bassler Ale, Gangster Light, Centennial Reserve Munich Helles, German Pilsner, Woody Nut Brown, Northwoods Red Ale, Raspberry Wheat, Spring Ale, Stout, South of the Border Light, Czech Pilsner, Aussie Lager, and others

TOURS: By request

BEER TO GO: Growlers, if you bring your own

FOOD: Selection of sandwiches, pastas, steaks, and pizza

AMENITIES: Free street parking, full bar, small selection of good guest taps, pool tables

PUB HOURS:

Summer Hours: Monday–Saturday: 11:00 A.M. to close

Winter Hours: Monday and Tuesday: 4:00 P.M. to close; Wednesday–Saturday: 11:00 A.M. to close

NEARBY ATTRACTIONS: Minocqua Brewing Company, Hodag Country Music Festival, disc golf, Rhinelander Logging Museum, water activities on nearby lakes, geocaching, Wisconsin River cruises

NOTES: Bugsy's is located right in the center of Rhinelander's downtown. Although it is called a sports bar, it feels more like a small-town Irish pub. The obligatory television screens are present but unobtrusive. Green-painted walls give the place a definite sense of St. Patrick's Day. It's a very casual and friendly place. It was easy to strike up conversations with the bartender and other patrons.

Bugsy Meinen brews his beers with a copper-clad extract system that sits in the front window of the pub. Unfortunately, on my visit they were doing a promotion, so I was only able to try one of the house beers. I was told that they typically have more available. The selection rotates constantly with no permanent, year-round beers.

Hearty bar food is on the menu. Portions are ample, and prices are very reasonable. Bugsy's is known in town for its pizza and burgers. I enjoyed a super-saucy half-rack of fall-off-the-bone ribs served with a big baked potato. If you go for a meal, you won't leave hungry.

Minocqua Brewing Company

ADDRESS: 238 Lakeshore Dr. Minocqua, WI 54548

TELEPHONE: 715–356–2600

EMAIL: brewer@minocquabrewingcompany.com

WEB SITE: www.minocquabrewingcompany.com

MICHAEL'S PICK: Minocqua Pale Ale: A shining star in a strong lineup, Minocqua Pale Ale brings to mind Sierra Nevada Pale Ale. It's light and dry with sharp but moderate bitterness. Floral and citrus hops are the highlight, but they rest comfortably on a biscuity bed of malt.

TYPE: Brewpub

DATE ESTABLISHED: 2006

OWNERS: Dave White, Loretta White, Dustin White, and Salena White

BREWMASTER: Ryan White

BREWING SYSTEM: 7.5-barrel Sanafab brewhouse

FLAGSHIP BEER: Wild Rice Lager

YEAR-ROUND BEERS: Whitey's Wheat, Minocqua Pale Ale (MPA), Wild Bill's Wild Rice Lager, Road Kill Red Ale, Bear Naked Brown Ale, Pudgy Possum Porter

SEASONAL BEERS: Oatmeal Stout, Scotch Ale, Honey Cranberry Ale, Vanilla Cream Ale

SPECIAL RELEASES: Black Dwarf IPA, Hefeweizen, Belgian Strong Ale

TOURS: No

BEER TO GO: Growlers

FOOD: Selection of brewpub favorites with some slightly upscale entrées: chops, steaks, seafood

AMENITIES: Parking lot, live music Thursday through Saturday upstairs in Divano Lounge, family-friendly, Mug Club

PUB HOURS: Tuesday–Sunday: 11:00 A.M. to close

NEARBY ATTRACTIONS: Water activities on area lakes, outdoor activities in nearby national and state forests—hiking, camping, snowshoeing, and snowmobiling

NOTES: Minocqua Brewing Company sits directly on the shores of Minocqua Lake. You couldn't invent a better location for a brewpub. In the summer the lake is skirted by pine and birch. In the winter it's a white expanse of ice and snow. Whether you have a window seat in the casual dining room or a table outside on a sunny summer evening, the view will encourage you to linger over several pints.

And you'll be glad you did. Brewer Ryan White maintains a solid lineup of mostly brewpub-standard styles. White had never brewed a drop of beer when his family bought the restaurant in 2005. He learned his craft doing internships at South Shore Brewery in Ashland and Stone Cellar Brewpub in Appleton. The thing he loves most about making beer is seeing the enjoyment people take from drinking his creations.

Minocqua is a classic North Country tourist town. Located in the Flambeau region of Wisconsin, it is surrounded by lakes and state forests that offer innumerable opportunities for outdoor activities. Whether you're into boating, fishing, hiking, snowmobiling, or cross-country skiing, you'll find something to do here in every season.

For pleasant ambience, good food, and tasty beer in a beautiful setting, Minocqua Brewing Company is certainly worth a stop in northern Wisconsin.

South Shore Brewery

ADDRESS: 808 W. Main St.
Ashland, WI 54806
TELEPHONE: 715–682–4200
EMAIL: info@southshorebrewery.com
WEB SITE:
www.southshorebrewery.com

MICHAEL'S PICK: Cream Ale: This is not your typical cream ale. Brewer Bo Bélanger calls it a "yin-yang" beer. Half of the wort is fermented as a lager for a clean, crisp character. The other half gets ale yeast for a subtle fruity note. Tinctures of lavender and wood betony provide curiously delicious melon and floral overtones that will have you scratching your head and asking, "What is that?"

TYPE: Brewpub

DATE ESTABLISHED: 1995

OWNER: Bo Bélanger

BREWMASTER: Bo Bélanger

BREWING SYSTEM: Ten-barrel PUB brewhouse

FLAGSHIP BEER: Nut Brown Ale

YEAR-ROUND BEERS: Red Lager, Nut Brown Ale, Northern Lights Ale, Honey Pils, Rhodes Scholar Stout, American Pale Ale

SEASONAL BEERS: Seasonal release monthly, including Mai Bock, Bavarian Wheat, Applefest Ale, Bracket and Porter, Wheat Doppelbock, Barley Legal Barleywine, Bourbon-Barrel Coffee Mint Stout

SPECIAL RELEASES: Roggenbier, Wet-Hopped Pale Ale, Alt, Dark Lager, Malt Liquor, and others

TOURS: By appointment

BEER TO GO: Growlers

FOOD: The Deep Water Grille features a wide selection of standard brewpub food and more upscale items, including Lake Superior whitefish. The Alley specializes in pizzas and burgers.

AMENITIES: Parking lot, full bar, happy-hour specials, seasonal outdoor seating on second-floor patio

PUB HOURS: Daily: 11:00 A.M. to 2:00 A.M.

NEARBY ATTRACTIONS: Lake Superior activities, including fishing and boating, all-season outdoor activities in area state parks and national forests, Apostle Islands National Lakeshore, Porcupine Mountains Wilderness State Park, Chequamegon National Forest, White Winter Meadery

NOTES: Bo Bélanger is on a mission to give his beers the true flavor of the upper Midwest. South Shore

South Shore Brewery brewmaster Bo Bélanger.

beers are brewed using only Wisconsin-grown base malts, either contracted with local farmers or grown on Bélanger's own forty-acre plot. As part of the Wisconsin Hops and Barley Coop, an organization that includes four other regional breweries, he is gradually expanding his use of locally grown hops. He hopes to transition to 100 percent Wisconsin-grown ingredients within a few years.

This emphasis on local reflects the attention to detail that goes into South Shore beers. Style-appropriate yeast strains are used for every beer. Malts are carefully selected not only for flavor but also for color. Bélanger's background in chemistry led him to build a quality-control lab, a rarity among similarly sized breweries. A sampler tray of South Shore beers looks like a row of jewels, and all the beers are clean and flavorful.

The brewery/restaurant sits just one block off of the Lake Superior shoreline. The second-floor balcony affords a nice view of the lake. The overall feel in the bar is of a nineteenth-century tavern with a vaguely nautical theme. The Deep Water Grille has a more elegant feel, while the alley is more like a casual sports bar.

Thirsty Pagan Brewing

ADDRESS: 1623 Broadway St.
Superior, WI 54880
TELEPHONE: 715–394–2500
EMAIL: steve@thirstypaganbrewing.com
WEB SITE: www.thirstypaganbrewing.com

MICHAEL'S PICK: Chillaxin Ale: Of the many hoppy ales on tap during my visit, the special-release Chillaxin Ale was the standout. I like IPAs with a strong malt backbone, and this one had it in spades, along with pronounced fruity esters that enhanced the juicy citrus hops. From the year-round offerings, I suggest Derailed Ale, a classic and balanced American pale ale with assertive bitterness and citrus and spice hop flavors.

TYPE: Brewpub

DATE ESTABLISHED: 1996

OWNER: Steve Knauss

BREWMASTER: Allyson Rolph

BREWING SYSTEM: Two-barrel custom-built electric brewhouse

FLAGSHIP BEER: Derailed Ale

YEAR-ROUND BEERS: North Coast Amber, Derailed Ale, Burntwood Black, Whitecap Wheat

SEASONAL BEERS: Check the Web site for constantly changing seasonals

SPECIAL RELEASES: New releases nearly every week

TOURS: By request, except on Friday and Saturday evenings. Call to schedule.

BEER TO GO: Growlers

FOOD: Pizzas are the specialty: build your own from a selection of toppings or choose one of six specialty pizzas. A small selection of sandwiches and appetizers is also available.

AMENITIES: Parking lot, free street parking, family-friendly, live music five nights a week, happy-hour specials, cask-conditioned selections, antique beer-sign collection

PUB HOURS: Sunday–Thursday: 4:00 P.M. to 2:00 A.M.; Friday and Saturday: 4:00 P.M. to 2:30 A.M.

NEARBY ATTRACTIONS: Multiple single-track mountain bike trails, downhill and cross-country skiing, Richard Bong Veterans Historical Center, East End Fire Department, Lake Superior Scenic Cruises, Canal Park and other Duluth attractions

NOTES: When describing what the brewpub looked like when he bought it in 2006, Thirsty Pagan owner Steve Knauss uses words like "crusty" and "cobwebby." In the intervening years he has transformed it from a dingy dive bar populated by grumpy old men into the fun, family-friendly place it is today.

The Thirsty Pagan retains a bit of the dive-bar ambience, but in a bright, nonintimidating way. Housed in an old dairy plant, the tile walls give it a sense of history. The bar is located in what had been an immense walk-in cooler. Old brewery signs cover the walls, including a spectacular Miller High Life mural taken from a defunct ninety-year-old jazz club. A look around the dining room reveals a broad mix of patrons, including twentysomethings, older regulars, and families with children.

The bar has a selection of nine house-brewed beers, including one hand-pumped, cask-conditioned selection. There were a lot of hoppy pale ales the night I was there, but the choices can vary considerably, as brewer Allyson Rolph crafts around 180 batches a year on the tiny two-barrel system. The beers, though a bit hit or miss, were generally solid. At the time of my visit there were plans to upgrade the brewery. An upgrade should resolve some slight issues.

EAST CENTRAL

3 Sheeps Brewing Company

ADDRESS: 1327 N. 14th St. Sheboygan, WI 53081

TELEPHONE: 920-395-3583

EMAIL: gpauly@3sheepsbrewing.com

WEB SITE: www.3sheepsbrewing.com

MICHAEL'S PICK: Baaad Boy Black Wheat: This baaad boy is just a tweak away from porter. It's mostly malt, with rich chocolate notes and just a touch of roast. You get the full mouthfeel of wheat, but wheaty flavor is more of an afterthought. Bitterness is low, but good attenuation keeps it light.

TYPE: Brewery

DATE ESTABLISHED: 2012

OWNER: Grant Pauly

BREWMASTER: Grant Pauly

BREWING SYSTEM: Ten-barrel Sprinkman brewhouse

FLAGSHIP BEERS: Enkel Biter Enkel, Baaad Boy Black Wheat

YEAR-ROUND BEERS: Enkel Biter Enkel, Really Cool Waterslides IPA, Baaad Boy Black Wheat, Cirque du Wit Wheat

SEASONAL BEERS: Rhubarb Brown Ale, Ginger Chocolate Stout

SPECIAL RELEASE: Bourbon Barrel Brett Porter

TOURS: See Web site for dates and times

BEER TO GO: Growlers and package

FOOD: None

AMENITIES: Parking lot, full bar

PUB HOURS: Tuesday–Saturday: 3:00 P.M. to close

NEARBY ATTRACTIONS: 8th Street Ale House, award-winning golf courses, University of Wisconsin–Sheboygan campus, John Michael Kohler Arts Center, Stefanie H. Weill Center for the Performing Arts, Above and Beyond Children's Museum, Sheboygan Theatre Company, boating and beaches on Lake Michigan, outdoor activities at Kettle Moraine State Forest, one hour from Milwaukee

NOTES: Grant Pauly once had a t-shirt with a picture of a gnome standing at a crossroads. One road led to fame, fortune, power, and success, the other to "really cool waterslides." For Pauly, 3 Sheeps is that really cool waterslide. Previous to opening the brewery, he was running his family's concrete-casting business. Staying there would have been to take the first road. He's much happier with the road he chose. "At the back door when you walk in, there is a casting there that I used to sell. Stepping over that every day when I come in is such a great reminder of what I used to be doing. And now I get to do this."

Pauly likes the creativity of brewing. He enjoys exploring flavor combinations that tweak the classics and play with drinkers' expectations. He describes the overarching theme of his beers as "one off normal." The description seems apt. Rather than the typical blond ale, his entry-level session beer is a Belgian single, the kind of beer monks brew for their own daily consumption. His year-round black beer isn't a porter or stout—it's a porter-like black wheat beer brewed with over 50 percent wheat malt, including roasted wheat for color and flavor.

At first glance you might think that 3 Sheeps is a brewpub. It's actually a production brewery operating inside of a bar. There are two separate entities that make up the operation. The brewery leases space in the building. The building's owner runs the bar, which purchases beer from the brewery. At the time of writing, the search was on for a restaurant partner to supply food.

Bull Falls Brewery

ADDRESS: 901 E. Thomas St.
Wausau, WI 54403
TELEPHONE: 715–842–2337
EMAIL: mikez@bullfallsbrewery.com
WEB SITE: www.bullfallsbrewery.com
MICHAEL'S PICK: Zwickel: An unfiltered German-style pilsner, this is dominated by spicy, black-licorice hop flavors and moderately high bitterness. The beer's sharpness is mellowed by the yeast that is left in suspension. The hops are supported by sweet, grainy, pilsner malt. A touch of sulfur lies underneath.
TYPE: Brewery
DATE ESTABLISHED: 2007
OWNERS: Don Zamzow and Michael Zamzow
BREWMASTER: Michael Zamzow
BREWING SYSTEM: Ten-barrel Sprinkman brewhouse
FLAGSHIP BEER: 5 Star Ale

YEAR-ROUND BEERS: White Water Ale, Holzhacker Lager, Zwickel, 5 Star Ale, Nut Brown Ale, Oatmeal Stout, Marathon, rotating wheat beers
SEASONAL BEERS: Oktoberfest, Edel Bock, Hefeweizen, Midnight Star
SPECIAL RELEASES: White Oak, Weizenbock
TOURS: By appointment
BEER TO GO: Growlers and kegs
FOOD: None
AMENITIES: Small parking lot, free street parking, tasting room, seasonal beer garden, frequent live music, annual Bockfest
PUB HOURS: Monday–Thursday: 4:00 to 11:00 P.M.; Friday: 4:00 P.M. to midnight; Saturday: 1:00 P.M. to midnight
NEARBY ATTRACTIONS: O'so Brewing Co., Red Eye Brewing Co., Great Dane Brewpub, Granite Peak Ski Area, Grand Theatre, Leigh Yawkey Woodson Art Museum, outdoor activities at Rib Mountain State Park, Nine-Mile County Park, mountain bike trails, international whitewater kayaking competitions throughout the summer

NOTES: Michael Zamzow calls himself a "beer drinker." When he goes out for beers, he wants to be able to have three or four without regretting it the next morning. This attitude is reflected in the beers that he makes. "I like the German lagers. That's where I live," he says. Indeed, aside from a couple of English-style ales, the beer list at Bull Falls is centered on classic German styles. You'll find very few beers over 6 percent ABV, seasonal bocks being the rare exceptions. It took him three years to put an IPA on the menu.

Zamzow began homebrewing in 1998. As his passion for beer grew, so did his batch size. He soon began making twenty-gallon batches at home. When a three-barrel professional system crossed his path, he bought it. Lacking a place to use it, it sat in storage for several years. When he and his father Don bought a building and began creating the brewery, they bought the current ten-barrel system. The three-barrel system was sold without ever being used.

Zamzow's "beer drinker" mentality is also reflected in the tasting-room patrons—mostly ordinary Wisconsinites who like to drink beer. The tasting room is a friendly place. The intimate size and simple, light-wood décor seem to encourage conversations. By the time I left, the place had completely filled with people sitting at tables or at the bar socializing over a pint and picking up growlers to take home.

While the beers were not all of uniform quality, they were by and large well-made and highly drinkable. True to Zamzow's preference, I found that the German styles trumped the others.

Central Waters Brewing Company

ADDRESS: 351 Allen St.
Amherst, WI 54406
TELEPHONE: 715–824–2739
EMAIL: info@centralwaters.com
WEB SITE: www.centralwaters.com
MICHAEL'S PICK: Illumination Double IPA: Massive dry-hopping lends this 9 percent ABV imperial IPA nose-grabbing tangerine and mango aromas that carry over into the flavor. It's plenty bitter, but overall it leans toward hop flavor. The malt provides an ample base but is dry enough to keep it very drinkable.
TYPE: Brewery
DATE ESTABLISHED: 1998
OWNERS: Paul Graham and Anello Mollica
BREWMASTER: Paul Graham
BREWING SYSTEM: Thirty-barrel DME brewhouse
FLAGSHIP BEERS: Ouisconsin Red Ale, Happy Heron Pale Ale, Mudpuppy Porter, Shine On, Glacial Trail IPA
YEAR-ROUND BEERS: Honey Blond, Shine On, Mudpuppy Porter, Glacial Trail IPA, Ouisconsin Red, Satin Solstice Stout, Happy Heron Pale Ale
SEASONAL BEERS: Whitewater Weizen, Oktoberfest
SPECIAL RELEASES: Bourbon Barrel Stout, Bourbon Barrel Barleywine, Bourbon Barrel Cherry Stout, Peruvian Morning, Kosmyk Charlie's Barleywine, Illumination Double IPA
TOURS: Fridays at 5:00 P.M. or by appointment
BEER TO GO: Growlers, kegs, and bottles
FOOD: None
AMENITIES: Parking lot, taproom
PUB HOURS: Friday: 4:00 to 9:00 P.M.; Saturday: 3:00 to 9:00 P.M.
NEARBY ATTRACTIONS: Stevens Point Brewing Company, O'so Brewing Company, Iola Winter Sports Club, seasonal outdoor activities and nearby state parks

NOTES: When Paul Graham and Anello Mollica bought Central Waters from the original owners in 2000, it was pretty rough going. The old building that housed the brewery was run down. The central Wisconsin market was not quite ready for craft beer. Retailers often didn't know what they were selling and didn't realize that the guys delivering the beer were also the ones making it. The cobbled-together brewing system led to inconsistent product and more than a few dumped batches.

After a long and steady period of growth, things have changed. Their new building in Amherst is a model of green construction with solar panels, efficient lighting, and radiant floor heat. A bigger, more modern brewhouse has resulted in greater consistency and improved quality. The changing market has also brought greater financial success. As Graham says, "The days of hanging my own check on the cork board are done."

Central Waters is known in Wisconsin as a stout brewery. Big barrel-aged stouts that are only available in the state have given them a reputation. Indeed, their barrel-aged beers are pretty amazing. But they produce a wide variety of beers from a light honey-blond ale to Belgian-style sours. Their mainstay beers don't go to extremes, focusing instead on balance and drinkability, designed to appeal to a wide range of palates. But hardcore beer fans will find something to enjoy in the barrel-aged and big beers.

Courthouse Pub

ADDRESS: 1001 S. 8th St.
Manitowoc, WI 54220
TELEPHONE: 920–686–1166
EMAIL: greatfood@courthousepub.com
WEB SITE: www.courthousepub.com
MICHAEL'S PICK: Crown Pilsner: The brewpub calls this an "English-style pilsner." I'm not sure what that means, but it is golden-colored with medium bitterness and graham-cracker malty sweetness. Excessive green apple flavors were certainly a flaw, but one that I actually found to be quite pleasant. It may not be a perfect beer, but I enjoyed it.
TYPE: Brewpub
DATE ESTABLISHED: 2001
OWNER: John Jagemann
BREWMASTER: Brent Boeldt
BREWING SYSTEM: Four-barrel Micropub International extract brewhouse
FLAGSHIP BEER: None
YEAR-ROUND BEERS: Beer list changes monthly
SEASONAL BEERS: Bailout Brewski, Trippel Jon, Canadian Ale, Sing-Thai, Czech Pilsner, Munich Helles, Crown Pilsner, Munich Helles, Oktoberfest 1516, Braxater Special, and others
SPECIAL RELEASES: None
TOURS: By request
BEER TO GO: Growlers
FOOD: Somewhat upscale entrées: steaks, pastas, and seafood. Lunch menu features signature sandwiches.
AMENITIES: Parking lot, private rooms available, catering, extensive wine list, full bar
PUB HOURS: Monday–Friday: 11:00 A.M. to 9:00 P.M.; Saturday: 3:30 to 9:00 P.M.
NEARBY ATTRACTIONS: Wisconsin Maritime Museum, performances at the Capital Civic Center, Rahr West Art Museum, Lincoln Park Zoo, S.S. *Badger* lake ferry

NOTES: The original building to occupy the site that is now the Courthouse Pub was built in 1885 to house F. Willinger's Beer Hall. The beer hall closed during Prohibition, and the building became the Court Café, named for the historic Manitowoc County Courthouse across the street. After Prohibition the building again changed names, becoming the Colonial Inn. The inn featured an open dining room with a long bar near the entrance.

The original building was torn down in 2002. The new building that houses the current pub was modeled on its predecessor. Even the interior retains the open feel and long bar of the Colonial Inn. It has a vaguely 1930s feel, but with a modern twist. The main bar area is light and airy with high ceilings and plenty of windows. The two smaller dining rooms are more intimate and formal.

The food at Courthouse is fantastic. The moderately fancy fare features unique combinations of ingredients like a turkey-breast sandwich with apple chutney. The house beers suffer many of the production flaws that seem to plague extract breweries, but you may find a star among those available. The pub has won two Awards of Excellence from *Wine Spectator* magazine for its extensive wine list.

Fox River Brewing Company and Restaurant/Fratello's Waterfront Restaurant

ADDRESS: 1501 Arboretum Dr.
Oshkosh, WI 54901
TELEPHONE: 920–232–2337
EMAIL: info@supplegroup.com
WEB SITE: www.supplerestaurantgroup.com
MICHAEL'S PICK: Oshkosh Best Bitter: Loaded with caramel and biscuit flavors, it's a malty bitter, to be sure. But bitterness isn't forgotten. It's got a sharp, hoppy bite at the top that gradually gives way mid-palate and makes a return on the finish. Light notes of orange and grass float on top.
TYPE: Brewpub
DATE ESTABLISHED: 1995
OWNER: Supple Restaurant Group
BREWMASTER: Kevin Bowen
BREWING SYSTEM: Thirteen-barrel Liquid Assets brewhouse
FLAGSHIP BEER: Caber Tossing Scottish Ale
YEAR-ROUND BEERS: Fox Light, Buzzin' Honey Ale, Winnebago Wheat, Caber Tossing Scottish Ale, rotating fruit/spice beer (Raspberry Wheat, Vanilla Cream Ale, Cherry Brau, Blü), rotating dark beer (Slam Dunkel, Trollycar Stout, Titan Porter, Breakfast Stout), rotating hoppy beer (Hoppy Face IPA, Optic IPA, Fox Tail Pale Ale, Juggernaut IPA, Oshkosh Best Bitter)

SEASONAL BEERS: Oktoberfest, Red Baron Alt, Upside Down Brown, Paine's Pilsner, Abby Normal, Vader's Imperial Stout
SPECIAL RELEASES: Bourbon Barrel Abby Normal, Friends of the Fox, and others
TOURS: By request
BEER TO GO: Growlers, kegs, and package
FOOD: Selection of moderately upscale dishes: steaks, seafood, pizza, salads
AMENITIES: Parking lot, full bar, extensive wine list, seasonal outdoor seating on the patio overlooking the Fox River, live music
PUB HOURS: Daily: 11:00 A.M. to close
NEARBY ATTRACTIONS: Grand Opera House, Paine Art Center, EAA AirVenture Museum, golf, boating on the Fox River

NOTES: Balance is a recurring theme of the Fratello's restaurants and Fox River Brewing Company. The franchise is owned by two brothers with very different personalities—one whose taste runs to the higher end, and one more in tune with the common man. This dichotomy is evident in the simultaneous focus on fine wine and house-brewed beer and in the juxtaposition of casual spaces with menus that are elevated in both content and presentation.

Balance is also important in the beer. It is a primary objective for brewer Kevin Bowen. His first encounter with good beer was drinking exquisitely balanced lagers in a Munich beer garden. Since becoming head brewer at Fox River, he has sought to make beers that are full-flavored without going too far in any one direction. He recognizes this as a trend for the Midwest in general, seeing the region as a "moderate voice between the crazy West Coast and traditional East Coast."

Balance is even reflected in the space at Fratello's in Oshkosh. First, there are two sides to the restaurant. One side is a full-on sports bar, full of flickering TVs. The other is a nice-casual dining room with white linen table cloths and a jewel-like wine case. Both overlook the Fox River through angular walls of windows. One would feel comfortable here in a suit or having just come off a boat on the river.

Fox River Brewing Co. and Restaurant

ADDRESS: 4301 W. Wisconsin Ave.
Appleton, WI 54915
TELEPHONE: 920–991–0000
EMAIL: info@supplegroup.com
WEB SITE: www.supplerestaurantgroup.com
MICHAEL'S PICK: Titan Porter: To me, this beer locates itself somewhere between a robust porter and a black

IPA. It's got the intense chocolate and roast of a porter, but with accentuated hop bitterness and flavor—too hoppy for one, too malty for the other. Cluster hops give it a kind of wild, rough edge. It's super flavorful, but still sessionable.

TYPE: Brewpub
DATE ESTABLISHED: 1997
OWNER: Supple Restaurant Group
BREWMASTER: Kevin Bowen
BREWING SYSTEM: Thirteen-barrel Liquid Assets brewhouse
FLAGSHIP BEER: Caber Tossing Scottish Ale
YEAR-ROUND BEERS: Fox Light, Buzzin' Honey Ale, Winnebago Wheat, Caber Tossing Scottish Ale, rotating fruit/spice beer (Raspberry Wheat, Vanilla Cream Ale, Cherry Brau, Blü), rotating dark beer (Slam Dunkel, Trollycar Stout, Titan Porter, Breakfast Stout), rotating hoppy beer (Hoppy Face IPA, Optic IPA, Fox Tail Pale Ale, Juggernaut IPA, Oshkosh Best Bitter)
SEASONAL BEERS: Oktoberfest, Red Baron Alt, Upside Down Brown, Paine's Pilsner, Abby Normal, Vader's Imperial Stout
SPECIAL RELEASES: Bourbon Barrel Abby Normal, Friends of the Fox, and others
TOURS: By request
BEER TO GO: Growlers, kegs, and package
FOOD: Selection of moderately upscale dishes: steaks, seafood, pizza, salads
AMENITIES: Parking lot, full bar, shopping at Fox River Mall
PUB HOURS: Daily: 11:00 A.M. to close
NEARBY ATTRACTIONS: Stone Cellar Brewery, the Building for Kids Children's Museum, Outagamie Museum/Houdini Historical Center, Fox Cities Performing Arts Center, Gordon Bubolz Nature Preserve, Memorial Park Arboretum and Gardens

NOTES: The Fratello's Appleton location at the Fox River Mall has a modern and slightly industrial feel. High ceilings and walls of windows keep it light and airy. It might be one of the only brewpubs in the country that is entered from a mall food court.

The Great Dane Pub and Brewing Co.

ADDRESS: 2305 Sherman St.
Wausau, WI 54401
TELEPHONE: 715–845–3000
EMAIL: info@greatdanepub.com
WEB SITE: www.greatdanepub.com
MICHAEL'S PICK: Crop Circle Wheat: A classic German-style wheat beer that was unexpectedly but pleasantly bitter. The characteristic yeast flavor leans toward

banana and citrus with nice lemony highlights. It's light and refreshing but still appropriately full-bodied.

TYPE: Brewpub
DATE ESTABLISHED: 2009
OWNERS: Rob LoBreglio and Eliot Butler
BREWMASTER: Pete McCabe
BREWING SYSTEM: Fifteen-barrel DME brewhouse
FLAGSHIP BEER: Scotch Ale
YEAR-ROUND BEERS: Landmark Light, George Ruder's German Pils, Crop Circle Wheat, Old Glory American Pale Ale, Stone of Scone Scotch Ale, Speedway India Pale Ale, Emerald Isle Stout, Parkers Publican Extra Pale Ale, rotating regulars (Wooly Mammoth Porter, Wooden Ships Extra Special Bitter)
SEASONAL BEERS: Velvet Hammer Bock, Oktoberfest, Bank Shot Nut Brown Ale, Mallard's Cream Ale, Cherry Ale, Belgian Pale Ale, Dominator Doppelbock, Tri-Pepper Pils, Old Scratch Barleywine
SPECIAL RELEASES: Oktoppel Bock, Über Bock, Amber Bock, and others
TOURS: By appointment
BEER TO GO: Growlers and kegs
FOOD: Selection of unique brewpub-style dishes: burgers, salads, sandwiches, pizzas, and assorted entrées. Interesting specialties include Bacon Mac and Cheese Pizza and Peanut Stew.
AMENITIES: Parking lot, billiards and shuffleboard tables, gluten-free and allergy menus, cask-conditioned selections, free Brew School on Monday nights, happy-hour specials, seasonal beer garden
PUB HOURS: Sunday–Thursday: 11:00 A.M. to 2:00 A.M.; Friday–Saturday: 11:00 A.M. to 2:30 A.M.; Sunday: 10:00 A.M. to 2:30 A.M. (Sunday brunch: 10:00 A.M. to 2:00 P.M.)
NEARBY ATTRACTIONS: Red Eye Brewing Company, Bull Falls Brewing Company, Granite Peak Ski Area, the Grand Theatre, Leigh Yawkey Woodson Art Museum, outdoor activities at Rib Mountain State Park, international whitewater kayaking competitions throughout the summer

NOTES: The Great Dane Brewpub chain has five locations in Madison and Wausau. While there is an assortment of chainwide recipes, each location (except Eastside in Madison) has a fully functional brewery and its own brewing staff who create a range of specialty beers unique to that store. Each location is also marked by its own particular ambience.

The Wausau location has an upscale-casual feel that reminded me of a stately English hunting club. I could almost imagine men in red jackets and jodhpurs tending their hounds. The dining room and bar areas both feature bar and table seating—the brewery is visible behind large windows from either. There are billiards tables for those who fancy a bit of pool.

The beers were a mixed bag, with most being quite acceptable. It was bock season when I visited, and there was an assortment of very tasty bocks to sample. The bittersweet-chocolaty Wooly Mammoth Porter served on cask was another standout.

Green Bay Brewing Company/Hinterland

ADDRESS: 313 Dousman St.
Green Bay, WI 54303
TELEPHONE: 920–438–8050
EMAIL: info@hinterlandbeer.com
WEB SITE: www.hinterlandbeer.com
MICHAEL'S PICK: Winterland: This is a beer that I wait for every season. A juniper-infused Baltic porter, it has significant but smooth roasted malt character with caramel sweetness lying underneath. The spruce flavor of juniper berries melds with the finishing hops, yielding a flavor that you can't quite put a finger on. It tastes like winter.
TYPE: Brewpub
DATE ESTABLISHED: 1995
OWNER: Bill Tressler and Michelle Tressler
BREWMASTER: Joe Karls
BREWING SYSTEM: Thirty-barrel Criveller brewhouse
FLAGSHIP BEERS: Luna Coffee Stout, Pale Ale
YEAR-ROUND BEERS: Pale Ale, Amber Ale, Luna Stout, India Pale Ale, Pub Draught
SEASONAL BEERS: Maple Bock, Cherry Wheat, Oktoberfest, Winterland
SPECIAL RELEASES: Bourbon Barrel Stout, Cab Franc Barrel-Aged Stout, White Out, Bourbon Barrel Strong Ale, Cocoa Nib Doppelbock, Saison, Grand Cru
TOURS: Saturdays by appointment. Cost $5.
BEER TO GO: Bottles
FOOD: Upscale starters and entrées featuring locally sourced ingredients and fresh seafood flown in daily
AMENITIES: Parking lot, happy-hour specials, full bar, seasonal outdoor seating
PUB HOURS: Monday–Saturday: 4:00 P.M. to close
NEARBY ATTRACTIONS: Titletown Brewing Company, Lambeau Field, University of Wisconsin–Green Bay campus, National Railroad Museum, Green Bay Children's Museum, Bay Beach Park and Wildlife Sanctuary, boat cruises on Green Bay, Grassy Island Range Lighthouse, NEW Zoo, Performances at Meyer Theatre, outdoor recreation at area parks on Green Bay

NOTES: Owner Bill Tressler and brewer Joe Karls approach beer from different directions. While Tressler loves bitterness and hops, Karls is all about malt. The two balance each other out, and that balancing act is reflected in Hinterland beers. Each beer is easy to drink and approachable while also being full-flavored with layered complexity. Hinterland beers are among the best currently coming out of Wisconsin.

Hinterland began as a production brewery in 1995. An editor at *Beer* magazine, Tressler felt that he needed to know more about the brewing process. He completed an associate's degree in fermentation science at the University of California–Davis. It was there that he decided to make brewing beer his career. With his wife Michelle, he opened the brewery in the small town of Denmark, Wisconsin. Early success led to an expansion and move to Green Bay. The restaurant opened in 2000.

Hinterland is not your typical brewpub. The menu and feel are decidedly upscale. In Tressler's words, "We put time into making the beer special. Why not make the food something special too?" There is a strong emphasis on locally sourced ingredients. Most of the produce and all of the beef comes from within one hundred miles of Green Bay. The space also reflects an interesting balance, with fixtures and furnishings adding elegance to the rawness of the historic industrial building.

Legends Brewhouse and Eatery–De Pere

ADDRESS: 875 Heritage Rd.
De Pere, WI 54115
TELEPHONE: 920–336–8036
EMAIL: jgosser@legendseatery.com
WEB SITE: www.legendseatery.com
MICHAEL'S PICK: Founders Honey Weiss: This American wheat beer features light, bready wheat and traces of honey sweetness around the edges. Medium levels of bitterness serve to provide balance.
TYPE: Brewpub
DATE ESTABLISHED: 2002
OWNERS: Jay Gosser, Julie Gosser, Greg DeCleene, and Ann DeCleene
BREWMASTER: Ken Novak
BREWING SYSTEM: Four-barrel Micropub International extract brewhouse
FLAGSHIP BEER: Duck Creek Dunkel
YEAR-ROUND BEERS: Longtail Light, Founders Honey Weiss, Acme Amber, Duck Creek Dunkel
SEASONAL BEERS: Jack Rabbit Red, Harvest Moon Oktoberfest, Rudolf's Red Nose Ale, Crocodile Lager, Scray's Hill Scottish Ale, Ixtapa Blond, Claude Allouez Indian Pale Ale, Nicolet Nut Brown Ale, Anniversary Ale, Celtic Golden Lager, Winterland Weizen Bock, Parmperin Park Porter, Half Moon Brick Belgian Tripel

SPECIAL RELEASES: None

TOURS: By request

BEER TO GO: Growlers

FOOD: Selection of standard brewpub favorites: burgers, entrées, wraps

AMENITIES: Parking lot, banquet room available, seasonal outdoor seating on a large deck

PUB HOURS: Monday–Thursday: 11:00 A.M. to 10:00 P.M.; Friday and Saturday: 11:00 A.M. to 11:00 P.M.; Sunday: 10:00 A.M. to 10:00 P.M.

NEARBY ATTRACTIONS: Hinterland Brewing Company, Titletown Brewing Company, golf, Oneida Nation Museum, Heritage Hill State Historic Park, Packers games at Lambeau Field, University of Wisconsin–Green Bay campus, cultural events at the Weidner Center for the Performing Arts

NOTES: Legends of De Pere sits on the southern outskirts of the village. It is surrounded by industrial buildings and housing developments, and yet it feels isolated, on the edge between urban and rural. Drive north and you enter a historic section of De Pere. Go south and it's all farmland.

Inside the place is a bustling sports bar. Television screens are everywhere, with multiple sporting events in play. During my visit, a regular stream of Packers fans stopped in for a pregame bite and beverage. It's a casual spot to enjoy a basket of Wisconsin cheese curds and a pint.

The pub keeps six house beers on tap, four year-round beers, and two rotating seasonals. They also stock a range of mass-market beers in bottles and draft.

Legends Brewhouse and Eatery–Howard

ADDRESS: 2840 Shawano Ave.
Green Bay, WI 54313

TELEPHONE: 920–662–1111

EMAIL: jgosser@legendseatery.com

WEB SITE: www.legendseatery.com

MICHAEL'S PICK: Duck Creek Dunkel: Molasses sweetness coupled with notes of chocolate are the dominant notes. Medium bitterness and spicy hop flavors fill in the background. Noticeable fermentation flaws detracted from the overall enjoyment.

TYPE: Brewpub

DATE ESTABLISHED: 1998

OWNER: Jay Gosser, Julie Gosser, Greg DeCleene, and Ann DeCleene

BREWMASTER: Ken Novak

BREWING SYSTEM: Four-barrel Micropub International extract brewhouse

FLAGSHIP BEER: Duck Creek Dunkel

YEAR-ROUND BEERS: Longtail Light, Founders Honey Weiss, Acme Amber, Duck Creek Dunkel

SEASONAL BEERS: Jack Rabbit Red, Harvest Moon Oktoberfest, Rudolf's Red Nose Ale, Crocodile Lager, Scray's Hill Scottish Ale, Ixtapa Blond, Claude Allouez Indian Pale Ale, Nicolet Nut Brown Ale, Anniversary Ale, Celtic Golden Lager, Winterland Weizen Bock, Pamperin Park Porter, Half Moon Brick Belgian Tripel

SPECIAL RELEASES: None

TOURS: By request

BEER TO GO: Growlers

FOOD: Selection of standard brewpub favorites: burgers, entrées, wraps

AMENITIES: Parking lot, banquet room available, happy-hour specials, Sunday brunch

PUB HOURS: Monday–Thursday: 11:00 A.M. to 10:00 P.M.; Friday and Saturday: 11:00 A.M. to 11:00 P.M.; Sunday: 10:00 A.M. to 10:00 P.M.

NEARBY ATTRACTIONS: Hinterland Brewing Company, Titletown Brewing Company, Captain's Walk Winery, Packers games at Lambeau Field, Bay Beach Amusement Park, Green Bay Botanical Gardens, NEW Zoo, National Railroad Museum, Oneida Bingo and Casino, Lake Michigan Cruises

NOTES: Stepping through the front door of the Legends Eatery in Howard, you pass the polished-copper brewing vessels in the tiny Brew Room to the left. You enter the dining room, a large hangar-like room with many levels and an oval bar at one end. Television screens are mounted all around so Packers fans won't miss the game. The room is dimly lit and a bit generic feeling, but not uncomfortable.

I was there during the Sunday brunch. The buffet had a wide range of items, including grilled chicken, roast beef, pork chops, and sauerkraut, as well as more typical breakfast fare, including made-to-order omelets. The food was good and reasonably priced.

The pub keeps six house beers on tap, four year-round beers, and two rotating seasonals. They also stock a range of mass-market beers in both bottles and draft.

O'so Brewing Company

ADDRESS: 3028 Village Park Dr.
Plover, WI 54467

TELEPHONE: 715–254–2163

EMAIL: brewmaster@osobrewing.com

WEB SITE: www.osobrewing.com

MICHAEL'S PICK: Rusty Red: This is not your average American amber ale. Brewed with mostly Munich and Vienna malts, it has a unique nutty and toasty profile that makes it stand out. Bitterness is moderate and the citrusy flavor hops have been reduced to allow that malt to shine. If you love malt, this one is for you.

TYPE: Brewery

DATE ESTABLISHED: 2009

OWNERS: Marc Buttera and Katina Buttera

BREWMASTER: Mike Krause

BREWING SYSTEM: Thirty-barrel Specific Mechanical brewhouse

FLAGSHIP BEERS: Hopdinger, Night Train

YEAR-ROUND BEERS: The Big O, Hopdinger, Rusty Red, Night Train

SEASONAL BEERS: O-toberfest, Doe in Heat, Black Scotch, Picnic Ants, Dank Imperial Red, Dominator Doppelbock, Dimwit Imperial Wit, Lupulin Maximus Imperial IPA

SPECIAL RELEASES: Jack's Lantern, Duzy Piwo, Floppin Opi, Black Cocker, Belgian Pale, Belgian Dark, Summer Storm, and others

TOURS: Saturday: 2:00, 3:00, and 4:00 P.M. Cost $2 charitable donation.

BEER TO GO: Growlers, kegs, and package

FOOD: None

AMENITIES: Parking lot, taproom, homebrew-supply store, live music

PUB HOURS: Monday–Friday: 3:00 to 9:00 P.M.; Saturday: noon to 9:00 P.M.

NEARBY ATTRACTIONS: Stevens Point and Central Waters Breweries, Green Circle Bicycle Trail, Mullins Cheese, skiing and hiking at Standing Rock Park, University of Wisconsin–Stevens Point

NOTES: O'so Brewery began in the back room of Point Homebrew Supply. The space was tiny. A big brewery was out of the question. This led to the adoption of one of the most unique brewing solutions I have seen. They operated two smaller brewhouses simultaneously to produce a combined fifteen-barrel batch. It made for a challenging brewday for brewer Mike Krause, as he constantly watched two clocks. When I asked how he managed it, he responded, "I drink a lot." Naturally, he meant the massive amounts of water and Gatorade he consumed to remain hydrated in the hot brewery.

O'so is the typical homebrewer's dream gone wild. The homebrew store came first, opening in 2003, when Marc and Katina Buttera grew tired of traveling to Appleton for supplies. As that business grew and moved into successively larger spaces, they began to consider exploring that homebrewing spirit of adventure on bigger scale. They cobbled together the first brewery in the storefront next to the store and began brewing beer as professionals.

They've come a long way since then. In late 2011 they relocated to a bigger space and left the dual-brewhouse system behind. The expansion and move has allowed them to greatly increase their production and distribution. When I visited, the beer was only available at the brewery; now you will find it in retail outlets across the state. It has also afforded them greater quality and consistency. As Marc told me, "If you can brew good beer on junk, you should really do well on better equipment."

Pigeon River Brewing Company

ADDRESS: W12710 U.S. Hwy 45 Marion, WI 54950

TELEPHONE: 715–256–7721

EMAIL: nknaack@gmail.com

WEB SITE: www.pigeonriverbrewing.com

MICHAEL'S PICK: Red IPA: Hop bitterness is the primary driver of this cross between American IPA and American amber ale. The hop load is appropriate to the former. The caramel and toasty malt flavors nudge it in the direction of the latter, but they don't quite provide the level of balance required for the amber style.

TYPE: Brewpub

DATE ESTABLISHED: 2012

OWNERS: Nate Knaack, Kayla Knaack, and Matt Wichman

BREWMASTER: Brett Hintz

BREWING SYSTEM: Six-barrel converted dairy-tank brewhouse

FLAGSHIP BEER: German Kölsch

YEAR-ROUND BEERS: Slippery Richard Oatmeal Stout, Black IPA, German Kölsch, American Wheat, Vienna Lager

SEASONAL BEER: Gingerbread Ale

SPECIAL RELEASE: Black Wit

TOURS: By request

BEER TO GO: Growlers and kegs

FOOD: Small selection of pizzas

AMENITIES: Parking lot, taproom, large selection of guest beers, seasonal beer garden

PUB HOURS: Wednesday–Friday: 4:00 P.M. to close; Saturday and Sunday: 11:00 A.M. to close

NEARBY ATTRACTIONS: Dupont Cheese Factory, Northstar Mohican Casino and Resort, year-round outdoor activities in nearby forest and wildlife preserves, forty-five miles from Appleton and Stevens Point

NOTES: The history of Pigeon River Brewing Company is an interesting story of crossed paths and coincidental meet-ups. It begins in high-school band class, where fellow tuba players Nate Knaack and Brett Hintz were reading a magazine about hops. "It just happened to be there," says Knaack. This inspired the pair to start homebrewing. They made—and drank—beer together until college took them in different directions.

In college, Knaack became the president of the brew club, where he met Matt Wichman. The two got to talking and discovered that they shared the dream of one day opening a brewery. As their friendship grew, they realized that they also shared something else—they both grew up in the small, northern Wisconsin town of Marion. It's a town where everyone knows each other, but somehow they had never met.

After college, the two returned to Marion and began pursuing their brewpub dream, along with Nate's wife Kayla. About that time, Knaack's old brewing partner Brett Hintz also returned to town. He signed on as brewer, closing the circle and completing the Pigeon River team.

Each of the partners brings a different skill set to the endeavor. Nate Knaack's expertise is marketing, while Kayla's is finance. Wichman is an experienced salesman. Hintz's biology studies leave him well suited to make the beer. They've got all the bases covered to run a successful business.

Pigeon River sits at the dividing line between the woods of northern Wisconsin and the farmland of the south. Its location along Highway 45 makes it a convenient stop for weekenders heading to the North Woods. To insure that the experience there is a good one, the Pigeon River crew trains their employees well, even requiring them to brew a batch of beer on the one-barrel pilot system.

Rail House Restaurant and Brewpub

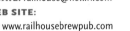

ADDRESS: 2029 Old Peshtigo Ct. Marinette, WI 54143
TELEPHONE: 715–732–4646
EMAIL: railhouse@new.rr.com
WEB SITE:
www.railhousebrewpub.com

MICHAEL'S PICK: Imperial Pilsner: There are very few imperial pilsner beers that I like. This is one of them. It's a full-bodied beer displaying honeyed pilsner-malt character and hints of fresh bread. Floral European hops offer secondary lemon and herb notes. It's bitter enough to deserve the double pilsner name, but it still lets the malt come through.
TYPE: Brewpub
DATE ESTABLISHED: 1997
OWNER: Ron Beyer
BREWMASTER: Ron Beyer

BREWING SYSTEM: Ten-barrel Northern Brew Systems brewhouse
FLAGSHIP BEER: Silver Cream
YEAR-ROUND BEERS: Oconto Premium, Silver Cream, Blueberry Draft, Brewer's Best Pilsner, Dumb Blond, Big Mac IPA, Honey Weiss, Scottish Ale, Oatmeal Stout, Bock, Caramel Cream, Nutty Brown Ale, Imperial Pilsner
SEASONAL BEERS: Zummer, Oktoberfest, Harvest Ale, Barleywine
SPECIAL RELEASES: None
TOURS: By request
BEER TO GO: Growlers
FOOD: Family restaurant fare: breakfast standards, pizza, burgers, pasta, and Mexican
AMENITIES: Parking lot, full bar, seasonal outdoor seating, daily food specials
PUB HOURS: Monday–Thursday: 11:00 A.M. to 10:00 P.M.; Friday and Saturday: 11:00 A.M. to 11:00 P.M.; Sunday: 11:00 A.M. to 9:00 P.M.
NEARBY ATTRACTIONS: All-season outdoor activities, including hiking and biking trails, lake kayaking, fishing, skiing, and snowmobiling, golf, Marinette County Scenic Waterfalls Tour, Theatre on the Bay

NOTES: From the homey dining-room décor to the vast and varied menu, Rail House feels like one of those small-town family restaurants that are so satisfying on long road trips. Step into the bar and you find yourself in the neighborhood tavern. It's simple and relatively unadorned, yet inviting—the kind of place where locals stop in for a quick cocktail or pint after work, and the bartender already knows what they want. It feels genuine. No corporate gloss here. This is the real deal.

There are a large number of beers to match the large number of items on the menu. Owner/brewer Ron Beyer keeps twelve house beers on tap in a wide variety of styles, including several lagers. Many of them, like the flagship Silver Cream, take their inspiration and their names from beers produced at the old Marinette Menominee Brewery that operated in the city until the 1960s. In this way the restaurant maintains a connection to the history of the community.

The beers at Rail House are flavorful and well-made, especially those at the lighter end of the spectrum. The twelve-beer sampler tray contained several standouts, including Silver Cream, Big Mac IPA, and the delicious Oconto Premium American-style lager. At only nine dollars, the sampler is a good bargain and a satisfying way to taste all of the brewpub's fine beers.

Red Eye Brewing Company

ADDRESS: 612 Washington St.
Wausau, WI 54403
TELEPHONE: 715–843–7334
EMAIL: info@redeyebrewing.com
WEB SITE: www.redeyebrewing.com
MICHAEL'S PICK: Conquest American
Rye ESB: English malts and American hops define this hybrid, strong pale ale. Full-flavored caramel malt is overlain by bright tangerine and tropical-fruit hops. While it has a bite, the focus is on hop flavor over bitterness. Rye offers a spicy surprise in the finish.
TYPE: Brewpub
DATE ESTABLISHED: 2008
OWNER: Kevin Eichelberger
BREWMASTER: Kevin Eichelberger
BREWING SYSTEM: Five-barrel Specific Mechanical brewhouse
FLAGSHIP BEERS: Bloom, Thrust!, Scarlet 7, Verruca Stout
YEAR-ROUND BEERS: Bloom, Thrust!, Scarlet 7, rotating dark beer
SEASONAL BEERS: Cart Ride to Mexico, Oktoberfest, Scotch Ale
SPECIAL RELEASES: Tough and Tender, Sticke Alt, Imperial American Wheat, Conquest American Rye ESB, Witbier, Serendipity, English Summer Ale, Black IPA, and others
TOURS: By appointment
BEER TO GO: Growlers and kegs
FOOD: Wood-fired pizza is the specialty, limited list of entrées, focus on locally sourced and organic ingredients
AMENITIES: Parking lot, full bar, group bike rides every Friday from the brewery
PUB HOURS: Monday–Saturday: 11:00 A.M. to 11:00 P.M.
NEARBY ATTRACTIONS: O'so Brewing Co., Bull Falls Brewing Co., Great Dane Brewpub, Granite Peak Ski Area, the Grand Theatre, Leigh Yawkey Woodson Art Museum, outdoor activities at Rib Mountain State Park, Nine-Mile County Park, mountain-bike trails, international whitewater kayaking competitions throughout the summer

NOTES: When Kevin Eichelberger opened Red Eye Brewing Co., he wanted to do something unique. While others in the area were brewing beers for the novice drinker, he went for more unique styles, like Belgians and black IPAs. He dabbles in the artistic side of brewing, experimenting with unusual ingredients, infusing his beers with the flavors of chamomile, caramelized figs, and flowers.

But it's not just about experimentation. Eichelberger is a firm believer in mastering the basics. As he told me, "If you can't brew a clean pilsner, then you shouldn't be throwing a lot of junk into beer." The quality of his beers attests to his brewing skills.

The artistic bent carries over to the décor. Inside and out the place has a creative, modern, artsy feel to it. The airy seating area is bookended by the long bar and the open kitchen. A connection to the local bicycling scene is evidenced by the bikes and bike paraphernalia all around.

Eichelberger believes that brewpubs are about providing local flavor. They grow much of their own produce and use local sources for the rest. Beef comes from area producers. Be sure to try the hamburger buns made with spent brewing grains. I ate one without the burger, and it was delicious.

Rowland's Calumet Brewing Company

ADDRESS: 25 N. Madison St.
Chilton, WI 53014
TELEPHONE: 920–849–2534
EMAIL: rcbrewing@gmail.com
WEB SITE:
www.rowlandsbrewery.com
MICHAEL'S PICK: Mittnacht Pilsner: This is a classic German schwarzbier. Pilsner-like body and crispness are layered with subtle roasted malt character. Hints of coffee and chocolate round it out. Bitterness is moderate, and the finish is dry and sharp.
TYPE: Brewpub/Brewery
DATE ESTABLISHED: 1990
OWNER: Patrick Rowland
BREWMASTER: Patrick Rowland
BREWING SYSTEM: Brewpub: Three-barrel JV Northwest brewhouse
PRODUCTION BREWERY: Seven-barrel PUB brewhouse
FLAGSHIP BEER: Oktoberfest
YEAR-ROUND BEERS: Calumet Amber, Calumet Dark, Calumet Oktoberfest, Calumet Rye, Fat Man's Nut Brown
SEASONAL BEERS: Bitter Bitch Belgian Ale, Bucholz Alt, Calumet Bock, Calumet Ice, Calumet Kölsch, Calumet Pilsner, Calumet Wheat, Conner John's Scotch Ale, Detention Ale, Guido's Grand Imperial Stout, Honey Lager, Hunter's Choice, Kelly's Irish Red Lager, Madison Street Lager, Mittnacht Pilsner Schwarzbier, Mortimer's Ale, Total Eclipse
SPECIAL RELEASES: None
TOURS: By appointment
BEER TO GO: Growlers and kegs

FOOD: Frozen pizza, beef jerky, turkey gizzards, and pickled eggs

AMENITIES: Parking lot, free street parking, full bar

PUB HOURS: Tuesday–Thursday: 2:00 P.M. to 2:00 A.M.; Friday and Saturday: noon to 2:30 A.M.; Sunday: noon to 2:00 A.M.

NEARBY ATTRACTIONS: Briess Malting Facility, Vern's Cheese, biking and snowmobile trails, Wisconsin Microbrewers Beer Fest in May, historic lime kilns at High Cliff State Park, underground cave trail at Ledgeview Nature Center

NOTES: The building that houses Rowland's Calumet Brewing Company was built sometime around 1870 to house Chilton's first fire department and city hall. It has served a number of purposes over the years, from dress shop to church. In 1937 it was converted to a tavern and has been one ever since.

Rowland's Calumet Brewing Company by night.

When Robert Rowland started making beer in the bar in 1990, the plan was to serve the beer only on site. Within just a few years, however, they started to pick up other draft accounts, stressing the capacity of the tiny three-barrel system. In 1997 he purchased a building down the street and put in another brewery to service that demand. Beer started flowing from Plant No. 2 in 2000.

From the faux-stone exterior on Chilton's Main Street to the 1920s vintage back-bar and rough-hewn simplicity, Rowland's Calumet feels every bit the small-town, neighborhood tavern that it has been for over seventy years. The long bar dominates and provides virtually the only seating. A pool table fills the middle of the floor. The walls are covered with historic memorabilia from the building, the town, and the Cal-

umet Brewing Co. that made beer here until 1942. It's a "No BS" zone where they'll make you feel like a local.

Brewer Patrick Rowland, son of the original Rowland, crafts generally solid beers in a variety of styles that include both ales and lagers. It's a bit hit or miss, but there are some real winners here. There hasn't been a non-house beer served here since 1996. With eleven beers always on tap, why would there be?

Shipwrecked Restaurant, Brew Pub, and Inn

ADDRESS: 7791 State Hwy 42
Egg Harbor, WI 54209

TELEPHONE: 888–868–2767

EMAIL: shipwrecked@itol.com

WEB SITE: www.shipwreckedmicrobrew.com

MICHAEL'S PICK: Spruce Tip Ale: It's a shame that this wonderful ale is only available seasonally. I would gladly drink it all year long. Spruce tips bring sprightly pine and blueberry overtones to a luscious base of toffee-flavored malt. Light and lingering bitterness combines with a faint, green tea–like astringency to gently counter the sweetness. Delightful.

TYPE: Brewpub

DATE ESTABLISHED: 1997

OWNER: Rob Pollman

BREWMASTER: Richard Zielke

BREWING SYSTEM: Fifteen-barrel Walker brewhouse

FLAGSHIP BEER: Door County Cherry Wheat

YEAR-ROUND BEERS: Bayside Blond, Captain's Copper, Door County Cherry Wheat, Lighthouse Light, Peninsula Porter

SEASONAL BEERS: India Pale Ale, Spruce Tip Ale, Pumpkin Patch, Milk Stout, Summer Wheat

SPECIAL RELEASES: None

TOURS: No

BEER TO GO: Growlers, kegs, and package

FOOD: Seasonal menus that change weekly, featuring a selection of Wisconsin-focused appetizers, salads, and sandwiches

AMENITIES: Free street parking, full bar, guest rooms at the inn, steps from the lake, Egg Harbor Marina is across the street

PUB HOURS:
May through October: Daily 11:00 A.M. to 10:00 P.M.
November through April: Friday–Sunday 11:00 A.M. to 8:00 P.M.

NEARBY ATTRACTIONS: Door Peninsula Winery, Harbor Ridge Winery, golf, boating, kayaking, and fishing on Lake Michigan, camping, quaint shops and galleries, pick-your-own cherries, berries, and apples at nearby orchards, White Cliff Fen and Forest State Natural Area, Peninsula State Park

NOTES: The Peninsula of Door County juts seventy miles into Lake Michigan on Wisconsin's north shore. Though only ten miles wide, its three hundred miles of shoreline, five state parks, cherry and apple orchards, and artist colonies make it the state's prime seasonal tourist destination. Lake resorts and bed and breakfasts abound. Loads of activities await. It's truly beautiful country.

Shipwrecked is nestled near the shoreline in the tiny town of Egg Harbor, toward the northern end of the peninsula. The building has been a tavern and inn since 1856, when it served lumberjacks and sailors. During the Roaring Twenties it became a favorite hideaway of the notorious gangster Al Capone, who reportedly used tunnels under the building for quick getaways. Lodging is still available at the inn, if you aren't afraid of the ghosts that reportedly inhabit the place.

Head Brewer Richard Zielke came to Shipwrecked in 2008, after twelve years at the Estes Park Brewery in Colorado. He finds the two to be similar. Both are small brewpub/packaging breweries in picturesque small towns with highly seasonal business. Looking at the broader picture, he reports that the current state of beer in the Heartland mirrors what happened ten years ago on the Colorado Front Range, now a national mecca for great beer.

Given the novice nature of his clientele, Zielke keeps the beers simple: no 100 IBU IPAs here. He tries to cover the bases, presenting a wide range of styles that often utilize local ingredients like spruce tips or the tart cherries that Door County is famous for.

Stevens Point Brewery

ADDRESS: 2617 Water St.
Stevens Point, WI 54481
TELEPHONE: 800-369-4911
EMAIL: info@pointbeer.com
WEB SITE: www.pointbeer.com

MICHAEL'S PICK: 2012 Black Ale: This beer is black and creamy like a sweet stout, but with the subtle roast and caramel flavor of a German schwarzbier. The rounder ale mouthfeel is primarily what separates it from its crisper lager cousin. Spicy hops and moderate bitterness are just enough to keep it balanced.

TYPE: Brewery
DATE ESTABLISHED: 1857
OWNERS: Joe Martino and Jim Wiechmann
BREWMASTER: John Zappa
BREWING SYSTEM: Two-hundred-barrel Robert Morton Ltd. brewhouse

FLAGSHIP BEER: Point Special Lager
YEAR-ROUND BEERS: 2012 Black Ale, Burly Brown Ale, Classic Amber, Cascade Pale Ale, Belgian White Wheat, Horizon Wheat, Special Lager, James Page Iron Range Amber Lager, James Page Burly Brown, James Page Voyaguer Extra Pale Ale, James Page White Ox Wheat Ale
SEASONAL BEERS: Einbeck, Nude Beach, Oktoberfest, St. Benedict's Winter Ale
SPECIAL RELEASES: Whole Hog Imperial Pilsner, Whole Hog Six-Hop IPA, Whole Hog Pumpkin Ale, Whole Hog Russian Imperial Stout
TOURS:
June through August: Monday–Saturday: 11:00 A.M., 12:00, 1:00, 2:00 P.M.
September through May: Monday–Friday: 1:00 P.M.; Saturday: 11:00 A.M., 12:00, 1:00, 2:00 P.M.
COST: $3 for ages twelve and up, $1 for ages five to eleven. Call for reservations.
BEER TO GO: Package
FOOD: None
AMENITIES: Parking lot, hospitality room, gift shop
PUB HOURS: During tours
NEARBY ATTRACTIONS: O'so and Central Waters Breweries, Green Circle Bicycle Trail, Mullins Cheese, skiing and hiking at Standing Rock Park, University of Wisconsin–Stevens Point, a variety of seasonal festivals in the historic downtown

NOTES: Stevens Point the brewery has existed longer than Stevens Point the town. Visiting the brewery, one senses that long history in the commingling of old and new. The modern brewhouse and canning line exist in harmony with the century-old grain scale that is still in use. Four-hundred-barrel stainless-steel fermenters now occupy rooms that once housed large wooden vessels. The brewery's original product, Point Special Lager, flows from those tanks alongside bold double IPAs and imperial stouts.

Unlike some larger breweries, where visitors are kept at a distance from the equipment, a tour at Stevens Point puts you up close. You climb the same steps the brewers use to get to the mash tun and kettle. There is nothing holding you back from stepping up to the packaging line as bottles and cans whiz past. And, of course, the tasting room at the end gives you a chance to get up close and personal with the beers.

Point's mainline selections could be called entry-level craft beers. The brewery is just fine with that designation. They are fond of saying that their beers are for "those who live in the craft-beer world or those who are just visiting." They don't challenge your palate, but each one is solidly crafted and very easy to drink. They are beers that you can and would have more than one of. If you are looking for more adventure, try the beers in their Whole Hog series.

Stone Cellar Brewpub

ADDRESS: 1004 S. Olde Oneida St. Appleton, WI 54915

TELEPHONE: 920–731–3322

EMAIL: steve@stonecellarbrewpub.com

WEB SITE: www.stonecellarbrewpub.com

MICHAEL'S PICK: Pilsner: Based on a recipe culled from the archives of the old Appleton Brewing and Malting Co., this is a delicious Bohemian-style pilsner. It has just the right balance of floral hops, graham-cracker sweetness, and crisp bitterness. It's a great example of the complexity possible in a relatively simple beer.

TYPE: Brewpub

DATE ESTABLISHED: 2004

OWNERS: Tom Lonsway and Steve Lonsway

BREWMASTER: Steve Lonsway

BREWING SYSTEM: Seven-barrel brewhouse, manufacturer unknown

FLAGSHIP BEERS: English Six Grain Ale, Tilted Kilt Scottish Ale

YEAR-ROUND BEERS: Houdini Honey Wheat, Marquette Pilsner, English Six Grain Ale, Pie Eyed Pale Ale, Tilted Kilt Scottish Ale, Stone Cellar Stout, Vanishing Vanilla Stout

SEASONAL BEERS: Pumpkin Spice, Wiley Rye Ale, Oktoberfest, Grand Cru, Smoked Porter, Imperial IPA, Red Pale Ale, Adler Brau, Imperial Six Grain, 666 Triple Six Grain, and others

SPECIAL RELEASES: Occasional barrel-aged releases

TOURS: By appointment

BEER TO GO: Growlers and package

FOOD: Selection of brewpub favorites featuring locally sourced and organic ingredients. Try the elk burger.

AMENITIES: Parking lot, full bar, seasonal beer garden, private room available, Mug Club, Beer School program

PUB HOURS: Daily: 11:00 A.M. to close

NEARBY ATTRACTIONS: Fratello's/Fox River Brewery at the Fox River Mall, the Building for Kids Children's Museum, Outagamie Museum/Houdini Historical Center, Fox Cities Performing Arts Center, Gordon Bubolz Nature Preserve, Memorial Park Arboretum and Gardens

NOTES: History and locality are two cornerstone principles at Stone Cellar. The connection to brewing history is immediately evident. The brewpub's bar and dining room are located in the former lagering cellars of the 1859 building that originally housed the Appleton Brewing and Malting Company. The beer garden is in the same space that welcomed nineteenth-century patrons to enjoy a summer afternoon beer.

The connection to local brewing history carries over into the beers as well. At least two of the beers, Pilsner and Adler Brau, are based on recipes from the archives of the predecessor brewery. Adler Brau even takes the name of one of that brewery's brands.

Stone Cellar aims to be Appleton's beer. Despite a recent expansion that tripled the brewery's capacity and allowed them to greatly increase off-site draft and package accounts, they have chosen to keep their market local. Sales are restricted to the area from Green Bay to the north and Oshkosh to the south. In addition, they get as many of their ingredients as possible for food and beer from local sources.

The beers at Stone Cellar are all exquisitely crafted. I had the nine-beer sampler, and there wasn't a bad one in the bunch. The homemade root beer is noteworthy for its lack of caramel coloring. I picked up the glass and said, "That is not root beer." I was quite surprised to find that it was indeed root beer, and tasty root beer at that.

Titletown Brewing Company

ADDRESS: 200 Dousman St. Green Bay, WI 54303

TELEPHONE: 920–437–2337

EMAIL: info@titletownbrewing.com

WEB SITE: www.titletownbrewing.com

MICHAEL'S PICK: Wild Train Rye'd: This amber ale rides a fine balance of rye spice, caramel sweetness, and citrusy hops. Bitterness is assertive but not overwhelming. The rye character comes through loud and clear, reminding me of rye flour. Underlying notes of chocolate and dark fruits add depth and complexity.

TYPE: Brewpub

DATE ESTABLISHED: 1996

OWNER: Brent Weycker

BREWMASTER: Dave Oldenburg

BREWING SYSTEM: Fifteen-barrel Specific Mechanical brewhouse

FLAGSHIP BEER: Johnny "Blood" Irish Red Ale

YEAR-ROUND BEERS: Canadeo Gold, "400" Honey Ale, Railyard Ale, Johnny "Blood" Irish Red Ale, Dark Helmet Schwartzbier, Hopasaurus Rex

SEASONAL BEERS: Daousman Street Wheat, Bridge Out Stout

SPECIAL RELEASES: Boathouse Pils, Wild Train Rye'd, Off Kilter, Big Boy Brown, Expect the Wurst, Trilithon

Tripel, Early Sunset Bitter, Ardennes Express, Slam Dunkel, Northwestern Export, Apricary Ale, Loose Caboose, Beeriodic Table, Dry Eyed Stout, Smoky the Beer, IrrationAle, and others

TOURS: By appointment or request

BEER TO GO: Growlers and kegs

FOOD: Standard brewpub fare with a few interesting diversions, including bison and elk burgers

AMENITIES: Parking lot, full bar, seasonal outdoor seating, Mug Club, pool tables and other games upstairs, private rooms available, Suds and Cinema nights

PUB HOURS: Daily: 11:00 A.M. to 9:00 P.M.

NEARBY ATTRACTIONS: Lambeau Field, University of Wisconsin–Green Bay campus, National Railroad Museum, Green Bay Children's Museum, Bay Beach Park and Wildlife Sanctuary, boat cruises on Green Bay, Grassy Island Range Lighthouse, NEW Zoo, Performances at Meyer Theatre, outdoor recreation at area parks on Green Bay

NOTES: Titletown Brewing Company is housed in an old Chicago & Northwestern Railway depot that dates to 1899. The building was left largely intact, right down to the original signage and railroad timetables that ornament the walls. The space evokes memories of a time when rail travel was an important part of the American landscape. You can almost feel the hustle and bustle of travelers coming and going. In fact, I'm told that visitors often share memories from the old days over a beer.

Titletown Brewing Company is housed in a rail depot from 1899.

The brewpub is a family-friendly place and a popular pregame destination for Packers fans. The downstairs dining room is open and airy. Wooden benches and simple accessories keep it casual. The brewery is visible behind the bar. Upstairs has a sports-bar feel

with billiard and shuffleboard tables and television screens to watch the game. Outdoor seating on the old train platforms offers a view of the bay. Come for the summertime Suds and Cinema series to enjoy a movie and beers.

Titletown brewers conjure up a wide array of solid beers that have garnered numerous local, regional, and national awards, including a recent gold medal win at the Great American Beer Festival. I found the Boathouse Pilsner, Hopasaurus Rex, and Railyard Alt especially tasty. They even pulled off the Wisconsin-original Expect the Wurst bratwurst beer. If they can do that, they can do anything. The brews are certainly worth a stop.

WEST CENTRAL

Blue Heron Brewpub

ADDRESS: 108 W. 9th St.
Marshfield, WI 54449

TELEPHONE: 715–389–1868

EMAIL: info@blueheronbrewpub.com

WEB SITE: www.blueheronbrewpub.com

MICHAEL'S PICK: Irish Red Ale: Creamy, super-caramel malt defines this one, but it's not overly sweet. Earthy hop flavors and moderate bitterness keep it balanced. A touch of roast adds a bit of depth. A most pleasant pint.

TYPE: Brewpub

DATE ESTABLISHED: 2005

OWNERS: Tom Hinke, Paula Hinke, Paul Meier, and Rita Meier

BREWMASTER: Corey Nebbeling

BREWING SYSTEM: Seven-barrel JV Northwest brewhouse

FLAGSHIP BEERS: Honey Blond, Tiger's Eye

YEAR-ROUND BEERS: Honey Blond, Loch Ness Scotch Ale, Tiger's Eye, rotating hoppy beer

SEASONAL BEERS: Dubilee Dubel, Hop Temper, Hub City Lager, Lil' Walt's Malt, Ol' Blue's Light, Possibly Wobbly, Soo Line Stout, Roddi's Bock, Oktoberfest, Witz End Wheat, Doc's Pale Wheat, Hannahweizen, Odyssey Weizenbock, Ryezome Red, Fool's Gold, Irish Red Ale, Winter Spice, Nut Brown Ale, Luscious Black, Panther Porter, Lazy Otter, and others

SPECIAL RELEASES: Arcturus Belgian Golden Ale, Deercamp Smoked Porter, Hub City Stout, Panther Porter, Parkin's Dark, Parkin's Pils, Reanimator Golden Quadruple, Rockstar IPA, Tappers Tripel, Witz End Wheat, and others

TOURS: By appointment

BEER TO GO: Growlers and kegs

FOOD: A wide selection of brewpub favorites: burgers, pizzas, wraps, salads, and Friday fish fry

AMENITIES: Parking lot, free street parking, full bar, happy-hour specials, catering and private dining areas, West 14th Restaurant upstairs offers fine dining option

PUB HOURS: Monday–Saturday: 11:00 A.M. to close

NEARBY ATTRACTIONS: State's largest round barn, Central Wisconsin fair, Jurrasic Park iron sculptures, Hub City Days festival in late July

NOTES: The dining room at the Blue Heron has the feel of a garage. That's appropriate, as it is located in what used to be the loading dock of a dairy plant. The fully windowed front wall recalls the bay doors that once allowed trucks in for loading and unloading. The super-casual atmosphere made for a most enjoyable lunch. It would be a fine place for a family-friendly dinner as well. If you're in the mood for something more upscale, head upstairs to the West 14th Restaurant. All the Blue Heron beers are available on tap in a more elegant setting.

The dining room at Blue Heron Brewpub.

The brewpub maintains a close relationship with the local homebrewing community. The M*A*S*H Tap program is a collaboration with the Marshfield Area Society of Homebrewers. Every couple of months, they collaborate on a recipe that is brewed and poured at the pub in a limited run. Luscious Black, a creamy imperial stout that is now a recurring seasonal offering, is one product of this collaboration.

While there was nothing outstanding, the beers I tasted on my visit were all well made and drinkable. The selection tended toward sessionable, brewpub standards. There was a change of brewers shortly after my visit. I was not able to return to sample the wares of the new brewer, Corey Nebbeling.

ADDRESS: 230 S. Knowles Ave. New Richmond, WI 54017

TELEPHONE: 715–246–9960

EMAIL: chris@bradysbrewhouse.com

WEB SITE: www.bradysbrewhouse.com

MICHAEL'S PICK: Midnight Chocolate Porter: This delightfully drinkable brown porter is made with real cocoa, and that character really comes through. A dry finish gives it the texture almost of cocoa powder, but there is sufficient caramel sweetness to keep it balanced. A bit of coffee roast and a light, spicy hop presence add interest. At just 4 percent ABV, you can have a few.

TYPE: Brewpub

DATE ESTABLISHED: 2010

OWNER: Chris Polfus

BREWMASTER: Luke Nirmaier

BREWING SYSTEM: Seven-barrel PUB Systems brewhouse

FLAGSHIP BEER: Hop Tornado IPA

YEAR-ROUND BEERS: Midnight Chocolate Porter, Harvester Oatmeal Stout, Sunny Golden Wheat, Hop Tornado IPA, Vagabond Irish Red

SEASONAL BEERS: None

SPECIAL RELEASES: Regular special releases, including Big Musky Pale Ale, St. Croix Crossing Steam, Aromarillo, and others

TOURS: By request

BEER TO GO: Growlers

FOOD: Stuffed burgers, pizzas, and wood-fire-grilled specialties. Six different ways to order French fries, from "Naked" to "Bacon and Bleu."

AMENITIES: Parking lot in back, free street parking, happy-hour specials, full bar with good guest-tap selection, live music, game room, meeting space and private room available

PUB HOURS: Monday–Thursday and Sunday: 11:00 A.M. to 11:00 P.M.; Friday and Saturday: 11:00 A.M. to 2:30 A.M.

NEARBY ATTRACTIONS: Golf, New Richmond Heritage Center, Old Gem Theatre, Park Art Fair and Willow River Blues and Brews Fest in June, Summer Fun Festival in July, Cedar Lake Speedway, art shows and performances at the Space, forty-five miles from the Twin Cities

NOTES: When you walk in the front door at Brady's, you are immediately enveloped in a symphony of smells. Wood fire, pizza crust, and grilling meat combine to create an inviting olfactory overload that makes you want to sit down and eat. Continue to the back of the restaurant on a brew day, and those smoky smells are joined by the thick, sweet aroma of boiling wort. If they could vent it to the street, the smells would be an irresistible draw to casual passersby.

The place has the feel of an upscale grill. Sleek lines, dark wood, and splashes of red create an atmosphere that is sophisticated but not stuffy. The open kitchen lets you in on the action, allowing a clear view to the wood-fired pizza oven and grills.

The beers are generally tasty and well made. You're unlikely to find anything flashy or over-the-top. The focus here is on subtle and nuanced session ales. The day I was there, the strongest house beer was only 6.5 percent ABV, and several were under 5 percent. If none of the seven house beers suits your fancy, the thirty-six guest taps are sure to offer something appealing. If you can't decide, treat yourself to a sampler flight of any of the currently available taps.

City Brewing Company

ADDRESS: 925 S. 3rd St.
La Crosse, WI 54601
TELEPHONE: 608-785-4200
EMAIL: inquiries@citybrewery.com
WEB SITE: www.citybrewery.com
MICHAEL'S PICK: No in-house brands
TYPE: Brewery
DATE ESTABLISHED: 2000
OWNER: Private investor group
BREWMASTER: Randy Hughes
BREWING SYSTEM: One-thousand-barrel brewhouse, manufacturer unknown
FLAGSHIP BEER: No in-house brands
YEAR-ROUND BEERS: No in-house brands
SEASONAL BEERS: No in-house brands

The boil kettles at City Brewing hold approximately two thousand barrels.

SPECIAL RELEASES: No in-house brands
TOURS: No
BEER TO GO: None
FOOD: None
AMENITIES: Free street parking
PUB HOURS: None
NEARBY ATTRACTIONS: Pearl Street Brewery, Mississippi River cruises, Mt. La Crosse Ski Area, Annual Oktoberfest, Children's Museum of La Crosse, golf, outdoor activities at Perrot and Merrick State Parks, Great River Road Bicycle Trail, river activities, including boating, fishing, and kayaking

NOTES: They have been making beer at the City Brewing Company facility in La Crosse for over 150 years. Its history traces the rise and decline of the American brewing industry from the local enterprises of the nineteenth century through the industry consolidation and rise of the megabreweries of the late twentieth century.

The company was founded in 1858 as the City Brewery, a partnership of prominent local brewers Gottlieb Heileman and John Gund. In 1872 Gund sold his share to Heileman, who continued to operate the brewery under the familiar G. Heileman Brewing Company name. The company quickly grew to regional and national prominence.

Having survived Prohibition, G. Heileman continued its rise. Through the 1970s and 1980s it acquired many of the smaller regional players that were succumbing to competitive pressure from the larger brewing concerns. It assembled an impressive array of brands that included Old Style, Special Export, Grain Belt, Sterling, Pfeiffer, and Schmidt. By the 1990s, however, the company was itself consumed by even larger entities. It was shuttered in 1999.

A private investor group bought the facility in 2000 and rechristened it City Brewing Company. Today the company produces over thirty beer brands under contract to other breweries. A large percentage of the brewery's ten-million-barrel capacity is devoted to energy drinks and flavored malt beverages. In addition to the plant in La Crosse, City Brewing Company operates facilities in Latrobe, Pennsylvania, and Memphis, Tennessee.

The Corner Pub

ADDRESS: 100 E. Main St.
Reedsburg, WI 53959
TELEPHONE: 608-524-8989
EMAIL: cornerpb@mwt.net
WEB SITE: None

Corner Pub owner/brewer Pete Peterson.

MICHAEL'S PICK: Porter: This light and drinkable porter leans a little bit toward the sweeter side, with some fruity highlights from fermentation. The sweetness doesn't take over, though. It's balanced by moderate hop bitterness and chocolaty roasted malt character.

TYPE: Brewpub

DATE ESTABLISHED: 1996

OWNER: Pete Peterson

BREWMASTER: Pete Peterson

BREWING SYSTEM: Two-barrel converted soup-kettle brewhouse

FLAGSHIP BEERS: Porter, India Pale Ale

YEAR-ROUND BEERS: American Pale Ale, Old Gold Lager, India Pale Ale

SEASONAL BEERS: Bock, Weiss, Oktoberfest, Milk Stout

SPECIAL RELEASES: Smoked Porter, Bourbon Scotch Ale

TOURS: By request

BEER TO GO: Growlers

FOOD: Simple pub fare, including burgers, salads, and seafood. Vegetarian options available. Homemade bread.

AMENITIES: Free street parking, limited full bar

PUB HOURS: Daily: 11:00 A.M. to midnight

NEARBY ATTRACTIONS: Moosjaw Brewpub, Port Huron Brewing Company, fifteen miles from Wisconsin Dells, "400" Bike Trail, House on the Rock

NOTES: The Corner Pub is situated in a cozy corner storefront on Reedsburg's Main Street. The spot has been a tavern since before Prohibition. It is the oldest continuously operating tavern in Sauk County. After operating under the same family ownership for over sixty-five years, it was sold in 1996 and became a sports bar. Pete Peterson had been running a restaurant and brewery further down the road. He bought the corner location in 2001 to move his business into downtown.

The Corner Pub feels like what it is: a small-town tavern in a rural community. It serves simple pub food along with the rural Wisconsin standards—taco Tuesday, fish fry on Friday, and prime rib on Saturday. The thing that sets it apart from other similar pubs is the two-barrel brewhouse in the basement and the homebrewed beer on tap.

Peterson began homebrewing in the 1990s, when he asked a buddy who brewed to help him make a batch of his own. He was hooked. After honing his skills at home, he decided to add homebrewed beer to his restaurant. He purchased some old industrial soup kettles from the school, retrofitted them into a brewery, and went to work. He describes his beers as "the closest thing to homebrew in a professional setting." They are made as naturally as possible, with no adjuncts and no filtering.

Das Bierhaus

ADDRESS: 120 6th Ave. West
Menomonie, WI 54751

TELEPHONE: 715–231–3230

EMAIL: bavarianbrewery@gmail.com

WEB SITE: www.dasbierhaus-wi.com

MICHAEL'S PICK: Schwarzbier: This one is as good as any I have had. The sweet malt base is complemented by light café-mocha roast. Moderate bitterness and a dry, crisp finish keep it fresh. Hints of sulfur in the background didn't detract from my enjoyment. Overall, this is a sessionable, easy-drinking black beer for those who think they don't like dark beers.

TYPE: Brewpub

DATE ESTABLISHED: 2007

OWNERS: Lee Quale and Marge Quale

BREWMASTER: Robert Wilber

BREWING SYSTEM: Seven-barrel brewhouse, unknown manufacturer

FLAGSHIP BEER: Pilsner

YEAR-ROUND BEERS: Pilsner, Dunkel, Märzen, Hefeweizen, Hefeweizen Dunkel, Schwarzbier

SEASONAL BEERS: Oktoberfest, Altbier, Kölsch, Gambrinator Doppelbock, Doppelbock Dark, Weizenbock

SPECIAL RELEASES: Rauchbier, Roggenbier, Dunkel Weizenbock, and others

TOURS: By request

BEER TO GO: Growlers

FOOD: Authentic German fare: schnitzel, fleischkäse, German sausages. Most items available as entrée or sandwich-basket options.

AMENITIES: Parking lot in back, Mug Club benefits

PUB HOURS: Monday–Thursday: 4:00 P.M. to 2:00 A.M.; Friday and Saturday: 11:00 A.M. to 2:30 A.M.; Sunday: 11:00 A.M. to 2:00 A.M.

NOTES: At Das Bierhaus they have a saying: "Import the brewmaster, not the beer." And that is indeed what they have done. Brewmaster Robert Wilber followed the traditional path of brewers in Germany and completed his extensive training at the famed Weihenstephaner School in Munich. Although he has been brewing in the United States for several years, he stays true to his German roots, brewing traditional lager styles that conform to the Reinheitsgebot, or German beer-purity laws.

That Wilber knows his stuff is immediately apparent in the beers, which, coupled with great traditional German food, make Das Bierhaus a hidden gem. These are clean, crisp lagers, made the way I remember them from many trips to Germany. The highly rated pilsner is sharply bitter with just the slightest hint of sulfur. The dunkel is smooth and toasty with a dry finish.

The German word *gemütlich* is difficult to translate. It means, roughly, cordial, welcoming, and comfortable. It could easily be applied to Das Bierhaus. The spare décor and small seating area aren't fancy, but they are inviting. The long bar seems like the kind of place where you could strike up a conversation with a stranger. German music plays over the sound system, and the one television over the bar only comes on during Packers games.

The food is well-done traditional German fare. Authentic German meats are procured from a butcher in Wheeling, Illinois. Co-owner Lee Quale boasts that the brats are the finer grind, less salty German style, instead of the typical Wisconsin brat. Dishes like schnitzel, fleischkäse, and Kasseler rippchen are available as entrées or in sandwich baskets.

Dave's BrewFarm

ADDRESS: 2470 Wilson St.
Wilson, WI 54027
TELEPHONE: 612–432–8130
EMAIL: davesbrewfarm@gmail.com
WEB SITE: www.brewfarm.com
MICHAEL'S PICK: Matacabras: A perfect example of Dave Anderson's style-confounding brew philosophy. Is this a Belgian barleywine? An English dubel? Or maybe an Anglo-Belgian imperial dunkel? Whatever you want to call it, it offers toasty bread-crust maltiness with layers of candied fruit flavors, brown sugar, and Belgian

yeast character. An herbal/spicy bite from rye malt and hops keeps it crisp.

TYPE: Brewery
DATE ESTABLISHED: 2009
OWNERS: Dave Anderson and Pam Dixon
BREWMASTER: Dave Anderson
BREWING SYSTEM: Seven-barrel "eclectic assemblage" brewhouse
FLAGSHIP BEER: BrewFarm Select
YEAR-ROUND BEERS: BrewFarm Select, Matacabras
SEASONAL BEERS: None
SPECIAL RELEASES: Frequent draft-only releases at the brewery include Mocha Diabla, AuBexxx, McAnderson, Lupulus Noir, and many others.
TOURS: Saturday open-house sessions at the brewery. Check Web site or Facebook page for times and dates.
FOOD: None
BEER TO GO: Growlers
AMENITIES: Free parking, taproom
PUB HOURS: None
NEARBY ATTRACTIONS: Das Bierhaus, Lucette Brewing Company, Rush River Brewing Company, sixty miles from the Twin Cities

NOTES: Dave's Brewfarm sits atop a ridge in the rolling rural landscape of western Wisconsin. Standing there, one feels far removed from everything. Wilson, the nearest town, is home to only about 180 people. A big sign set with heavy timbers at the top of the drive is almost the only thing that distinguishes the brewery from the farmsteads that dot the countryside around it.

The brewery is built on an ethos of sustainability. According to owner/brewer Dave Anderson, "We're not just a brewery. I call it a demonstration project." The brewery generates power from the wind and uses a geothermal unit for heating and cooling. The building is plumbed for solar/thermal panels that will eventually be installed on the roof. Additionally, the drains all lead to a five-thousand-gallon tank for reusing gray water. The idea of sustainability is literally built into the business.

Anderson says of his business, "This is a true farmhouse brewery. We are on thirty-eight acres. We grow our own hops and other supplemental herbs. I've got a neighbor across the way who wants to do some heirloom barleys." The rustic red building housing the brewery is a live/work space with living quarters upstairs and the aptly titled "labrewatory" downstairs.

Anderson doesn't brew to style. He takes his influence from the Belgian brewers' willingness to experiment. He employs herbs, spices, and other exotic ingredients, as well as unusual yeast selection, to craft intriguing concoctions that aren't easily pigeonholed into conventional categories. But it's not about pushing the limits as far as they can go. Another trait that Anderson takes from the Belgians is a desire for drinkability. He makes beers that challenge expectations but don't necessarily tax sensibilities.

Hudson Brewing Company

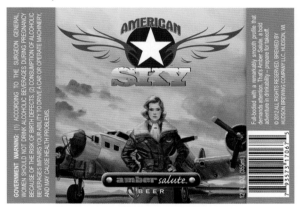

ADDRESS: 1510 Swasey St.
Hudson, WI 54016
TELEPHONE: 651-503-3165
EMAIL:
molly@americanskybeer.com
WEB SITE: www.americanskybeer.com
MICHAEL'S PICK: Dry Stout: This taproom-only specialty falls somewhere between a dry Irish stout and an oatmeal stout. It's got the coffee roastiness and bitter finish of the former, but the silky mouthfeel and cookie-dough taste of the latter. Its light body and low alcohol allow for several pints.
TYPE: Brewery
DATE ESTABLISHED: 2012
OWNERS: Greg Harris and Molly Harris
BREWMASTER: Greg Harris
BREWING SYSTEM: Fifteen-barrel Newlands Systems brewhouse
FLAGSHIP BEERS: American Sky Tailgunner Gold, American Sky Amber Salute, American Sky IPA
YEAR-ROUND BEERS: American Sky Tailgunner Gold, American Sky Amber Salute, American Sky IPA
SEASONAL BEERS: Planned
SPECIAL RELEASES: Dry Stout, Pumpkin Ale, Vanilla Oatmeal Stout, Creamed Ale, Double Pilsner
TOURS: By appointment
BEER TO GO: Growlers and package
FOOD: None
AMENITIES: Parking lot, taproom, brewery available for private events
PUB HOURS: Thursday–Friday: 3:00 to 7:00 P.M.; Saturday: noon to 7:00 P.M.; Sunday: 11:00 A.M. to 5:00 P.M.
NEARBY ATTRACTIONS: Boating and water activities on the St. Croix River, hiking and cross-country skiing in nearby state parks, Afton Ski Area, Octagon House Museum, shops, restaurants, and antique stores in nearby Stillwater, Minnesota, thirty miles from the Twin Cities

NOTES: Greg and Molly Harris take great pride in being American. Service to country runs deep in both of their families. Greg's own time in the army was a continuation of a family tradition that goes all the

way back to World War I. They feel deeply and speak passionately about the sacrifices that built the nation.

This patriotism infuses their brand. The American Sky name and the romanticized images of World War II bombers on the labels reflect this. Mottos like "let freedom pour" and "bold as America herself" are a further indication of what motivates the couple. For them, building the brewery is as much about realizing the American dream as it is about making beer.

Greg and Molly see this ethos reflected in the type of beers they make as well. They aren't out for extremes. American Sky beers are brewed for wider appeal. They reflect the tastes of the local market, with an emphasis on malt character and low hop bitterness. As Greg himself describes them, they are easy-drinking crossover beers—the kind of beers that might lure dedicated drinkers of macro lagers over to fuller-flavored brews. A small pilot-batch system though allows for occasional flights of fancy in taproom-only beers.

The taproom has an aeronautic theme that stems from Greg's love of recreational flying. The metal top on the circular bar is shaped like an airplane wing. Images of airplanes adorn the walls.

Jacob Leinenkugel Brewing Company

ADDRESS: 124 E. Elm St.
Chippewa Falls, WI 54729
TELEPHONE: 888-534-6437
EMAIL: leinielodge@leinenkugels.com
WEB SITE: www.leinie.com
MICHAEL'S PICK: Creamy Dark: Creamy Dark is aptly named. Its velvety mouthfeel enhances its ease of drinking. Smooth and chocolaty with only light roast bitterness, it falls somewhere between a Munich-style dunkel and a stout. It would go equally well on a cold winter night or a hot summer day.

TYPE: Brewery

DATE ESTABLISHED: 1867

OWNERS: MillerCoors

BREWMASTER: John Buhrow

BREWING SYSTEM: 165-barrel Ziemann brewhouse

FLAGSHIP BEER: Leinenkugel Original

YEAR-ROUND BEERS: Original, Light, Sunset Wheat, Berry Weiss, Red Lager, Creamy Dark

SEASONAL BEERS: Summer Shandy, Oktoberfest, Fireside Nut Brown, 1888 Bock, Berry Shandy

SPECIAL RELEASES: Leinenkugel's Limited, Big Eddy Series including Russian Imperial Stout, Double India Pale Ale, Scotch Ale, and Baltic Porter

TOURS: Monday–Thursday and Saturday every half hour from 9:30 A.M. to 4:00 P.M.; Friday every half hour from 9:30 A.M. to 6:30 P.M.; Sunday every half hour from 11:30 A.M. to 3:00 P.M.

BEER TO GO: None

AMENITIES: Parking lot, Leinie Lodge gift shop and tasting area

LEINE LODGE HOURS: Monday–Saturday: 9:00 A.M. to 5:00 P.M.; Sunday: 11:00 A.M. to 4:00 P.M.

NEARBY ATTRACTIONS: Hyde Center for the Arts, Irvine Park and Zoo, Old Abe Bicycle Trail, pick-your-own seasonal fruits and apples at Connell's Orchard or John McIlquham Orchard, Autumn Harvest Winery, the Cook-Rutledge Mansion, summer and winter recreational opportunities in nearby state and county parks

NOTES: The Jacob Lienenkugel brewery in Chippewa Falls is a strange time warp. Most of the buildings date from the 1890s. The original well house covering the Big Eddy spring that once provided the company's brewing water still stands to one side of the old brewhouse. From the outside, the experience is one of stepping back 140 years into Wisconsin brewing history.

Once you step inside the brewery, it's a different story. Squeezed uncomfortably inside the nineteenth-century building is a state-of-the-art twenty-first-century brewery. Gleaming stainless-steel vessels are crammed into tiny rooms meant to hold much smaller vessels. Intricate pathways of pipe move beer up and down in a multifloor brewing sequence that defies easy comprehension. The new packaging house, the most recent addition, holds an impressively massive bottling line and pasteurization system.

Leinenkugel is one of America's oldest breweries. In 1988, the company was purchased by Miller Brewing Company in a deal that many thought would com-

promise the brewery's product and independence. This has not proven to be the case. A direct descendent of founder Jacob Leinenkugel still serves as president, and the company operates with its own board of directors. The beer has not changed as a result of the merger.

Leinenkugel makes primarily lagers that run straight down the middle of the road. There is nothing wrong with that. Their beers are of consistently high quality, and there are some full-flavored standouts among them. The limited-release Big Eddy ales are outstanding examples.

Lazy Monk Brewing

ADDRESS: 320 Putnam St. Eau Claire, WI 54703

TELEPHONE: 715–271–5887

EMAIL: info@lazymonkbrewing.com

WEB SITE: www.lazymonkbrewing.com

MICHAEL'S PICK: Bohemian Pilsner: As a native Czech, Leos Frank knows pilsner, and he brews a pretty decent one. The characteristic balance of bready-sweet malt and bitterness is there. So is the perfumed character of Saaz hops.

TYPE: Brewery

DATE ESTABLISHED: 2011

OWNER: Leos Frank

BREWMASTER: Leos Frank

BREWING SYSTEM: 5.5-barrel custom-built electric brewhouse

FLAGSHIP BEERS: Bohemian Pilsner, Bohemian Dark Lager

YEAR-ROUND BEERS: Bohemian Pilsner, Bohemian Dark Lager

SEASONAL BEERS: Märzen, Mai Bock, Oktoberfest Lager, Baltic Porter, Winter Lager, Bock

SPECIAL RELEASES: Regular special releases in the taproom

TOURS: By request

BEER TO GO: Growlers and kegs

FOOD: None

AMENITIES: Parking lot, taproom

PUB HOURS: Wednesday–Friday: 5:00 to 8:00 P.M.

NEARBY ATTRACTIONS: Chippewa River Bike Trail, performances at the Eau Claire Regional Arts Center/State Theatre, Chippewa Valley Museum, Children's Museum, Paul Bunyan Logging Camp Museum

NOTES: Leos Frank quit drinking beer after he moved to the United States from what was then still Czechoslovakia. Accustomed to the full-flavored lagers of his homeland, he couldn't understand why Americans thought of the light, premium lagers produced by the big breweries as "heavy" beers. He thought, "Why keep drinking beer if I'm going to be disappointed every time?"

But then someone told him about homebrewing. He picked up the hobby and quickly became obsessed. Making more beer than he could consume, he kept his neighbors happy with a steady stream of homemade brews. Like many homebrewers, he considered opening a brewery, but the risk didn't seem worth leaving his steady job and benefits.

When he was laid off from that job, the opportunity seemed too good to pass up. He designed a brewery that was really just a scaled-up homebrew system, had it fabricated by a local metal shop, and Lazy Monk was born.

Frank focuses on producing the kind of lagers he enjoyed in the Old Country. In another nod to European practice, he uses returnable growlers for his packaged product. Consumers can buy the growlers in stores and return them for a deposit. It's less expensive and better for the environment.

Lucette Brewing Company

ADDRESS: 910 Hudson Rd.
Menomonie, WI 54751
TELEPHONE: 715–233–2055
EMAIL: info@lucettebrewing.com
WEB SITE:
www.lucettebrewing.com
MICHAEL'S PICK: Shining Dawn
Golden Belgian Ale: A simply made beer with many flavors but only 5 percent ABV, I call this a sessionable version of the Belgian strong golden style. Sweet pilsner malt is balanced by herbal, black-licorice hop flavors and a dry finish. The bitterness is fairly assertive, despite the brewer's claim of a mere 15 IBU. A proprietary yeast strain yields subtle Belgian banana ester character.
TYPE: Brewery
DATE ESTABLISHED: 2010
OWNERS: Michael Wilson and Tim Schletty
BREWMASTER: Jon Christiansen
BREWING SYSTEM: Fifteen-barrel Specific Mechanical brewhouse
FLAGSHIP BEER: Easy Rider Pale Ale
YEAR-ROUND BEERS: Slow Hand Stout, Shining Dawn Golden Belgian Ale, Easy Rider Pale Ale, The Farmer's Daughter
SEASONAL BEERS: None
SPECIAL RELEASES: Double Dawn

TOURS: Saturdays at 2:00 P.M.
BEER TO GO: None
FOOD: None
AMENITIES: Parking lot
PUB HOURS: None
NEARBY ATTRACTIONS: Das Bierhaus, Red Cedar Bike Trail, Jacob Leinenkugel Brewing Company, University of Wisconsin–Stout campus

NOTES: If enthusiasm is a requirement for a new brewery's success, then the guys at Lucette should have a bright future. The leadership trio is electrified as they describe what lies ahead for them. The energy is contagious.

Their diverse backgrounds should also serve them well in the competitive craft-beer industry. Michael Wilson worked for a beer distributor after college. Tim Schletty comes from retail sales. Brewer Jon Christiansen started his career interning at the De Koninck brewery in Belgium. He completed the diploma course at the Siebel Institute before working professionally at several breweries.

They are after sessionable complexity in their product. They want Lucette beers to have broad appeal in the regional market, but they also want to nudge that market toward more full-flavored beers. They succeed at both. Each of their three launch beers showcases one ingredient—malt, hops, or yeast. Starting with classic styles, they give them just the slightest tweak, such as adding a Belgian yeast strain, to bring nuance and depth.

The brewery sits on the banks of the Red Cedar River, right next to the Red Cedar Bike Trail.

Moosejaw Pizza and Dells Brewing Co.

ADDRESS:
110 Wisconsin Dells Parkway South
Wisconsin Dells, WI 53965
TELEPHONE: 608–254–1122
EMAIL: info@dellsmoosejaw.com
WEB SITE: www.dellsmoosejaw.com
MICHAEL'S PICK: Pilsner: Jamie Martin's pilsner is a malty Bohemian style that verges on a Munich helles. Grainy-sweet pilsner malt is balanced by relatively moderate bitterness. Spicy European hops give anise notes and just the slightest hint of citrus.
TYPE: Brewpub
DATE ESTABLISHED: 2002
OWNER: Private ownership group
BREWMASTER: Jamie Martin

BREWING SYSTEM: Fifteen-barrel Bohemian
   Breweries brewhouse

FLAGSHIP BEER: Rustic Red

YEAR-ROUND BEERS: Golden Lager, Honey Ale,
   Raspberry Creme Ale, Kilbourn Hop Ale, Dells Pilsner,
   Rustic Red

SEASONAL BEERS: Blond Bock, Dunkel, Milk Stout,
   Oktoberfest, Winter Warmer

SPECIAL RELEASES: American IPA, Cherry Ale, Delton
   Dark Ale, Smoked Porter, Stand Rock Bock, Apple Ale,
   Betty's Black Ale, Wyatt's Barleywine, Schmidt's Pale
   Ale No. 5, Imperial Stout, Belgian Golden, and others

TOURS: By appointment

BEER TO GO: Growlers

FOOD: Large selection of family-friendly favorites: pizza,
   burgers and sandwiches, steaks and seafood, build-
   your-own pasta dishes

AMENITIES: Parking lot, full bar, family-friendly

PUB HOURS: Daily: 11:00 A.M. to midnight

NEARBY ATTRACTIONS: Port Huron Brewing
   Company, The Corner Pub, Wisconsin Dells attractions,
   water parks, theme parks, Dells boat tours, Wisconsin
   Dells Ducks, Tommy Bartlett Thrill Show, Hiking and
   Cross Country Skiing, Tunnels of Moosejaw

NOTES: Jamie Martin is one of only a few women
brewers in the industry. She's the only woman in
charge of a brewery in Wisconsin. While she says that
it may have made it harder for her to get a foot in the
door at the beginning, now that she's established,
being a woman has some advantages. "I get a lot of
press," she says.

Martin is a process-oriented brewer; she gets ex-
cited learning about new equipment and processes.
She loves trying out new fermentation regimes or fig-
uring out ways to fix things when they break. With a
background in biotech, she geeks out on lab analysis.
This attention to process allows her to be relaxed in
the brewery. She's learned over the years how to deal
with whatever issues might arise.

Moosejaw's transient, tourist clientele gives Martin some latitude in how she brews. With very few
regulars, she isn't tied to certain flavor profiles. If
a particular hop variety is in short supply, she can
switch to another. But it also means that she has to
keep things fairly tame. The majority of customers
aren't beer connoisseurs. Most of her beers lean to the
sweet side to accommodate palates unaccustomed
to bolder and more bitter flavors. But she does get to
spread her wings on occasion, with beers like Smoked
Porter or a hoppy imperial stout fermented with a
Belgian yeast strain.

The Moosejaw dining room feels like a Wisconsin
hunting lodge. The log-cabin construction is adorned
with trophy animal heads, and antler chandeliers
hang from the high ceiling. It's a great place to take
the kids after a day at the water park.

Northwoods Brewpub and Grill

ADDRESS:
   3560 Oakwood Mall Dr.
   Eau Claire, WI 54701

TELEPHONE: 715-552-0510

EMAIL: info@northwoodsbrewpub.com

WEB SITE: www.northwoodsbrewpub.com

MICHAEL'S PICK: Kelly's Stout: This one starts out
   sweet and finishes dry and roasty. In between there is a
   play of caramel, chocolate, and roast with light earthy/
   herbal hops to round it out. It's too light and dry to
   stand up to dessert, but it works well as a stand-alone
   beer or with one of the Norwegian lefse wraps on the
   menu.

TYPE: Brewpub

DATE ESTABLISHED: 1997

OWNER: Jerry Bechard

BREWMASTER: Tim Kelly

BREWING SYSTEM: Seven-barrel DME brewhouse

FLAGSHIP BEER: Floppin' Crappie

YEAR-ROUND BEERS: Mouthy Muskie Light, Kelly's
   Stout, White Weasel Light Ale, Half Moon Gold,
   Bumbl'n Bubbas Buzz'n Brew, Prickly Pike's Pilsner,
   Floppin' Crappie, Whitetail Wheat, Birchwood Pale Ale,
   Red Cedar Red, Lil' Bandit Brown Ale, Poplar Porter,
   Walter's Beer

SEASONAL BEERS: Irish Red Ale, Dunkel Weizen,
   Ripplin' Red Raspberry Wheat, Oktoberfest Lager, IPA

SPECIAL RELEASES: Occasional

TOURS: By request

BEER TO GO: Growlers, kegs, party pigs, and package

FOOD: Norwegian-themed items from the Norske Nook,
   breakfast, lunch, and dinner

AMENITIES: Parking lot, happy-hour specials, full bar,
   Mug Club, pool tables, live music on Thursday nights

PUB HOURS: Daily: 7:00 A.M. to 2:00 A.M.

NEARBY ATTRACTIONS: Jacob Leinenkugel Brewing
   Company, Lazy Monk Brewing Company, Chippewa
   River Bike Trail, Chaos Water Park, Children's Museum
   of Eau Claire, Country Jam USA in July, Paul Bunyan
   Logging Camp Museum, nearby cross-country ski trails

NOTES: When Tim Kelly was approached about becoming head brewer at Jerry Bechard's new brewpub,
he was managing a farm. At the time he had no brewing experience. But the idea was intriguing enough

that he went off to Chicago's Siebel Institute to learn the craft and then interned at a now-defunct brewpub in Madison. After all these years, he still enjoys making fine beers tailored to the western Wisconsin palate.

He doesn't make extreme beers. Eau Claire is a light-lager-drinking town, so Tim crafts balanced and drinkable beers that offer full flavor without pushing the envelope too far. There are always fourteen house beers on tap, so there is something to appeal to everyone.

All of the beers share a crisp, dry character and sharp bitterness that I found appealing. However, there is a sameness to them, a house character that could stand a little shaking up.

The ambience is cozy, like a North Woods log-cabin lodge. It's a good place to bring the family. The food is from the Norske Nook, a small Wisconsin chain sometimes described as "a Norwegian Perkins." The menu is full of traditional Scandinavian dishes like meatballs and lefse, a Norwegian flatbread. I had a meatball lefse wrap that was smothered in gravy and seemed a bit bland, but bland is kind of the nature of the beast with Scandinavian fare. If you crave basic meat-and-potatoes kind of food, this is the place. Burgers, pizza, and other non-Norwegian dishes are also available.

Pearl Street Brewery

ADDRESS: 1401 St. Andrew St.
La Crosse, WI 54603
TELEPHONE: 608–784–4832
EMAIL: info@pearlstreetbrewery.com
WEB SITE: www.pearlstreetbrewery.com
MICHAEL'S PICK: DTB Brown Ale: Chocolate, toast, molasses, and brown sugar lead the way in this classic English brown ale. It's light-bodied but full of flavor. Medium bitterness keeps it balanced, and light grassy hop flavors add depth. This is a sessionable brown that would go down equally well on a hot summer day or a crisp fall afternoon.
TYPE: Brewery
DATE ESTABLISHED: 1999
OWNERS: Anthony Katchever and Joseph Katchever
BREWMASTER: Joseph Katchever
BREWING SYSTEM: Thirty-barrel Newlands Systems brewhouse
FLAGSHIP BEER: DTB Brown Ale
YEAR-ROUND BEERS: DTB Brown Ale, Pearl Street Pale Ale, El Hefe Bavarian Style Hefeweizen, That's What I'm Talkin' 'bout Organic Rolled Oat Stout!, Dankenstein Imperial India Pale Ale

SEASONAL BEERS: Harvest Ale, Evil Doppelganger Double Mai Bock, Tamboise, Smokin' Hemp Porter
SPECIAL RELEASES: Proven Performance Pale Ale, Cherry Stout, Bedwetter Barleywine, Holy Matrimony Altbier, Rubber Mills Pils, Hochey Brown Apple Ale, bourbon-barrel-aged selections, and others
TOURS: Saturday: noon to 5:00 P.M., and by appointment
BEER TO GO: Growlers and package
FOOD: Free wings on Tuesdays
AMENITIES: Parking lot, taproom, Friday-night happy hours with live music, Free-wheelin' Wednesdays offer one free beer to patrons arriving by bike, free wireless internet, available for private parties
PUB HOURS: Tuesday–Friday: 4:00 to 8:00 P.M.; Saturday: noon to 5:00 P.M.
NEARBY ATTRACTIONS: City Brewing Company, Mississippi River cruises, Mt. La Crosse Ski Area, Annual Oktoberfest, Children's Museum of La Crosse, golf, outdoor activities at Perrot and Merrick State Parks, Great River Road Bicycle Trail, river activities, including boating, fishing, and kayaking

NOTES: There's nothing fancy about Pearl Street Brewery. Housed in the raw industrial space of a nineteenth-century rubber mill, the tasting room and brewery have a distinctly blue-collar feel. The brewhouse stands behind the bar like some steaming machine from the building's past. Worn tables and simple stools make the taproom area resemble an employee break room.

From the beers to the people who make them, this down-to-earth, grassroots character is what Pearl Street is all about. "We want to be eye-to-eye with the customer," says Tami Plourde, Chief Beer Ambassador. "We're very Wisconsin, blue-collar. We aren't hoity-toity people here. We make beer and sling it out the door."

The beer at Pearl Street isn't about rare ingredients or obtuse styles. They are focused on making tangible and accessible beers that will appeal to a wide range of drinkers, from the novice to the beer nerd. While some breweries try to keep twenty or thirty different beers going, the Pearl Street brewers concentrate on making a few styles well.

Port Huron Brewing Company

ADDRESS: 805 Business Park Rd.
Wisconsin Dells, WI 53965
TELEPHONE: 608–253–0340
EMAIL: porthuronbeer@gmail.com
WEB SITE: www.porthuronbeer.com
MICHAEL'S PICK: Honey Blond: This reminds me of a light Czech pilsner, with a delicate balance of bitter

and sweet, full-flavored but easy to drink. Toasty flavors of Vienna malt add character and complexity. Gentle pine and citrus hops along with a dry finish make it refreshing. It's a great patio brew.

TYPE: Brewery
DATE ESTABLISHED: 2012
OWNER: Tanner Brethorst
BREWMASTER: Tanner Brethorst
BREWING SYSTEM: Twenty-hectoliter Specific Mechanical brewhouse
FLAGSHIP BEER: Honey Blond
YEAR-ROUND BEERS: Honey Blonde, Porter, Hefeweizen, Alt
SEASONAL BEERS: Planned
SPECIAL RELEASES: Planned
TOURS: Saturdays. Check Web site for times and dates.
BEER TO GO: Growlers
FOOD: None
AMENITIES: Parking lot, taproom
PUB HOURS: Friday: 3:00 to 9:00 P.M.; Saturday: noon to 9:00 P.M. Hours subject to change; please check Web site for updated hours.
NEARBY ATTRACTIONS: Moosejaw Pizza and Dells Brewing Co., The Corner Pub, Wisconsin Dells attractions, water parks, theme parks, Dells boat tours, Wisconsin Dells Ducks, Tommy Bartlett Thrill Show, hiking, cross-country skiing, Tunnels of Moosejaw

NOTES: The Port Huron from which the brewery takes its name is not a place but a tractor. The 1918 Port Huron steam tractor has been in Tanner Brethorst's family for sixty years, and it is central to the brewery's identity. The taproom has an aura of early twentieth-century industry, with original blueprints from the Port Huron manufacturer adorning the walls and a small steam engine to power the belt-driven ceiling fans. Brethorst has plans for an annual Harvest Ale, using the tractor to reap and winnow grain grown by nearby farmers. He would like to brew a "Steam" beer, but he has to find a way to work around Anchor Brewing Company's trademark on the term.

Brethorst first became interested in beer in 1999, when his father started a running-and-beer group. With that group, he sampled beers from the bourgeoning Wisconsin craft-beer scene and went on occasional brewery tours. He started homebrewing in 2002 while still in college. After a summer job at Tyranena Brewing Company, he was hooked. He went to brewing school at the Siebel Institute and worked for several years at Lake Louie Brewing and Capital Brewery before members of his family approached him about starting his own brewery.

Port Huron is a family enterprise, says Brethorst. Every investor is either a relative or old family friend. He's a one-man show on most days, but he relies heavily on the help of family members who volunteer their skills in carpentry, bookkeeping, and mechanical maintenance to reduce some of the burden and keep things running smoothly. This help allows him to remain focused on what is most important to him: producing a wide range of high-quality beers that are consistent from batch to batch.

Rush River Brewing Company

ADDRESS: 990 Antler Ct.
River Falls, WI 54022
TELEPHONE: 715–426–2054
EMAIL: Form on Web site
WEB SITE: www.rushriverbeer.com
MICHAEL'S PICK: The Unforgiven Amber Ale: A solid midwestern amber ale, this beer forefronts smooth, sweet caramel malt. Hop bitterness balances but isn't as aggressive as West Coast examples of the style. Bright, citrusy hops fill in the high notes on top. The Unforgiven is a go-to brew when I want an easy-drinking beer that won't tax my senses.
TYPE: Brewery
DATE ESTABLISHED: 2004
OWNERS: Dan Chang and Nick Anderson
BREWMASTERS: Dan Chang and Nick Anderson
BREWING SYSTEM: Nineteen-barrel DME mash tun, twenty-two-barrel DME brew kettle
FLAGSHIP BEER: The Unforgiven Amber Ale
YEAR-ROUND BEERS: Lost Arrow Porter, The Unforgiven Amber Ale, Small Axe Golden Ale, Bubblejack India Pale Ale, Double Bubble Imperial IPA
SEASONAL BEERS: Winter Warmer, Über Alt, Lyndale Brown Ale, Nevermore Chocolate Oatmeal Stout
SPECIAL RELEASES: Planned
TOURS: By appointment
BEER TO GO: Growlers
FOOD: None
AMENITIES: Parking lot, small sampling bar
PUB HOURS: None
NEARBY ATTRACTIONS: University of Wisconsin–River Falls, Kansas City Chiefs summer training camp, summer and winter outdoor activities at Willow River Falls State Park, kayaking on the Kinnickinnic River, thirty-five miles from the Twin Cities

NOTES: Dan Chang and Nick Anderson love session beers, and session beers are the foundation of their business. Their core lineup consists primarily of middle-of-the-road, easy-to-drink ales. "Nothing to blow your socks off," in Chang's words. But Rush River beers are middle-of-the-road only when compared to the beer world's extremes. Rest assured that these are full-flavored and satisfying brews, well suited to the palates of beginners and beer connoisseurs alike.

Anderson and Chang are natives of the upper Midwest, hailing from Minneapolis and Milwaukee, respectively. They met while working together at Mac and Jack's Brewery in Seattle, starting as keg washers and eventually working their way up to head brewers. The desire to run a microbrewery of their own brought them back to the Midwest in 2000, where Anderson tended bar while Chang took a job on the brewing staff at Summit in St. Paul.

When they opened the brewery in 2004, there weren't many craft beers available in the region. With the local palate not yet developed, the pair started out making beers that were suited to their market. They have worked slowly and steadily in the years since to develop that market and achieve success. Although production has expanded year after year, they sometimes can't keep up with demand. The beer selection has expanded as well. Year-round offerings now include a not-so-sessionable 9 percent Double IPA. A hi-test Sticke Altbier and an 8 percent chocolate oatmeal stout have become regular seasonal releases.

Sand Creek Brewing Company

ADDRESS: 320 Pierce St.
Black River Falls, WI 54615
TELEPHONE: 715–284–7553
EMAIL: Form on Web site
WEB SITE: www.sandcreekbrewing.com
MICHAEL'S PICK: One Planet Ale: This is a flavorful multigrain session ale made with mostly Wisconsin ingredients. A blend of wheat, oats, rye, and barley provide a lightly sweet, honey-tinged malt profile. Tasty orange citrus flavors swirl through the nose and palate. Listening back to my interview, I gave up counting the times that I said, "I could drink a lot of this."
TYPE: Brewery
DATE ESTABLISHED: 1999
OWNERS: Jim Wiesender and Todd Krueger
BREWMASTER: Todd Krueger
BREWING SYSTEM: Twenty-barrel JV Northwest brewhouse
FLAGSHIP BEERS: Sand Creek Hard Lemonade, Oscar's Chocolate Oatmeal Stout
YEAR-ROUND BEERS: Sand Creek Golden Ale, One Planet Ale, Sand Creek English Style Special Ale, Wild Ride IPA, Woody's Wheat, Oscar's Chocolate Oatmeal

Stout, Badger Porter, Cranberry Special Ale, Pioneer Black River Red, Groovy Brew, Sand Creek Hard Lemonade
SEASONAL BEERS: Cranberry Special Ale, Black River Red, Oktoberfest
SPECIAL RELEASES: Sand Creek Reserve Series: Wisconsin Scottish Ale, Ulrich's Doppelbock, Double Chocolate Oatmeal Stout, and others
TOURS: Saturday at 3:00 P.M. From May through September, tours are also available on Saturday from noon to 5:00 P.M. Other times available by appointment.
BEER TO GO: Kegs and package
FOOD: None
AMENITIES: Small parking lot, free street parking, tasting room
PUB HOURS: Friday: 3:00 to 5:00 P.M.; Saturday: noon to 5:00 P.M.
NEARBY ATTRACTIONS: Majestic Pines Casino, outdoor activities including hiking, biking, canoeing, skiing, snowmobiling, hunting, and fishing, Jackson County Forest, and Black River State Forest

NOTES: Sand Creek has the reputation of being the craft-beer contract brewer for the upper Midwest. Indeed, they make beer for a number of other entities that don't yet have the means or intention to invest in a brewery of their own. They have been the beer-making springboard for several regional brewers that later went on to build their own facilities, such as Fulton and Liftbridge in Minnesota and Half Acre in Chicago.

But Sand Creek isn't just a contract brewer. They produce an extensive and popular brand of their own. Brewer Todd Krueger has won prestigious brewing awards, including two gold medals at the World Beer Cup. These beers have been successful enough that the company is considering expansion, building a separate fifty-barrel production facility to produce their own beers while keeping the current one for contract clients and specialty beers.

The Sand Creek lineup of beers features a wide variety of styles from light golden ale to a gargantuan 12 percent ABV doppelbock, all of which are clean, complex, and well made.

The building that houses Sand Creek is itself a part of Wisconsin brewing history. It was originally the home of the Oberbolz Brewery. Founded in 1856 by Swiss immigrants, it was the first large-scale brewing operation in western Wisconsin.

Valkyrie Brewing Company

ADDRESS: 234 W. Dallas St.
Dallas, WI 54733
TELEPHONE: 715–837–1824
EMAIL: brewer@valkyriebrewery.com
WEB SITE: www.valkyriebrewery.com
MICHAEL'S PICK: Rubee: Rubee is an easy-drinking Märzen-style lager with an appropriately malt-forward profile. Toasty caramel malt is balanced by moderate bitterness and subtle spicy hop flavors from European hops. It finishes reasonably dry with some lingering bitterness.
TYPE: Brewery
DATE ESTABLISHED: 1994
OWNERS: Randy Lee and Ann Lee
BREWMASTER: Randy Lee
BREWING SYSTEM: Six-barrel converted dairy-tank brewhouse
FLAGSHIP BEER: Rubee
YEAR-ROUND BEERS: Rubee, War Hammer, Dragon Blade
SEASONAL BEERS: Velvet Green, Supernova, Night Wolf, Lime Twist, Abbey Normal, Whispering Embers, Blaze Orange, Crimson Wonder, Hot Chocolate, Golden Horn, Big Swede, Invader
SPECIAL RELEASES: Berserk Barleywine
TOURS: Saturdays at 1:00 P.M. or by appointment
BEER TO GO: Growlers
FOOD: None
AMENITIES: Free street parking, taproom
PUB HOURS: Hours change seasonally. Check Web site.
NEARBY ATTRACTIONS: Pine Crest Golf Course, Barron County Historical Society Pioneer Village Museum, fishing and boating on the Chetek chain of lakes, ATV and snowmobile trails, bike trails, trout fishing, hiking on the Ice Age Trail

NOTES: Valkyrie Brewing Company began life as Viking Brewing Company. In 2011 they sold the trademark to an Icelandic brewery of the same name that was hoping to start distribution in the United States. That set off a yearlong period of reconceptualizing and rebranding. In essence, after seventeen years in the business, the Lees had the opportunity to start over again. As Ann Lee puts it, "There are not a lot of times in your life where you get to say, 'I'm going to be somebody else now, but I like this part of me, so I'm going to keep that.'" She literally dreamed up the name Valkyrie in the middle of the night. She has been having a great time ever since creating the story to go along with it.

The brewery has been a family affair from the beginning. When Randy and Ann Lee met, they were both looking to get back to their small-town Wisconsin roots. They also wanted to do something that they could work on together. The limited opportunities of small-town life meant that they would have to create that thing for themselves. Randy was already making beer at home, so a brewery seemed like a good way to go. Their two children were enlisted to help with bottling, and they now have an interest in continuing with the business after college.

Visiting Valkyrie, I felt a connection to the brewing history of the region. From the small-town location to the old building that houses the brewery and the equipment inside, it hearkens back to a day when every town had a brewery that sold beer within a limited area around that town. The ghosts of the nineteenth century were alive in Dallas, Wisconsin, on the day I visited.

SOUTHEAST

Geneva Lake Brewing Company

ADDRESS: 750 Veterans Dr., Suite 107
Lake Geneva, WI 53147
TELEPHONE: 262–248–2539
EMAIL: info@glbrewing.com
WEB SITE:
www.genevalakebrewingcompany.com
MICHAEL'S PICK: No Wake IPA: Tangerines and tropical fruits rest comfortably on a grainy bed of caramel and biscuit. Bitterness is aggressive, but by no means tongue-scraping. The well-attenuated, dry finish allows the bitterness to linger long after swallowing.
TYPE: Brewery
DATE ESTABLISHED: 2012
OWNERS: Pat McIntosh and Jon McIntosh
BREWMASTER: Jon McIntosh
BREWING SYSTEM: Seven-barrel PUB brewhouse
FLAGSHIP BEERS: No Wake IPA, Cedar Point Amber Ale, Weekender Wheat Beer
YEAR-ROUND BEERS: No Wake IPA, Cedar Point Amber Ale, Weekender Wheat Beer, Narrows Kölsch, Black Point Oatmeal Stout
SEASONAL BEERS: Pumpkin Ale, others planned
SPECIAL RELEASES: None
TOURS: By request during taproom hours
BEER TO GO: Growlers and package
FOOD: None
AMENITIES: Small parking lot, free street parking, taproom

PUB HOURS: Thursday and Friday: 3:00 to 7:00 P.M.; Saturday and Sunday: 11:00 A.M. to 3:00 P.M.

NEARBY ATTRACTIONS: Water activities and cruises on Geneva Lake, Golf, Yerkes Observatory, Lake Geneva Theatre Company, Studio Winery, World Class Driving Adventures, Lake Geneva Canopy Tours, Dan Patch riding stable

NOTES: Lake Geneva, Wisconsin, is called by some the "Hamptons of the Midwest." Situated on the shore of Geneva Lake near the Illinois state line, it is a popular destination for tourists from Chicago and Milwaukee. The 5,500-square-acre lake is, of course, the main draw. Its entire circumference is dotted with resorts and attractions. The lake offers fishing, boating, and waterskiing in the warmer months, but ice fishing, snowmobiling, and skiing make the area a year-round draw.

Pat McIntosh is quick to point out that the brewery is named for the lake, not the town. Their beer belongs to the entire region. This tie to the lake is reflected in the beer names. Black Point is the lake's deepest spot. A jut of land projecting from the southern shore creates a place called the Narrows. He adds that while they have a strong local following, it is the tourist traffic that drives their taproom business.

Geneva Lake is a family business. The father-and-son team of Pat and Jon McIntosh do the heavy lifting. Pat runs the business, while Jon makes the beer. Pat's daughter helps out with social media and merchandising, and a daughter-in-law does the books. Anytime you visit the brewery, you are likely to see at least one of them chatting with customers or pouring beer.

Gray Brewing Company

ADDRESS: 2424 W. Court St.
Janesville, WI 53548
TELEPHONE: 608–754–5150
EMAIL: office@graybrewing.com
WEB SITE: www.graybrewing.com
MICHAEL'S PICK: Busted Knuckle Irish Ale: Light-bodied and lager-like, Busted Knuckle rides a line between dark American lager and Irish red ale. It features moderate grainy malt sweetness with subtle overtones of caramel and toast. Bitterness is reasonably high and accentuated by earthy hop flavor and a crisp, dry finish. Slight fermentation issues detract somewhat from the overall enjoyment.
TYPE: Brewery
DATE ESTABLISHED: 1856
OWNER: Robert R. Gray II

BREWMASTER: Robert R. Gray II
BREWING SYSTEM: Thirty-barrel converted dairy-tank brewhouse
FLAGSHIP BEERS: Busted Knuckle Irish Ale, Oatmeal Stout
YEAR-ROUND BEERS: Oatmeal Stout, Honey Ale, Rathskeller Amber Ale, Busted Knuckle Irish Ale, Bully Porter
SEASONAL BEERS: Rock Hard Red, Wisco Wheat
SPECIAL RELEASES: None
TOURS: No
BEER TO GO: None
FOOD: None
AMENITIES: Small parking lot
PUB HOURS: None
NEARBY ATTRACTIONS: Randy's Fun Hunter's Brewery, Rotary Botanical Garden, Robert O. Cook Memorial Arboretum, Janesville Haunted Mansion, Janesville Performing Arts Center

NOTES: Gray Brewing Company's modern beer business rose literally from ashes. The brewery was founded in 1856 by Irish immigrant Joshua Gray. It made beer and soda until 1912, when growing anti-alcohol sentiment caused the firm to cease beer production. Soda making carried the business through Prohibition and continued until an arson fire gutted the plant in 1992. Robert "Fred" Gray saw the fire as an opportunity to restore the company to its roots. When the facility was rebuilt, it included a small brewhouse for the production of beer.

Gray's beers found immediate success, taking home two gold medals at the 1994 Great American Beer Festival and a bronze at the 1996 World Beer Cup. While most of the beer is sold in Wisconsin, Gray's distributes throughout the region, including Minnesota, Illinois, Iowa, and Michigan. The company also owns the Gray's Tied House Restaurant outside Madison.

Soda still makes up a large percentage of the brewery's total output. They also do some contract brewing of soda and beer for other companies.

Public Craft Brewing Company

ADDRESS: 716 58th St.
Kenosha, WI 53140
TELEPHONE: 262–652–2739
EMAIL: info@publiccraftbrewing.com
WEB SITE: www.publiccraftbrewing.com
MICHAEL'S PICK: None available for sample
TYPE: Brewery
DATE ESTABLISHED: 2012
OWNER: Matt Geary

BREWMASTER: Matt Geary

BREWING SYSTEM: 3.5-barrel Psycho Brew brewhouse

FLAGSHIP BEERS: Public American Pale Ale, Hop in the Sack IPA, Perception Porter, K-Town Brown

YEAR-ROUND BEERS: Public American Pale Ale, Hop in the Sack IPA, Perception Porter, K-Town Brown

SEASONAL BEERS: The Tober, Getaway Wit, others planned

SPECIAL RELEASES: Stout No. 4, Barrel Aged Old Ale, others planned

TOURS: By request

BEER TO GO: Growlers

FOOD: None

AMENITIES: Free street parking, free parking in city lot across the street, taproom

PUB HOURS: Thursday and Friday: 3:30 to 8:30 P.M.; Saturday: noon to 8:30 P.M.

NEARBY ATTRACTIONS: Dinosaur Discovery Museum, Civil War Museum, Great Lakes Dragaway, Wilmont Raceway, Pringle Nature Center, Bristol Renaissance Fair, Electric Streetcar Circulator, Jelly Belly Visitor Center, forty miles from Milwaukee

NOTES: For Matt Geary, "public" is more than just a word. The name gets to the heart of what he wants his brewery to be. He's striving to revive the traditional public house, a community gathering place where locals can forge bonds over beers. The taproom is set up for this. It's got a casual, cafe-type feel with no televisions to distract from conversation. A collection of board games promotes communal activity. Donations from regulars have turned a small collection of mostly beer and brewing books into a full-fledged mini library with subjects ranging from serious literature to politics.

Geary's beers contribute to the communal experience. He brews mostly lower-alcohol, English-style session ales that showcase malt. Get him started about hops, and he's likely to jump onto his soapbox. He believes that the American obsession with super-hoppy IPAs has run its course. He calls them the "Justin Bieber of the beer world—everywhere and overdone." He aims for balance in his brews.

Geary's background is in graphic design. He still does all of brewery's design work. His homebrewing hobby, though, held his passion. When he soured on his profession, he turned to his hobby for a career change. Rather than talk about "if" he opened a brewery, Geary began to speak in terms of "when." After a course at the Siebel Institute and months of build-out he was finally able to open the front door. He says that he felt a great rush of pride to walk through that door,

a door he had walked through a million times during construction, and see a room full of people enjoying his beer.

Randy's Restaurant and Fun Hunter's Brewery

ADDRESS: 841 E. Milwaukee St. Whitewater, WI 53190

TELEPHONE: 262–473–8000

EMAIL: info@funhunters.net

WEB SITE: www.funhunters.net

MICHAEL'S PICK: Amber Lager: This Vienna-style lager is malt-forward, but beautifully balanced and crisp. Toffee and bread-crust malt leads the way with European hops offering a spicy contrast. Moderate bitterness and a dry finish make it a beer that demands seconds.

TYPE: Brewpub

DATE ESTABLISHED: 1972, brewing began in 1994

OWNERS: Pat Cruse and Randy Cruse

BREWMASTER: Randy Cruse

BREWING SYSTEM: Seven-barrel Specific Mechanical brewhouse

FLAGSHIP BEERS: Warhawk Wheat, Amber Lager

YEAR-ROUND BEERS: Warhawk Wheat, Amber Lager, IPA, Oatmeal Stout

SEASONAL BEERS: Annual Rye, Brown Ale, Oktoberfest, Maibock

SPECIAL RELEASES: Golden Pilsner, Barleywine

TOURS: By appointment

BEER TO GO: Growlers

FOOD: Reasonably priced, supper-club selections: steaks, chops, seafood, and sandwiches. Thursday-night pasta bar and Friday-night fish fry.

AMENITIES: Parking lot, full bar, private room available, catering

PUB HOURS: Tuesday–Thursday: 11:00 A.M. to 9:00 P.M.; Friday and Saturday: 11:00 A.M. to 10:00 P.M.; Sunday: 10:30 A.M. to 8:30 P.M.

NEARBY ATTRACTIONS: University of Wisconsin–Whitewater campus, cross-country biking in Kettle Moraine State Forest, camping, hiking, and cross-country skiing in Kettle Moraine State Park, water activities on Whitewater, Lauderdale, Geneva, and Delevan Lakes, Fireside Theatre in Fort Atkinson, American Players Theatre in Lake Geneva, one hour to Milwaukee and Madison

NOTES: Randy's Restaurant is a Whitewater institution. While Pat and Randy Cruse have run the place for forty years, there has been a restaurant at the location since the 1930s. Three generations have grown up there. Grandparents who came when they were kids now bring their grandchildren. It's the place where people celebrate special events, from graduation parties to wedding receptions and retirement sendoffs.

I could feel that sense of community while I was there. The bartender knew the patrons, the patrons knew each other, and Randy Cruse seemed to know everybody. The place serves up fine food in an elegant atmosphere, but with a casual attitude. It's nice enough for a reception or a fancy date, but not at all stuffy. Randy's is a popular stop for motorcyclists taking rides in Kettle Moraine State Forest.

When an arson fire in 1989 forced them to rebuild, Cruse wanted to add something special to the restaurant. He thought of brewing but was told that the lack of small-scale equipment at the time made adding a brewery a daunting task. But when the brewery boom of the 1990s began, he decided to take the leap. He took a short course at the Siebel Institute and enlisted Karl Strauss, the former Pabst brewmaster turned brewery consultant, to show him the ropes.

You won't find anything crazy at Randy's. You will find clean, well-made, and flavorful beers brewed to classic styles. As Cruse describes them, "Nothing off the wall. Nothing that will knock you off the stool after two beers." But when paired with a portabella fillet, one of the restaurant's signature steaks, they don't disappoint.

Riverside Brewery and Restaurant

ADDRESS: 255 S. Main St.
West Bend, WI 53095
TELEPHONE: 262–334–2739
EMAIL: Form on Web site
WEB SITE: www.riversidebreweryandrestaurant.com
MICHAEL'S PICK: Bee Home Soon Honey Ale: This beer took me by surprise. I expected the typical brewpub blond ale. What I got was a full-bodied, aggressively malty beer with loads of lingering honey flavor. The malt is balanced by moderate bitterness and sharp, spicy hop flavors. Topping 6 percent ABV, it is a pleasantly assertive and flavorful "light" selection.
TYPE: Brewpub
DATE ESTABLISHED: 2005
OWNERS: Wayne Kainz and Dana Kainz
BREWMASTER: Chris George
BREWING SYSTEM: Seven-barrel Walker brewhouse
FLAGSHIP BEER: Main Street Amber Ale
YEAR-ROUND BEERS: Main Street Amber Ale, Bee Home Soon Honey Ale, Dizzy Blond Weiss, Bent River Berry Weiss, Feelin' Lucky Irish Stout

SEASONAL BEERS: Don't Worry, Be Hoppy IPA, Flying Squirrel Nut Brown Ale, LuenBrew Chocolate Oatmeal Stout, Clev's Aged Old World Oktoberfest, Dubliner's Downfall Imperial Stout, Abbey Ale
SPECIAL RELEASES: Occasional bourbon-barrel-aged beers
TOURS: Most Fridays or by appointment
BEER TO GO: Growlers
FOOD: Moderately upscale versions of brewpub favorites with an emphasis on steaks and ribs
AMENITIES: Free street parking, parking in Century Bank lot across the street after 5:00, daily food specials, private rooms available, live music on Saturdays, Mug Club, family-friendly, happy-hour specials, seasonal outdoor seating on deck overlooking the river
PUB HOURS: Monday–Thursday: 11:00 A.M. to midnight; Friday and Saturday: 11:00 A.M. to 12:30 A.M.; Sunday: 11:00 A.M. to 8:00 P.M.
NEARBY ATTRACTIONS: Silver Creek Brewing Co., Water Street Brewery–Grafton, West Bend Art Museum, golf, outdoor activities at Cedarburg Bog State Natural Area and Jackson Marsh State Wildlife Area, Schauer Center for the Arts in nearby Hartford, forty-five minutes from downtown Milwaukee

NOTES: About halfway through my beer sampler I began to notice a trend. All the beers at Riverside were surprisingly big and bold, even the weissbier and the "light" honey blond ale. That's when brewer Chris George informed me that very few of his beers come in under 6 percent ABV. "It's not a soft palate of beers," he explained. Indeed, they were all well-made, full-flavored, and yet easy to drink. It was a pleasing sampler all around.

The amped-up beer profile fits with the overall concept at Riverside. Owner Wayne Kainz calls it "upper-casual." The décor is based on pre-Prohibition-era saloons. It's casual, but with an intimate and elegant twist. The menu consists of classic brewpub fare, but the focus on steaks and ribs, along with signature panini sandwiches, gives it an upscale flair. As Kainz explained, "You can come in dressed-up for your tenth anniversary or just wearing jeans and a t-shirt and be comfortable either way."

I took advantage of the Thursday rib special while I was there. The ribs were literally fall-off-the-bone tender. With a choice of four sauces, from zingy mango-habanero to maple-bourbon, you really can't go wrong.

ADDRESS: 510 56th St.
Kenosha, WI 53140
TELEPHONE: 262–320–7623
EMAIL: info@rusticbrewing.com
WEB SITE: www.rusticbrewing.com
MICHAEL'S PICK: None available for sample
TYPE: Brewery
DATE ESTABLISHED: 2012
OWNERS: Greg York and Michelle York
BREWMASTER: Greg York
BREWING SYSTEM: Two-hundred-liter Speidel
brewhouse
FLAGSHIP BEERS: Southport Wheat, Simmons Island
Imperial Blonde
YEAR-ROUND BEERS: Southport Wheat, Accommo-
dation Amber, Simmons Island Imperial Blonde
SEASONAL BEERS: Kenosha Pale Ale (KPA), Rustic
Farmhouse Ale, Downtown Double American Pale Ale,
and others
SPECIAL RELEASES: Planned
TOURS: By request
BEER TO GO: Growlers
FOOD: Planned small menu of lighter fare
AMENITIES: Free street parking, Brew-It-Yourself classes,
Mug Club, live music
PUB HOURS: Wednesday and Thursday: 5:00 to 10:00
P.M.; Friday: 4:00 P.M. to close; Saturday: noon to close;
Sunday: noon to 5:00 P.M.
NEARBY ATTRACTIONS: Civil War Museum, Kenosha
Public Museum, concerts at the Rhode Center for the
Arts, artisan shops downtown, Frank's Diner, Kenosha
Streetcar Society, sprint-car races at Wilmot Raceway,
forty miles from Milwaukee, sixty miles from Chicago

NOTES: Wisconsin is a motorcycle-loving state. It ranks among the top ten states for motorcycle ownership per capita. Rustic Road owner and brewer Greg York loves to ride. He especially loves the sense of freedom that comes from taking to Wisconsin's back roads, many of which are protected by the state's Rustic Road Preservation Program. Unfortunately for York, Kenosha County has only one such rustic road. They are mostly located in the northern part of the state. With Rustic Road Brewing Company, he's trying to bring a little bit of that freewheeling feeling back to southeastern Wisconsin.

York had been homebrewing for over a decade before taking the leap to go pro. Like many homebrewers, the thought of opening a brewery was always in the back of his mind, but he only thought of it as an option for later in life. Starting a brewery was some-

thing to do in retirement. But over the years, he says, he heard too many stories of people dying before realizing their goal. Why wait for something that might never happen?

At just two hundred liters, or just over 1.5 barrels, Rustic Road is operating on a nano scale, a difficult thing to maintain in a business that is said to depend on volume. But York is sanguine about his prospects. His beer is only available in the brewery taproom. Selling direct to the public gives him a higher margin than breweries that package for distribution. He's keeping overhead low and hasn't yet had to quit his day job. If the brewery even turns a small profit, he'll be satisfied.

Keeping it small is also part of his brewing philosophy. He wants Rustic Road to hearken back to the days when breweries made beer for their local market. He's trying to speak the beer language of Kenosha—to meet the local public where they are. If that public appreciates it, that's frosting on the cake.

ADDRESS: N57W6172 Portland Rd.
Cedarburg, WI 53012
TELEPHONE: 262–375–4444
EMAIL: info@silvercreekbrewing.com
WEB SITE: www.silvercreekbrewing.com
MICHAEL'S PICK: Porter: This Baltic-style porter is
much lighter-bodied than its 7.5 percent ABV would
indicate. Flavors of coffee and cocoa are offset by
moderate caramel sweetness. It finishes crisp and dry,
leaving you ready for another.
TYPE: Brewpub
DATE ESTABLISHED: 1999
OWNERS: Steve Venturini, Todd Schneeberger, and Steve
Roensch
BREWMASTER: Steve Venturini
BREWING SYSTEM: Fifteen-barrel McCann Fabrication
brewhouse
FLAGSHIP BEERS: Hefe-Weiss, Porter
YEAR-ROUND BEERS: Pacific Coast Lager, Hefe-Weiss,
India Pale Ale, Porter, ESBlack
SEASONAL BEERS: Imperial Mai Bock, Oktoberfest,
Vintage Ale
SPECIAL RELEASES: New Harvest Lager, Spiced Porter
TOURS: By request
BEER TO GO: Growlers, party pigs, and kegs
FOOD: None
AMENITIES: Free street parking, happy-hour specials,
live music on select Saturdays, seasonal outdoor
seating in the beer garden overlooking Cedar Creek,
good selection of guest taps

PUB HOURS: Tuesday–Thursday: 5:00 P.M. to close; Friday: 3:00 P.M. to close; Saturday: 2:00 P.M. to close; Sunday: noon to close

NEARBY ATTRACTIONS: Riverside Brewery and Restaurant, Water Street—Grafton, Cedarburg's quaint bed and breakfasts, unique shops, museums, and good restaurants, seasonal festivals on Cedarburg's historic Main Street, Cedar Creek Winery, Chiselled Grape Winery, Cedarburg Performing Arts Center

NOTES: Silver Creek Brewing Company was born of the owners' desire to create the most appealing beer garden in the state. Indeed, nestled under shade trees on the bank of Cedar Creek just below a waterfall, it is an idyllic spot to enjoy a cold beer on a warm summer day. Achieving this dream, though, required a three-year labor of love to reclaim the basement of a 150-year-old flour mill. "In hindsight," says co-owner Todd Schneeberger, "we were psychotic to have taken it on."

Their efforts, along with those of an army of volunteer tradespeople, resulted in a cozy spot to savor a pint either indoors or out. The place reeks of history. Stepping through the stone-arch entrance to the taproom, you cross a bridge over the original mill race that once turned the gears that drove the mill. Much of the material removed from the space has been repurposed. An old steep stairway now serves as a bookshelf. Oak grain-hoppers were turned into bar railings.

The brewery sits at one end of the taproom, lit as though on stage. The room is tiny and intimate, the kind of space that encourages conversation. The clientele is a mix of young and old, tourists who drive the town's economy and local regulars who stop in weekly to catch up with friends and neighbors. They don't serve food, but they do have menus from nearby restaurants to order carry-out or delivery.

Sweet Mullets Brewing Company

ADDRESS: N58W39800 Industrial Rd., Suite D, Oconomowoc, WI 53066

TELEPHONE: 262–456–2843

EMAIL: info@sweetmulletsbrewing.com

WEB SITE: www.sweetmulltesbrewing.com

MICHAEL'S PICK: Wild-Hopped Buckwheat Ale: This award-winning, easy-drinking ale features Wisconsin-grown hops and buckwheat. There's a little caramel, a little toast, and a little sweetness. Buckwheat lends some nutty notes and a bit of aromatic funk. Restrained

hops offer fruity and bitter contrast to the malt. It's not overly complex, but certainly a pleasure to drink.

TYPE: Brewpub

DATE ESTABLISHED: 2012

OWNERS: Mark Duchow and Barbara Jones

BREWMASTER: Mark Duchow

BREWING SYSTEM: Fifteen-barrel CDC brewhouse

FLAGSHIP BEER: Rye Bob

YEAR-ROUND BEERS: 505 Export Stout, Rye Bob

SEASONAL BEERS: None

SPECIAL RELEASES: 501 Red Ale, Wild-Hopped Buckwheat, Jorge Jalapeno Ale, MECO (Main Engine Cutoff) Wheat, Belgian IPA, Baltic Porter, Flanders Red Ale

TOURS: Saturdays. See Web site for times.

BEER TO GO: Growlers

FOOD: Small plate selection of baked, steamed, and fresh foods, pretzels, cheeses, and house-made chips and dips

AMENITIES: Parking lot, monthly Beer Appreciation nights, selection of Wisconsin guest taps, limited selection of Wisconsin wines and spirits

PUB HOURS: Wednesday and Thursday: 4:00 to 10:00 P.M.; Friday: 4:00 to 11:00 P.M.; Saturday: noon to 11:00 P.M.; Sunday: noon to 10:00 P.M.

NEARBY ATTRACTIONS: Golf, Theatre on Main, boating, fishing, and swimming on nearby lakes, forty-five minutes from Milwaukee

NOTES: Mark Duchow loves everything about brewing. He geeks out on the science, digs into the physicality of the process, and delights in indulging his creative side to explore new and interesting flavor combinations. He stumbled into it in 1992, when he started washing kegs at the Water Street Brewery in Milwaukee. Within three years he had worked his way up to brewmaster and discovered his chosen career. He told himself then that he would go back to school when brewing stopped being fun. All these years later, he says, "I haven't worked in twenty years."

This love of the craft shows in the range of beers he makes at Sweet Mullets. Resisting the idea of recurring seasonals and year-round, core beers, Duchow likes to brew according to whim. He plans to continuously rotate beers through the lineup, possibly turning them over as often as every three or four weeks. You should expect something new every time you go in.

You should also expect something interesting. Duchow says that drinkability and uniqueness define his brews. He is constantly looking for the thing that isn't being made elsewhere, like a beer brewed with one-third barley, one-third wild grapes, and one-third walnuts. He's made a traditional stein beer, using hot rocks to bring the wort to a boil. Besides producing an interesting beer, the process also makes for a great show that involves customers more deeply with the process of making the beer. "Education is a large part of industry," he says. "When people get to know something better they want to explore it more."

This creativity carries over into the food and atmosphere at Sweet Mullets. The menu is more like tapas than traditional pub grub. They describe the ambiance as "English pub meets industrial warehouse." The dining room is made up of 90 percent recycled materials, including tables and bar made from old pallets and wainscoting that was once a barn roof.

SOUTHWEST

The Brewery Creek Brewing Company

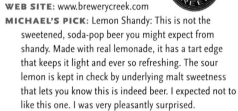

ADDRESS: 23 Commerce St.
Mineral Point, WI 53565
TELEPHONE: 608–987–3298
EMAIL: info@brewerycreek.com
WEB SITE: www.brewerycreek.com

MICHAEL'S PICK: Lemon Shandy: This is not the sweetened, soda-pop beer you might expect from shandy. Made with real lemonade, it has a tart edge that keeps it light and ever so refreshing. The sour lemon is kept in check by underlying malt sweetness that lets you know this is indeed beer. I expected not to like this one. I was very pleasantly surprised.

TYPE: Brewpub

DATE ESTABLISHED: 1998

OWNERS: Deborah Donaghue and Jeff Donaghue

BREWMASTER: Jeff Donaghue

BREWING SYSTEM: Fifteen-barrel Criveller brewhouse

FLAGSHIP BEER: None

YEAR-ROUND BEERS: The constantly rotating selection always includes something light, something dark, and a couple in between. Examples include Golden Ale, India Pale Ale, Lemon Shandy, Scottish Porter, Irish Stout, Helles Lager, Dortmunder, Amber Ale, Wit, and Kristal Weiss.

SEASONAL BEERS: None

SPECIAL RELEASES: Occasional barrel-aged selections

TOURS: By request

BEER TO GO: Growlers

FOOD: Selection of beef, chicken, and salmon sandwiches, salads, burgers, and entrées, featuring locally sourced and organic ingredients. Large vegetarian selection.

AMENITIES: Parking lot, lodging at the Brewery Street Inn, daily food specials

PUB HOURS:
June to October: Tuesday–Thursday: 11:00 A.M. to 8:00 P.M.; Friday and Saturday: 11:30 A.M. to 8:30 P.M.; Sunday: 11:30 A.M. to 3:00 P.M.
November to May: Thursday: 11:30 A.M. to 8:00 P.M.; Friday and Saturday: 11:30 A.M. to 8:30 P.M.

NEARBY ATTRACTIONS: Hook's Cheese Company, House on the Rock, Taliesen, American Players Theater, outdoor activities at Governor Dodge and Yellowstone State Parks, bicycling on local rural roads

NOTES: Deborah and Jeff Donaghue actually have three businesses in one at Brewery creek: brewery, restaurant, and inn. The three work together in a symbiotic relationship to make the location a delightfully peaceful getaway destination. The inn and restaurant go together naturally. Homemade beer adds magic to the experience. The historic and picturesque village of Mineral Point is an easy drive from Madison, Milwaukee, and Chicago.

Accommodations at Brewery Creek Inn are gorgeous. Spacious rooms feature exposed stone walls, plush queen-size beds, and fireplaces. A separate breakfast area offers guests a cozy morning meal. If you don't want to stay at the main inn, rooms are available in two nearby cabins, former homes to the lead miners that built the town.

Brewery Creek owner/brewer Jeff Donaghue.

Jeff Donaghue began homebrewing in 1967. He admits that his first attempts at beer making were not altogether successful. But the experience lit a fire in him that eventually inspired him to give up his corporate day job and start a professional brewing career. At Brewery Creek he has made a name for himself with his shandy. What began as a summer seasonal has become a more-or-less year-round offering due to customer demand. At Wisconsin beer fests he is known to pour several different varieties along with other traditional beer/soda concoctions, like radler and colaweizen.

Minhas Craft Brewery

ADDRESS: 1208 14th Ave.
Monroe, WI 53566
TELEPHONE: 800-233-7205
EMAIL: Contact form on Web site
WEB SITE: www.minhasbrewery.com
MICHAEL'S PICK: Chocolate Bunny Stout: The bottle says that this stout is brewed with chocolate, but the flavor is very subtle. It's really just a full-flavored sweet stout with overtones of bittersweet chocolate and licorice. Coffee-like roast is balanced by some caramel sweetness. Earthy hop flavors peek out from the background. It's surprisingly full-bodied for its 5 percent ABV.
TYPE: Brewery
DATE ESTABLISHED: 1845
OWNERS: Ravinder Minhas and Manjit Minhas
BREWMASTER: Kris Kalav
BREWING SYSTEM: 350-barrel Vendome brewhouse
FLAGSHIP BEERS: Huber Bock, Boxer Lager, Mountain Crest Classic Lager
YEAR-ROUND BEERS: Mountain Crest Classic Lager, Boxer Lager, Boxer Light, Boxer Ice, Clear Creek Ice, Huber Premium, Huber Bock, Lazy Mutt "Farmhouse" Ale, 1845 Pils, Shergill IPA, Swiss Amber, Axehead, Thunderbolt, Perfect 10, Chocolate Bunny Stout, Mystical Jack American Strong Ale, Traditional Jack American IPA, Imperial Jack Double IPA
SEASONAL BEERS: Minhas Oktoberfest
SPECIAL RELEASES: Occasional cask-conditioned beers
TOURS: Monday: 11:00 A.M.; Tuesday–Thursday: 1:00 P.M.; Friday and Sunday: 1:00 and 3:00 P.M. Cost $10, includes tour, complementary glass, and a take-home sampler pack.
BEER TO GO: Growlers and package
FOOD: None
AMENITIES: Free street parking, Haydock World of Beer Memorabilia Museum, gift shop, tasting room
PUB HOURS: Monday–Friday: 8:00 A.M. to 5:00 P.M.; Saturday: noon to 4:00 P.M.
NEARBY ATTRACTIONS: New Glarus Brewing Company, Whistle Stop Restaurant and Brewery, historic Monroe town square and courthouse, bike trails, Silver-Lewis Cheese Factory Co-op, one hour from Madison

NOTES: They have been brewing beer at this plant on 14th Avenue for a very long time. It is the oldest con-tinuously operating brewery in the Midwest and the second oldest in the United States. It began in 1845 as the Monroe Brewery. In 1947 it became the Joseph Huber Brewing Company, which at one point was one of the largest regional breweries in the country. The brewery survived the industry consolidations of the 1970s and 1980s under a variety of owners. It became Minhas Craft Brewing in 2006.

Like many old breweries, this one expanded piece-meal, with additions occurring through the years. Walking through the facility is a trip through time. Each threshold is a portal into another era. The central brewhouse, featuring nineteenth-century brick-vaulted cellaring rooms, is surrounded by buildings and tanks dating through the 1950s.

Between its own beers and contracted beer, Minhas currently produces about thirty different brands. Among the more familiar contract brands brewed here are Berghoff and the Trader Joe's line of beers. An interesting sideline is the production of bulk beer for use by manufacturers of beer batters.

Be sure to leave time to check out the three rooms of the Haydock World of Beer Memorabilia Museum. The museum displays artifacts from the private collection of Herb and Helen Haydock. It includes original lithographs dating from the mid-1800s through the 1960s, as well as a large assortment of growlers, tap handles, promotional trinkets, and toy cars, trucks, and trains.

Potosi Brewing Company

ADDRESS: 209 S. Main St.
Potosi, WI 53820
TELEPHONE: 608-763-4002
EMAIL: info@potosibrewery.com
WEB SITE: www.potosibrewery.com
MICHAEL'S PICK: Gandy Dancer Porter: This classic brown porter features moderate chocolate roast character enhanced by balancing caramel sweetness. Notes of dark-roasted coffee hang in the background. Hop bitterness is low, but mild earthy and herbal hop flavors provide a nice grounding.
TYPE: Brewery
DATE ESTABLISHED: Original 1852, current 2008
OWNER: Potosi Foundation
BREWMASTER: Steve Buszka
BREWING SYSTEM: Fifteen-barrel Specific Mechanical brewhouse
FLAGSHIP BEERS: Good Old Potosi, Snake Hollow India Pale Ale

YEAR-ROUND BEERS: Good Old Potosi, Potosi Pure Malt Cave Ale, Snake Hollow India Pale Ale, Czech Style Pilsner

SEASONAL BEERS: Steamboat Shandy, Wee Stein Wit, Gandy Dancer Porter, Fiddler Oatmeal Stout, Brown Ale, ESB, Honey Cream Ale, Tangerine IPA, Holiday Bock, Pumpkin Ale, Black Ale, Harvest Pale Ale

SPECIAL RELEASES: Brandy-barrel-aged Scotch Ale, other barrel-aged releases

TOURS: Self-guided, anytime during business hours

BEER TO GO: Growlers, kegs, and package

FOOD: Selection of sandwiches, burgers, and entrées, including seafood and steaks

AMENITIES: Parking lot, National Brewing Museum, Potosi Brewing Company Transportation Museum, private room available, seasonal outdoor seating, gift shop

PUB HOURS:

March 13 through December: Daily: 10:00 A.M. to 9:00 P.M.
January through March 12: Wednesday–Sunday: 11:00 A.M. to 9:00 P.M.

NEARBY ATTRACTIONS: St. John's Mine, Grant River Recreation Area and National Wildlife Refuge, Nelson Dewey State Park, Potosi Passage through Time Museum, eagle watching along the Great River Road scenic byway, National Mississippi River Museum and Aquarium, Stonefield State Historic Site

NOTES: The current Potosi Brewing Company was built literally on the ruins of the brewing industry's past. The original brewery was founded in 1852. At its peak it was the fifth largest brewery in Wisconsin, shipping beer to destinations throughout the United States. By the 1960s the brewery began a downward trajectory that mirrored the fate of many regional breweries. It closed its doors in 1972, and the buildings sat vacant for a quarter century.

The faithfully restored nineteenth-century brewery building at Potosi Brewing Company.

When Gary David bought the buildings in the mid-1990s, they were a near-total loss. His passion to save them inspired the involvement of the local community. A local board was established, money was raised, and the brewery was beautifully restored. It continues to be a community effort, with locals volunteering to help with maintenance and day-to-day operations.

The brewery is a fitting home for the National Brewing Museum. The rotating collection features thousands of artifacts showcasing the proud history of American brewing. It is a must-see for anyone interested in beer and brewing.

Sitting in the dining room, one can feel the history of the place, from the old stone walls to the tables made from staves of wooden fermenters removed during renovation. Brewer Steve Buszka came to Potosi from the Bell's Brewery. He crafts solid brews intended to appeal to a wide audience, some of which are reminiscent of the kinds of beer that might have been brewed here a hundred years ago.

Woodman Brewery/Whistle Stop

ADDRESS: 401 Main St. Woodman, WI 53827

TELEPHONE: 608-533-2200

EMAIL: Form on Web site

WEB SITE: www.woodmanwi.com

MICHAEL'S PICK: Arctic IPA: A mint-infused IPA? I admit that I approached this one with trepidation, but it proved to be surprisingly pleasant. Though the aroma is intense, the spearmint flavor is just enough to enhance the already minty Northern Brewer hops. Bitterness is bracing, but it and the mint are tempered by a good amount of caramel malt.

TYPE: Brewpub

DATE ESTABLISHED: Brewing began in 2010

OWNERS: Dennis Erb and Leslie Erb

BREWMASTER: Dennis Erb

BREWING SYSTEM: Fifteen-gallon homemade electric brewhouse

FLAGSHIP BEER: 77 Draft Ale

YEAR-ROUND BEERS: 77 Draft Ale, American Pale Ale, Irish Stout, American Honey Wheat

SEASONAL BEERS: Thanksgiving Novi Bock, Hazelnut Red Stout, S'mores Porter, Amber Bock, 69 on the Beach, Maple Wheat, Shocktoberfest, and others

SPECIAL RELEASES: Caribbean Stout, Raspberry Ale, New Zealand Pilsner, Pistachio Kölsch, Badger Ale, Nugget India Pale Ale, Hard Apple Cider, Scotch Ale, Almond Brown Ale, Santa's Xmas Ale, Oatmeal Porter, Jalapeno Blond Ale, Russian Ale, Arctic IPA, Italian Ale, Rose Red Ale, and others

TOURS: No

BEER TO GO: Package

FOOD: Reasonably priced menu of sandwiches, burgers, steaks, and pizzas

AMENITIES: Parking lot, free street parking, daily food and drink specials, also serves as the town post office

PUB HOURS: Daily: 9:00 A.M. to close

NEARBY ATTRACTIONS: Potosi Brewery, Brewery Creek Inn, outdoor activities, hunting, fishing, ATV riding, snowmobiling, Wyalusing State Park, Wauzeka Bottoms State Natural Area, Kickapoo Indian Caverns, Eagle Cave, Prairie du Chien historic sites

NOTES: In almost every way, the Whistle Stop is what you would expect from a tavern in a tiny Wisconsin town. The décor is simple. Miller Lite posters adorn the walls. The tables are covered with the requisite red-and-white checked tablecloths. Tuesday is taco night, and Friday features an all-you-can-eat fish fry. The food is simple but good. The one thing that makes it different is the beer. It's made on site, and it's like no place else.

Ordering beer at the Whistle Stop is a bit of a crap-shoot. About half of the beers I tried had gone sour—unintentional, but not always entirely bad. Those that hadn't "gone Belgian" were actually quite tasty and absolutely unique.

Dennis Erb refers to his brewery as "Dogfish Head on a smaller scale." The comparison is not entirely undeserved. Many of his beers are one of a kind. There's Pistachio Kölsch, Hazelnut Red Stout, the minty-bitter Arctic IPA, and Rose Red, a red ale brewed with rose hips and rose extract. Erb takes inspiration from all around him. Sometimes it's something he sees in the grocery store. Or maybe he reads about an exotic location and sets about translating it into beer. The experiments don't always work, but when they do they are surprisingly delicious. And you have to give him credit for going out on a limb in a place where Miller Lite is king.

FERMENTERIES

GRANITE CITY FOOD AND BREWERY—MADISON

Address: 72 West Towne Mall
Madison, WI 53719
Telephone: 608–829–0700
Web site: http://www.gcfb.net/location/madison

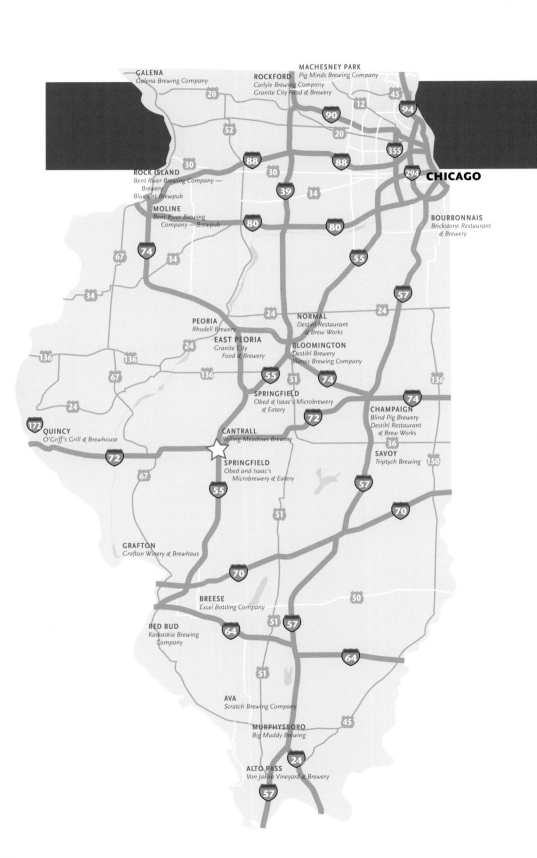

GALENA
Galena Brewing Company

ROCKFORD
Carlyle Brewing Company
Granite City Food & Brewery

MACHESNEY PARK
Pig Minds Brewing Company

CHICAGO

ROCK ISLAND
Bent River Brewing Company —
Brewery
Blue Cat Brewpub

MOLINE
Bent River Brewing
Company — Brewpub

BOURBONNAIS
Brickstone Restaurant
& Brewery

PEORIA
Rhodell Brewery

NORMAL
Destihl Restaurant
& Brew Works

EAST PEORIA
Granite City
Food & Brewery

BLOOMINGTON
Destihl Brewery
Illinois Brewing Company

SPRINGFIELD
Obed & Isaac's Microbrewery
& Eatery

CHAMPAIGN
Blind Pig Brewery
Destihl Restaurant
& Brew Works

QUINCY
O'Griff's Grill & Brewhouse

CANTRALL
Rolling Meadows Brewery

SAVOY
Triptych Brewing

SPRINGFIELD
Obed and Isaac's
Microbrewery & Eatery

GRAFTON
Grafton Winery & Brewhaus

BREESE
Excel Bottling Company

RED BUD
Kaskaskia Brewing
Company

AVA
Scratch Brewing Company

MURPHYSBORO
Big Muddy Brewing

ALTO PASS
Von Jakob Vineyard & Brewery

With the second-highest number of breweries in the region and a city of the size and sophistication of Chicago, one might expect that the Illinois brewing industry was long established. But that would be a mistake. Over 60 percent of the state's breweries opened after 2006, and 38 percent of them after 2010. What the Illinois beer scene lacks in longevity, it makes up for in variety. The state is home to breweries of all sizes, making everything from traditional German lagers to tongue-punishing imperial and Belgian IPAs. While midwestern balance is still the rule, breweries like the Haymarket Pub and Brewery and Pipeworks Brewing Company are pushing at its edges with hopped-up, spiced-up, and high-gravity creations. Good food has always been a part of life in Chicago, and that influence carries into the beer scene in the chef collaborations at the Goose Island brewpubs. And the Goose Island Fulton Street Brewery has an enormous barrel-aging program that includes extensive experimentation with wild fermentation. From the craft-beer novice to the most extreme beer geek, Illinois truly has something for everyone.

Because nearly all of its breweries are clustered into three easily-drivable areas, Illinois is a beer-traveler's dream. Forty-nine of the seventy breweries operating in the state at this writing are located in the Chicago metro area. It's a large area—one hundred miles from the southernmost brewery in Bourbonnais to the northernmost in Zion—but it is easily sliced into manageable chunks. Eighteen breweries and brewpubs await you within the Chicago city limits, among them some of the best in the state. In the northern suburbs stretching from I-90 north, you'll find fourteen breweries to explore. There are eleven in the western suburbs between I-90 and I-55. South of the city, between I-55 and the Indiana state line,

there are six. From there, it's an easy drive across the state line to visit Three Floyds in Munster, Indiana.

Across the state to the west, the Quad Cities offer five breweries for your inspection. On the Illinois side of the Mississippi there is the Bent River Brewing Company brewpub in Moline and the Bent River production brewery and Blue Cat brewpub in Rock Island. Across the river in Davenport, Iowa, you can grab a sample and a sixpack at the Great River Brewery or stop in for a bite and a beer at the Front Street Brewery. The two are nearly across the street from one another, so why not do both? And if you're traveling across the state, a quick trip up I-39 gets you to Rockford for a stop at the Carlyle Brewing Company and Pig Minds Brewing Company.

Springfield, Bloomington-Normal, and Champaign form an easily drivable triangle in the center of the state. The towns lie just an hour to an hour-and-a-half apart and together give access to eight breweries. The stylish Destihl restaurants have locations in Champaign and Normal. Illinois Brewing Company in Bloomington offers gritty entertainment, with bands and billiards. Check out the Blind Pig in Champaign for the cozy feel of an English pub. Triptych Brewing is just south of downtown in Savoy. In the capital city of Springfield, you can spend the day taking in the historic Lincoln sites and then settle in for a pint at Obed and Isaac's. Be sure to take the short drive out of town to visit the environmentally conscious Rolling Meadows Microbrewery. Peoria and the John S. Rhodell brewery lie just outside the triangle, forty-five minutes from Bloomington.

If you are looking for an escape from the hustle and bustle of urban life, you can get away to the beauty of the Shenandoah National Forest in the southern tip of the state. It's a great area for hiking, camping, and other outdoor activities. It's also where you'll find the Big Muddy Brewing Company, Scratch Brewing Company, and Von Jakob Vineyard and Brewery. Alternatively, take a step back in time to enjoy the quaint ambience of a historic Mississippi River town in Quincy. O'Griff's Irish Pub and Brewery is right on the old town square.

The Illinois Brewing Industry at a Glance
(Based on 2012 Data)

LARGEST BREWERY: Goose Island Beer Co. Fulton Street Brewery, Chicago (130,000 barrels)*

SMALLEST BREWERY: Light the Lamp Brewery, Grayslake (10 barrels**)

LARGEST BREWPUB: Rock Bottom Restaurant and Brewery, Chicago (2,223 barrels**)

SMALLEST BREWPUB: Lunar Brewing, Villa Park (126 barrels**)

BREWERIES PER CAPITA: .0000052 per capita, or 189,254 persons per brewery***

* *Crain's Chicago Business*, July 27, 2012, http://www.chicago business.com/article/20130228/NEWS07/130229730/ goose-island-bottles-to-hit-all-50-states
**Brewers Association Data, *New Brewer* 30.3 (May/June 2013): 86–156.
***Based on 2011 population estimates from the U.S. Census Bureau (http://quickfacts.census.gov/qfd/states/17000.html) and the author's brewery list as of December 31, 2012.

Illinois Contract Breweries:

Ale Syndicate, Chicago
Baderbräu Brewing Company, Chicago
Big Shoulders Beer Company, Chicago
Black Toad Brewing Company, Chicago
Chicago Beer Company, Chicago
Hopothesis Beer Company, Chicago
Millrose Brewing, South Barrington
Pabst Brewing Company, Woodridge
Pizza Beer Company, St. Charles
Ram/Bighorn Brewery, Rosemont
Trinity Brewing, Chicago

Illinois Breweries in Planning (as of March 2013):

4 Paws Brewing, Chicago
Abby Ridge, Alton Pass
Admiral Sasquatch, Summit
Against the Grain Brewery and Alehouse, Rock Island
Ale Syndicate, Chicago
Alto Pass Brewing Company, Alto Pass
Arcade Brewery, Chicago
Belleville Brewing Company, Belleville
Big Dick's Brewing Company, Chicago

Breakroom Brewery, Chicago
Buckledown Brewing, Lyons
Brutally Honest Brewing, Chicago
Chicago Beer Company, Chicago
Copper Hills Brewing Company, Rockford
Destihl Restaurant and Brew Works, Burr Ridge
Doubleheart Brewing Company, Chicago
DryHop Brewers, Chicago
Durkin Brewing, Barrington
East Wind Brewing, Staunton
Elevated Brewing Co., Chicago
Empirical Brewery, Chicago
English Prairie Brewery, Spring Grove
Engrained Brewing Co., Springfield
Eureka Springs Brewing Company, Princeton
Hopvine Brewing Company, Aurora
Hailstorm Brewing Company, Orland Park
Illuminated Brew Works, Oak Park
J. T. Walker's Restaurant and Sports Bar, Mahomet
Knight and Gunner Brewing Co., Chicago
Lagunitas Brewing Company, Chicago
Last Bay Beer Company, Chicago
Little Egypt Beer, Murphysboro
Low Dive Brewing, Chicago
Misfit Craft Brewery, Oswego
Moody Tongue Brewery, Chicago
Off Key Brewing, Oak Park
Old Pilsen Brewery, Chicago
Oval Brewing Company, Chicago
Panic Brewing, Chicago
Powell Brew House, Chicago
Ridgebrook Brewing Company, Godrey
Rude Boy Brewing Company, Chicago
San Vicente Enterprises, Chicago
Schalkhausser Brewing Co., Peoria
South Loop Brewing Company, Chicago
St. Nicholas Brewing Company, Du Quoin
Stockyard Brewing Company, Chicago
Strange Pelican Brewing Company, Chicago
Sub-Urban Brewing, Plainfield
Temperance Beer Company, Evanston
Two Buddies Brewery, Chicago
Two Tree Beer Company, Chicago
Une Année, Chicago
Unknown Brewing Company, Chicago
Urban Legend Brewing Company, Westmont

Illinois Beer Festivals:

Chicago Beer Festival, Chicago, March (http://thechicagobeerfestival.com/)
Peoria Jaycee's International Beer Festival, Peoria, April (http://www.peoriajaycees.org/events/international-beer-festival/)

Tinley Park Brew and Vine Festival, Tinley Park, April
(www.tinleyparkbrewandvinefest.com)

Barrington Brew Fest, Barrington, July
(www.barringtonbrewfest.com)

Wheaton Brew Fest, Wheaton, August
(http://www.wheatonparkdistrict.com/brewfest/)

Oak Park Microbrew Review, Oak Park, August
(www.sevengenerationsahead.org)

Brüegala Beer Festival, Bloomington, August
(www.bruegala.com)

Springfield Oyster and Beer Festival, Springfield, September
(www.sobfestival.com)

Screw City Beer Festival, Rockford, September
(www.screwcitybeerfest.com)

Big Muddy Monster Brew Festival, Murphysboro, October
(http://www.bigmuddymonsterbrewfest.com/)

Festival of Wood and Barrel-Aged Beer, Chicago, November
(www.illinoisbeer.com)

Chicago Beer Hoptacular, Chicago, November
(www.beerhoptacular.com)

Chicago Beer Society Fall Tasting, Chicago, November
(www.chibeer.org)

CHICAGO METRO

5 Rabbit Cerveceria

ADDRESS: 6398 W. 74th St.
Bedford Park, IL 60638

TELEPHONE: 312-895-9591

EMAIL: info@5rabbitbrewery.com

WEB SITE: www.5rabbitbrewery.com

MICHAEL'S PICK: 5 Vulture: This is brown ale with a kick. Toast and caramel notes predominate, with some burnt-sugar character filling in the edges. Cocoa nibs bring in bittersweet chocolate notes. Ancho chilies yield dark, raisiny flavors and a subtle, lingering heat. It's not an intense chili beer, but one with just a note of spicy intrigue.

TYPE: Brewery

DATE ESTABLISHED: 2011

OWNERS: Andrés Araya and Randy Mosher

BREWMASTER: John J. Hall

BREWING SYSTEM: Thirty-barrel DME brewhouse

FLAGSHIP BEERS: 5 Rabbit Golden Ale, 5 Lizard Wheat Ale, 5 Vulture Dark Ale, 5 Grass

YEAR-ROUND BEERS: 5 Rabbit Golden Ale, 5 Lizard Wheat Ale, 5 Vulture Dark Ale, 5 Grass

SEASONAL BEERS: Vida y Muerte Muertzenbier, Huitzi Mid-winter Ale, Ki'Chun Ale

SPECIAL RELEASES: Planned

TOURS: See Web site for times

BEER TO GO: Growlers

FOOD: None

AMENITIES: Small parking lot, free street parking, near Chicago Midway Airport

PUB HOURS: See Web site for hours

NEARBY ATTRACTIONS: Hiking and biking in Waterfall Glenn County Forest Preserve and Paw Paw Woods Nature Preserve, White Sox games at U.S. Cellular Field, horse racing at Hawthorne Race Course, DuSable Museum of African American History, twenty-five minutes from the Chicago Loop

NOTES: "Píixan" is an old Mayan term loosely meaning "free spirit." It's also the motto of 5 Rabbit Cerveceria, the nation's first Latin American brewery. That free-spiritedness is embodied in the name of the brewery as well as the names of the beers: 5 Rabbit, 5 Lizard, 5 Vulture, 5 Grass, and 5 Flower are the Aztec deities representing pleasure and excess, an expression of the role alcohol played in that culture as a pathway to the spirit world. Free-spirited also describes the way 5 Rabbit approaches beer. They take inspiration from the food, art, and culture of the Latin American community to craft Latin twists on classic styles.

Since embarking on the 5 Rabbit project, the team has had to figure out what exactly it means to be a "Latin American" brewery. They want to upset the stereotype of Latin beer as only light, Mexican-style lagers. Their goal is to do for beer what the renowned chef Rick Bayless did for the region's food. To achieve this, they take a culinary approach to their recipes. Using ingredients from Central America, they produce beers intended to complement the full range of Latin foods, from shrimp to steak and barbacoa. Lime peel and passion fruit add zip to their witbier instead of the traditional orange peel. Their brown ale is flavored with cocoa, ancho chilies, and piloncillo sugar.

In order to reach out to Chicago's large Latin American population, the brewery team is staying engaged with community organizations and charity groups. Their beer has been poured at the Mexican Fine Art Museum and other cultural venues.

Argus Brewery

ADDRESS: 11314 S. Front Ave.
Chicago, IL 60628

TELEPHONE: 773-941-4050

EMAIL: localbrew@argusbrewery.com

WEB SITE: www.argusbrewery.com

MICHAEL'S PICK: Country House Red Ale: Rich caramel malt is overlaid with notes of biscuit from English malts. The sweetness is contrasted by the fresh, grassy

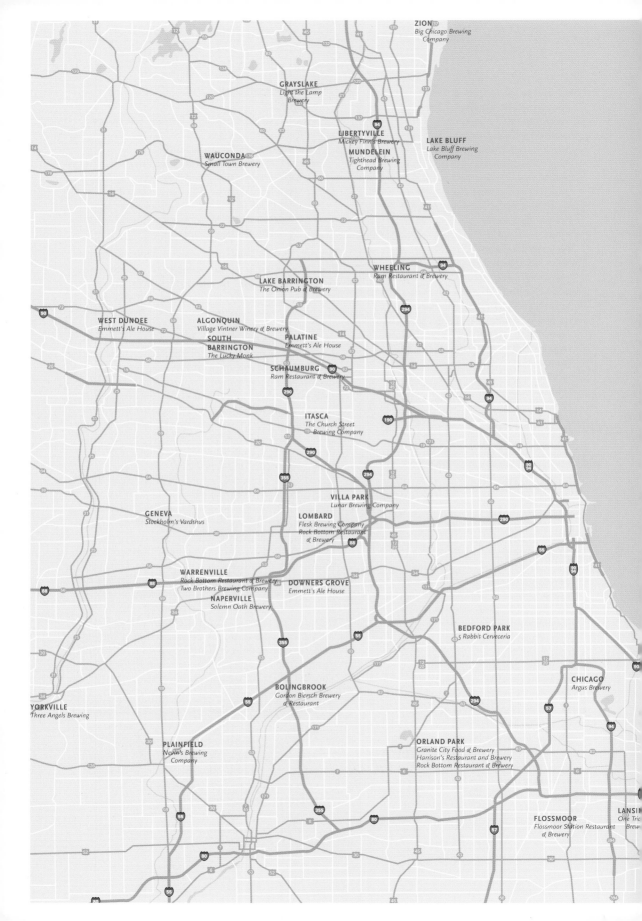

ZION
Big Chicago Brewing
Company

GRAYSLAKE
Light the Lamp
Brewery

LIBERTYVILLE
Mickey Finn's Brewery

LAKE BLUFF
Lake Bluff Brewing
Company

WAUCONDA
Small Town Brewery

MUNDELEIN
Tighthead Brewing
Company

WHEELING
Ram Restaurant & Brewery

LAKE BARRINGTON
The Onion Pub & Brewery

WEST DUNDEE
Emmett's Ale House

ALGONQUIN
Village Vintner Winery & Brewery

**SOUTH
BARRINGTON**
The Lucky Monk

PALATINE
Emmett's Ale House

SCHAUMBURG
Ram Restaurant & Brewery

ITASCA
The Church Street
Brewing Company

VILLA PARK
Lunar Brewing Company

GENEVA
Stockholm's Vardshus

LOMBARD
Flesk Brewing Company
Rock Bottom Restaurant
& Brewery

WARRENVILLE
Rock Bottom Restaurant & Brewery
Two Brothers Brewing Company

DOWNERS GROVE
Emmett's Ale House

NAPERVILLE
Solemn Oath Brewery

BEDFORD PARK
5 Rabbit Cerveceria

CHICAGO
Argus Brewery

YORKVILLE
Three Angels Brewing

BOLINGBROOK
Gordon Biersch Brewery
& Restaurant

PLAINFIELD
Nevin's Brewing
Company

ORLAND PARK
Granite City Food & Brewery
Harrison's Restaurant and Brewery
Rock Bottom Restaurant & Brewery

FLOSSMOOR
Flossmoor Station Restaurant
& Brewery

LANSIN
One Tric
Brew

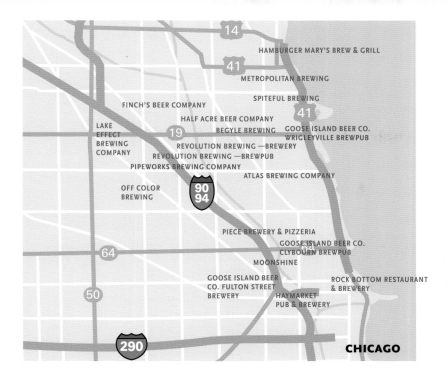

HAMBURGER MARY'S BREW & GRILL

METROPOLITAN BREWING

SPITEFUL BREWING

FINCH'S BEER COMPANY

HALF ACRE BEER COMPANY

LAKE EFFECT BREWING COMPANY

BEGYLE BREWING

GOOSE ISLAND BEER CO. WRIGLEYVILLE BREWPUB

REVOLUTION BREWING — BREWERY
REVOLUTION BREWING — BREWPUB

PIPEWORKS BREWING COMPANY

ATLAS BREWING COMPANY

OFF COLOR BREWING

PIECE BREWERY & PIZZERIA

GOOSE ISLAND BEER CO. CLYBOURN BREWPUB

MOONSHINE

GOOSE ISLAND BEER CO. FULTON STREET BREWERY

ROCK BOTTOM RESTAURANT & BREWERY

HAYMARKET PUB & BREWERY

CHICAGO

flavors of English hops. Moderate bitterness and a dry finish keep it utterly sessionable. A very pleasant and very drinkable beer.

TYPE: Brewery

DATE ESTABLISHED: 2009

OWNERS: Robert Jensen and Patrick Jensen

BREWMASTER: Grant Johnston

BREWING SYSTEM: Ten-barrel Liquid Assets brewhouse

FLAGSHIP BEER: Pegasus IPA

YEAR-ROUND BEERS: Agrus California Steam, Argus Hopsteiner, Pegasus IPA, McCaffrey's Irish Cream Ale, Country House Red Ale

SEASONAL BEERS: Ballydoyle

SPECIAL RELEASES: None

TOURS: By appointment

BEER TO GO: None

FOOD: None

AMENITIES: Taproom available for private parties, free street parking, convenient to Metra trains

PUB HOURS: None

NEARBY ATTRACTIONS: Twenty minutes from the Chicago Loop, located in the Pullman State Historic Site, casinos in Hammond, Indiana

NOTES: The Argus Brewery is literally surrounded by history. The building in which it is located was originally built in 1906 to stable the horses that pulled Schlitz beer wagons. It is the only building remaining from what was once a vast brewery complex. Across the railroad tracks that run directly in front of the brewery lies the Pullman State Historic Site, the still mostly intact company town built by the railroad magnate George Pullman in 1880 to house workers at his massive sleeping-car-production factory. This history alone makes a visit to Argus worth the trip.

The brewery focuses on low-gravity session beers with delicate but full-flavored profiles. Brewer Grant Johnston is inspired by English brewing traditions. He loves malt and hops in balance. "So many beers today are too extreme, too bitter," he says. You won't find any knock-your-socks-off-and-slap-you-in-the-face beers in the Argus lineup. What you will find are beers that are nuanced, layered, and full-flavored. These are beers meant for drinking.

Johnston honed his brewing skills over a long career that includes breweries on the West Coast and London. He made his first batch of homebrew in 1987. In 1989 he got his first professional brewing job at Marin Brewing Company in Larkspur, California. From there, he moved around among many Bay Area breweries before being asked to open the Zero Degree Brewpub in London. He recalls the time spent brewing in England as among the best in his career.

Atlas Brewing Company

ADDRESS: 2747 N. Lincoln Ave.
Chicago, IL 60614

TELEPHONE: 773–295–1270

EMAIL: ben@atlasbeer.com

WEB SITE: www.atlasbeer.com

MICHAEL'S PICK: For Those Who Are Ready to Rock Bock: I would characterize this Americanized bock as

a West Coast imperial amber lager. Citrusy hop flavors and aggressive bitterness are balanced by bock-like, toasty-caramel malt sweetness. It's chewy in your mouth but goes out with a dry, crisp, lager finish.

TYPE: Brewpub

DATE ESTABLISHED: 2012

OWNERS: Ben Saller and Steven Soble

BREWMASTERS: Ben Saller and John Saller

BREWING SYSTEM: Seven-barrel Premier Stainless brewhouse

FLAGSHIP BEERS: Atlas Golden Ale, Diversy Pale Ale, 1871 Smoked Porter

YEAR-ROUND BEERS: Atlas Golden Ale, Diversy Pale Ale, 1871 Smoked Porter, Brother Mauro Double Mild, Demeter Wheat Ale, Hyperion Double IPA

SEASONAL BEERS: Nyad Belgian Summer Pale Ale and others

SPECIAL RELEASES: Oktoberfest, Black Doppelbock, Belgian Strong Dark Holiday Ale, and others

TOURS: By appointment

BEER TO GO: Growlers and kegs

FOOD: Elevated pub food, featuring a selection of unique burgers, salads, pizzas, mussels, and entrées

AMENITIES: Metered street parking, full bar, selection of guest taps, signature cocktails, bowling alley

PUB HOURS: Monday–Wednesday and Sunday: 5:00 P.M. to midnight; Thursday: 5:00 P.M. to 1:00 A.M.; Friday: 5:00 P.M. to 2:00 A.M.; Saturday: 5:00 P.M. to 3:00 A.M.

NEARBY ATTRACTIONS: Half Acre Beer Company, Kingston Mines Blues Club, Apollo Theatre, Vic Theatre, Victory Gardens Theatre, Briar Street Theatre, Athenaeum Theatre, Chicago Lakefront activities

NOTES: While brainstorming a name for the new brewpub, Steve Soble tossed out the word "Atlas." While he was thinking of a cartographic theme, the Saller brothers, Ben and John, went straight to mythology. When that name was chosen, they decided to go in both directions, riffing on of the multiple interpretations of the word in the names of their beers. Demeter Wheat and Hyperion Double IPA share tap space with Brother Mauro Double Mild, named after a fifteenth-century monk credited with creating a surprisingly accurate map of the known world in 1450.

The team at Atlas is trying to elevate the brewpub experience. Soble describes the aesthetic as "modern apothecary." Colorful bottles sparkle like jewels behind the bar, and chandeliers are made from the bottoms of beer growlers. The place has a sleek, upscale feel, featuring a black soapstone bar and rich woodwork. The menu includes signature items like a short rib burger with tomato jam and brie, grilled pear salad, and an assortment of mussels with differ-

ent preparations. Despite the upscale vibe, prices are reasonable.

Ben and John Saller describe their brewing as ingredient-focused. They want all of the components of a beer to show through. Their hoppy IPAs must also have an interesting malt profile. Malt-focused beers emphasize nuanced flavors instead of just an overload of caramel.

Begyle Brewing

ADDRESS: 1800 W. Cuyler Ave. Chicago, IL 60613

TELEPHONE: 773-661-6963

EMAIL: oh.hey@begylebrewing.com

WEB SITE: www.begylebrewing.com

MICHAEL'S PICK: Crash Landed: The guys at Begyle call this an American pale wheat ale, and that is a very apt description. A burst of tangerine and orange peel greet the nose as you raise the glass. Citrusy orange follows through to the flavor, accompanied by some hoppy spice. It all sits on a bed of softly sweet wheat malt. Reasonably high bitterness and 7 percent ABV put this "session" beer into IPA range.

TYPE: Brewery

DATE ESTABLISHED: 2012

OWNERS: Brendan Blume, Matt Ritchey, and Kevin Cary

BREWER: Matt Ritchey

BREWING SYSTEM: Ten-barrel Newlands Systems brewhouse

FLAGSHIP BEERS: Crash Landed Pale Wheat Ale, Flannel Pajamas Oatmeal Stout, Begyle Pale Ale, Begyle Blonde Ale

YEAR-ROUND BEERS: Crash Landed Pale Wheat Ale, Flannel Pajamas Oatmeal Stout, Begyle Pale Ale, Begyle Blonde Ale

SEASONAL BEERS: Black IPA, Neighborly, others planned

SPECIAL RELEASES: Winter Warmer, Allium Beta Beer, others planned

TOURS: Planned. See Web site for more information.

BEER TO GO: Growlers, kegs, and package

FOOD: None

AMENITIES: Parking lot, tasting room, convenient to the Brown Line "L" trains

PUB HOURS: Check Web site for hours.

NEARBY ATTRACTIONS: Metropolitan Brewing Company, Half Acre Brewing Company, Shattered Globe Theatre, standup comedy at the Lincoln Lodge, Old Town School of Folk Music, Graceland Cemetery, Wrigley Field

NOTES: Aside from the obvious desire to make great beer, Begyle Brewing is driven by three big ideas:

community, collaboration, and supporting local small businesses. Community is built into the business model. The inspiration comes from the community-supported agriculture (CSA) movement, in which subscribers purchase a share of a farmer's crop. Begyle subscribers can choose from a variety of membership levels: one growler a month or many, and on up to kegs. Shareholders receive a discounted price. The brewery also supports the neighborhood's thriving arts scene by leasing excess brewery space to local artists for use as studios. This partnership gives Begyle greater visibility in the community, as those artists spread the word about the beer.

Begyle's brewer and chef collaborations encourage the already-strong camaraderie that exists among Chicago's brewers and restaurateurs. Brewer Matt Ritchey has built several collectively created beers with other Chicago brewers. One such collaboration even involved the owner of a hop farm. They have an ongoing collaborative relationship with the chef at Allium restaurant in downtown Chicago, who shares their locavore mentality. He has brought a culinary viewpoint and unique ingredients to the beers, including items foraged from the surrounding landscape.

Begyle's three owners all come from entrepreneurial families. That small-business background is in part what led them to launch the brewery. It also is the driving force behind their desire to support other small businesses. Nearly all of their hops are purchased from small growers in Wisconsin. They are looking into working with small-scale barley farmers and artisanal maltsters in New England. They source as much of their raw material from small, local suppliers as they can.

Big Chicago Brewing Company

ADDRESS:
    2701 Deborah Ave., Building 4
    Zion, IL 60099
TELEPHONE: None
EMAIL: russ@bigchicagobrew.com
WEB SITE: www.bigchicagobrew.com
MICHAEL'S PICK: None available for tasting
TYPE: Brewery
DATE ESTABLISHED: 2012
OWNER: Russ Sher
BREWMASTER: Todd Britt
BREWING SYSTEM: Sixteen-barrel JV Northwest
    brewhouse
FLAGSHIP BEER: None
YEAR-ROUND BEERS: None
SEASONAL BEERS: None

SPECIAL RELEASES: None
TOURS: Check Web site for days and times.
BEER TO GO: No
FOOD: None
AMENITIES: Free street parking, private tasting room
    for clients
PUB HOURS: None
NEARBY ATTRACTIONS: Raven's Glen and Chain
    o' Lakes Forest Preserves, Illinois Beach State Park,
    performances at the Genesee Theatre in Waukegan,
    Dungeon of Doom Haunted House, Platen Press
    Printing Museum, Six Flags Great America, 1.25 hours
    from the Chicago Loop, one hour from Milwaukee

NOTES: Big Chicago Brewing Company began life in 1996 at the Flatlanders Restaurant and Brewery, tucked into the quaint Village Green Shopping Center in Lincolnshire, Illinois, a northern suburb of Chicago. In 2011 the decision was made to separate the brewery from the restaurant. The equipment was removed and trucked north to the town of Zion, near the Wisconsin state line.

The new entity operates strictly as a contract-brewing and private-label production facility. Big Chicago began with enough capacity to brew ten thousand barrels annually. Plans are to expand up to sixty thousand by year five. They produce beer for a wide range of clients, including the Flatlanders restaurant, which relocated west to Vernon Hills.

Brickstone Restaurant and Brewery

ADDRESS: 557 William Latham Dr.
    Bourbonnais, IL 60914
TELEPHONE: 815–936–9277
EMAIL: brickstonebrewery@yahoo.com
WEB SITE: www.brickstonebrewery.com
MICHAEL'S PICK: Golden Promise IPA: This beer takes
    its name from Golden Promise malt, which gives
    it flavorful biscuit and toffee character. The brew's
    elevated strength is revealed in its malty richness.
    But it's not all about the malt—this is an IPA, after
    all. Grassy English hop flavors ride over the top,
    accompanied by faint notes of orangy citrus. Assertive
    bitterness lingers well into the finish.
TYPE: Brewpub
DATE ESTABLISHED: 2006
OWNERS: George Giannakopoulos and Tom Vasilakis
BREWMASTER: Tom Vasilakis
BREWING SYSTEM: Ten-barrel Newlands Systems
    brewhouse
FLAGSHIP BEERS: 557 Light Lager, Cherry Ale,
    American Pale Ale, Golden Promise IPA, Forbidden
    Wheat, Irish Red

YEAR-ROUND BEERS: 557 Light Lager, Cherry Ale, American Pale Ale, Golden Promise IPA, Forbidden Wheat, Irish Red, rotating dark

SEASONAL BEERS: Oktoberfest, Rye IPA, Blood Orange Hefeweizen

SPECIAL RELEASES: Robust Porter, American Red, Oatmeal Stout, Märzen, Belgian Dubbel, Blond Ale, Heady Betty Double IPA, Hop Sinner, occasional barrel-aged selections, and others

TOURS: By appointment

BEER TO GO: Growlers and kegs

FOOD: Somewhat upscale American fare with a bit of a Greek twist: sandwiches, salads, steaks, and chops. Try the Greek-style center-cut pork chops.

AMENITIES: Parking lot, full bar, good selection of guest taps, private room available, Mug Club

PUB HOURS: Sunday–Thursday: 11:00 A.M. to midnight; Friday and Saturday: 11:00 A.M. to 2:00 A.M.

NEARBY ATTRACTIONS: Flossmoor Station Brewpub, Harrison's Brewpub, Rock Bottom–Orland Park, Three Floyds Brewery, scuba diving at Haigh Quarry, golf, Kankakee River State Park, sixty miles from the Chicago Loop

NOTES: Brickstone Brewery was a surprising find. Located in a rural area between Chicago and Champaign, small-town Bourbonnais is not the place you would expect to find a brewpub, especially not one as good as Brickstone. From the comfortably classy, casual-upscale atmosphere to the finely crafted brews and wonderfully prepared food, this place has it all.

Brickstone is totally family-owned and -operated. George Giannakopoulos and Tom Vasilakis are cousins. George's brother is the chef. Another cousin works there too, along with Mom and Dad. The sense of family extends to the customers as well. The brewpub is a gathering place for locals. It's a "Cheers" kind of vibe, where everybody knows your name. It's not uncommon to see people moving from table to table in the dining room greeting their friends and neighbors. I felt right at home chatting with the other patrons at the bar.

Should you find yourself cruising along Interstate 57 between Chicago and Champaign, Brickstone is certainly worth a stop.

The Church Street Brewing Company

ADDRESS: 1480 Industrial Dr., Unit C
Itasca, IL 60143

TELEPHONE: 630–438–5725

EMAIL: info@churchstreetbrew.com

WEB SITE: www.churchstreetbrew.com

MICHAEL'S PICK: Heavenly Helles: The name says it all. It's a Munich helles style lager and it's pretty good.

Grainy-sweet pils malt meets gentle, spicy hops and moderate bitterness.

TYPE: Brewery

DATE ESTABLISHED: 2012

OWNERS: Joe Gregor and Lisa Gregor

BREWMASTER: Joe Gregor

BREWING SYSTEM: Thirty-barrel Pacific Brewing Systems brewhouse

FLAGSHIP BEER: Church Street Helles Lager

YEAR-ROUND BEERS: Church Street Helles Lager, Church Street Continental Lager, Church Street Scottish Ale, Church Street Red Rye

SEASONAL BEERS: Planned

SPECIAL RELEASES: Church Street IPA and others

TOURS: By request during taproom hours

BEER TO GO: Growlers

FOOD: None

AMENITIES: Parking lot, taproom

PUB HOURS: Thursday–Friday: 4:00 to 7:00 P.M.; Saturday: 1:00 to 5:00 P.M.

NEARBY ATTRACTIONS: Lunar Brewing, Rock Bottom–Lombard, Ram Restaurant and Brewery–Schaumburg, several nearby golf courses, Ned Brown Forest Preserve, events at Allstate Arena, Pirates' Cove Children's Theme Park, close to Chicago O'Hare International Airport, thirty-five minutes from the Chicago Loop

NOTES: Several years ago, Joe Gregor's son decided that his father needed a hobby, so he bought him a homebrew kit. The elder Gregor took to it immediately. A chemical engineer by trade, the process of making beer was an extension of his expertise. And so the seeds for Church Street Brewing Company were sowed.

Fast forward a few years: Joe Gregor is nearing retirement and looking for a project. Having developed his homebrewing skills and found that others enjoyed the beer he made, a commercial brewery seemed the thing. Plans were drawn. A space was secured. Equipment was ordered. And in September 2012 that seed blossomed into beer.

But founding a brewery wasn't all easy. There was the paperwork and licensing to get through—a challenge for every would-be brewer. The building that was declared to have seventeen-foot ceilings was found—after equipment had been ordered—to have a sloping roof. Everything had to be shortened by six inches, and all of the ordered sixty-barrel fermenters had to be replaced with a twice as many thirty-barrel tanks.

In his chemical-engineering career, Joe Gregor had frequent opportunities to travel overseas, where he loved sampling the local beers. It was on one of these trips that he developed a love of German-style lagers.

Consumed fresh, these crisp, clean brews were unlike the import versions he was accustomed to at home. A desire to share the taste of freshly brewed, well-crafted lagers drives the Church Street lineup. Gregor's focus is on brewing the classics as true to style as possible, even using the more labor- and energy-intensive decoction method to brew his German-style beers. In addition to the lagers, he also makes a selection of English-style brews with the same attention to stylistic authenticity.

Emmett's Ale House–Downers Grove

ADDRESS: 5200 Main St.
Downers Grove, IL 60515
TELEPHONE: 630–434–8500
EMAIL: Form on Web site
WEB SITE: www.emmettsalehouse.com
MICHAEL'S PICK: McCarthy Red: Caramel and biscuit malt are the stars of the show in this American amber ale. Bitterness is firm, but it never quite overwhelms the malt. Citrus and pine hop flavors are layered on top, with light floral notes in the background. It's sharp, finely layered, and very drinkable.
TYPE: Brewpub
DATE ESTABLISHED: 2004
OWNERS: Andrew Burns, Matthew Burns, and Timothy Burns
BREWMASTER: Ryan Clooney
BREWING SYSTEM: Fifteen-barrel Specific Mechanical brewhouse
FLAGSHIP BEERS: Munich Light, 1 A.M. Ale, Victory Pale Ale, McCarthy Red Ale, Double Barrel Oatmeal Stout
YEAR-ROUND BEERS: Munich Light, 1 A.M. Ale, Victory Pale Ale, McCarthy Red Ale, Double Barrel Oatmeal Stout
SEASONAL BEERS: Doppelbock, Belgian Tripel, Maibock, Hefeweizen, Kölsch, Pilsner, Belgian Blond, ESB, Imperial Stout, Oktoberfest, Barleywine, Porter, Munich Dunkel
SPECIAL RELEASES: Irish Dry Stout, Scottish Ale, American Barleywine, Nitro Black IPA, Rye IPA, Saison, and others
TOURS: By request
BEER TO GO: Growlers, package, and kegs
FOOD: Selection of slightly upscale pub fare. Emphasis on organic, hormone-free, and locally sourced ingredients.
AMENITIES: Parking lot, free street parking, convenient to Downers Grove Metra station, nightly drink and food specials, private rooms and banquet services available, full bar
PUB HOURS: Monday–Wednesday: 11:00 A.M. to midnight; Thursday–Saturday: 11:00 A.M. to 1:00 A.M.; Sunday: noon to 10:00 P.M.

NEARBY ATTRACTIONS: Two Brothers Brewing Company, Rock Bottom–Warrenville, Rock Bottom–Lombard, Limestone Brewing Company, hiking in nearby forest preserves, Morton Arboretum, twenty-five miles from the Chicago Loop

NOTES: The Emmett's franchise brings a fine-dining feel to the brewpub concept. The ambience in all three locations has a similar air of sophistication, reinforced by dim lighting, dark wood, and servers in long aprons. Were it not for the statewide smoking ban, one could easily imagine fine gentlemen smoking cigars in the bar. It's nice, but not stuffy. Emmett's is a comfortable place to just hang out with friends at the bar over beers. Call it upscale casual or fine-dining lite.

The beer at Emmett's is fairly traditional. It's that way by design. Head Brewer Ryan Clooney and his crew craft beers according to classic styles using only the traditional four ingredients: water, malt, hops, and yeast. You'll find all the brewpub standards—light lager, amber ale, pale ale, porters, and stouts—along with a couple of bolder seasonal and special-release beers. While they may not push boundaries, they are all well-made with nicely defined layers of flavor.

I found that different beers stood out at different locations. Was this due to water, equipment, or just my mood? I can't say.

Emmett's Ale House–Palatine

ADDRESS: 110 N. Brockway St.
Palatine, IL 60067
TELEPHONE: 847–359–1533
EMAIL: Form on Web site
WEB SITE: www.emmettsalehouse.com
MICHAEL'S PICK: Munich Light: A beautifully balanced Munich helles lager, Munich Light highlights bready, pilsner-malt sweetness. Moderate bitterness and the licorice-like flavors of Continental hops round out the experience. It's crisp, clean, and very well made.
TYPE: Brewpub
DATE ESTABLISHED: 2007
OWNERS: Andrew Burns, Matthew Burns, and Timothy Burns
BREWMASTER: Ryan Clooney
BREWING SYSTEM: Ten-barrel DME brewhouse
FLAGSHIP BEERS: Munich Light, 1 A.M. Ale, Victory Pale Ale, McCarthy Red Ale, Double Barrel Oatmeal Stout
YEAR-ROUND BEERS: Munich Light, 1 A.M. Ale, Victory Pale Ale, McCarthy Red Ale, Double Barrel Oatmeal Stout
SEASONAL BEERS: Doppelbock, Belgian Tripel, Maibock, Hefeweizen, Kölsch, Pilsner, Belgian Blond,

ESB, Imperial Stout, Oktoberfest, Barleywine, Porter, Munich Dunkel

SPECIAL RELEASES: Irish Dry Stout, Scottish Ale, American Barleywine, Nitro Black IPA, Rye IPA, Saison, and others

TOURS: By request

BEER TO GO: Growlers, package, and kegs

FOOD: Selection of slightly upscale pub fare. Emphasis on organic, hormone-free, and locally sourced ingredients.

AMENITIES: Parking lot, convenient to the Palatine Metra station, seasonal outdoor seating, nightly drink and food specials, private rooms and banquet services available, full bar

PUB HOURS: Monday–Thursday: 11:30 A.M. to 11:00 P.M.; Friday and Saturday: 11:30 A.M. to 12:30 A.M.; Sunday: 11:30 A.M. to 9:00 P.M.

NEARBY ATTRACTIONS: Ram Restaurant and Brewery in Schaumburg and Wheeling, the Lucky Monk, The Onion Pub, thirty miles from the Chicago Loop, hiking in Deer Grove and Paul Douglas Forest Preserves

NOTES: See listing for Emmett's–Downers Grove

Emmett's Ale House–West Dundee

ADDRESS: 128 W. Main St.
West Dundee, IL 60118

TELEPHONE: 847–428–4500

EMAIL: Form on Web site

WEB SITE: www.emmettsalehouse.com

MICHAEL'S PICK: Victory Pale Ale: This hoppy American pale ale is all about the hops. Citrus-pith hop flavors are highlighted. It's got a bitter bark, but it doesn't bite. Underneath it all is a gentle malty sweetness with hints of biscuit and caramel. It's no surprise that this beer medaled in both the Great American Beer Festival and the World Beer Cup.

TYPE: Brewpub

DATE ESTABLISHED: 1998

OWNERS: Andrew Burns, Matthew Burns, and Timothy Burns

BREWMASTER: Ryan Clooney

BREWING SYSTEM: Seven-barrel JV Northwest brewhouse

FLAGSHIP BEERS: Munich Light, 1 A.M. Ale, Victory Pale Ale, McCarthy Red Ale, Double Barrel Oatmeal Stout

YEAR-ROUND BEERS: Munich Light, 1 A.M. Ale, Victory Pale Ale, McCarthy Red Ale, Double Barrel Oatmeal Stout

SEASONAL BEERS: Doppelbock, Belgian Tripel, Maibock, Hefeweizen, Kölsch, Pilsner, Belgian Blond, ESB, Imperial Stout, Oktoberfest, Barleywine, Porter, Munich Dunkel

SPECIAL RELEASES: Irish Dry Stout, Scottish Ale, American Barleywine, Nitro Black IPA, Rye IPA, Saison, and others

TOURS: By appointment

BEER TO GO: Growlers, package, and kegs

FOOD: Selection of slightly upscale pub fare. Emphasis on organic, hormone-free, and locally sourced ingredients.

AMENITIES: Free parking on street and in public lots, nightly drink and food specials, private rooms and banquet services available, full bar

PUB HOURS: Monday–Thursday: 11:30 A.M. to 11:00 P.M.; Friday and Saturday: 11:30 A.M. to 12:30 A.M.; Sunday: 11:30 A.M. to 9:00 P.M.

NEARBY ATTRACTIONS: The Lucky Monk, The Onion Pub, hiking in nearby Forest Preserves, Des Plaines River Bike Trail, Spring Hill Mall, Grand Victoria Casino, forty miles from the Chicago Loop

NOTES: See listing for Emmett's–Downers Grove

Finch's Beer Company

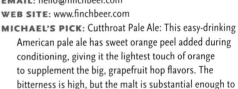

ADDRESS: 4565 N. Elston Ave.
Chicago, IL 60630

TELEPHONE: 773–283–4839

EMAIL: hello@finchbeer.com

WEB SITE: www.finchbeer.com

MICHAEL'S PICK: Cutthroat Pale Ale: This easy-drinking American pale ale has sweet orange peel added during conditioning, giving it the lightest touch of orange to supplement the big, grapefruit hop flavors. The bitterness is high, but the malt is substantial enough to keep it balanced. Some caramel and biscuit notes add complexity.

TYPE: Brewery

DATE ESTABLISHED: 2011

OWNERS: Benjamin Finch, Paul Finch, and Richard Grant

BREWMASTER: Richard Grant

BREWING SYSTEM: Fifteen-barrel Pacific Brewing Systems brewhouse

FLAGSHIP BEERS: Golden Wing Blond Ale, Cutthroat Pale Ale

YEAR-ROUND BEERS: Golden Wing Blond Ale, Cutthroat Pale Ale, Threadless India Pale Ale, Fascist Pig Ale, Secret Stache Stout

SEASONAL BEERS: Planned

SPECIAL RELEASES: Altus Gravitas Barleywine, Toasted Summer, and others

TOURS: Two Saturdays per month. Check Web site for dates. Cost $10.

BEER TO GO: None

FOOD: None

AMENITIES: Free street parking

PUB HOURS: None

NOTES: Finch's head brewer Richard Grant started
homebrewing while he was studying photography at
the School of the Art Institute of Chicago. His initial
batch was intended to be part of a project. As the campus was dry, his idea didn't go over so well.

He continued to brew after graduation, eventually
deciding that brewing was the career he wanted to
pursue. He attended the Siebel Institute and soon
after landed an assistant-brewer position at the Orland Park Rock Bottom. From Rock Bottom he became assistant brewer at Flossmoor Station, eventually working his way up to head brewer.

Grant feels that his background in photography
has helped him as a brewer. Like brewing, photography blends both art and science. Both require a creative vision coupled with the process-knowledge to
see that vision through to fruition. Grant continues
to homebrew when time allows, saying that it affords
him an opportunity to explore the creative side.

The mission at Finch's Beer Company is to provide
fresh, well-crafted, sessionable beers to the local Chicago market. Their beers can be found at many local
taps and in cans at stores.

Flesk Brewing Company

ADDRESS: 844 N. Ridge Ave.
Lombard, IL 60148
TELEPHONE: 630–233–4997
EMAIL: info@fleskbrewing.com
WEB SITE: www.fleskbrewing.com
MICHAEL'S PICK: None available for sample
TYPE: Brewery
DATE ESTABLISHED: 2012
OWNERS: William O'Brien and James O'Brien
BREWMASTER: James O'Brien
BREWING SYSTEM: 1.5-barrel Psycho Brew brewhouse
FLAGSHIP BEER: None
YEAR-ROUND BEERS: None
SEASONAL BEERS: None
SPECIAL RELEASES: Force of Nature Belgian IPA, Feral
Cat American Wheat, Gnomon Saison, Front Toward
Enemy IPA
TOURS: By request
BEER TO GO: Package
FOOD: None
AMENITIES: Parking lot
PUB HOURS: None

NOTES: As a youth, William and James O'Brien's father went to Ireland to explore his Gaelic roots. There
he visited the ruins of Flesk Castle. He returned from
the place with "relics," rusted iron spikes that he kept
encased in a glass box tucked away on a shelf. Years
later, the elder O'Brien regaled the brothers with stories about the castle. The "relics"—which they were
instructed never to touch—presented a tangible connection to the ghosts and sprites that inhabited its
crumbling walls.

Years later, as the O'Briens were building an identity for their fledgling brewery, they were reminded
of those stories. Naming the brewery after the castle seemed an obvious choice. They've incorporated
their Irish heritage in other ways as well. The arm and
sword in their logo is an element from the O'Brien
family crest.

The two feel that their small scale gives them freedom to pursue an eclectic brewing style. They don't
brew any year-round beers, opting instead for an ever-evolving lineup of specialties and one-offs. They
are letting the community have a say in the beers they
make by soliciting suggestions from their customers
over social media. If drinkers demand a particular
style or unique ingredient, the O'Briens say that they
will make it happen.

One note of interest: at the time of writing, James
O'Brien is also head brewer at the nearby Lunar
Brewing.

Flossmoor Station Restaurant and Brewery

ADDRESS: 1035 Sterling Ave.
Flossmoor, IL 60422
TELEPHONE: 708–957–2739
EMAIL: flossmoorstation@yahoo.com
WEB SITE: www.flossmoorstation.com
MICHAEL'S PICK: Rail Hopper IPA: Sharp bitterness at
the start quickly gives way to a juicy burst of citrus and
tropical fruit from ample application of American hops.
It's supported on a sweet and simple malt base. There
is plenty of hop character, but the amped up malt leads
me to label this a classic Midwest-style IPA.
TYPE: Brewpub
DATE ESTABLISHED: 1996
OWNERS: Dean Armstrong and Carolyn Armstrong
BREWMASTER: Bjorn Johnson
BREWING SYSTEM: Fifteen-barrel Specific Mechanical
brewhouse

Bags of grain cover the brewhouse at Flossmoor Station Restaurant and Brewery.

FLAGSHIP BEERS: Pullman Brown Ale, Rail Hopper IPA

YEAR-ROUND BEERS: Zephyr Golden Ale, Gandy Dancer Honey Ale, Station Master Wheat Ale, Chessie, Roundhouse Raspberry, Panama Limited Red Ale, Pullman Brown Ale, Rail Hopper IPA, Iron Horse Stout, rotating fruit beer

SEASONAL BEERS: None

SPECIAL RELEASES: Spoonless Winter Warmer, Belgian Abbey Ale, Overtime 2X IPA, Restless Wind, No Show ESB, Kellehers Bruin, Bear Claw, Intercontinental Pale Lager, Maple Wheat, occasional sour and barrel-aged beers, and others

TOURS: By request

BEER TO GO: Growlers, package, and kegs

FOOD: Selection of standard brewpub favorites: burgers, sandwiches, salads, and entrées.

AMENITIES: Free street parking, private room available, full bar, family friendly, convenient to the Flossmoor Metra station

PUB HOURS: Monday–Thursday: 11:30 A.M. to midnight; Friday and Saturday: 11:30 A.M. to 1:00 A.M.; Sunday: 11:30 A.M. to 11:00 P.M.

NEARBY ATTRACTIONS: Three Floyds Brewing, Brickstone Brewery and Restaurant, Rock Bottom–Orland Park, Harrison's Brewery and Restaurant, golf, concerts at the First Midwest Bank Amphitheatre, thirty miles from the Chicago Loop

NOTES: The historic train station in Flossmoor was once the pivotal stop on a rail line that ferried Chicago's moneyed elite to the area's exclusive golf clubs. It's now the home of the Flossmoor Station Restaurant and Brewery. When the Metra commuter-rail line was moved to a platform behind the building, the old station quickly fell into disrepair. Dean and Carolyn Armstrong purchased the building and carefully restored it, preserving as much of its original character as possible, right down to the iron-grated ticket booth that now serves as the host stand.

Through the pub and off-premises retail beer sales, Flossmoor Station has built a regional reputation for high-quality brews. The assortment is broad. With fifteen or more beers on tap, the ever-rotating selection includes everything from light, golden ales to big-bruiser, barrel-aged beers and sours.

Flossmoor Station has a casual pub atmosphere that retains much of the feel of the old train depot. Whether you pull up a stool at the bar or grab a table in the dining room, it's a fun place to converse with friends over great food and beer.

Goose Island Beer Co. Clybourn Brewpub

ADDRESS: 1800 N. Clybourn Ave. Chicago, IL 60614

TELEPHONE: 312-915-0071

EMAIL: info@gooseisland.com

WEB SITE: www.gooseisland.com

MICHAEL'S PICK: Tingly Tongue: This is a great example of the pub's culinary approach to brewing. Made in collaboration with Chef Stephanie Izard of Girl and the Goat restaurant, it is a black witbier with peppercorns, yuzu, Thai chilis, and orange peel. It's light, with floral, spicy, and citrus overtones. A mild tingle of chili heat comes in long after the swallow. This is a beer to sit and ponder.

TYPE: Brewpub

DATE ESTABLISHED: 1988

OWNER: John Hall

BREWMASTER: Nick Barron

BREWING SYSTEM: Ten-barrel JV Northwest brewhouse

FLAGSHIP BEER: Honkers Ale

YEAR-ROUND BEERS: 312 Urban Wheat Ale, Green Line Pale Ale, India Pale Ale, Matilda

SEASONAL BEERS: Rotating dark beers in winter, rotating light beers in summer

SPECIAL RELEASES: New release every week. Examples include Cherrywood Smoked Bock, Curbside Saison, Double D Belgian Dubbel with Brettanomyces, Oatmeal Stout, Tingly Tongue, Sour Shimmy, Luciana, Citrine Bombshell, and Sahti

TOURS: Saturdays at 12:30 and 2:00 P.M.; Sundays at 1:30, 3:00, and 4:30 P.M. Reservations are required.

BEER TO GO: Growlers, kegs, and package

FOOD: An eclectic menu of unique sandwiches and small plates with an emphasis on locally sourced ingredients. The menu has an upscale feel, but pricing is reasonable.

AMENITIES: Limited parking lot, free street parking, convenient to Brown and Red Line "L" trains, full bar, MBA Passport program, cask-conditioned selections

PUB HOURS: Daily: 11:00 A.M. to close

NEARBY ATTRACTIONS: Chicagoland breweries, Steppenwolf Theatre, Royal George Theatre, centrally located in Chicago's North Side, quick train ride to the Chicago Loop, Chicago History Museum

NOTES: The Goose Island Clybourn Brewpub is the original home of the Goose Island Brewing Company. It's one of my favorite places to grab a beer and a bite when I'm in the Windy City. I often refer to it as my "Chicago office." The atmosphere is cozy and casual, the perfect setting for a night out with friends or for getting work done at the bar. The constantly changing beer list is of consistently high quality. And the super-knowledgeable bar staff is ready to answer any questions you might have about a particular brew.

Head brewer Nick Barron came to Goose Island from the Flossmoor Station Restaurant and Brewery in Chicago's southern suburbs. His approach to brewing is a culinary one. He starts with a vision of the final brew and then tries different combinations of ingredients to coax the desired flavors from his raw materials. He's not afraid to venture into using vegetables, spices, fruit, or whatever else suits his fancy or his mood. This leaves him well placed to carry on the food-focused brewing style established by his predecessor chef/brewer Jared Rouben.

Many of the beers at Goose Island reflect Barron's love of low-alcohol session beers. English bitters and ESBs are among his favorites. But you can expect to see some high-gravity bombers on tap as well.

Goose Island Beer Co. Fulton Street Brewery

ADDRESS: 1800 W. Fulton St. Chicago, IL 60612
TELEPHONE: 312–226–1119
EMAIL: info@gooseisland.com
WEB SITE: www.gooseisland.com
MICHAEL'S PICK: Bourbon County Brand Stout: This is one of the world's great beers. Rich, thick, and packing a potent punch, it remains velvety smooth and beautifully drinkable. It weaves a complex web of flavors, including chocolate, roast, vanilla, caramel, and smoke. Perfect when fresh, it gets even better with age.
TYPE: Brewery
DATE ESTABLISHED: 1998
OWNER: Anheuser-Busch In-Bev
BREWMASTER: Brett Porter

BREWING SYSTEM: Fifty-barrel JV Northwest brewhouse
FLAGSHIP BEER: Honker's Ale
YEAR-ROUND BEERS: 312 Urban Wheat Ale, Green Line Pale Ale, Honker's Ale, India Pale Ale, Matilda, Pere Jacques, Sofie, Fleur, Pepe Nero, Demolition, Marisol, Nut Brown, Oatmeal Stout
SEASONAL BEERS: Summertime, Harvest Ale, Mild Winter, Christmas Ale
SPECIAL RELEASES: Juliet, Lolita, Madame Rose, Night Stalker, Big John, Bourbon County Brand Stout, Bourbon County Brand Coffee Stout, King Henry, Rare Bourbon County Brand Stout, Bourbon County Brand Vanilla Stout, Dominique, and others
TOURS: By appointment
BEER TO GO: None
FOOD: None
AMENITIES: Free street parking
PUB HOURS: None
NEARBY ATTRACTIONS: Games and concerts at the United Center, University of Illinois at Chicago, Redmoon Theatre, Haymarket Brewpub, Piece Pizzeria and Brewpub, Wicker Park shops and music clubs, Lyric Opera, Willis Tower

NOTES: Goose Island is a brewery headed in many directions at once. While maintaining the Classic Line of beers that helped pioneer the American craft-beer movement, they are continuing to innovate with their Vintage Line of Belgian-style and barrel-aged beers. In addition, the brewery maintains an active beer-education program aimed at increasing public knowledge about beer in general and beer/food pairing in particular.

The brewery's Belgian-inspired lineup makes use of the "wild" Brettanomyces yeast strain for the unique, earthy flavors it imparts. Fermentation with that yeast can be wildly unpredictable. In some barrels the character will show up quickly, while in others it can take a very long time. Bottles and kegs develop differently, resulting in different-tasting beers.

Brewmaster Brett Porter is spearheading an extensive research-and-development program to study the fermentation characteristics of these yeast strains with the goal of making better and more consistent beer. Using high-tech analytical tools and rigorous brewing practices, they want

Beer aging in barrels at the Goose Island Fulton Street Brewery.

to discover how Brettanomyces functions in order to make its results as predictable as normal brewing yeast. It is groundbreaking research for the industry.

The recent acquisition of Goose Island Beer Co. by brewing giant Anheuser-Busch In-Bev has separated the production brewery from the brewpubs. In addition to the brewery, Goose Island also has an entire building across Fulton Street that houses its enormous barrel-aging cellar.

Goose Island Beer Co. Wrigleyville Brewpub

ADDRESS: 3535 N. Clark St.
Chicago, IL 60657
TELEPHONE: 773–832–9040
EMAIL: info@gooseisland.com
WEB SITE: www.gooseisland.com
MICHAEL'S PICK: Green Line Pale Ale: Simply a solid American-style pale ale. Moderately high bitterness balances grainy-sweet malt with biscuit overtones. Pine resin and citrus hops nicely complement the malt character. This is a good sessionable beer that would be great before a Cubs home game.
TYPE: Brewpub
DATE ESTABLISHED: 1988
OWNER: John Hall
BREWMASTER: Nick Barron
BREWING SYSTEM: Fifteen-barrel JV Northwest brewhouse
FLAGSHIP BEER: Cubby Blueberry Ale
YEAR-ROUND BEERS: 312 Urban Wheat Ale, Green Line Pale Ale, India Pale Ale, Matilda, Cubby Blueberry Ale
SEASONAL BEERS: Summertime, Harvest Ale, Mild Winter, Christmas Ale
SPECIAL RELEASES: Rotating dark beers in winter, rotating light beers in summer
TOURS: Saturdays at 12:30 and 2:00 P.M.; Sundays at 1:30, 3:00, and 4:30 P.M. Reservations are required.
BEER TO GO: Six packs, kegs, and package
FOOD: Slightly upscale pub food, with more of an emphasis on burgers and sandwiches than at the Clybourn location
AMENITIES: Metered street parking or paid lots, convenient to Red Line "L" trains, steps from Wrigley Field, full bar, MBA Passport program, live music, private dining room available, upstairs bar for private parties
PUB HOURS:
Cubs home-game day hours: Sunday–Thursday: 11:00 A.M. to midnight; Friday and Saturday: 11:00 A.M. to 2:00 A.M.
Regular Hours: Sunday–Wednesday: 11:00 A.M. to 11:00 P.M.; Thursday: 11:00 A.M. to midnight; Friday and Saturday: 11:00 A.M. to 2:00 A.M.

NEARBY ATTRACTIONS: Chicagoland breweries, Wrigley Field, Wrigleyville bars and restaurants, Vic Theatre, Graceland Cemetery, Chicago Lakefront and Belmont Harbor, Sydney R. Morovitz Golf Course

NOTES: The Goose Island Wrigleyville location features beers from the same brewers as the original Clybourn brewpub. The brews are mostly the same, although the selection is more limited. Cubby Blueberry Ale—brewed to commemorate the Chicago Cubs, who play at the nearby Wrigley Field—is the one brew that is exclusive to this store. It is a moderately bitter amber ale with toast and caramel malt notes and pronounced earthy/tart blueberry flavors.

The pub is spacious, with soaring ceilings and plenty of standing room for pre- and postgame crowds. Dark wood, brass railings, and red, white, and blue bunting evoke a 1910 saloon. Exposed concrete and abundant television screens add a modern sports-bar edge to the nostalgia. The brewery is just visible behind glass opposite the bar. A more intimate back dining room would seem to offer a quieter respite from what could become a noisy front bar area.

Gordon Biersch Brewery and Restaurant

ADDRESS: 639 E. Boughton Rd., Suite 100
Bolingbrook, IL 60440
TELEPHONE: 630–739–6036
EMAIL: None
WEB SITE: www.gordonbiersch.com
MICHAEL'S PICK: Czech Pilsner: Pilsner is the perfect beer, and Gordon Biersch makes a good one. It's crisp and clean with sharp bitterness that is backed up by rich, bready pilsner malt sweetness. The real star is the floral aroma and flavor of Czech Saaz hops. It's subtle, but not without complexity, just as pilsner should be.
TYPE: Brewpub
DATE ESTABLISHED: 2008
OWNER: Craftworks Restaurants and Breweries Inc.
BREWMASTER: John Wyzkiewicz
BREWING SYSTEM: Twenty-barrel Specific Mechanical brewhouse
FLAGSHIP BEERS: Golden Export, Hefeweizen, Czech Pilsner, Märzen, Schwarzbier
YEAR-ROUND BEERS: Golden Export, Hefeweizen, Czech Pilsner, Märzen, Schwarzbier
SEASONAL BEERS: Vienna Lager, Eisbock, Dunkel, Goze, Weizenbock, Rauchbier, Altbier, Sommerfest, Winterbock
SPECIAL RELEASES: Roggenbier, occasional barrel-aged beers
TOURS: By request
BEER TO GO: Growlers and kegs (reservation required for kegs)

FOOD: Moderately upscale selection of brewpub favorites: salads, burgers, steaks, and seafood

AMENITIES: Parking lot, seasonal outdoor seating, private rooms available, full bar, happy-hour specials, Stein Club, family-friendly

PUB HOURS: Monday–Thursday: 11:00 A.M. to midnight; Friday and Saturday: 11:00 A.M. to 1:00 A.M.; Sunday: 11:00 A.M. to 11:00 P.M.

NEARBY ATTRACTIONS: Emmett's Ale House–Downers Grove, Nevins Brewing Company, Harrison's Brewery and Restaurant, Rock Bottom–Orland Park, Rock Bottom–Warrenville, Two Brothers Brewing Company, hiking at nearby forest preserves, Cyprus Grove Family Aquatic Park, Naper Settlement Museum, Morton Arboretum, thirty miles from the Chicago Loop

NOTES: Founded by Dan Gordon and Dean Biersch, the first Gordon Biersch restaurant opened in Palo Alto, California, in 1988. The franchise currently operates in over thirty locations throughout the country.

Dan Gordon is a graduate of the master-brewer program at the Weihenstephan Brewery outside Munich, Germany. His training guided Gordon Biersch's focus on finely crafted German-style lagers and ales. The chain boasts of its adherence to the German purity laws and its use of malt and hops imported from Germany. The beers have won many awards in national and international competition.

Gordon Biersch brewers follow strict protocols to insure consistency from location to location, including sending samples to the corporate laboratory for analysis. You can be assured that the beer you loved at one location will be just as good at another. When the beer is well made, that's not a bad thing.

Half Acre Beer Company

ADDRESS: 4257 N. Lincoln Ave.
Chicago, IL 60618

TELEPHONE: 773–248–4038

EMAIL: hello@halfacrebeer.com

WEB SITE: www.halfacrebeer.com

MICHAEL'S PICK: Over Ale: A hoppy brown porter? A modestly hopped black IPA? Who knows? Who cares? It's got chocolate roast. It's got caramel sweetness. And it's got piney hops. As the can says, "It's quite possibly exactly what you think it is."

TYPE: Brewery

DATE ESTABLISHED: 2006

OWNERS: Gabriel Magliaro and Matt Gallagher

BREWMASTER: Matt Gallagher

BREWING SYSTEM: Fifteen-barrel Century brewhouse

FLAGSHIP BEER: Daisy Cutter Pale Ale

YEAR-ROUND BEERS: Daisy Cutter Pale Ale, Half Acre Over Ale, Gossamer Golden Ale

SEASONAL BEERS: None

SPECIAL RELEASES: Double Daisy Cutter, Baumé, Ginger Twin India Red Ale, Big Hugs Imperial Stout, Magnus, The Invasion Helles Bock, Shewolf India Pale Ale, Freedom of '78 Pure Guava Wheat India Pale Ale, Bairn Farmhouse, StickyFat American Dark Ale, The Empty Sea, Buckingham Green Amber, Marty Stouffer's Wild America Barley Wine, Ambrosia Drop, and many others

TOURS: Saturdays at 1:00 P.M. Cost $10. Reservations required.

BEER TO GO: Growlers, kegs, and package

FOOD: None

AMENITIES: Free street parking, tasting room and swag store, convenient to the Brown Line "L" trains

PUB HOURS: Tuesday–Friday: noon to 8:00 P.M.; Saturday: 11:00 A.M. to 7:00 P.M.; Sunday: 11:00 A.M. to 5:00 P.M.

NEARBY ATTRACTIONS: Chicago-area breweries, Finch's Brewing Company and Metropolitan Brewing nearby, Old Town School of Folk Music, Aragon Ballroom, Music Box Theatre, Shattered Globe Theatre, American Theatre Company, Graceland Cemetery

NOTES: When the Half Acre guys moved to Chicago the mid-2000s, there wasn't much homegrown beer. Goose Island, Piece Pizza, and Rock Bottom were about it. Having come from Boulder, a town with a well-established beer culture, they had to ask, "Where's the beer?" Not finding it, they took matters into their own hands.

With no background in brewing, aside from a few batches of homebrew, they took the leap. Their first beers, contract brewed at the Sand Creek Brewing Co. in Wisconsin, were an immediate hit. The next step was to build a brewery. The first Half Acre beers brewed at their own facility were released in late 2008.

Half Acre's approach is to produce unique takes on classic microbrew styles. High gravity and super-hoppy beers are not their mainstays. As Gabriel Magliaro explained it, they start with a base style and then work outward in concentric circles. Once they have an understanding of one thing, they push it another step further to the next plateau. This step-by-step approach has led to a lineup that encompasses everything from a classic golden ale to an imperial rye stout and a saison brewed with lemon and chamomile.

Ultimately, for Magliaro beer drinking is not about the beer. "It's about sitting down with others and having beer to put a cap on the moment in time. You might be drinking the most coveted beer in the world, but it's not so much fun if you're drinking it alone with a notepad."

Hamburger Mary's Brew and Grill

ADDRESS: 5400 N. Clark St.
Chicago, IL 60640

TELEPHONE: 773-784-6969

EMAIL: chicago@hamburgermarys.com

WEB SITE: www.hamburgermarys.com/chicago

MICHAEL'S PICK: Apple Pie Wheat: It really does taste like apple pie. A wheaty crust is overlain with cinnamon spice and juicy, cooked apples. Clove phenols from the hefeweizen yeast put the finishing touches on the apple-pie spicing. I didn't expect to like it, but I did.

TYPE: Brewpub

DATE ESTABLISHED: 2006, brewing began in 2009

OWNERS: Brandon Wright and Ashley Wright

BREWMASTER: Brandon Wright

BREWING SYSTEM: Fifty-five-gallon Blichmann Engineering brewhouse

FLAGSHIP BEERS: Blond Bombshell Organic Golden Ale, Mary Hoppins Pale Ale

YEAR-ROUND BEERS: Blond Bombshell Organic Golden Ale, Mary Hoppins Pale Ale, Gangster Hopped-up Amber Ale, rotating IPA selection including Hippity-Hoppity, Black Widow, and Belgian IPA

SEASONAL BEERS: Apple Pie Wheat, Capone Imperial Red, Mary Christmas Ale, Busta Nut Brown Ale, Strawberry Blond Bombshell, Rye of the Tiger Red Rye Ale

SPECIAL RELEASES: Gluten Free Sleeping Beauty, Ancho-Pilonchillo, Smokin' Scotty, Honey-Ginger Mead, Hibiscus Wit, Peanut Butter Porter, Mary's Queen of Scotts, Mrs. O'Leary Stout, Raspberry Lambic-Saison, Van Dam Good IPA, Sweet Potato Ale

TOURS: No

BEER TO GO: Growlers

FOOD: Diner-like menu that includes homey favorites like macaroni and cheese and tater tots. Hamburgers are obviously the specialty.

AMENITIES: Metered street parking, full bar, live music in the attic, daily drink specials

PUB HOURS:
Dining Room: Monday–Friday: 11:30 A.M. to 11:00 P.M.; Saturday and Sunday: 10:30 A.M. to 11:00 P.M.
Mary's Attic: Wednesday–Friday and Sunday: 8:00 P.M. to 2:00 A.M.; Saturday: 8:00 P.M. to 3:00 A.M.
Mary's Rec Room: Monday–Wednesday: 5:00 P.M. to midnight; Thursday and Friday: 5:00 P.M. to 1:30 A.M.; Saturday: 12:00 P.M. to 2:30 A.M.; Sunday 12:00 P.M. to midnight

NEARBY ATTRACTIONS: The Hopleaf, Metropolitan Brewing Co., Andersonville shopping and restaurants, The Neo-Futurists Theater, Organic Theatre, Chicago Filmmakers, Swedish American Museum, Aragon Ballroom, Riviera Theatre

The fermentation room at Hamburger Mary's.

NOTES: The Hamburger Mary's franchise has its roots in the gay and lesbian community of San Francisco, but it is about much more than that. Calling itself an "open-air bar and grille for open-minded people," the concept is really about fun and food. While there are ten locations scattered throughout the country, Chicago is the only one with a brewery.

Hamburger Mary's Chicago has three different spaces, each with its own distinct feel. The main dining room is all kitsch and camp, with red-velvet curtains, beaded lamps, and multiple flower-print wallpapers. Next door, the Rec Room has a comfortable, sports-bar feel. It's a good place to watch the game over a beer. Upstairs in Mary's Attic you can enjoy the nearly nightly live music events.

Brewer Brandon Wright calls his beers "Mary's Homebrew." He brews them on a stove-top system that he says is a "glorified homebrew system." The results are mixed, but the fun and food balance it all out. Come to Mary's for the atmosphere and the fantastic burgers and enjoy a homebrewed beer while you're there.

Harrison's Restaurant and Brewery

ADDRESS: 15845 S. La Grange Rd.
Orland Park, IL 60462

TELEPHONE: 708-226-0100

EMAIL: harrisonsbrewpub@sbcglobal.net

WEB SITE: www.harrisonsbrewpub.com

MICHAEL'S PICK: Harrisons Red: Caramel malt and subtle but lingering roast mark this as an Irish-style red ale. The bitterness is moderate but hangs on into the finish, supported by light earthy hop notes. It's rounded out by hints of fruit.

TYPE: Brewpub

DATE ESTABLISHED: 1998

OWNER: Family-owned

BREWMASTER: Joachim Mekoum

BREWING SYSTEM: Fifteen-barrel Newlands Systems brewhouse

FLAGSHIP BEER: Millennium Pale Ale

YEAR-ROUND BEERS: Millennium Pale Ale, La Grange Golden Light, Harrison's Lager Lite, Harrison's Wheat, Raspberry Wheat, Harrison's Red, Imperial Black Diamond Stout, Category 3 Triple IPA, Harrison's Brown Ale, rotating fruit beer

SEASONAL BEERS: Oktoberfest, Pilsner, Lazy Dog Lager, Butterscotch Ale, Barleywine, Hefeweizen

SPECIAL RELEASES: Hoppy Dog Lager, Triple Sec Bock, Bourbon Barrel Stout, and others

TOURS: By request

BEER TO GO: Growlers and kegs

FOOD: Large selection of brewpub favorites: wings, ribs, sandwiches and burgers, steaks, and chops

AMENITIES: Parking lot, seasonal outdoor seating, full bar, Mug Club, daily food specials

PUB HOURS: Sunday–Thursday: 11:00 A.M. to 1:00 A.M.; Friday and Saturday: 11:00 A.M. to 2:00 A.M.

NEARBY ATTRACTIONS: Rock Bottom–Orland Park, Flossmoor Station Brewpub, Three Floyds Brewing, Brickstone Restaurant and Brewery, hiking and cross-country skiing in nearby forest preserves, concerts at First Midwest Bank Amphitheatre, Lake Katherine Botanic Gardens, twenty-five miles from the Chicago Loop

NOTES: Harrison's head brewer Joachim Mekoum loves the social aspect of beer. Growing up in France and Germany, he is familiar with both wine and beer culture. To him, wine is best consumed at home with family. Beer is what you drink while out with friends or when stopping by the pub on the way home from work.

This social focus means his favorite beers are session beers. He likes flavorful, low-alcohol beers that allow you to drink a few pints without losing control. As he is fond of saying, "If you drink beer to get drunk, drink vodka instead. It's faster." This preference is reflected in the beer he brews at Harrison's. While he makes all styles, the majority of them are on the lighter end of the spectrum. He wants his customers to drink more than one.

Harrison's has a casual, family-friendly vibe. The atmosphere falls somewhere between an English pub and one of those Greek-owned family restaurants. Portions are huge—burgers are ten ounces—so be prepared to take home a doggy bag if you order appetizers before your entrée.

Haymarket Pub and Brewery

ADDRESS: 737 W. Randolph St. Chicago, IL 60661

TELEPHONE: 312–638–0070

EMAIL: Form on Web site

WEB SITE: www.haymarketbrewing.com

MICHAEL'S PICK: Living Wage American-Belgo Pale Ale: This was my go-to beer on every visit. It's an easy-drinking, low-alcohol session ale with a light Belgian flair. Hops are the focus. Crisp bitterness and bright citrusy flavors compliment subtle spiciness from Belgian yeast.

TYPE: Brewpub

DATE ESTABLISHED: 2010

OWNERS: John Neurauter and Pete Crowley

BREWMASTER: Pete Crowley

BREWING SYSTEM: Fifteen-barrel ABT brewhouse

FLAGSHIP BEER: Mathias Double IPA

YEAR-ROUND BEERS: None. Beers that are frequently available include Speakerswagon Pilsner, Living Wage, Six Point Golden Lager, Mathias Double IPA, Mojo Abbey Style Dubbel, Last Chance Belgian IPA, and Midnight Hour Porter

SEASONAL BEERS: Oktoberfest Märzen Bier and others

SPECIAL RELEASES: I'm So Lonely Belgian Single, Hard Times American IPA, Black Wobbly Robust Porter, Ti Jean Belgian Pale Ale, Dynamite and Roses Belgian IPA, Peace Frog American IPA, Anarchy Double IPA, Devil in the Wit City, The Saison Also Rises, Chicago Amnesia Apricot Wheat, 7GA IPA, Clare's Right Hook Bourbon Barrel Aged Barleywine, BUK Black Rye Bock, and others

TOURS: By request

BEER TO GO: Growlers

FOOD: "Craft pub food": interesting twists on classic brewpub fare, with a focus on locally sourced ingredients and homemade, beer-infused sausages. The spicy porter mustard is a must-try.

AMENITIES: Home of the Drinking and Writing Theatre, good selection of guest taps and bottle beers, full bar, seasonal outdoor seating, private room available

PUB HOURS: Sunday–Friday: 11:00 A.M. to 2:00 A.M.; Saturday: 11:00 A.M. to 3:00 A.M.

NEARBY ATTRACTIONS: Goose Island Fulton Street Brewery, Willis Tower, Goodman Theatre, Art Institute of Chicago, Lyric Opera, Cadillac Palace Theatre, Chicago Theatre, Chicago Cultural Center, Jane Addams Hull-House Museum, Site of the 1886 Haymarket Riot, Randolph Street Market District, sporting events at the United Center

NOTES: Haymarket owner/brewer Pete Crowley brews the kind of beers that he likes to drink. What he likes are Belgians and hops. No other brewpub in Chicago focuses on Belgian-style beers to the same extent. Among the more than ten house beers on tap you'll find an ever-changing array of styles, from light and fruity witbiers to bold and bitter Beligan IPAs, with a few traditional Abbey-style beers scattered among them. Also present are American-style IPAs and double IPAs.

If you're not a fan of those styles, don't fret. Pete also brews awesome porters and stouts as well as a first-rate pilsner. A large selection of guest taps and bottles from American craft brewers fill in the stylistic gaps.

The place has the feel of an upscale beer bar. It's elegant, but still casual enough to hang out for conversation over a few pints. It has an intimacy that defies the nearly three-hundred-person seating capacity. Be sure to take note of the beautiful tile mosaic floors.

During an extended stay in the city, Haymarket joined the Goose Island Clybourn pub to become my second "Chicago office." It's a must-visit when you are in the Windy City.

Lake Bluff Brewing Company

ADDRESS: 16 E. Scranton Ave.
Lake Bluff, IL 60044
TELEPHONE: 224–544–5179
EMAIL: info@lbbrew.com
WEB SITE: www.lbbrew.com
MICHAEL'S PICK: Bohemian Blonde: Built on the base of a Bohemian pilsner, but made with clean-fermenting ale yeast, Bohemian Blonde is not your run-of-the-mill, beginner's blond ale. It's sharply bitter and loaded with flavor. It's a "smack-you-in-the-face" easy-drinker that highlights hops.
TYPE: Brewery
DATE ESTABLISHED: 2010
OWNERS: Rodd Specketer and David Burns
BREWMASTER: David Burns
BREWING SYSTEM: Three-barrel Premier Stainless brewhouse
FLAGSHIP BEER: Hard Tail Imperial IPA
YEAR-ROUND BEERS: Bohemian Blonde Ale, Soft Tail IPA, Hard Tail Imperial IPA, Inspiration Pale Ale, Easy Rider English Ale, Black Squirrel Bourbon Stout
SEASONAL BEERS: Weeee!!!! Heavy Scotch Ale, Cosmic Speculation Barleywine, 'Tis the Saison, Belgian Monkey Dark Strong Ale
SPECIAL RELEASES: Hefeweizen, Americana Wheat 101, and others
TOURS: By appointment or request
BEER TO GO: Growlers
FOOD: Limited menu of sandwiches and small-bites from local Lake Bluff vendors
AMENITIES: Parking lot in rear, free street parking, tasting room, limited wine selection, seasonal outdoor seating, easy access to Chicago from the Metra train
PUB HOURS: Sunday: 1:00 to 6:00 P.M.; Wednesday and Thursday: 5:00 to 10:00 P.M.; Friday and Saturday: 5:00 P.M. to midnight

NEARBY ATTRACTIONS: Mickey Finn's Brewpub, Tighthead Brewing Company, the park across the street has summer concerts and farmers market, located in the quaint downtown Lake Bluff shopping area, midway between Chicago and Milwaukee, North Shore Distillery, Lake Michigan North Shore, easy access to bike trails, Ravinia Festival

NOTES: Lake Bluff is a cozy, relatively affluent bedroom community located about thirty-five miles north of Chicago on the North Shore of Lake Michigan. Its quaint downtown, organized around a central park, features the trendy boutiques and assortment of coffee shops and intimate restaurants that typify the towns of the area. Lake Bluff Brewing Company fits right in.

The brewery is nestled on the edge of downtown. Its historic-looking storefront is across the street from the park. The inside has a comfortable and casual, minimalist feel. A popular stop for commuters headed to or coming from Chicago on the train, it's a place where you can feel at home in jeans or a suit. There are televisions for watching the game, but they are unobtrusively placed, and the sound is usually turned off. The wooded park and small-town feel make the patio a great place for a pint on a summer evening.

David Burns and Rodd Specketer lean toward big beers and bold flavors. As they told me, "We're targeting people who already enjoy or want to enjoy craft beer, not the average Joe." They are meeting with a good response, already finding it difficult to meet demand selling only from their taproom. The day I was there they had freshly sold out of all but two of their own beers. I found those two to be clean, well-made, and worthy of a stop.

Lake Effect Brewing Company

ADDRESS: 4727 W. Montrose Ave.
Chicago, IL 60641
TELEPHONE: 312–919–4473
EMAIL:
clint@lakeeffectbrewing.com
WEB SITE:
www.lakeeffectbrewing.com
MICHAEL'S PICK: Belgian IPA: This Americanized version of the style showcases the bold flavors of citrusy Citra and piney Simcoe hops that combine with yeasty esters to create a tropical, fruit-punch impression. The bitterness has a bite, but a moderate one. A touch of sweetness and hints of biscuit bring balance.
TYPE: Brewery
DATE ESTABLISHED: 2012

OWNERS: Clint Bautz and Lynn Ford

BREWMASTER: Clint Bautz

BREWING SYSTEM: Four-barrel Psycho Brew brewhouse

FLAGSHIP BEERS: BESB, Lake-Effect Snow Wit Bier, Bitchin' Blonde, Fresh Coast IPA

YEAR-ROUND BEERS: Fresh Coast IPA, Lake-Effect Snow Wit Bier, Fresh Coast Pale Ale, Milk Stout

SEASONAL BEERS: Kölsch Style Ale, Smoked Lager, Imperial IPA, Märzen, Barrel-aged Imperial Stout

SPECIAL RELEASES: Lager, Malty Medley English Strong

TOURS: By appointment

BEER TO GO: Growlers

FOOD: None

AMENITIES: Parking lot, free street parking, taproom, convenient to the Montrose stop on the Blue Line "L" and the Metra/Mayfair station

PUB HOURS: Check Web site

NEARBY ATTRACTIONS: Finch's Beer Company, Independence Tap beer bar, Irish American Heritage Center, LaBagh Woods and Forest Glenn Woods Forest Preserves, Old Town School of Folk Music, Portage Theatre

NOTES: Lake Effect Brewing Company sees itself first and foremost as a neighborhood establishment. Before it opened, the up-and-coming northwestern Chicago neighborhoods in which it is located didn't have much to offer residents in the way of good beer. Owners Clint Bautz and Lynn Ford aim to fill that void, distributing their small-batch brews primarily to accounts near the brewery. They want locals to view their taproom as a friendly place to pop in for a pint or pick up a freshly made growler as they step off the train on their way home from work.

The name of the brewery doesn't only reference the lake-effect snows that frequently snarl traffic in the city during the winter months. It reflects a local focus that is broader than just the neighborhood. Lake Effect sources most of its raw materials from the region surrounding Lake Michigan. The brewers grow some of their own hops; the rest come from farms in Michigan and Wisconsin. Briess Malting in Chilton, Wisconsin, supplies the malt. And, of course, they use fresh Lake Michigan water.

Bautz and Ford joke that their signature style might just be that they don't really have a signature style. They are focused on crafting a wide-ranging lineup of twelve beers that runs the gamut from witbier and Belgian blond ale to smoked lager and imperial stout. Of course, there's a hoppy IPA in there as well. The mix reflects the pair's view of beer as a beverage of endless variety. They want their customers to be able to explore as many different paths as possible.

ADDRESS: 10 N. Lake St., Unit 107
Grayslake, IL 60030

TELEPHONE: 847–752–8489

EMAIL: cofb4@yahoo.com

WEB SITE: www.lightthelampbrewery.com

MICHAEL'S PICK: Sin Bin Stout: Sometimes it is difficult to distinguish between porter and stout, and Sin Bin is one of those beers that blur the line. Moderate roasted bitterness is supported by dark chocolate and dry, toasted malt flavors. A bit of caramel sweetness gives some contrast. It finishes dry with lingering coffee-like notes.

TYPE: Brewery

DATE ESTABLISHED: 2012

OWNERS: Bill Hermes, Don Chatten, Jeff Sheppard, Dave Cavanaugh, and Kurt Engdahl

BREWMASTER: Bill Hermes

BREWING SYSTEM: Fifteen-gallon Sabco Systems brewhouse

FLAGSHIP BEER: 1980 Miracle American Ale

YEAR-ROUND BEERS: Power Play IPA, 1980 Miracle American Ale, Sin Bin Stout, Bench Minor Blond, Red Line Ale

SEASONAL BEERS: Highsticking Holiday Ale, Light the Lamp Oktoberfest, Wraparound Wheat

SPECIAL RELEASES: Hattrick Hefeweizen, Yard Sale Ale, Shorthanded IPA

TOURS: By request

BEER TO GO: Growlers

FOOD: Small selection of pizzas and snacks

AMENITIES: Parking lot, free street parking, seasonal outdoor seating, available for private events

PUB HOURS: Friday: 4:00 P.M. to midnight; Saturday and Sunday: noon to midnight. Check Web site for additional open hours during hockey games.

NEARBY ATTRACTIONS: Historic Grayslake downtown, Six Flags Great America, Lake County Fairgrounds, water activities on nearby lakes, fifty miles from the Chicago Loop

NOTES: What happens when a group of homebrewing fiftysomething hockey dads goes to the Munich Oktoberfest? They come home and start a brewery, of course.

It was hockey that brought the Light the Lamp team together. They all have sons who played the sport as teammates and competitors. The men met while attending games or coaching those teams. Some of them have played pond hockey together. Getting together to watch the Chicago Blackhawks play is a favorite pastime. Naturally, beer is involved.

It was the Oktoberfest experience that led them to start homebrewing together. Munich was a side stop in a trip to watch the Blackhawks play in Helsinki. While enjoying liters of lager under the tents, Bill Hermes, Don Chatten, and Jeff Sheppard decided to resume the hobby that they had left some time before. As their passion grew, they developed labels, logos, and all the trappings of a commercial brewery. When their kids were finally grown and gone, they decided to take it all the way.

Hockey infuses everything in the brewery. The lamp in the name refers to the light behind the net that is lit whenever a goal is scored. The beers all have hockey names: Hat Trick, Power Play, and Yard Sale, which refers to the scattering of equipment on the ice during a bench-clearing fight. Tap handles are the taped-up butt-ends of hockey sticks with pucks mounted on top.

The taproom has a sports-bar feel. The red walls recall the Blackhawk team colors. Their signature drink is a modified black and tan made with Sin Bin Stout and Red Line Ale, another reference to the black and red of the beloved hometown team. Of course, there is a large-screen television for watching the games.

The Lucky Monk

ADDRESS: 105 Hollywood Blvd. S
South Barrington, IL 60010
TELEPHONE: 847–898–0500
EMAIL: info@theluckymonk.com
WEB SITE: www.theluckymonk.com
MICHAEL'S PICK: Gr'ale Belgian-Style Amber Ale: This Belgian-style amber ale features a complex malt profile that mingles notes of toast, caramel, and biscuit. Spicy hops are enhanced by a subtle, peppery Belgian yeast influence. It's a style-bending beer that I describe as "English bitter goes to Belgium."
TYPE: Brewpub
DATE ESTABLISHED: 2009
OWNER: Private family–owned
BREWMASTER: Anthony Carollo
BREWING SYSTEM: Ten-barrel PUB brewhouse
FLAGSHIP BEERS: Gr'ale Belgian-Style Amber Ale, Cardinal Sin Pilsner
YEAR-ROUND BEERS: Triticale Weiss Beer, Gr'ale Belgian-Style Amber Ale, Cardinal Sin Pilsner, Fallen Angel Vienna-Style Lager, Confessional IPA, Solitude Oatmeal Stout
SEASONAL BEERS: Bishop's Brown Ale, Belgian Dubbel, Bock
SPECIAL RELEASE: Belgian Tripel
TOURS: By request

BEER TO GO: Growlers, kegs, and package
FOOD: A selection of brewpub favorites, with some moderately upscale options
AMENITIES: Parking lot, live music on Thursdays, seasonal patio seating on two levels, private dining rooms available
PUB HOURS: Monday–Thursday: 11:00 A.M. to 11:00 P.M.; Friday and Saturday: 11:00 A.M. to midnight; Sunday: 11:00 A.M. to 10:00 P.M.
NEARBY ATTRACTIONS: Emmett's Ale House, The Onion Brewpub, Morton Arboretum, Sears Center events, Allstate Arena events, Spring Creek Valley Forest Preserve, forty-five minutes from the Chicago Loop

Lucky Monk head brewer Anthony Carollo.

NOTES: The name Lucky Monk might lead you to expect an emphasis on Belgian-style ales. While brewer Anthony Carollo does dabble in Belgians, the range of beer styles at the restaurant is broader than that. The list of house beers retains a distinctly Anglo and European focus, featuring a wide assortment of traditional English ales and German lagers. You won't find many classic American styles here.

This selection reflects what Carollo likes to drink. He tends toward easy-drinking session beers—bitters, porters, mild ales, and pilsners. He appreciates the tradition and history that go into making those beers. He also believes that this narrowed focus has an impact on quality. Rather than trying to be all things to all people, he wants to concentrate on doing just a few things and doing them well.

The focus on sessionable beers also seems appropriate to the place. The bar area features a circular bar with the brewery visible behind it. It's a comfortable space where I could easily imagine sitting for a pint or three. The spacious dining room is sleek and modern. Two patios, one with a large fire pit, offer inviting outdoor dining.

Lunar Brewing Company

ADDRESS: 54 E. St. Charles Rd.
Villa Park, IL 60181

TELEPHONE: 630–530–2077

EMAIL: lunarbrewco@hotmail.com

WEB SITE: www.myspace.com/Lunarbrewingco

MICHAEL'S PICK: Moondance IPA: A full, rich mouthfeel makes this IPA seem bigger than its 6 percent ABV. Hops are king, with aggressive bitterness and juicy citrus and tropical fruit flavors. Hints of ninety-weight oil that are typical of Amarillo hops hang in the background.

TYPE: Brewpub

DATE ESTABLISHED: 1996

OWNER: Charlie Tierney

BREWMASTER: James O'Brien

BREWING SYSTEM: 1.5-barrel converted soup-kettle brewhouse

FLAGSHIP BEER: Moondance IPA

YEAR-ROUND BEERS: Jumping Cow Cream Ale, Space Cadet Stout, Moondance IPA

SEASONAL BEERS: Neil Armstrong Tripel, Big Bang Barleywine, Illuminator Doppelbock, Christmas in the Caribbean

SPECIAL RELEASES: Black Trappist Moon, Belgian IPA, Belgian Scottish Ale, Dark Side Dubbel, Chateau de Lune, E.xtra S.tellar B.itter, Raspberry Cream, 162, Full Moon, Harvest Ale, and others

TOURS: By request

BEER TO GO: Growlers

FOOD: Limited selection of frozen pizzas

AMENITIES: Parking lot in back, free street parking, full bar, good selection of guest taps and bottles, Mug Club program

PUB HOURS: Monday–Thursday: noon to 1:00 A.M.; Friday and Saturday: noon to 2:00 A.M.; Sunday: noon to 10:00 P.M.

NEARBY ATTRACTIONS: Morton Arboretum, golf, Elmhurst Art Museum, Emmett's Ale House, Rock Bottom–Lombard, thirty minutes from the Chicago Loop

NOTES: Despite a statewide smoking ban that has been in place in Illinois since 2008, Lunar Brewing still has the faint aroma of old cigarettes. Not enough to be unpleasant, it's just enough to remind you that this space has been a tavern for over sixty years. It's the kind of place that you can imagine your grandfather—or even great-grandfather—going to for a beer. It's the classic Chicago neighborhood tavern, right down to the dart boards, worn fixtures, and antique cooler behind the bar.

Aside from a limited selection of frozen pizzas, the bar doesn't serve food. That's because the kitchen is the brewery. The brewhouse is a cobbled-together contraption of converted soup kettles, mix-and-match fermenters, and an old homebrew system. Water is heated on the homebrew system and transferred in buckets to the brewing vessels. It's a wonky and labor-intensive process that somehow seems appropriate to the place.

Despite this unconventional brewery, Lunar manages to make good beer. They've won numerous awards in regional competition. They even have a small barrel-aging program. The brewery has initiated a series of collaborative brews with other Illinois breweries, including Lucky Monk, Haymarket, and Blue Cat. In addition to the fine house beers, Lunar keeps a great selection of draft and bottled guest beers.

Metropolitan Brewing

ADDRESS: 5121 N. Ravenswood Ave.
Chicago, IL 60640

TELEPHONE: None

EMAIL: minion@metrobrewing.com

WEBSITE: www.metrobrewing.com

MICHAEL'S PICK: Iron Works Alt Style: There are only a few really good U.S.-brewed Altbiers out there, and this is one of them. It showcases rich caramel and melanoidin Munich malt character with toasty and nutty highlights. The malt is balanced by a crisp, dry finish and moderate bitterness. Spicy Mt. Hood hop aromas waft delicately over the top.

TYPE: Brewery

DATE ESTABLISHED: 2009

OWNERS: Doug Hurst and Tracy Hurst

BREWMASTER: Doug Hurst

BREWING SYSTEM: Fifteen-barrel ABT brewhouse

FLAGSHIP BEERS: Krankshaft Kölsch, Dynamo Copper Lager, Flywheel Bright Lager, Iron Works Alt Style

YEAR-ROUND BEERS: Krankshaft Kölsch, Dynamo Copper Lager, Flywheel Bright Lager, Iron Works Alt Style

SEASONAL BEERS: None

SPECIAL RELEASES: India Pale Lager, Ginger Infused I-Beam Alt, Baltic Porter, Maibock, Eifel Tower Eisbock, Doppelbock, Arc Welder Dunkel Rye, and others

TOURS: Check Web site for dates and times. Reservations required. Cost $5.

BEER TO GO: None

FOOD: None

AMENITIES: Free street parking

PUB HOURS: None

NEARBY ATTRACTIONS: Chicago-area breweries, Old Town School of Folk Music, Andersonville shops and restaurants, the Hopleaf beer bar, The Neo-Futurists Theater, shares the building with Koval Distillery

Fermentation tanks at Metropolitain Brewing.

NOTES: While doing an internship in Munich to complete his diploma course at the Siebel Institute brewing school, Doug Hurst was surprised by the lager beers he tasted. They were the same beers that were available at home, but they tasted better. The secret was freshness. By the time these beers reached the United States, they were losing their flavor.

This experience of freshness led him to focus Metropolitan Brewing on German-style lagers and ales. He is drawn to lager brewing for its nuance. They are beers that make a statement without hitting you over the head. As he put its, he doesn't want to be the "Oliver Stone of brewing." He wants to make beers with more subtle complexity.

This focus on lagers is somewhat unusual in craft brewing. Lagers take longer to brew than ales. Extended conditioning ties up tanks, which necessitates a bigger investment in fermenter capacity. But Metropolitan is making it work. The reception of the beers in the Chicago market has been such that they sell all the beer they can make with only local distribution.

Local is how they want to keep it. According to Tracy Hurst, they don't see the brewery growing beyond a narrow regional market. Once they have grown into the neighboring states, they intend to stop expanding geographically, growing the business instead by introducing new brands. As she puts it, "We will always give our neighbors something to be proud of."

At the time of writing, there was talk of expansion and a move to a new location. Further details were not available.

Mickey Finn's Brewery

ADDRESS: 412 N. Milwaukee Ave.
Libertyville, IL 60048
TELEPHONE: 847-362-6688
EMAIL: info@mickeyfinnsbrewery.com
WEB SITE: www.mickeyfinnsbrewery.com
MICHAEL'S PICK: Yorkie Bitter: A classic Yorkshire bitter that is only served cask-conditioned. It features moderate hop bitterness that just balances luscious caramel and biscuit malt. There's a bitter bite early on, but earthy/grassy hop flavors play a minor role in the middle, allowing the malt to remain at center stage. Velvety smooth mouthfeel and low alcohol make this an extremely enjoyable session beer.
TYPE: Brewpub
DATE ESTABLISHED: 1994
OWNER: Brian Grano
BREWMASTER: Greg Browne
BREWING SYSTEM: Ten-barrel Specific Mechanical brewhouse
FLAGSHIP BEER: 847 Suburban Wheat
YEAR-ROUND BEERS: 847 Suburban Wheat, Mickey Finn's Amber Ale, rotating pale ale, rotating dark ale
SEASONAL BEERS: Will Rock Doppelbock, Märzen Madness, Dog Days of Summer, Bear Down Brown, Cerveza, Katarina Wit Bier, McFinn's Wee Heavy, Santa's Magic, Valkyrie Pilsner, Little Finn's Cream Ale, Winter Weiss Bock, Fifth of Rye, Mickey Finn's Kölsch Ale, Mutha's Milk, Oktoberfest, Pineapple Express Double IPA, Dunkel Lager, Yorkie Bitter
SPECIAL RELEASES: BigHead Pale Ale, Hop Garden Helles, Amber Lite, Barrel Aged Delusion, BBQ Bock, Bill's Oatmeal Stout, Bohemian Pilsner, British Invasion Pale Ale, Butler Ballpark Ale, Czech Pils, Dusseldorf Brown, ESB, Extra Stout Porter, Four Dogs, Goudendark Dunkel Weizen, Hackett Irish Stout, Hop Garden Helles, Imperial Delusion, Legspinner Barleywine, Little Fort Porter, Matt's Hop Slap IPA, Q-Dog Pale Ale, R.K.'s IPA, Rudolph's Red Ale, Rudolph's Revenge, Rudolph's Winterfest Red Lager, Paint It Black, and others
TOURS: By request
BEER TO GO: Growlers, kegs, and package
FOOD: Selection of standard pub fare
AMENITIES: Daily drink and food specials, live music in the Amber Room on Friday and Saturday, private banquet rooms available, cask-conditioned selections, easily accessible from the Metra train
PUB HOURS: Monday–Thursday: 11:30 A.M. to 11:30 P.M.; Friday and Saturday: 11:30 A.M. to 1:15 A.M.; Sunday: 11:30 A.M. to 9:00 P.M.
NEARBY ATTRACTIONS: Lake Bluff Brewing Company, Tighthead Brewing Company, quaint shops in

Libertyville downtown, the Firkin beer bar, fifty minutes from the Chicago Loop

NOTES: Chicago has been a bit behind the curve in the recent craft-beer boom. It is only in the last three to four years that the scene has taken off. Within that scene, Mickey Finn's is a venerable elder statesman. Other brewpubs came and went with the boom and bust in the mid-1990s, but Mickey Finn's has survived, serving well-crafted beers to a loyal local following for twenty years.

Brewer Greg Browne worked at a number of those other breweries before landing here in 2004. He brews beers according to classic styles, eschewing trends toward extreme beers and exotic ingredients. "That's the audience for the place, anyway," he says. The beers won't blow your socks off at Mickey Finn's, but you will find a wide selection of well-crafted and drinkable brews.

It's a family-friendly place with a fun, casual feel. The bar area has served that purpose for over one hundred years. At the time of writing, the brewpub was planning to move to a larger location across the street.

Moonshine

ADDRESS: 1824 W. Division St.
Chicago, IL 60622
TELEPHONE: 773–862–8686
EMAIL: Form on Web site
WEB SITE: www.moonshinechicago.com
MICHAEL'S PICK: Rye Pale Ale: Bright aromas of tropical fruit and tangerines from Amarillo and Simco hops reach your nose before you even pick up the glass. Twenty percent rye malt in the grist gives delicious spicy and earthy undertones. At only 6 percent ABV, this one has the flavor and feel of a double IPA, but the punch of an IPA.
TYPE: Brewpub
DATE ESTABLISHED: 2008
OWNER: Private investor group
BREWMASTER: J. D. McCormick
BREWING SYSTEM: Ten-barrel Century brewhouse
FLAGSHIP BEERS: Moonlight Golden Ale, Able Danger IPA
YEAR-ROUND BEERS: Moonlight Golden Ale, Able Danger IPA
SEASONAL BEERS: Neel Young
SPECIAL RELEASES: Rye Pale Ale, Smoked Porter, Cascadian IPA, Action Club Bitter, Kronic Hemp Ale, Wry Wit, Putin Britches, White Lightning, Piston Broke Chicago Pale Ale, Second City Dry Irish Stout, Angel Bones
TOURS: By appointment
BEER TO GO: Growlers

FOOD: Wide range of classic pub foods interspersed with some interesting upscale dishes: pizzas, burgers, pastas, tacos, and entrées. Focus on locally grown ingredients.
AMENITIES: Good selection of guest taps, daily food specials, full bar with specialty martinis and cocktails, Bloody Mary bar, dog-friendly, seasonal outdoor seating, convenient to Blue Line "L" trains
PUB HOURS: Monday: 5:00 P.M. to 2:00 A.M.; Tuesday–Friday: 11:00 A.M. to 2:00 A.M.; Saturday: 10:00 A.M. to 3:00 A.M.; Sunday: 10:00 A.M. to 2:00 A.M.
NEARBY ATTRACTIONS: Chicago-area breweries, Piece Pizza and Brewery, Chopin Theatre, restaurants and nightlife of Wicker Park neighborhood

NOTES: When I visited Moonshine, brewer J. D. McCormick had only recently taken over from the previous brewer. He was just beginning to make his mark, tweaking the old recipes and trying out new ones. If the beers I tasted were any indication, he is taking the bar in the right direction. The beers that bore his impression were clean, flavorful, and well-made.

McCormick sees brewing as an inspiration for learning in general. To him, it is a craft that pulls together disparate areas of knowledge from history and art to math and science. He loves digging into old brewing stories and dead styles. As he continues to find his way at Moonshine, he would like to branch out and experiment with different styles and new yeast strains. But he admits that he has to keep the clientele in mind. He will continue to brew the easy-drinking beers that people come there for.

The general feel of the place is upscale casual. Located in a trendy district of the city, it can take on a clubby tone on weekend nights. It's not a sports bar, but there are many television screens above the bar, and sporting events are a popular draw.

Nevin's Brewing Company

ADDRESS: 12337 S. Route 59
Plainfield, IL 60585
TELEPHONE: 630–428–4242
EMAIL: None
WEB SITE: www.nevinsbrewing.com
MICHAEL'S PICK: None available for sample
TYPE: Brewpub
DATE ESTABLISHED: 2012
OWNERS: Steve Cin and Rohit Sahajpal
BREWMASTER: Marc Wilson
BREWING SYSTEM: Fifteen-barrel Zhongde Equipment Co. brewhouse
FLAGSHIP BEERS: None
YEAR-ROUND BEERS: To be determined

SEASONAL BEERS: None

SPECIAL RELEASES: Planned

TOURS: Check Web site for times

BEER TO GO: Growlers

FOOD: A large selection of traditional American pub fare

AMENITIES: Parking lot, seasonal outdoor seating, full bar featuring craft cocktails, private banquet space

PUB HOURS: Monday–Thursday: 11:00 A.M. to 1:00 A.M.; Friday and Saturday: 11:00 A.M. to 2:00 A.M.; Sunday: 11:00 A.M. to midnight

NEARBY ATTRACTIONS: Spring Brook Trail Forest Preserve, Western Du Page Bike Trail, golf, canoeing on the Fox River, Railroad Museum, Historic Downtown Pedestrian District, forty-five minutes from the Chicago Loop

NOTES: The Tommy Nevins family of Irish-themed restaurant/pubs is well known in the Chicago area. The first location opened in 1990 in the northern suburb of Evanston. In my table-waiting days, it was a favorite after-shift hangout for me and my colleagues, a comfy place to grab a beer after work. A Naperville location opened in 2007 and another in Frankfurt near Joliet in 2009.

Nevin's Brewing Company is a bit of a departure for the group. Gone is the Irish pub theme. This space has a more contemporary feel. Floor-to-ceiling windows offer an unobstructed view into the brewery. When you belly up to the soapstone and corrugated-steel bar, you can choose from an assortment of craft cocktails in addition to the six to eight house beers and an array of local guest taps. The main room is a large cocktail area with high-top tables and a stage for live music. Seated dining is in another side room.

Brewer Marc Wilson came to Nevin's from the Rock Bottom chain. He got his professional start as assistant brewer in the Chicago location, moving from there to the head brewer position in Warrenville. As a brewer, he goes for balance. Whatever the style, from light cream ale to imperial stout, he doesn't want any particular component of the beer to "knock you around." He embraces the notion that there is a beer for every occasion, saying that he enjoys all styles at different times.

Plainfield is on the far outer edge of the Chicago metro area, making Nevin's a bit of an island in the beer landscape. But Wilson doesn't see that as an excuse to brew bland beers. His goal is to bring the taste of the city out to the suburbs. He wants to give patrons the experience of full-flavored beers without having to make the trek into Chicago.

Off Color Brewing

ADDRESS: 3925 W. Dickens Ave. Chicago, IL 60647

TELEPHONE: None

EMAIL: offcolorbrewing@gmail.com

WEB SITE: www.offcolorbrewing.com

MICHAEL'S PICK: None available for sample

TYPE: Brewery

DATE ESTABLISHED: 2013

OWNERS: John Laffler and Dave Bleitner

BREWMASTERS: John Laffler and Dave Bleitner

BREWING SYSTEM: Twenty-barrel Newlands Systems brewhouse

FLAGSHIP BEERS: Gose, Kottbuss

YEAR-ROUND BEERS: Gose, Kottbuss

SEASONAL BEERS: Grätzer, Doppelbock, Eisbock, Tripel, Belgian Strong Dark Ale, Bière de Garde, Grapefruit and Honey Saison, and others

SPECIAL RELEASES: Planned

TOURS: Check Web site for times

BEER TO GO: None

FOOD: None

AMENITIES: Street parking

PUB HOURS: None

NEARBY ATTRACTIONS: Restaurants, galleries, and clubs in Wicker Park neighborhood, historic Logan Square memorial

NOTES: For John Laffler, brewing is more than just making beer. As a practitioner of one of humanity's oldest crafts, he feels a connection to history and culture. He sees beer as a connecting thread through civilization. It's not just a beverage; it's an expression of ideas. Beer is art.

"Art is the least effective way of communicating," he told me. "But I think that's what makes it so beautiful. Beer is part of that. It's about being part of culture. Expanding culture. Expressing ideas. Making people comfortable. Making people uncomfortable. It's artistry."

Laffler describes what they are doing at Off Color as "avant-garde brewing." This intentionally vague term expresses his belief that labels like "craft beer" are limiting and need to be reimagined and redefined. He doesn't want his brewery to be pigeonholed into any one thing. That he and co-owner Dave Bleitner draw inspiration from the deep well of brewing's past is evident from their flagship beers, Gose and Kottbuss—both nearly extinct historical styles. But they aren't just re-creating history. They take that influence and tweak it to fit the present, resulting in creations such as Half Bock, a low-alcohol interpretation of the traditional German bock beer.

Laffler and Bleitner are the yin to each other's yang. Laffler calls himself the "flash and pizazz" of the partnership. Bleitner handles the "make sure things work" side. His business card lists his title as "the other guy." Both are accomplished brewers with impressive pedigrees. They met while studying at the Siebel Institute. Both interned at Metropolitan Brewing in Chicago. In 2009 Bleitner achieved the highest score on the General Certificate in Brewing exam given by the Institute of Brewing and Distilling in London, earning him the Worshipful Company of Brewers award for that year. Laffler went on to manage the barrel-aging program at Goose Island Fulton Street Brewery, where he cut his teeth making experimental beers.

One Trick Pony Brewery

ADDRESS: 17933 Chappel Ave.
Lansing, IL 60438
TELEPHONE: 708–213–7995
EMAIL: onetrickponybrewery@rocketmail.com
WEB SITE: www.onetrickponybrewery.com
MICHAEL'S PICK: None available for sample
TYPE: Brewery
DATE ESTABLISHED: 2012
OWNER: Mark Kocol
BREWMASTER: Mark Kocol
BREWING SYSTEM: Two-barrel homemade brewhouse
FLAGSHIP BEERS: Spotted Saddle American Pale Ale, Warlander Imperial IPA, Kisber Felver Black IPA
YEAR-ROUND BEERS: Spotted Saddle American Pale Ale, Walkaloosa American IPA, Warlander Imperial IPA, Brabant Belgian Golden Ale, Kisber Felver Black IPA, Marsh Tacky American Stout
SEASONAL BEERS: Christmas Stallion, Georgia Grande Imperial Peach Hefeweizen, Hannoverian Wheat, Black Jack Smoked Porter, Prometia Belgian Tripel, Pumpkin Ale, Harvest Ale
SPECIAL RELEASES: Kentucky Mountain Barrel-Aged Old Ale, Roger Leo IPA, McCurdy Oatmeal Stout, Cleveland Bay Robust Porter, Holsteiner Dunkelweizen, Shire Extra Special Bitter, Storm Cat and Nelson Experimental Amber Ales, Horse Collar Imperial Rye IPA, and others
TOURS: By appointment
BEER TO GO: Growlers and kegs
FOOD: None
AMENITIES: Parking lot, taproom, cash only
PUB HOURS: Monday–Thursday: 3:00 P.M. to 9:00 P.M.; Friday and Saturday: 3:00 P.M. to 10:00 P.M.; Sunday: 2:00 P.M. to 6:00 P.M.
NEARBY ATTRACTIONS: Flossmoor Station Brewery and Restaurant, Three Floyds Brewing, golf, concerts at the First Midwest Bank Amphitheatre, thirty miles from the Chicago Loop

NOTES: An immigration lawyer by day and brewer by night, Mark Kocol's journey into good beer began with a pint passed to him in his law office one afternoon. It was a beer made by a small Indiana brewery. He loved it. He began making regular trips to visit breweries in his neighboring state, getting deeper into beer with every trip. His first attempt to open a brewpub in 2008 stalled when the economy crashed. As things slowly picked up, the idea resurfaced, this time as a brewery/taproom.

The brewery's name comes from an offhand remark Kocol made to his buddy Dave, who asked to homebrew with him. Dave loved hoppy IPAs and little else. But Kocol refused to limit his brewing to that one style, telling him, "I will not be a one-trick pony." The name has given Kocol a convenient approach to naming his beers. Worried that he would overthink the process, he decided simply that all of his beer names would be horse-related.

The taproom at One Trick Pony has the rough-and-ready feel of a juke joint or roadhouse. It's a cozy place where regulars and newcomers are equally welcome. The bare walls and concrete floors are softened by 150-plus growlers that hang from the ceiling. One wall is covered by a large map of the Chicagoland area, on which is kept a running record of the metro's breweries and brewpubs. Kocol's friend Dave will likely greet you at the door and entertain you by spinning vinyl records from the 1980s and 1990s.

The Onion Pub and Brewery

ADDRESS: 22221 N. Pepper Rd.
Lake Barrington, IL 60010
TELEPHONE: 847–381–7308
EMAIL: info@onionpub.com
WEB SITE: www.onionpub.com
MICHAEL'S PICK: Paddy Pale Ale: This easy-to-drink, hop-centric American pale ale has overtones of mandarin orange and spice. Malty sweetness stays well in the background. It's bitter, but the focus is really on hop flavor and aroma.
TYPE: Brewpub
DATE ESTABLISHED: 1995
OWNERS: Kainz family
BREWMASTER: Pete Janusas
BREWING SYSTEM: Twenty-hectoliter Specific Mechanical brewhouse
FLAGSHIP BEER: Paddy Pale Ale
YEAR-ROUND BEERS: Paddy Pale Ale, Louis Light, CentenniAle, Jack Stout, Hop Slayer Double IPA, Brau Bohemian Pilsner, Kainz Nut Brown Ale, Hefty Weiss

SEASONAL BEERS: Instigator Doppelbock, Winter Warmer, Summer Wit, Oktoberfest, Pumpkin Ale, Solstice Jo

SPECIAL RELEASES: King Paddy, Take It Off, Java Jack, Belgian Golden

TOURS: By request

BEER TO GO: Growlers and kegs

FOOD: Selection of brewpub standards: pizza, burgers, sandwiches, and entrées

AMENITIES: Parking lot, live music Thursday and Friday, full bar, seasonal patio seating overlooking an eleven-acre lake, daily food specials, frequent-diner rewards program, Mug Club, Metra trains run nearby, banquet rooms available

PUB HOURS: Tuesday–Thursday: 11:00 A.M. to 11:00 P.M.; Friday and Saturday: 11:00 A.M. to midnight; Sunday: 11:00 A.M. to 8:00 P.M.

NEARBY ATTRACTIONS: Flint Creek drainage wildlife areas, Grassy Lake Forest Preserve, Spring Creek Valley Forest Preserve, Volo Auto Museum, golf, one hour from the Chicago Loop

NOTES: The Onion opened in 1995 as a production brewery, but the owners' plan from the beginning had been to open a brewpub. Given Lake Barrington's distance from Chicago, they sensed a need for a local spot where people could enjoy a good meal with locally crafted beer. In 2003 they purchased land and built the brewpub from the ground up, with room enough in the basement to move the packaging operation there as well.

The restaurant was built with sustainability in mind. Timbers milled from trees that had already fallen give the main dining room a rustic feel. Eighteen-inch-thick, insulated walls help maintain a comfortable temperature year-round. An old quarry pit on the property was turned into a pond that not only provides a view from the outdoor balcony but also holds a geothermal unit that helps with heating and cooling. They compost their spent brewing grains and turn waste vegetable oil into biodiesel.

The focus of the beer lineup is lighter, sessionable ales and lagers. For owner Mike Kainz, the bottom line is that when he goes out for beers, he likes to drink more than one. Taking his cue from the Brits, he says, "They have low-alcohol bitters for a reason." The Onion does, however, make some more extreme beers, like Hop Slayer Double IPA, to satisfy that craving.

Piece Brewery and Pizzeria

ADDRESS: 1927 W. North Ave.
Chicago, IL 60622

TELEPHONE: 773-772-4422

EMAIL: piecechicago1@aol.com

WEB SITE: www.piecechicago.com

MICHAEL'S PICK: Golden Arm: This Kölsch-style beer is light, delicate, and brimming with subtle complexity. The bready sweetness of pilsner malt is underscored with sprightly fruitiness and the slightest hint of sulfur. Gentle bitterness and low spiciness from continental hops add balance and depth. It's a beautiful example of the style.

TYPE: Brewpub

DATE ESTABLISHED: 2001

OWNER: Bill Jacobs

BREWMASTER: Jonathan Cutler

BREWING SYSTEM: Seven-barrel PUB brewhouse

FLAGSHIP BEERS: Golden Arm, Top Heavy Hefeweizen

YEAR-ROUND BEERS: Worryin Ale, Golden Arm, Top Heavy Hefeweizen, Wingnut Double IPA, rotating hoppy selection (Dysfunctionale, Full-Frontal Pale Ale, Capt. Kickass), rotating dark selection (Flat Iron Stout, Fornicator Doppelbock, Prodigal Porter)

SEASONAL BEERS: Festivus, Oktoberfist

SPECIAL RELEASES: Bier de Garde, Wackjob Double IPA, Camel Toe, Amarillo Brillo, Big Black Mariah, Dark Beer, Crucial Pale Ale, Hoppy Ending, Swingin' Single, Dolomite Malt Liquor, Dark-n-Curvy Dunkelweizen, Big-n-Curvy, Imperial Hefeweize, Lectis Weiss, Barrel-aged It's Something, OMFG!, and others

TOURS: No

BEER TO GO: Growlers

FOOD: Delicious thin-crust pizza with either red or white sauce. You add an assortment of toppings. A small selection of appetizers, salads, and sandwiches is also available.

AMENITIES: Live-band karaoke, live music, daily food and drink specials, valet parking after 5:00, convenient to the Blue Line "L" trains, good selection of guest taps and bottles

PUB HOURS: Monday–Thursday: 11:00 A.M. to 1:30 A.M.; Friday: 11:00 A.M. to 2:00 A.M.; Saturday: 11:00 A.M. to 3:00 A.M.; Sunday: 11:00 A.M. to 1:00 A.M.

NEARBY ATTRACTIONS: Chicago-area breweries, Goose Island Clybourn Brewpub, Around the Coyote Arts Festival, Wicker Park shops and music clubs, United Center, Chopin Theatre

NOTES: When Piece opened in 2001, it was only the third brewpub in Chicago. Over the intervening years it has established itself as one of the best. Jonathan Cutler has racked up numerous World Beer Cup and

Great American Beer Festival medals for his creations. In 2006, brewpub and brewer won the prestigious World Beer Cup Champion Small Brewery and Brewmaster Awards.

Indeed, Piece had the best and most consistent overall lineup of all the brewpubs on my Chicago visit. From a delicate Kölsch to a slap-you-in-the-face, 9.5 percent alcohol Double IPA, every beer was exceptionally well made and terrifically drinkable.

Piece operates with a "keep it simple" philosophy. Pizza and beer are pretty much all they do, and they do both very well. The pizzas are excellent. A small pie looks huge, but the cracker-thin crust makes it manageable as a single serving.

The dining room is open and airy, and very casual. It's the kind of place where you might end up sharing a table with strangers. The old wooden trusses supporting the rounded ceiling combine with the sleek furnishings and long bar to suggest a hipster roadhouse in an airplane hangar. It's a space that screams noise and fun.

Pipeworks Brewing Company

ADDRESS: 1675 N. Western Ave. Chicago, IL 60647

TELEPHONE: 847–910–9493

EMAIL: info@pipeworksbrewing.com

WEB SITE: www.pipeworksbrewing.com

MICHAEL'S PICK: Smoked Porter 20%: A blend of beechwood- and cherrywood-smoked malt makes up 20 percent of the grist in this creamy 7 percent ABV porter. It brings a background of meaty and charpit smoke that melds nicely with the rather gentle touch of roast. Caramel sweetness gives life to the middle, while cocoa bitterness grabs the sides of the tongue in the finish.

TYPE: Brewery

DATE ESTABLISHED: 2012

OWNERS: Beejay Oslon, Gerrit Lewis, and Scott Coffman

BREWMASTER: Beejay Oslon

BREWING SYSTEM: Three-barrel Psycho Brew brewhouse

FLAGSHIP BEERS: None

YEAR-ROUND BEERS: None

SEASONAL BEERS: None

SPECIAL RELEASES: End of Days, Smoked Porter, Ninja vs. Unicorn, Glaucus Barleywine, Abduction Imperial Stout, Last Kiss Wee Heavy, Learning to Fly Berliner Weiss, Bottled Up Baltic Porter, Xenophon's Wine, Pipedream IPA, Small Animal Big Machine, and others

TOURS: Check Web site for information

BEER TO GO: Growlers and package

Label art for Unicorn's Revenge Double IPA Ale.

FOOD: None

AMENITIES: Free street parking, bottle shop selling package beer and brewery merchandise, convenient to Blue Line "L" trains

PUB HOURS: None

NEARBY ATTRACTIONS: Chicago breweries, Revolution Brewing, Piece Pizzeria, Moonshine Brewpub, Goose Island Clybourn, concerts at the Congress Theatre, Wicker Park restaurants and nightclubs, the Map Room beer bar

NOTES: Beejay Oslon describes Pipeworks' style as "beer geeks brewing beer for beer geeks." Pipeworks doesn't brew beer for the mass market. Their beers are big, bold, and boundary-pushing. They don't list year-round beers because they seldom brew the same thing twice. The thought of making the same brew again and again seems restrictive to these former artists. Their creative bent drives them to reach for unconventional flavor combinations and unusual ingredients.

Olsen met Garrit Lewis while working at West Lakeview Liquor, a haven for Chicagoland beer geeks. When these homebrewing buddies decided to go pro, they arranged an internship with brewer Urbain Coutteau at the highly regarded De Struise Brewery in Belgium, a brewery known for crafting exceptional and unconventional brews. While there, they got a crash course in brewing, learning everything from recipe conception to packaging.

While their size gives them flexibility to play—they never have to worry about selling fifteen barrels of any one creation—it also limits their ability to distribute. In the near term, they intend to remain a neighborhood brewery, maintaining a limited number of draft accounts while selling most of their beer in growlers and bottles in Chicagoland retail stores. I expect it won't be long before demand forces an expansion.

Ram Restaurant and Brewery–Schaumburg

ADDRESS: 1901 McConnor Pkwy. Schaumburg, IL 60173

TELEPHONE: 847–517–8791

EMAIL: None

WEB SITE: www.theram.com/illinois/schaumburg.html

MICHAEL'S PICK: 71 Pale Ale: Don't expect a citrusy, American hop bomb. This pale ale is more British in nature. Earthy and floral hop flavors are enhanced by spicy notes from a touch of rye added to the grist. Bitterness is modest, but enough to balance the caramel and biscuit malt.

TYPE: Brewpub

DATE ESTABLISHED: 2001

OWNER: Ram International

BREWMASTER: Tom Nelson

BREWING SYSTEM: Fifteen-barrel JV Northwest brewhouse

FLAGSHIP BEERS: Chicago Blond Ale, Buttface Amber Ale

YEAR-ROUND BEERS: Chicago Blond Ale, Big Horn Hefeweizen, Big Red Ale, 71 Pale Ale, Buttface Amber Ale, Total Disorder Porter

SEASONAL BEERS: S'no Angel, Irish Red, Barefoot Wit, Bighorn Oktoberfest, Icebreaker Stout (different every year), Bighorn Maibock, Uncle John's, Bohemian Norm

SPECIAL RELEASES: Occasional Belgian-style ales

TOURS: By request

BEER TO GO: Growlers and kegs

FOOD: Selection of brewpub standards

AMENITIES: Parking lot, happy-hour drink specials, full bar, Mug Club, catering and banquets, private room available

PUB HOURS: Daily: 11:00 A.M. to close

NEARBY ATTRACTIONS: Emmett's Ale House–Palatine, the Lucky Monk, thirty miles from the Chicago Loop, Ned Brown and Poplar Creek Forest Preserves, performances at the Prairie Center for the Arts, Legoland Discovery Center, Improv Comedy Club

NOTES: The layout and feel of Ram–Schaumburg is almost exactly like that of the Wheeling location: it's like an upscale sports bar. An extra-large television screen behind the main bar goes nearly to the top of the high, arched ceiling. You can belly up to one of the two bars or get cozy in a high-backed booth. Orange-tinted wood and leather upholstery give it a classy ruggedness.

The six year-round beers and most of the seasonals are standardized across the Ram chain. But this doesn't mean they are bad. Ram brews have won numerous medals in national and international competition. Brewer Tom Nelson does get some room to play. There are always a couple of nonstandard taps available. I tasted a very nice pilsner and an American strong ale called Uncle John's.

If you eat at the Ram, expect huge portions of good old American-style fare. Lots of fried food, big burgers, steaks, ribs, and salads. Take a stab at conquering the five-pound Behemoth burger: finish the whole thing in one sitting to win a one-of-a-kind t-shirt.

Ram Restaurant and Brewery–Wheeling

ADDRESS: 700 N. Milwaukee Ave. Wheeling, IL 60090

RAM.
Restaurant & Brewery

TELEPHONE: 847–520–1222

EMAIL: None

WEB SITE: www.theram.com/illinois/wheeling.html

MICHAEL'S PICK: Buttface Amber: Toffee and caramel malt take center stage in this classic midwestern amber ale. Bitterness is on the low end for the style, and the bright, citrusy hop flavors seem to ride over the top.

TYPE: Brewpub

DATE ESTABLISHED: 2001

OWNER: Ram International

BREWMASTER: Lanny Fetzer

BREWING SYSTEM: Fifteen-barrel JV Northwest brewhouse

FLAGSHIP BEERS: Chicago Blond Ale, Buttface Amber Ale

YEAR-ROUND BEERS: Chicago Blond Ale, Big Horn Hefeweizen, Big Red Ale, 71 Pale Ale, Buttface Amber Ale, Total Disorder Porter

SEASONAL BEERS: S'no Angel, Irish Red, Barefoot Wit, Bighorn Oktoberfest, Icebreaker Stout (different every year), Bighorn Maibock

SPECIAL RELEASES: Occasional Belgian-style ales

TOURS: By request

BEER TO GO: Growlers and kegs

FOOD: Selection of brewpub standards

AMENITIES: Parking lot, happy-hour drink specials, full bar, Mug Club, catering and banquets

PUB HOURS: Daily: 11:00 A.M. to close

NEARBY ATTRACTIONS: Chicago Botanical Gardens, Mickey Finn's Brewpub, the Firkin beer bar, Lake Bluff Brewery, Lynfred Winery tasting room, Cooper's Hawk Winery, Ravinia Festival, Historic Long Grove, thirty miles from the Chicago Loop

NOTES: Lanny Fetzer's entire brewing career has been at Ram. He was hired as an assistant brewer at the Portland, Oregon, store in 1996, the year the chain began making beer. Over the years he has brewed at several locations, opening some and installing breweries at others. In 2001 he opened the Wheeling brewpub and has been there ever since.

Ram brewpubs have six beers that are standard across the chain, several of which have won medals in international competition. Fetzer doesn't view this standardization as a hindrance. He sees many of these beers as gateways to bring more people into the craft-beer fold; start people off with Chicago

Blond Ale and gradually move them up to the Butt-face Amber. Eventually they are drinking the more full-flavored seasonal beers.

It's with the seasonals that Fetzer gets a chance to play. Those beers are all his. He approaches them from a culinary perspective. He loves to cook and loves picking apart recipes, looking for just the right ingredients to achieve desired flavor combinations, like orange and oats in a hoppy pale ale. He appreciates beers with complexity, or as he puts it, "beers that reveal themselves." With ten beers on tap at any given time, he always has four opportunities to experiment.

The ambience at Ram–Wheeling is like an upscale sports bar. An extra-large television screen behind the main bar goes nearly to the top of the high, arched ceiling. You can sit at one of the two bars or cozy up in a high-backed booth. Orange-tinted wood and leather upholstery give it a classy ruggedness.

The fermentation cellar at Revolution Brewing.

Revolution Brewing–Brewpub

ADDRESS: 2323 N. Milwaukee Ave.
Chicago, IL 60647
TELEPHONE: 773-227-2739
EMAIL: info@revbrew.com
WEB SITE: www.revbrew.com
MICHAEL'S PICK: Tart with a Heart: Take a 10 percent ABV brown ale and age it in bourbon barrels, then add Italian plum puree and blend it all together with a smoked Scottish Wee Heavy, and you end up with this sweet/tart delight. Rich caramel malt is balanced by a lightly sour fruitiness. Big vanilla and bourbon flavors and background smokiness give it cavernous depth. It's dangerously easy to drink.
TYPE: Brewpub
DATE ESTABLISHED: 2010
OWNER: Josh Deth
BREWMASTER: Wil Turner
BREWING SYSTEM: Fifteen-barrel Bohemian brewhouse
FLAGSHIP BEERS: Bottom Up Wit, Anti-Hero IPA, Eugene Porter
YEAR-ROUND BEERS: Bottom Up Wit, Iron Fist Pale Ale, Anti-Hero IPA, Cross of Gold, Eugene Porter
SEASONAL BEERS: Mild, Märzen, Coup d'Etat Saison, Rosa Hibiscus, Christmas Ale
SPECIAL RELEASES: Thirty-five different styles each year, including Tart with a Heart, Samahdi, Willie Wee Heavy, Baphomet, Pablo Picasso, and many others
TOURS: Saturdays at noon
BEER TO GO: Growlers
FOOD: Elevated pub food; upscale takes on brewpub classics. Sausages and breads made on premises. Bacon-fat popcorn is a must-try.

AMENITIES: Metered street parking, convenient to the Blue Line "L" trains, full bar, live music upstairs, private rooms available, cask-conditioned beers
PUB HOURS: Monday–Friday: 11:00 A.M. to 2:00 A.M.; Saturday and Sunday: 10:00 A.M. to 2:00 A.M.
NEARBY ATTRACTIONS: Chicago-area breweries, Wicker Park restaurants and nightlife, Logan Square restaurants and nightlife, Piece Pizzeria and Brewery, Moonshine Brewpub, concerts at the Congress Theatre

NOTES: Whatever you want in terms of beer, Revolution Brewing has it. They make over thirty-five different beer styles throughout the year, ranging from light cream ale to big, barrel-aged bruisers. Their large guest-beer selection even includes King Cobra Malt Liquor, Old Style, and Pabst Blue Ribbon.

Beer is the focus at Revolution, and the team of Josh Deth and founding brewer Jim Cibak have the depth of experience to keep it sharp. Deth started brewing professionally in 1995, and his career has included work at Grizzly Peak in Ann Arbor and at Goose Island. In 2003 he quit brewing to become a restaurateur. Cibak is a fellow Goose Island alum who also brewed at Three Floyds Brewing in Indiana. Their partnership produces well-crafted, layered beers with food to match. Cibak has since left the brewpub to run Revolution's new production facility. Former assistant brewer Wil Turner has taken his place.

That beer focus is reflected in the space. The large oval bar is the first thing you see upon entering; carved-wood fists, appropriate to a place called Revolution, defiantly support the arched back bar. The downstairs dining room has a sleek, artsy feel with barrel-stave designs on the walls and a buff stone fireplace anchoring a small lounge area. There is more seating upstairs, along with another bar and a stage for live music.

Revolution Brewing–Brewery

ADDRESS: 3344 N. Kedzie Ave.
Chicago, IL 60618
TELEPHONE: 773–588–2267
EMAIL: info@revbrew.com
WEB SITE: www.revbrew.com
MICHAEL'S PICK: None available for sample
TYPE: Brewery
DATE ESTABLISHED: 2012
OWNER: Josh Deth
BREWMASTER: Jim Cibak
BREWING SYSTEM: Sixty-barrel Newlands Systems brewhouse
FLAGSHIP BEERS: Bottom Up Wit, Anti-Hero IPA, Eugene Porter
YEAR-ROUND BEERS: Bottom Up Wit, Anti-Hero IPA, Eugene Porter
SEASONAL BEERS: Cross of Gold, Double Fist Double Pale Ale, Oktoberfest, Coup d'Etat Saison, Iron Fist Pale Ale, Fistmas Ale, Rosa Hibiscus Ale, Mad Cow
SPECIAL RELEASES: Straight Jacket Bourbon Barrel Barleywine, Very Mad Cow Bourbon Barrel Milk Stout, and others
TOURS: Wednesday–Saturday: 6:00 P.M.
BEER TO GO: Growlers, kegs, and package
FOOD: None
AMENITIES: Free street parking, taproom
PUB HOURS: Wednesday–Saturday: 2:00 to 10:00 P.M.
NEARBY ATTRACTIONS: Chicago-area breweries, Revolution Brewing Brewpub, Factory Theatre, Prop Theatre, Logan Square restaurants, Wicker Park music clubs and restaurants

NOTES: According to Josh Deth, a production brewery was in the long-term plan for Revolution Brewery from the very beginning. It didn't take them long to make that plan a reality. Just one year after the brewpub opened, the process was already under way. It made sense. The brewpub system had quickly reached maximum capacity, and there was demand for Revolution beer in the market. The added capacity will free them up to do some different things in the brewpub, such as brewing lagers. The extra tank time required for these beers has always made that impractical in the past. They have also already taken steps to greatly expand their barrel-aging program.

A new canning line means that Revolution beers will be available in retail stores, as well as other restaurants and bars. But you don't have to pick up a four pack to enjoy beer from the new place. The brewery taproom features a sixty-foot wooden bar made by the same group that built the bars for the brewpub. Seventeen taps wait to quench your thirst.

Rock Bottom Restaurant and Brewery–Chicago

ADDRESS: 1 W. Grand Ave.
Chicago, IL 60654
TELEPHONE: 312–755–9339
EMAIL: chicago@rockbottom.com
WEB SITE: www.rockbottom.com/chicago
MICHAEL'S PICK: Smoked Märzen: This is an altogether quaffable smoked beer. The spicy, salami-like smoke never quite takes over, letting the rich caramel malt of the underlying Märzen-style beer come through. Low alcohol and a crisp lager finish mean you can drink two or three. This is a great beer with rare beef.
TYPE: Brewpub
DATE ESTABLISHED: 1995
OWNER: CraftWorks Restaurants and Breweries Inc.
BREWMASTER: Hayley Shine
BREWING SYSTEM: Twelve-barrel JV Northwest brewhouse
FLAGSHIP BEERS: Kölsch, White Ale, Red Ale, IPA
YEAR-ROUND BEERS: Kölsch, White Ale, Red Ale, IPA, Chicago Gold, Terminal Stout
SEASONAL BEERS: Scotch Ale, Rye Lager, Blond, Amber Bock, Black Lager, Strong Belgian Bold, Firehouse Red Ale, Heller Bock, Czech Pilsner, American Dream IPA, Vienna Lager, Saison, Rocktoberfest, Anniversary Ale, Belgian Dubbel, Imperial Red Ale
SPECIAL RELEASES: Smoked Märzen, Smoked Helles, Coffee Stout, a variety of barrel-aged beers, and others
TOURS: By request. Large groups should call for an appointment.
BEER TO GO: Growlers
FOOD: Standard Rock Bottom Restaurant menu: pub food, sandwiches and burgers, salads, chili, and a range of entrées. Good selection of steaks. Some more upscale items.
AMENITIES: Metered street parking, paid parking in nearby ramps, convenient to Red Line "L" trains, full bar, Saturday and Sunday brunch menu, Beer School programs first Tuesday of every month, happy-hour specials, Mug Club program, monthly tapping events, cask-conditioned selections, seasonal roof deck, private rooms available
PUB HOURS: Monday–Friday: 11:00 A.M. to 2:00 A.M.; Saturday and Sunday: 10:00 A.M. to 2:00 A.M.
NEARBY ATTRACTIONS: Navy Pier, Water Tower Place, boat rides on the Chicago River, concerts at House

of Blues, Chicago Loop, Grant Park and Buckingham Fountain, Millennium Park, Chicago Theatre, Goodman Theatre, Field Museum, Soldier Field, Art Institute of Chicago, Museum of Contemporary Art, John Hancock Building, shopping on Michigan Ave.

NOTES: When Hayley Shine returned to Long Beach from an October vacation in Chicago, her supervisor at Rock Bottom asked her what she thought of the city. She said, "I love Chicago. I'd move there in a hot minute." Little did she know that by December she would be doing just that.

A desire for good beer at the lowest possible cost led Shine to start homebrewing in college. At one point, she says, she had it down to fifty cents per bottle. But as happens with homebrewers, the deeper into the hobby she got, the more expensive it became, as equipment expansions and the purchase of more and more expensive beers ate into those initial savings.

Her professional brewing career began at the Rogue Ales Public House in San Francisco. She trained at the Rogue brewery in Newport, Oregon, and ran the brewery's Issaquah brewpub before being hired on at Rock Bottom.

The Chicago store has a slightly different feel than most of the other Rock Bottom locations. One side of the restaurant is a chop-house-style dining room with white-linen tablecloths. The main bar/dining room is casual, with exposed brick and large wooden beams that evoke Chicago's industrial past.

Rock Bottom Restaurant and Brewery—Lombard

ADDRESS: 94 Yorktown Center
Lombard, IL 60148
TELEPHONE: 630–424–1550
EMAIL: yorktown@rockbottom.com
WEB SITE: www.rockbottom.com/lombard-yorktown-center
MICHAEL'S PICK: Lighter Shade of Pale XPA: This is an attempt to make an India Pale Ale that is truly pale. The grain bill consists of just a single pale malt, giving the beer a light golden color and simple grainy-sweet profile. Hops are the focus. The bitterness is assertive but not unbalanced. Citrus and pine hop flavors dominate, with hints of melon and tangerine in the background. It finishes refreshingly crisp and dry.
TYPE: Brewpub
DATE ESTABLISHED: 2006
OWNER: CraftWorks Restaurants and Breweries Inc.
BREWMASTER: Jim Wolfer
BREWING SYSTEM: Eight-barrel Newlands Systems brewhouse
FLAGSHIP BEERS: Kölsch, White Ale, Red Ale, IPA
YEAR-ROUND BEERS: Kölsch, White Ale, Red Ale, IPA

SEASONAL BEERS: None
SPECIAL RELEASES: Popcorn Malt Liquor, Bishop Belgian Tripel, Nibs Chocolate Porter, Bourbon Barrel Imperial Stout, Lighter Shade of Pale XPA, All That It Takes Russian Imperial Stout, Lord Infamous Pumpkin Bock, and others
TOURS: By request
BEER TO GO: Growlers
FOOD: Standard Rock Bottom Restaurant menu: pub food, sandwiches and burgers, salads, chili, and a range of entrées. Good selection of steaks. Some more upscale items.
AMENITIES: Parking lot, full bar, seasonal outdoor seating, located at Yorktown Mall
PUB HOURS: Sunday–Thursday: 11:00 A.M. to 1:00 A.M.; Friday and Saturday: 11:00 A.M. to 2:00 A.M.
NEARBY ATTRACTIONS: Emmett's Ale House—Downers Grove, Lunar Brewing, Two Brothers Brewing Company, Rock Bottom—Warrenville, Gordon Biersch, Morton Arboretum, twenty miles from the Chicago Loop

NOTES: When asked what he loves about brewing, Jim Wolfer responds, "What's not to love?" He enjoys the physical work and the fact that every day is different. He likes seeing people at the bar enjoying the fruits of his labors. He takes pleasure in the creative process of recipe development. And on brewdays he is enveloped in the aromas of grain and hops. He's right. What's not to love?

Wolfer approaches brewing from the artistic side. Recipe ideas sometimes come to him in the middle of the night, forcing him to get out of bed and write them down. He fleshes out his recipes by tasting grains and smelling hops. It's only after finding the right combination of flavors that he turns to pencil-and-paper calculations. His approach seems to work. The beers I tasted ranged in style from a simple brown ale to a spiced-up imperial American wheat. They were all clean and bright with finely articulated layers of flavor.

The ambience and menu at Rock Bottom are standardized across the chain. Look for slightly upscale pub food with some nicer items tossed in. That said, the food is always delicious and the casual, craftsman atmosphere is always inviting.

Rock Bottom Restaurant and Brewery—Orland Park

ADDRESS: 16156 S. La Grange Rd.
Orland Park, IL 60467
TELEPHONE: 708–226–0021
EMAIL: orlandpark@rockbottom.com
WEB SITE: www.rockbottom.com/orland-park
MICHAEL'S PICK: Oatmeal Stout: A huge addition of malted oats in the grist give this inky brew a velvety-

smooth texture. Dark-roast coffee character is there, but kept in check by a good amount of molasses-like sweetness. Licorice added to the brew gives an interesting anise twist.

TYPE: Brewpub
DATE ESTABLISHED: 2007
OWNER: CraftWorks Restaurants and Breweries Inc.
BREWMASTER: Iain Wilson
BREWING SYSTEM: Eight-barrel Newlands Systems brewhouse
FLAGSHIP BEERS: Kölsch, White Ale, Red Ale, IPA
YEAR-ROUND BEERS: Kölsch, White Ale, Red Ale, IPA, Orland Park Light, Lumpy Dog Brown, Rotating Stout, Rotating Hoppy Beer
SEASONAL BEERS: King of Hearts, Copper Weiss, Firechief, Honey Blond, Rocktoberfest, Winter Wheat, Cinco de Mayo, Monster Mash, Naughty Scot, and others
SPECIAL RELEASES: Powerhouse Pale Ale, Eric the Red, Vienna Lager, Select Pils, Line Drive Lager, M&B Peanut Butter Brown, Mindbender ESB, Schwarz Hacker, Circle City Light, and others
TOURS: By request
BEER TO GO: Growlers and kegs
FOOD: Standard Rock Bottom Restaurant menu: pub food, sandwiches and burgers, salads, chili, and a range of entrées. Good selection of steaks. Some more upscale items.
AMENITIES: Parking lot, seasonal outdoor seating, full bar, cask-conditioned selections, semi-private space available
PUB HOURS: Sunday–Tuesday: 11:00 A.M. to midnight; Wednesday and Thursday: 11:00 A.M. to 1:00 A.M.; Friday and Saturday: 11:00 A.M. to 2:00 A.M.
NEARBY ATTRACTIONS: Harrison's Restaurant and Brewery, Flossmoor Station Brewpub, Three Floyds Brewing, Brickstone Restaurant and Brewery, hiking and cross-country skiing in nearby forest preserves, concerts at First Midwest Bank Amphitheatre, Lake Katherine Botanic Gardens, twenty-five miles from the Chicago Loop

NOTES: Scotsman Iain Wilson calls himself a "lager brewer that also makes ales." This is contrary to the majority of craft brewers, who primarily focus on ales. Before coming to the United States he worked at larger breweries in Scotland, primarily making lagers. He says that his system at Rock Bottom is particularly well suited to making these crisp, bottom-fermented beers. His lager beers have won him several medals in competition. He boasts particularly of his Orland Park Light Lager, which won a gold medal at the Great American Beer Festival in a category typically dominated by the big breweries.

Wilson believes in giving his customers choice. He typically has fourteen to fifteen beers on tap, along with a cask-conditioned selection. This is more than at most Rock Bottoms. He says that he gets bored easily. Keeping up with such a large selection gives him something to do. But it also keeps people coming back. Customers know that they will always find something new, and they will always find something they like.

The ambience and menu at Rock Bottom are fairly standardized across the chain. Look for slightly upscale pub food with some nicer items tossed in. That said, the food is always delicious, and the casual, craftsman atmosphere is always inviting.

Rock Bottom Restaurant and Brewery—Warrenville

ADDRESS: 28256 Diehl Rd.
Warrenville, IL 60555
TELEPHONE: 630–836–1380
EMAIL: warrenville@rockbottom.com
WEB SITE: www.rockbottom.com/warrenville
MICHAEL'S PICK: Sled Dog Imperial Red Ale: A blend of noble and American hops gives this hop-forward red ale an earthy/citrus stamp. Bitterness is sharp and assertive but stops short of tongue-scraping. Caramel and toffee malt provide a smooth counterbalance to the hops.
TYPE: Brewpub
DATE ESTABLISHED: 1999
OWNER: CraftWorks Restaurants and Breweries Inc.
BREWMASTER: Todd Britt
BREWING SYSTEM: Ten-barrel JV Northwest brewhouse
FLAGSHIP BEERS: Kölsch, White Ale, Red Ale, IPA
YEAR-ROUND BEERS: Kölsch, White Ale, Red Ale, IPA, Rotating Dark
SEASONAL BEERS: Oktoberfest, Firechief, Irish Dry Stout, Belgian IPA, Sled Dog Imperial Red
SPECIAL RELEASES: Barleywine, Lumpy Dog Brown, Winter Wheat, Bock, occasional barrel-aged selections, including Doppelbock and Sled Dog Imperial Red, and others
TOURS: By request
BEER TO GO: Growlers
FOOD: Standard Rock Bottom Restaurant menu: pub food, sandwiches and burgers, salads, chili, and a range of entrées. Good selection of steaks. Some more upscale items.
AMENITIES: Parking lot, full bar, seasonal outdoor seating
PUB HOURS: Monday–Thursday: 11:00 A.M. to 1:00 A.M.; Friday: 11:00 A.M. to 2:00 A.M.; Saturday: 11:30 A.M. to 2:00 A.M.; Sunday: 11:30 A.M. to midnight
NEARBY ATTRACTIONS: Two Brothers Brewing Company, Rock Bottom—Lombard, Emmett's Ale

House—Downers Grove, Nevin's Brewing Company, Stockholm's Vardshus, hiking in nearby forest preserves, golf, Fermilab National Accelerator Laboratory tours, forty miles from the Chicago Loop

NOTES: Todd Britt's brewing career has come full circle. He got his start in the industry as an eager volunteer at the very Rock Bottom location where he is now head brewer. In between was a two-year run as assistant brewer at the Goose Island Brewpub and a short stint at the Rock Bottom Chicago store.

It was under the tutelage of Jared Rouben, former head brewer at Goose Island, that Britt says he learned all he knows. With his background as a chef, Rouben taught him how to taste beer and really understand the nuances of its flavor. He came to think of beer as food, opening up his mind and palate to a greater range of flavors than one normally associates with beer.

This understanding has made him a very purposeful brewer. He makes sure that every flavor from every ingredient has a reason to be there. He doesn't add things just to add things. Each new element has to complement or contrast a flavor that is already in the beer.

Britt is a fan of the English brewing traditions. He likes sessionable beers that allow for several pints over an evening with friends. But he doesn't want to be known as a one-trick pony. He's not averse to tossing the occasional strong beer or hop monster into the mix.

The ambience and menu at Rock Bottom are fairly standardized across the chain. Look for slightly upscale pub food with some nicer items tossed in. That said, the food is always delicious, and the casual, craftsman atmosphere is always inviting.

Small Town Brewery

ADDRESS: 441 W. Bonner Rd.
Wauconda, IL 60084
TELEPHONE: 815–566–0415
EMAIL: timkovac@smalltownbrewery.com
WEB SITE: www.smalltownbrewery.com
MICHAEL'S PICK: 20% Root Beer: Root beer with a faint vodka bite is the best way to describe this concoction. Brewer Tim Kovac calls this "root beer the way it used to be made"—with barley malt, honey, vanilla, and other ingredients. I'm skeptical of his claim that this ferments up to 20 percent alcohol, but that is what he says. In any case, it was pretty tasty.
TYPE: Brewery
DATE ESTABLISHED: 2010
OWNERS: Tim Kovac and John Dopak

BREWMASTER: Tim Kovac
BREWING SYSTEM: Two fifty-gallon converted soup kettles
FLAGSHIP BEER: Main Street Amber
YEAR-ROUND BEERS: Main Street Stout, Main Street Amber, Main Street IPA
SEASONAL BEERS: Holiday Christmas Ale, Summer Pirate Ale, Winter Pirate Ale, Apple Cider Ale, Pumpkin Ale
SPECIAL RELEASES: 20% Root Beer, 1801 Stout, 1600s Porter, 1600s Winter Spiced Ale, Agave Ale, Agave Lime Ale, Honey Nut Brown Ale
TOURS: By appointment
BEER TO GO: None
FOOD: None
AMENITIES: Parking lot
PUB HOURS: None
NEARBY ATTRACTIONS: Tighthead Brewing Company, Mickey Finn's Brewpub, The Onion Pub, Lake County Discovery Museum, Volo Auto Museum, hiking and cross-country skiing at nearby forest preserves and parks, forty-five miles from the Chicago Loop

NOTES: Small Town Brewery was born of a homebrewing hobby and a very old recipe book. Tim Kovac started brewing as a way to spend more time with his son. His homebrews received praise from friends and family, leading him to take the leap and go pro. When he informed his mother of his plans, she told him the story of a long-ago ancestor and handed him a very special old book.

In the early 1600s, this ancestor had been a bit of a gambler. He won a brewery in a game of chance. For many years he made and sold beer in London. He later became the captain of a ship that brought colonists to the New World and eventually settled in Boston. The book that Kovac's mother kept secreted away in a chest was a book of brewer's logs and beer recipes from the 1600s. It is these recipes that Kovac says are the inspiration for Small Town beers.

I must confess that, having spent an hour with Kovac, I left the brewery feeling less clear about what he is doing than when I arrived. It's obvious to me that his understanding of the brewing process and history are limited at best. With simple brewing calculations, it is impossible to re-create the beers he is making using the methods he describes. However, without actually seeing his process, I'll have to take what he says at face value. And the root beer was quite good. Small Town has plans to open a distillery in the near future.

Solemn Oath Brewery

ADDRESS: 1661 Quincy Ave.
Naperville, IL 60540
TELEPHONE: 630–995–3062
EMAIL: hello@solemnoathbrewery.com
WEB SITE: www.solemnoathbrewery.com
MICHAEL'S PICK: Sweet Sweet Whisper Kisses: This is
a version of the Whisper Kisses saison that has been
infused with locally produced honey. The flavor of honey
shines through, providing a nice balance to the yeast-
derived black pepper notes. The light body and dry finish
make this 9 percent behemoth drink more like 6 percent.
TYPE: Brewery
DATE ESTABLISHED: 2012
OWNERS: John Barley and Joe Barley
BREWMASTER: Tim Marshall
BREWING SYSTEM: Fifteen-barrel Premier Stainless
brewhouse
FLAGSHIP BEERS: None
YEAR-ROUND BEERS: None
SEASONAL BEERS: Kidnapped by Vikings, Khlöros,
Oubliette, Ultra High Frequency, Yarnbomb,
Snaggletooth Bandana
SPECIAL RELEASES: E-Ville, Nourri au Fourrage,
Pernicieux, Coffee Infused Khlörost, Radth, bourbon-
and wine-barrel-aged beers, and others
TOURS: By appointment
BEER TO GO: Growlers and kegs
FOOD: None
AMENITIES: Parking lot, taproom
PUB HOURS: Thursday and Friday: noon to 9:00 P.M.;
Saturday: 11:00 A.M. to 7:00 P.M.; Sunday: 11:00 A.M.
to 5:00 P.M.
NEARBY ATTRACTIONS: Two Brothers Brewing Com-
pany, Rock Bottom—Warrenville, Emmett's Ale House—
Downers Grove, Stockholm's Vardshus, hiking in nearby
forest preserves, golf, Fermilab National Accelerator
Laboratory tours, forty miles from the Chicago Loop

Solemn Oath Brewery in Naperville, Illinois.

NOTES:

There was three kings into the east,
Three kings both great and high,
An' they hae sworn a solemn oath
John Barleycorn should die.

Those opening lines of Robert Burns's anti-alcohol
poem "John Barleycorn" provided the inspiration for
Solemn Oath Brewery's moniker. The fact that one
of the founders is named John Barley made it a no-
brainer. But rest assured, as a purveyor of craft ales,
he is no advocate of abstinence.

Solemn Oath's mission is to bring boldly flavored
beers to Chicago's western suburbs. While they tend
to brew with a Belgian slant, that's not all they do.
Imperial stouts, brown ales, and varied versions of
IPA are also part of their repertoire. Unusual and unexpected flavor combinations are also in the mix, like
Belgian witbier infused with coffee beans from a local
artisanal roaster.

The lineup at Solemn Oath is customer-driven.
In the first year of operation, the brewery produced
over thirty different beers with the intention of letting
their audience tell them what to stick with. Beers are
tweaked, rebrewed, or retired based on the feedback
of drinkers.

They try to involve the community in other ways
as well. Monthly homebrewing classes give fans the
opportunity to spend a couple hours at the brewery
learning how to make their own beer at home. Joe Barley says that some of the best beers they have tasted
were homebrews, and they want to share with others
the secrets to brewing good beer.

Even the layout of the taproom promotes customer
involvement. Patrons are practically sitting in the
brewery. "If someone holds your chair," says Barley,
"you can reach out and touch our hot liquor tank."

Spiteful Brewing

ADDRESS: 1815 W. Berteau Ave., Unit 15
Chicago, IL 60613
TELEPHONE: 773–315–0828
EMAIL: info@spitefulbrewing.com
WEB SITE: www.spitefulbrewing.com
MICHAEL'S PICK: Burning Bridges Brown Ale: This
super-roasty American brown ale seems to aspire to
become a stout. The aroma is all chocolate. Coffee-
grounds and dark chocolate flavors give a café mocha
effect. The roastiness is perhaps slightly overdone.
It conspires with resinous hops to produce a fairly
high-level bitterness. Herbal and minty hop flavors
give cooling overtones.

TYPE: Brewery

DATE ESTABLISHED: 2012

OWNERS: Brad Shaffer and Jason Klein

BREWMASTERS: Brad Shaffer and Jason Klein

BREWING SYSTEM: Three-barrel Portland Kettle Works brewhouse

FLAGSHIP BEERS: GFY PoP Stout, Bitter Biker Imperial Pale Ale, Irish Ale

YEAR-ROUND BEERS: GFY PoP Stout, Bitter Biker Imperial Pale Ale, Irish Ale

SEASONAL BEERS: Winter Ale, Dunkeweizen

SPECIAL RELEASES: American Brown Ale

TOURS: By request

BEER TO GO: None

FOOD: None

AMENITIES: Free street parking, free bike parking, convenient to the Montrose and Irving Park stops on the Brown Line "L"

PUB HOURS: None

NEARBY ATTRACTIONS: Chicago-area breweries, Old Town School of Folk Music, Andersonville shops and restaurants, the Hopleaf beer bar, the Neo-Futurists Theater, Music Box Theatre, Mercury Theater, Graceland Cemetery

NOTES: Ask a craft brewer how they got into the business, and chances are the story will begin, "Well, I started homebrewing. . . ." But Brad Shaffer and Jason Klein came at it from the opposite direction. They started homebrewing only after deciding to go pro.

Returning to Chicago after college, the two childhood friends were unhappy with their prospects. Schaffer was unemployed, and Klein was working an unsatisfying job in the family business. They both wanted careers that they were passionate about. "We wanted to wake up happy to go to work every day," said Klein. A shared passion for beer led Klein to make the unlikely suggestion, "Why don't we do a microbrewery?"

The two embarked on a path of "aggressive homebrewing," making two or three batches of beer every weekend to shorten their learning curve. They started with extract kits on the stove and quickly advanced to brewing all-grain recipes in ever-larger volumes. They read every book they could find on the subject of beer and brewing. Eventually Schaffer left his job to work at Pipeworks Brewing Company for some hands-on experience while they completed a business plan and applied for licenses.

In terms of footprint, Spiteful Brewing is certainly one of the smallest breweries in the region. Seven five-barrel fermenters, the three-barrel brewhouse, cold room, and all of the ingredients and miscellaneous equipment are crammed into a room that is just less than eight hundred square feet. To make it work, they've had to go vertical. Shelving that towers from floor to ceiling allows them to take full advantage of what little space they have.

Stockholm's Vardshus

ADDRESS: 306 W. State St. Geneva, IL 60134

TELEPHONE: 630–208–7070

EMAIL: info@stockholmsbrewpub.com

WEB SITE: www.stockholmsbrewpub.com

MICHAEL'S PICK: Lorazz Weiss: Most fruity wheat beers tend toward the sweet side. This one is decidedly tart and crisp. The raspberry flavor is somewhat subtle, allowing the wheat to share the stage. Higher-than-expected bitterness and a dry finish help keep this fruit beer refreshing.

TYPE: Brewpub

DATE ESTABLISHED: 2002

OWNER: Michael Oleson

BREWMASTER: Michael Oleson

BREWING SYSTEM: Ten-barrel "Frankenstein" extract brewhouse

FLAGSHIP BEER: State St. Pilsner

YEAR-ROUND BEERS: Blend of Silk, Lorazz Weiss, Mike's Blend, Aegir's Ale, SWB, State St. Pilsner, Doc's Porter, Downtown Honey Brown, Third Street Ale, Older but Weisser

SEASONAL BEERS: Iron Vice Weiss, Summertime Kölsch, Winter Bock, American IPA, Abbey Ale, SBSB, Oktoberfest

SPECIAL RELEASES: None

TOURS: By request

BEER TO GO: One-liter growlers

FOOD: Selection of upscale pub favorites: sandwiches, burgers, steaks, and seafood. Italian and seasonal specialties.

AMENITIES: Free street parking, full bar, seasonal outdoor seating

PUB HOURS: Monday–Thursday: 11:00 A.M. to 1:00 A.M.; Friday and Saturday: 11:00 A.M. to 2:00 A.M.; Sunday: noon to midnight

NEARBY ATTRACTIONS: Two Brothers Brewing Company, Rock Bottom–Warrenville, Geneva Ale House beer bar, downtown Geneva shopping and art galleries, Fox River Bike Trail, Fermilab National Accelerator Laboratory tours, golf, nearby forest preserves, thirty-five miles from the Chicago Loop

NOTES: Stockholm's location has been a tavern since 1938. Owner Michael Oleson has childhood memories of coming there with his grandfather. It still has a 1930s neighborhood-tavern feel. But a look at the menu and a taste of the food reveals that this is not your granddaddy's bar. Oleson describes it as "white tablecloth quality without the stuffed shirt." Every item is prepared to order from scratch using top quality ingredients like sushi-grade fish and aged beef.

Oleson has dreamed of opening Stockholm's at this location since 1985 when he first tried to purchase the building. Having been outbid, he had to wait sixteen years for another shot. When the building came up for sale in 2001, he leapt at the chance. The place has been a success. Oleson claims a large number of regulars, and the small dining room fills daily at lunch and dinner. There was a solid lunchtime crowd on the day of my visit.

All of Oleson's beers are unfiltered and naturally carbonated through refermentation in the keg. He believes that this gives them a more complex flavor profile. One interesting offering is beer blends. Mike's blend is a one-to-two mix of the pilsner and brown ale. SWB combines the Aegir's English pale ale with the porter.

Three Angels Brewing

ADDRESS: 10842 Ashley Rd.
  Yorkville, IL 60560
TELEPHONE: 630–553–5622
EMAIL:
  jason@threeangelsbrewing.com
WEBSITE: www.threeangelsbrewing.com
MICHAEL'S PICK: None available for sample
TYPE: Brewery
DATE ESTABLISHED: 2012
OWNERS: Jason Leslie and Boyd Ingemunson
BREWMASTER: Jason Leslie
BREWING SYSTEM: Two-barrel converted dairy-tank brewhouse
FLAGSHIP BEERS: None
YEAR-ROUND BEERS: None
SEASONAL BEERS: None
SPECIAL RELEASES: Blackball Bourbon Barrel Stout, Our Daily Bread, RHF India Pale Ale, and others
TOURS: By appointment
BEER TO GO: Growlers planned
FOOD: None
AMENITIES: Free parking, retail store and taproom planned, seasonal outdoor seating
PUB HOURS: Check Web site
NEARBY ATTRACTIONS: Nevins Brewing Company, Solemn Oath Brewing Company, Raging Wave Water Park, Mies van der Rohe–designed Farnsworth House, Geneva Kayak Center, Silver Spring State Park, Rich Harvest Farms Golf Course

NOTES: At Three Angels Brewing, music is as much a part of the mission as beer. Music is so important, in fact, that the original plan was to sell Three Angels beer exclusively at music events organized by Rogue Barrister, a music-promotion company owned by brewery cofounder Boyd Ingemunson. It was about cross-promoting two loves. People who come for the music will drink the beer. Those who come for the beer will hear the music. It's a win/win situation for both bands and brews. This remains the brewery's primary mode of operation, but they have started placing Three Angels beer in local bars, primarily those that also serve as venues for live music.

The brewery's headquarters is in Ingemunson's law office. The actual brewery is located outside of town on a farm. When their first choice site was denied by the state, Leslie and Ingemunson accepted a friend's offer to put the brewery in his 1850s barn. This friend also happened to be a first-class contractor. He set to work converting the rough-hewn structure into a fully functioning and duly licensed beer factory, complete with a complex water-treatment system and variable-frequency drives to power the sanitary pumps. Given the building's former use, it seems fitting that the crew opted to make their brewhouse out of repurposed dairy tanks.

Leslie and Ingemunson have plans to expand into microdistilling in the near future.

Tighthead Brewing Company

ADDRESS: 161 N. Archer Ave.
  Mundelein, IL 60060
TELEPHONE: 847–970–9174
EMAIL: info@tightheadbrewing.com
WEBSITE: www.tightheadbrewing.com
MICHAEL'S PICK: Boxcar Porter: A round belly of caramel and milk chocolate forms the body of this beer. Coffee-like roasted malt flavor and the subtle earth and orange marmalade of East Kent Golding hops are delicately layered on top. It finishes with lingering roasted malt bitterness. I love this beer.
TYPE: Brewery
DATE ESTABLISHED: 2011
OWNER: Bruce Dir
BREWMASTER: Bruce Dir
BREWING SYSTEM: Fifteen-barrel Newlands Systems brewhouse
FLAGSHIP BEER: Scarlet Fire Red Ale
YEAR-ROUND BEERS: Comfortably Blond, Scarlet Fire Red Ale, Irie IPA
SEASONAL BEERS: Boxcar Porter, Hat Trick Tripel, Barleywine

SPECIAL RELEASES: Extra Pale Ale, others planned

TOURS: Saturday and Sunday: 2:00 and 4:00 P.M.

BEER TO GO: Growlers and kegs

FOOD: None

AMENITIES: Parking lot, tasting room, Mundelein Metra station is just across the parking lot

PUB HOURS: Wednesday–Friday: 4:00 to 10:00 P.M.; Saturday: noon to 10:00 P.M.; Sunday: noon to 6:00 P.M.

NEARBY ATTRACTIONS: Lake Bluff Brewing Company, Small Town Brewing Company, Mickey Finn's Brewpub, Six Flags Great America, Almond Marsh Forest Preserve, golf courses, Volo Auto Museum, forty miles from the Chicago Loop

NOTES: It was unemployment that motivated home-brewer Bruce Dir to open a brewery. Like many home-brewers, the idea had been in the back of his mind for some time. After being laid off from two corporate jobs in as many years, he got permission from his wife and got to work. Dir supplemented his homebrewing experience with courses at Chicago's Siebel Institute brewing school and served a yearlong internship at the now-defunct Flatlander's Brewpub. He enlisted American Brewers Guild–trained Billy Oaks, who was managing a local homebrew store, to be head brewer. Construction on the brewery began in April 2011. The first beer flowed seven months later in November.

At the time of my visit in January 2012, the pair was still working to define Tighthead's identity. Their initial releases were met with enthusiasm, and the number of draft accounts was building. The majority of their distribution was within twenty miles of the brewery, and they were looking to keep things as local as possible.

Their beers shoot straight down the center of stylistic guidelines—nothing too extreme in any direction. They craft a broad assortment of styles designed to appeal to a wide range of palates, from novice to beer nerd.

If their early efforts are any indication of what's to come, Tighthead is a brewery to watch. The beers that I had the opportunity to taste were all clean and crisp, with well-defined layers of flavor. While the porter stood out, there wasn't a loser in the lot.

Two Brothers Brewing Company

ADDRESS: 30W315 Calumet Ave. Warrenville, IL 60555

TELEPHONE: 630–393–4800

EMAIL: beerguys@twobrosbrew.com

WEBSITE: www.twobrosbrew.com

MICHAEL'S PICK: Cane and Ebel: The brothers call this a "hopped-up red rye ale." That description is apt, but

it's not an unbalanced beer. A touch of Thai palm sugar in the brew brings a raisiny sweetness that enhances the toasty, nutty, and caramel malt flavors. Firmly bitter, its spice and citrus hop character is pumped up by the spicy edge of rye. This is a beer that makes me say "wow."

TYPE: Brewery

DATE ESTABLISHED: 1996

OWNERS: Jim Ebel and Jason Ebel

BREWMASTER: Jason Ebel

BREWING SYSTEM: Fifty-barrel Newlands Systems brewhouse

FLAGSHIP BEER: Domaine DuPage

YEAR-ROUND BEERS: Domaine DuPage, The Bitter End, Ebel's Weiss, Prairie Path Ale, Cane and Ebel, J-Series Oak Foudre Aged Beers, including Resistance IPA and Long Haul Session Ale

SEASONAL BEERS: Monarch White, Dog Days Lager, Heavy Handed IPA, Northwind Imperial Stout, Hop Juice IIPA, Hop Juice Black, Atom Smasher, Bare Tree Wheat Wine

SPECIAL RELEASES: Heavier Handed, Moaten, Hoodwink, Cocoa Northwind Imperial Stout, Askew, Door County Cherry Stout, Hoppy Porter, and others

TOURS: Saturday: 1:00 and 2:30 P.M.; Sunday: 1:00 P.M.

BEER TO GO: Growlers

FOOD: Small selection of pub favorites: burgers, sandwiches, pizza, and light entrées. Emphasis on organic ingredients.

AMENITIES: Parking lot, Two Brothers Tap House is a full-service brewpub

PUB HOURS: Monday–Thursday: 3:00 to 11:00 P.M.; Friday and Saturday: noon to midnight; Sunday: noon to 9:00 P.M.

NEARBY ATTRACTIONS: Rock Bottom–Warrenville, Stockholm's Brewpub, hiking in nearby forest preserves, golf, Fermilab National Accelerator Laboratory tours, thirty miles from the Chicago Loop

NOTES: Jim and Jason Ebel opened Two Brothers at the peak of the 1990s brewery boom. It was a time when scores of investors looking to cash in on craft beer were producing less-than-stellar product. But the brothers had a different perspective. Travels in Europe had introduced them to a different kind of beer culture. Beer wasn't the yellow fizzy stuff that Dad drank during football games. It was stuff that brought people together and that they enjoyed with meals. The pair became enamored of that lifestyle and that kind of vision.

With its mainline beers, Two Brothers strives for balance and drinkability. At 8 percent ABV, North-wind Imperial Stout is at the low end for the style. It avoids the cloying sweetness of some stronger versions. The pale ales and IPAs highlight hops, without tongue-scraping levels of bitterness. But rest assured, they manage to maintain quaffability without sacrificing flavor or letting go of innovation. The use of unique ingredients like Thai palm sugar or the practice of aging beer in oak foudres lends even their lightest beers onion-like layers of complexity.

If you are in the western suburbs, the taproom is worth a stop even if you aren't taking the tour. An impressive selection of guest beers complements the several house beers on tap, some of which aren't available elsewhere. You can grab a bite if you're hungry.

Village Vintner Winery and Brewery

ADDRESS: 2380 Esplanade Dr.
Algonquin, IL 60102
TELEPHONE: 847–658–4900
EMAIL: info@thevillagevintner.com
WEB SITE: www.thevillagevintner.com
MICHAEL'S PICK: None available for sample
TYPE: Brewpub
DATE ESTABLISHED: 2012
OWNER: Steve Boyer
BREWMASTER: Steve Boyer
BREWING SYSTEM: Three-barrel Stout Tanks and Kettles brewhouse
FLAGSHIP BEERS: Vanilla Cream Ale, Red Head Ale, Vit Ale, Hop Rocket, No Doubt Double Oat Stout, Pilsner
YEAR-ROUND BEERS: Vanilla Cream Ale, Red Head Ale, Vit Ale, Hop Rocket, No Doubt Double Oat Stout, Pilsner
SEASONAL BEERS: Scottish Ale, Octobierfest, Dunkelweizen, Holiday Ale, Hefeweizen, Maibock, Belgian Dubbel
SPECIAL RELEASES: Black Rye IPA, Nut Brown Ale, Coconut Porter, Chocolate Vanilla Stout, Bourbon Barrel Stout
TOURS: By request
BEER TO GO: Growlers
FOOD: Upscale pub fare: wood-fired pizza, fire-roasted ribs, burgers, sandwiches, and entrées
AMENITIES: Parking lot, full bar, house-made wines, separate wine- and beer-tasting bar, seasonal outdoor seating, take-out menu, Wine and Mug Clubs
PUB HOURS: Monday: 5:00 to 11:00 P.M.; Tuesday–Thursday: 11:00 A.M. to 11:00 P.M.; Friday and Saturday: 11:00 A.M. to midnight; Sunday: 11:00 A.M. to 10:00 P.M.
NEARBY ATTRACTIONS: Emmett's Ale House–West Dundee, The Onion Pub, hiking in nearby forest preserves, Des Plaines River Bike Trail, Metropolis Performing Arts Center, Raue Center for the Arts, Grand Victoria Casino, forty-three miles from the Chicago Loop

NOTES: Village Vintner is one of only two establishments in the region that makes both wine and beer. It is the only one that makes beer entirely on-site and from scratch. When Steve Boyer first opened the business, it was just a winery. Although he had dreamed of a pizzeria that served its own beer and wine, his lack of restaurant experience and the cost of brewing equipment at the time put that goal out of reach. Six years later, as the brewery boom was picking up, he saw the potential to draw more customers by adding food and beer to the winery. He returned to his dream, but on a much bigger scale than before.

Boyer is both brewer and vintner. He enjoys doing both, but he says that each has its pluses and minuses. Brewing beer is more difficult than making wine; all of the ingredients have to be carefully balanced to consistently produce a pleasant drink. But the variety of ingredients offers more opportunity to explore. The process is also quick—a few hours to brew, and he's done except for fermentation. Winemaking requires a two-week process of crushing and pressing the grapes before it goes into barrels. But winemaking is more about the fruit than the winemaker. With good grapes, he says, it's not hard to make good wine. With bad grapes, there isn't much that he can do.

With house-made beer and wine as well as a full cocktail bar, Village Vintner offers something for everyone. If there's a wait for a table, you can belly up to the tasting bar for sampler flights of brewer/vintner's wares.

NORTHERN

Bent River Brewing Company–Brewpub

ADDRESS: 1413 5th Ave.
Moline, IL 61265
TELEPHONE: 309–797–2722
EMAIL: info@bentriverbrewing.com
WEB SITE: www.bentriverbrewery.com
MICHAEL'S PICK: Dry Hopped Pale Ale: Big tangerine and tropical-fruit aromas greet your nose as you raise the glass. Your tongue is met with a clean, sharp bitterness that is balanced by ample caramel malt. It seems bigger than its modest 6 percent ABV. Resinous and tropical-fruit hop flavors float on top and carry through to a dry, bitter finish.
TYPE: Brewpub
DATE ESTABLISHED: 1997
OWNERS: Tim Koster and Gary Freeman
BREWMASTER: Steve Ratcliff

BREWING SYSTEM: Fifteen-barrel Bohemian Breweries brewhouse

FLAGSHIP BEER: Uncommon Stout

YEAR-ROUND BEERS: Mississippi Blond, American Wheat, Uncommon Stout, Oatmeal Stout, Pale Ale, Strawberry or Raspberry Wheat

SEASONAL BEERS: Jingle Java, DeSoto Lager, Dry Hopped Pale Ale, Jerry's Honey Bear Porter, Jalapeño Pepper Ale, Sweet Potato Ale

SPECIAL RELEASES: English Strong Ale, 2 Dave Strong Stout, and others

TOURS: No

BEER TO GO: Growlers

FOOD: Selection of standard brewpub fare

AMENITIES: Free street parking, paid city parking lot in back, Mug Club, seasonal patio seating, three-dollar burger basket from 11:00 A.M. to 2:00 P.M. daily, full bar, cookouts on summer weekends, music on Saturday nights

PUB HOURS: Daily: 11:00 A.M. to 3:00 A.M.

NEARBY ATTRACTIONS: I Wireless Center events, John Deere Commons, John Deere family homes, Great River Brewery, Front Street Brewpub, Blue Cat Brewpub, Moline River Walk, river cruises

NOTES: You can't help but be impressed by the brewery at Bent River Brewpub. It's the first thing you see when you walk in the door. Crowded behind the bar, its copper-clad, fifteen-barrel brewhouse and row of shiny, thirty-barrel fermenters appear massive. Despite this, they have maxed out its capacity and built a production brewery down the street in Rock Island.

It was almost by accident that Steve Ratcliff came to brew on that monster system. A friend of the former brewer, he started as an assistant, washing kegs and learning the ropes. After just three months of on-the-job training, that brewer left, and Ratcliff stepped up to fill his shoes. A former jack-of-all-trades, he never saw himself as a brewer until it happened. Now that he is one, he loves it. "People love it. It's not like they come to me to fix their car. I'm the beer guy."

Despite his lack of prior experience, Ratcliff makes some very good beer. His lineup includes the brewpub-standard blond and pale ale, along with some more challenging brews like jalapeño ale and sweet-potato ale. I will attest to the tastiness of the latter. The former is not my style.

The ambience is casual, loose, and lively. Multiple television screens show sports, while loud music provides an upbeat soundtrack. The staff calls it a "casual neighborhood bar" that attracts a varied mix of people from students to locals. You might see middle-aged workers from the John Deere plant conversing over a beer with students from nearby Augustana University.

Bent River Brewing Company–Brewery

ADDRESS: 2324 5th Ave.
Rock Island, IL 61201

TELEPHONE: 309–283–4811

EMAIL: info@bentriverbrewing.com

WEB SITE: www.bentriverbrewery.com

MICHAEL'S PICK: None available for sample

TYPE: Brewery

DATE ESTABLISHED: 2012

OWNERS: Tim Koster and Gary Freeman

BREWMASTER: Steve Ratcliff

BREWING SYSTEM: Thirty-barrel Zhongde Equipment Co. brewhouse

FLAGSHIP BEER: Uncommon Stout

YEAR-ROUND BEERS: Mississippi Blond, Uncommon Stout

SEASONAL BEERS: None

SPECIAL RELEASES: None

TOURS: See Web site for days and times

BEER TO GO: Growlers

FOOD: None

AMENITIES: Parking lot, taproom, Uncommon Beverage Station drive-thru selling coffee drinks and growlers

PUB HOURS: Monday–Thursday: 3:00 P.M. to 1:00 A.M.; Friday: 3:00 P.M. to 2:00 A.M.; Saturday: noon to 2:00 A.M.; Sunday: noon to 10:00 P.M.

NEARBY ATTRACTIONS: Blue Cat Brewpub, Bent River Brewpub, Great River Brewery, Front Street Brewpub, I Wireless Center events, John Deere Commons, John Deere historic homes, river cruises

NOTES: Although it appears massive, crammed into the tiny space behind the bar, the fifteen-barrel brewhouse at the Bent River Brewpub in Moline could not satisfy demand, especially for the brewery's flagship Uncommon Stout. Seeing an immediate need to expand, the owners purchased an old car wash on a corner of Rock Island that had been considered an eyesore and built a brewery. The building's previous use proved perfect for installing a brewhouse. Water hookups and floor drains were abundant. The new facility will initially produce Uncommon Stout and Mississippi Blond, the company's two most popular beers. Packaging will also happen there for retail distribution.

Also on the property was a defunct coffee stand. It seemed a shame to let that go to waste, and so the Uncommon Beverage Station was born. The one-of-a-kind, drive-thru outlet sells both coffee drinks and growlers of Bent River beer.

Blue Cat Brewpub

ADDRESS: 113 18th St.
Rock Island, IL 61201
TELEPHONE: 309–788–8247
EMAIL: bluecatbrew@bluecatbrewpub.com
WEB SITE: www.bluecatbrewpub.com
MICHAEL'S PICK: Count Magnus Dark Belgian Ale: A bruiser of a Belgian ale, Count Magnus clocks in at 10 percent ABV, but it carries it well. A bready base supports sumptuous caramel, vanilla, and raisiny, dried-fruit flavors. The cotton-candy, banana, and spice of Belgian yeast add complexity. The silky mouthfeel gives way to a dry finish that keeps it light.
TYPE: Brewpub
DATE ESTABLISHED: 1994
OWNERS: Dan Cleaveland and Martha Cleaveland
BREWMASTER: Dan Cleaveland
BREWING SYSTEM: Ten-barrel Newlands Systems kettle and Specific Mechanical mash tun
FLAGSHIP BEER: Off the Rail Pale Ale
YEAR-ROUND BEERS: Wigged Pig Wheat, Off the Rail Pale Ale, Big Bad Dog Olde English Ale, rotating stout selection
SEASONAL BEERS: Blue Cat Porter, Gunther Bock, Tuxtenacious Tripel, Olivia's Cranberry Ale, Coriander and Orange, Pumpkin Ale, Baltic Porter
SPECIAL RELEASES: Rambling Raspberry, Audrey's Brown Ale, Wee Bit Scotch Ale, River Back Jack, Crescent Moon ESB, AKA Pilsner, Mallard Ale, Red Toad, and many others
TOURS: By appointment
BEER TO GO: Growlers and kegs
FOOD: Standard pub favorites and an eclectic scattering of regional and more upscale items
AMENITIES: Metered street parking and paid parking in public lot across the street, weekly beer and food specials, Beer School classes, second-floor bar with pool tables, beer dinners every three months
PUB HOURS: Monday–Saturday: 11:00 A.M. to 3:00 A.M.
NEARBY ATTRACTIONS: Great River Brewery, Front Street Brewpub, Bent River Brewery, Rock Island Brewing Company beer bar, located in "The District," a two-block area hosting frequent street festivals, Bix Beiderbecke Festival, Davenport Blues Festival, Quad Cities Criterium Bicycle Race

NOTES: From the gray-blue exterior with its blue-striped awning to the elegantly casual dining room, the Blue Cat Brewpub has the feel of a place that should groove with the soothing sounds of jazz. The blue-painted walls and the old Bull Durham advertizing mural discovered during the renovation give it a comfy, classy vibe. The brewery is visible on two levels behind the first-floor bar. Upstairs there is additional seating with pool tables and a second bar.

When brewer Dan Cleaveland opened the place with his sister Martha, he had no formal brewing experience, but his former career as a chemist served him well. As he explains it, "Learning to brew was really just learning a new chemical process." He spent a week at the Wynkoop Brewpub in Denver to learn the ropes and then leapt in.

Cleaveland is inspired by learning about beer styles. His beers are rooted in style guidelines, but he'll tweak his recipes to showcase particular ingredients and flavors. His tastes lean toward Belgian ales and malt-forward beers. This is reflected in the tap selection, but those who prefer a lighter beer or love the hops will find something for them as well. The area's hard water is good for making dark beers, so he also brews a lot of stouts.

Carlyle Brewing Company

ADDRESS: 215 E. State St.
Rockford, IL 61104
TELEPHONE: 815–963–2739
EMAIL: ro@carlylebrewing.com
WEB SITE:
www.carlylebrewing.com
MICHAEL'S PICK: West Coast Red Ale: Hardly as assertive as a true "West Coast" red ale, it is still firmly hoppy. Medium-high bitterness bites early before giving way to rich caramel malt. Pine-resin and grapefruit-pith hop flavors carry through from start to finish and linger a while after swallowing.
TYPE: Brewpub
DATE ESTABLISHED: 2003
OWNER: Don Carlyle
BREWMASTER: Don Carlyle
BREWING SYSTEM: Ten-barrel Newlands Systems brewhouse
FLAGSHIP BEERS: Humulus Lupulus IPA, Vanilla Cream Ale
YEAR-ROUND BEERS: Stout, Vanilla Cream Ale, Humulus Lupulus IPA, Scottish Ale, Irish Red
SEASONAL BEERS: Black Walnut Stout, Hefeweizen, Oktoberfest, Holiday Spice, Belgian Trippel
SPECIAL RELEASES: West Coast Red, Rockinator Doppelbock, Honey Ale, California Common, Coffee Porter, IPAIPA, Baby Huemey Pale Ale, Defroster (barleywine), Harvest Ale (a brown IPA), Bourbon Barrel Stout, Saison, Vienna Lager, Roggenbier, Helles, and others
TOURS: No
BEER TO GO: Growlers

Carlyle Brewing Company in Rockford, Illinois.

FOOD: Limited menu of simple pub standards, sandwiches, and pizza

AMENITIES: Free parking in lot across the street and ample free street parking, seasonal beer garden, located centrally in downtown Rockford

PUB HOURS: Monday: 3:00 to 10:30 P.M.; Tuesday–Wednesday: 3:00 to 11:00 P.M.; Thursday: 3:00 P.M. to midnight; Friday: 3:00 P.M. to 1:00 A.M.; Saturday: Noon to 1:00 A.M.

NEARBY ATTRACTIONS: Pig Minds Brewing Company, Discovery Center Museum, Burpee Museum of Natural History, Klehm Arboretum, events at Rockford Metro Center, Midway Village Museum, Anderson Japanese Gardens, apple picking at Curran's Orchard, Coronado Theatre, Tinker Swiss Cottage, Rock Cut State Park

NOTES: The German word "Gemütlichkeit" is used to denote an atmosphere of informality and friendliness. It describes a comfortable place where one can feel at home. This evocative word can be aptly applied to Carlyle Brewing Co.

To brewer/owner Don Carlyle, beer is a social drink, and the pub is built to encourage friendly interactions over a pint. The front bar is an intimate space. The ambience is that of a casual neighborhood bar crossed with a German beer hall. Heavy, dark-wood tables line the walls with benches for seating. There are no television screens to distract you from your conversation. Music plays, but the volume is kept low, so you'll never have to shout to be heard above it. It is a place where strangers can become friends.

It is also a place that is all about the beer. There are no wines or cocktails served at this bar. There are always twelve beers on tap, all brewed on the premises. The selection on my visit ran the gamut from the light and refreshing Honey Ale to the monstrous 9 percent ABV Rockinator Doppelbock. Overall, the beers leaned to the sweeter side, but I found the hoppier selections to be nicely balanced, and many of them were certainly worth a pint.

Galena Brewing Company

ADDRESS: 227 N. Main St.
Galena, IL 61036

TELEPHONE: 815–776–9917

EMAIL: Form on Web site

WEB SITE: www.galenabrewery.com

MICHAEL'S PICK: Miner's Treasure Amber Ale: This is a great everyday drinking beer. Its crisp and clean profile showcases caramel malt with subtle, dark fruitiness that brings to mind raisin bread. The bitterness is moderate, but there is plenty of pine and citrus hop flavor to keep the caramel in check.

TYPE: Brewpub

DATE ESTABLISHED: 2010

OWNERS: Warren Bell and Kathy Cameron

BREWMASTER: Steve Winter

BREWING SYSTEM: Ten-barrel Premier Stainless brewhouse

FLAGSHIP BEER: Miner's Treasure Amber Ale

YEAR-ROUND BEERS: Uly's Dark Oatmeal Stout, Miner's Treasure Amber Ale, Annabelle's IPA, Farmer's Cream Ale, Uptown Nut Brown Ale, Chocolate Oatmeal Stout

SEASONAL BEERS: Wheat Wine, Wee Hefty Scotch Ale, Paradox Ale, Hefeweizen, Oktoberfest, Yuletide, and others

SPECIAL RELEASES: None

TOURS: Daily at 3:00 and 6:00 P.M. Cost $5.

BEER TO GO: Growlers and package

FOOD: Simple menu of sandwiches, salads, and an assortment of tapas items

AMENITIES: Free street parking, daily food and drink specials, live music, full bar featuring local wines, family-friendly

PUB HOURS: Monday: noon to 9:00 P.M.; Tuesday and Wednesday: 4:00 to 8:00 P.M.; Thursday–Sunday: 11:00 A.M. to 11:00 P.M.

NEARBY ATTRACTIONS: Potosi Brewing Company, National Brewing Museum, shops and restaurants on Galena's historic Main Street, National Mississippi River Museum and Aquarium, Massbach Ridge Winery, Rocky Waters Vineyard and Winery, Galena Cellars Winery, Apple River Fort State Historic Site, Galena River Hiking and Biking Trail, Apple River Canyon State Park, kayaking on area waterways, Chestnut Mountain Ski Resort

NOTES: Walking along Galena's Main Street, one gets a sense of what nineteenth-century "big city" life was like. The town was once a major hub of Mississippi River travel, and the narrow cobblestone streets of downtown are lined with buildings that date from that era. The town once boasted no fewer than eight breweries, including the Fulton Brewery, where the familiar Red Stripe beer was reportedly first brewed before the brand was sold to a firm in Jamaica, although this story cannot be confirmed.

Galena Brewing Company is located toward the north end of Main Street in what appears from the outside to be one of the few buildings of more recent construction. The dining room is large and open with a high vaulted ceiling. The brewery sits on a raised platform behind the bar, giving the impression of a church altarpiece. It has the feel of a roadhouse minus the peanut shells on the floor.

The brewhouse behind the bar at Galena Brewing Company.

The food and beer make Galena Brewing worth a visit. The brews are generally clean and flavorful. If you like lighter beers, the cream ale is a standout. And be sure to try the award-winning chocolate oatmeal stout. The tapas selection provides a pleasant opportunity to graze on small-plate items that are just a bit fancier than the atmosphere would suggest.

Pig Minds Brewing Company

ADDRESS: 4080 Steele Dr.
Machesney Park, IL 61115
TELEPHONE: 779-423-2147
EMAIL: info@pigmindsbrewing.com
WEB SITE: www.pigmindsbrewing.com
MICHAEL'S PICK: American Hardcore: Packing a 7 percent alcohol punch, this is not your typical American wheat beer. It's medium-full-bodied with a center of bready wheat. Hops and malt ride a razor's-edge balance that just barely tilts in favor of the grain. It comes across like a wheaty Dortmunder lager.
TYPE: Brewpub
DATE ESTABLISHED: 2012

OWNERS: Brian Endl and Randy Yunk
BREWMASTER: Carson Souza
BREWING SYSTEM: Seven-barrel PUB brewhouse
FLAGSHIP BEERS: Blue Collar, Southy Bitch Slap American Irish Red
YEAR-ROUND BEERS: Blue Collar, Southy Bitch Slap American Irish Red
SEASONAL BEERS: Oktoberfest
SPECIAL RELEASES: Hopcore American Pale Ale, The Killer IPA, Life of Brian American Porter, American Hardcore Wheat, No Regrets Imperial IPA, Fuzzy Nuts and Bolts, PD California Ale, Boats and Hoes, Flame Thrower, Donkey Punch, The Rated, Shitz and Gigs, Reign Supreme, Yelp's Pig Slop, Coffee Express, Smokie Scott, Special Smokie Scott, Beer Geek, Something Dramatic, Randy's Basement, Ester the Wild Bitch, Praying Mantis, and others
TOURS: By request
BEER TO GO: Growlers
FOOD: Vegan versions of classic pub favorites
AMENITIES: Parking lot, limited wine list, live music
PUB HOURS: Monday–Thursday: 3:00 to 11:00 P.M.; Friday and Saturday: noon to 1:00 A.M.; Sunday: noon to 8:00 P.M.
NEARBY ATTRACTIONS: Carlyle Brewing Company, Discovery Center Museum, Burpee Museum of Natural History, Klehm Arboretum, Events at Rockford Metro Center, Midway Village Museum, Anderson Japanese Gardens, apple picking at Curran's Orchard, Coronado Theatre, Tinker Swiss Cottage, Rock Cut State Park

NOTES: In brewer Carson Souza's own words, he "doesn't conform well." With a degree in jazz composition and a longtime love affair with hardcore punk rock, he embraces an ethos of boundary pushing and risk taking. The hardcore attitude—along with roasted poblano peppers, mangos, vanilla beans, and an assortment of other unusual ingredients—is infused into every beer that he makes. As he told me, "There are too many guys that do the same thing. I didn't get into this business to do the same thing."

Souza rejects the idea of a "standard lineup." With only two year-round beers, he's always looking toward what's next. Sedate, session beers are not the norm. When I visited, there were no beers containing less than 6 percent ABV. Even the beer names—Southy Bitch Slap, The Killer, No Regrets—reflect an outlaw disposition.

The brewpub's menu takes nonconformity to the next level. Pig Minds is, to my knowledge, the only totally vegan brewpub in the country. The food is familiar—burgers, tacos, and hot wings—but instead of meat they are made with mushrooms, beans, and seitan. Don't let this scare you. The food is great. The Magic Mushroom Marinated Portobello sandwich is to die for.

The décor is spare and industrial. The long, stainless steel–and-wood bar wraps around the brewery, putting you face-to-face with where the beer is made.

CENTRAL

Blind Pig Brewery

ADDRESS: 120 N. Neil St.
Champaign, IL 61820
TELEPHONE: 217–398–5133
EMAIL: startatab@blindpigbrewery.com
WEB SITE: www.blindpigbrewery.com
MICHAEL'S PICK: Belgo-American IPA: Intensely dry and sharply bitter are the two main descriptors that I would use to characterize this beer. A high degree of attenuation makes the malt a mere afterthought to the hops. Spicy and herbal hop flavors accentuate the underlying notes of pepper and fruit from the Belgian yeast.
TYPE: Brewpub
DATE ESTABLISHED: 2009
OWNER: Chris Knight
BREWMASTER: Bill Morgan
BREWING SYSTEM: Two-barrel Specific Mechanical brewhouse
FLAGSHIP BEER: American Pale Ale
YEAR-ROUND BEERS: None
SEASONAL BEERS: Red Rye Ale, Belgo-American IPA, Cherry Milk Stout, Winter Warmer, Oat Stout, Cyser, Extra Pale Ale, Oatmeal Stout, Blueberry Wheat, Ordinary Bitter
SPECIAL RELEASES: Rauch Heller Bock, Maibock, Samburro Chili Beer, American Dark Ale, and others
TOURS: By appointment
BEER TO GO: None
FOOD: None
AMENITIES: Metered street parking or paid parking structures, limited full bar, seasonal outdoor seating, good selection of guest taps and bottles, including cellared selections
PUB HOURS: Daily: 3:00 P.M. to 2:00 A.M.
NEARBY ATTRACTIONS: Destihl Brewpub, Blind Pig Co. beer bar, Triptych Brewing, Orpheum Children's Science Museum, performances and films at the Virginia Theatre, University of Illinois campus, Spurlock Ethnographic Museum, Krannert Art Museum

NOTES: The Blind Pig Brewery feels like a place lifted from the pages of a Dickens novel. The black-and-gold-painted storefront with its many-paned windows suggests a nineteenth-century English pub. Approaching it, one can almost smell the soot-laden air of Victorian London. Once inside, you enter a cozy space; the tightness of quarters is intensified by dim lighting and dark wood. It feels like night even at midday. Booth tables nearly disappear into cubbies in the wall. Heavy wooden timbers enhance the illusion of age.

Founded in 2009, the brewery springs from the partnership of two beer lovers. Owner Chris Knight had been successfully operating the Blind Pig Co. beer bar since 2003. The popular beer and music venue, located around the corner from the brewery on Walnut Street, had been rated among the top beer bars in the nation. But Knight saw another hole in the Champaign beer scene that needed filling. He wanted to open a brewery.

Enter Bill Morgan. Morgan first became interested in beer when he accidentally stumbled on a copy of Michael Jackson's *Pocket Guide to Beer.* After perusing its pages, he picked up a mixed six pack, and his mind was blown. That experience led to a two-decade career in beer that spans multiple countries and includes winning the first gold medal for sour beers at the Great American Beer Festival in 1997. But Morgan was looking to slow things down a bit. He had moved back to Champaign-Urbana to pursue a master's degree when he was approached by Knight about opening the brewery.

Morgan has freedom to play at Blind Pig. He seldom brews the same beer twice. His selections include everything from classic styles to chili beers.

Destihl Brewery

ADDRESS: 1616 General Electric Rd.,
Unit 1
Bloomington, IL 61704
TELEPHONE: 877–572–7563
EMAIL: Brewery@destihl.com
WEB SITE: www.destihlbrewery.com
MICHAEL'S PICK: None available for sample
TYPE: Brewery
DATE ESTABLISHED: 2013
OWNER: Matt Potts
BREWMASTER: Matt Potts
BREWING SYSTEM: Thirty-barrel brewhouse, manufacturer unavailable
FLAGSHIP BEERS: Normal Blonde, Road Block Red, Red Bird Ale, Black Angel Stout, Hoperation Overload, Black Torrent, Dead Head Double Red, Vertex IPA, Weissenheimer Hefeweizen, Downstate Pale Ale

YEAR-ROUND BEERS: Normal Blond, Road Block Red, Red Bird Ale, Black Angel Stout, Hoperation Overload, Black Torrent, Dead Head Double Red, Vertex IPA, Weissenheimer Hefeweizen, Downstate Pale Ale

SEASONAL BEERS: Strawberry Blonde, Nit Wit, Lawnmower Ale, Hawaii 5-Ale, Saison de Ruisseau, Malus Apple Blonde, Samhain Pumpkin Ale, Märzen Oktoberfest

SPECIAL RELEASES: Hopweizen, Tripel, Obatar, Nutty Brown Ale, Jivaro Oatmeal Espresso Stout, 120 Shilling Scotch Ale, Antigluten Cherry Belgian-Style Ale, Bamberger Rauchbier, Rivale, Quadrupel, Ambassador AM-Belgo Double Pale Ale, Altercation, All the Wiser, Antigluten Double Pale Ale, Kölsch Style, Bière Brune, Baldock IPA, Dark Side, Destihlinator Doppelbock, Bar Sinister Mild Ale, Saint Dekkera Sours, assorted barrel-aged beers, and others

TOURS: By appointment

BEER TO GO: None

FOOD: None

AMENITIES: Parking lot

PUB HOURS: None

NEARBY ATTRACTIONS: Illinois Brewing Company, Destihl brewpub, Bloomington Center for the Performing Arts, Heartland Theatre, Children's Discovery Museum, Miller Park Zoo, Illinois State University campus, Illinois Wesleyan University campus, sporting events and performances at the U.S. Cellular Coliseum

NOTES: In states where the law allows it, there is a growing trend for brewpubs to open separate production breweries. This trend is especially evident in Illinois. Goose Island did it in the 1990s. Revolution Brewing and Bent River Brewing followed in 2012, and now Destihl is jumping on the train. As the enthusiasm for craft beer grows, these businesses see opportunity in expanded capacity and packaging capability. A larger facility allows them to increase output, not only for sale in the pubs but for outside retail distribution as well.

For Destihl, the production brewery allows for expansion of distribution into neighboring states, starting with draft and eventually adding bottles and cans. Five hundred oak barrels and a number of large, oak foudres from France will enable Destihl to ramp up the barrel-aged and sour-beer program to meet increasing demand. According to brewmaster Matt Potts, most of the Destihl beers will be produced here in one form or another and at various times during the year on a rotating, seasonal, or special-release basis.

Destihl Restaurant and Brew Works

ADDRESS: 301 N. Neil St. Champaign, IL 61820

TELEPHONE: 217–356–0301

EMAIL: Form on Web site

WEB SITE: www.destihl.com

MICHAEL'S PICK: Miner's Ruin: It's not that often that you find a great California Common–style beer at a brewpub. The deep caramel and toast malts that greeted my tongue on the first sip made me say "wow." The bitterness is enough to keep it balanced and sharp. It lingers into the finish, along with the classic, rough-edged, woody/earthy hop flavors.

TYPE: Brewpub

DATE ESTABLISHED: 2011

OWNER: Matt Potts

BREWMASTER: Matt Potts

BREWING SYSTEM: Ten-hectoliter Premier Stainless brewhouse

FLAGSHIP BEER: Weissenheimer Hefeweizen

YEAR-ROUND BEERS: Champaign Blonde Ale, Weissenheimer Hefeweizen, Roadblock Red Ale, Black Angel Stout, DeadHead Double Red Ale, rotating hoppy beer (Downstate Pale Ale, Vertex IPA, Hoperation Overload Double IPA), rotating fruit beer

SEASONAL BEERS: Lawnmower Ale, Saison de Ruisseau, Oktoberfest, Samhain Pumpkin Porter, Snowblower Winter Bock, Christmas Ale, and others

SPECIAL RELEASES: St. Dekkera Reserve Series Sour Ales, Vertex IPA, Tripel, Roggenbier, Pappy's Porter, Obatar Ordinary Bitter, Nit Wit, Miner's Ruin, Lost in Space American Wheat Stout, Drunken Weasel Dunkel Weizen, Dosvidanya Russian Imperial Stout, Destihlinator Doppelbock, Clarice Belgian Strong Dark Ale, and others

TOURS: By request

BEER TO GO: Growlers and kegs

FOOD: Upscale versions of classic brewpub favorites

AMENITIES: Metered street parking and paid parking ramps, loyalty-rewards program, extensive wine list and signature cocktails, private room available, cask-conditioned beers

PUB HOURS: Monday–Thursday: 11:00 A.M. to 10:00 P.M.; Friday–Saturday: 11:00 A.M. to midnight; Sunday: 10:00 A.M. to 9:00 P.M.

NEARBY ATTRACTIONS: Blind Pig Brewery, Triptych Brewing, Orpheum Children's Science Museum, performances and films at the Virginia Theatre, University of Illinois campus, Spurlock Ethnographic Museum, Krannert Art Museum

NOTES: The Destihl restaurants take the brewpub idea and step it up a notch, adding a casual fine-dining flare to the familiar concept. From the food to the décor, it feels familiar but just a little bit higher-class. The fish tacos aren't just whitefish, they're swordfish. The pizzas are wood-fired and feature unique combinations like asparagus, bacon, and herbed goat cheese with a balsamic vinegar glaze. House beers are served alongside high-end wines and spirits. The dining room has the brewpub-standard motifs, stone veneers and dark wood, but given a contemporary, industrial-arts twist.

The Champaign location is situated in the city's newly revitalized downtown. Until recently a rundown area, it is now a bustling hub of trendy shops, restaurants, and coffee houses. Destihl fits right in.

The tap list of eleven house beers includes a wide range of styles, with a large number of Belgians. The overall quality of the beers is very high. A few standouts include Ambassador, a sharply bitter and full-bodied Belgian IPA, and Black Angel Stout, a nearly 7 percent ABV American-style stout. But the brewers try to keep things mixed up. If you don't find these beers on your visit, I'm sure something else will tickle your taste buds.

Destihl Restaurant and Brew Works

ADDRESS: 318 S. Towanda Ave. Normal, IL 61761
TELEPHONE: 309–862–2337
EMAIL: Form on Web site
WEB SITE: www.destihl.com
MICHAEL'S PICK: St. Dekkera Reserve: The St. Dekkera series consists of barrel-aged, sour versions of other Destihl offerings. During my visit the base beer was their Dead Head Red strong American red ale. Hints of caramel malt were still evident beneath the ample acidity. Earthy, barnyard flavors rounded it out. It made a surprisingly good partner with the coffee-encrusted ribeye that I had for dinner.
TYPE: Brewpub
DATE ESTABLISHED: 2007
OWNER: Matt Potts
BREWMASTER: Matt Potts
BREWING SYSTEM: Ten-hectoliter Beroplan brewhouse
FLAGSHIP BEER: Weissenheimer Hefeweizen
YEAR-ROUND BEERS: Normal Blonde Ale, Weissenheimer Hefeweizen, Redbird Ale, Black Angel Stout, DeadHead Double Red Ale, rotating hoppy beer (Downstate Pale Ale, Vertex IPA, Hoperation Overload Double IPA), rotating fruit beer

SEASONAL BEERS: Lawnmower Ale, Saison de Ruisseau, Oktoberfest, Samhain Pumpkin Porter, Snowblower Winter Bock, Christmas Ale, and others
SPECIAL RELEASES: St. Dekkera Reserve Series Sour Ales, 120 Shilling Scotch Ale, All-the-Wiser Imperial Hefeweizen, Altercation, Antigluten Double Pale Ale, Baltic Porter, Bar Sinister Mild Ale, Chocolate Raspberry Imperial Stout, Dampfbier, Jacob's Ladder American Brown Ale, Miner's Ruin, Quadrupel, Vienna Lager, and others
TOURS: By request
BEER TO GO: Growlers and kegs
FOOD: Upscale versions of classic brewpub favorites
AMENITIES: Parking lot, loyalty-rewards program, extensive wine list and signature cocktails, seasonal outdoor seating, private room available, cask-conditioned beers
PUB HOURS: Monday–Thursday: 11:00 A.M. to 10:00 P.M.; Friday–Saturday: 11:00 A.M. to 11:00 P.M.; Sunday: 10:00 A.M. to 9:00 P.M.
NEARBY ATTRACTIONS: Illinois Brewing Company, Bloomington Center for the Performing Arts, Heartland Theatre, Children's Discovery Museum, Miller Park Zoo, Illinois State University campus, Illinois Wesleyan University campus, sporting events and performances at the U.S. Cellular Coliseum

NOTES: The Destihl restaurants take the brewpub idea and steps it up a notch, adding a casual fine-dining flare to the familiar concept. From the food to the décor, it feels familiar, but just a little bit higher-class. The fish tacos aren't just whitefish, they're swordfish. The pizzas are wood-fired and feature unique combinations like asparagus, bacon, and herbed goat cheese with a balsamic vinegar glaze. House beers are served alongside high-end wines and spirits. The dining room has the brewpub-standard motifs, stone veneers and dark wood, but given a contemporary, industrial-arts twist.

Brewmaster Matt Potts has received some high praise from beer lovers and fellow brewers for his barrel-aged, sour beers. I had the opportunity to sample several at the Normal location, and the congratulations are well deserved. Except for a fantastic Flanders Red Ale, most of these tart treats are soured versions of the brewery's regular offerings, like the Blond or the Dead Head Red. They are all unblended, single-barrel vintages. The sour beer du jour is listed on the menu as St. Dekkera Reserve.

Illinois Brewing Company

ADDRESS: 102 N. Center St. No. 111
Bloomington, IL 61701

TELEPHONE: 309–829–2805

EMAIL: None

WEB SITE: https://www.facebook.com/pages/
Illinois-Brewing-Company/136256266386813

MICHAEL'S PICK: Newmarket Pale Ale: Hops dominate
this classic American pale ale. Flavors of citrus-pith and
spice are just barely supported on a bed of lightly sweet
malt. Moderately high bitterness lingers into the finish.
It's not a complex beer, but it goes down easy.

TYPE: Brewpub

DATE ESTABLISHED: 1999

OWNER: Jeff Skinner

BREWMASTER: Jeff Skinner

BREWING SYSTEM: Seven-barrel CDC brewhouse

FLAGSHIP BEER: Newmarket Pale Ale

YEAR-ROUND BEERS: O'Turly's Lyte, Wee Willy's
Wheat Ale, Clover Hill Honey Ale, Trendy Cream Ale,
Maggie's Irish Red, Illinois Amber Ale, Newmarket Pale
Ale, Big Beaver Brown Ale, Stumblin Stout, Porter from
Hell, Colonel Harrington Imperial Pale Ale, Red Lager

SEASONAL BEERS: None

SPECIAL RELEASES: None

TOURS: By appointment

BEER TO GO: Growlers and kegs

FOOD: Small selection of simple pub standards: burgers,
brats, wings, and pizza

AMENITIES: Free street parking, homebrew-supply
store, full bar, daily beer specials, live music, karaoke,
selection of guest taps and bottles

PUB HOURS: Monday–Thursday: 11:00 A.M. to 1:00 A.M.;
Friday and Saturday: 11:00 A.M. to 2:00 A.M.; Sunday:
noon to 1:00 A.M.

NEARBY ATTRACTIONS: Destihl Brewpub,
Bloomington Center for the Performing Arts, Heartland
Theatre, Children's Discovery Museum, Miller Park
Zoo, Illinois State University campus, Illinois Wesleyan
University campus, sporting events and performances
at the U.S. Cellular Coliseum

NOTES: If the trend is to make brewpubs ever-more
upscale, Illinois Brewing Company isn't going along.
More brew-bar than brew-pub, it is a no-frills, what-
you-see-is-what-you-get establishment with a kind of
dingy, dive-bar appeal. The building shows signs of
decay and neglect. Seating is limited mostly to stools
at the bar, but there is plenty of room to stand at rails
along the wall. If the live music in the back doesn't
suit your taste, you can entertain yourself up front
with pinball, pool, and darts.

The beer at Illinois Brewing is appropriate for the
place. There are no overhyped bourbon-barrel beers
here. Sour-beer fans should seek solace elsewhere.
Owner/brewer Jeff Skinner makes straightforward
beers brewed to classic styles. His seven rotating
house taps encompass a range of ales and lagers,
from hoppy IPA to roasty porter and "lyte" lager, all
a bit rough around the edges but very drinkable. If
the house beers aren't your thing, there is a decent
selection of guest taps and bottles. As Skinner says,
"We don't get snobby about that. If you want Busch
Light, I'll give you Busch Light."

The food is equally unpretentious. Burgers, brats,
wings, and bar snacks provide the perfect accompa-
niment to the brews and the ambiance. The burgers
are huge and really quite tasty.

Obed and Isaac's Microbrewery and Eatery

ADDRESS: 500 S. 6th St.
Springfield, IL 62701

TELEPHONE: 217–670–0627

EMAIL: Form on Web site

WEB SITE: www.obedandisaacs.com

MICHAEL'S PICK: English Pale Ale: This simple English
bitter starts with a snappy bitter bite that quickly gives
way to toffee-tinged malt. Grassy hop flavors with a kiss
of orange marmalade complete the effect. It's a light
and drinkable beer that welcomes a second pint.

TYPE: Brewpub

DATE ESTABLISHED: 2012

OWNERS: Court Conn and Karen Conn

BREWMASTER: Adam Conn

BREWING SYSTEM: Seven-barrel Premier Stainless
brewhouse

FLAGSHIP BEERS: Obed's Pride Amber Ale, Ditzy
Blond, Black IPA

YEAR-ROUND BEERS: Obed's Pride Amber Ale, The
Long Nine IPA, Mother Road Route 66 Pale Ale, Ditzy
Blond, Black IPA

SEASONAL BEERS: Strawberry Blond, Wheat, Holiday
Ale, Watermelon Wheat, Springfield Oktoberfest Beer
(SOB)

SPECIAL RELEASES: Scottish Ale, Silly Pants Stout,
ESB, Kölsch, Wheat Ale, English Pale Ale

TOURS: By reservation or request

BEER TO GO: Growlers and kegs

FOOD: Eclectic selection of pub food, lamb specialties

AMENITIES: Small parking lot, metered street parking,
full bar, dog-friendly, Sunday brunch, seasonal outdoor
seating in spacious beer garden

PUB HOURS: Daily: 11:00 A.M. to 11:30 P.M.

NEARBY ATTRACTIONS: Illinois State Capital, Old State Capital Historic Site, Abraham Lincoln Sites, Abraham Lincoln Presidential Library, Dana-Thomas House, Lost Bridge Bike Trail, outdoor activities on Lake Springfield

NOTES: Springfield is a city that oozes American history. Abraham Lincoln's home and the carefully preserved buildings that surround it give visitors a visceral connection to the nation's sixteenth president and the tumultuous time in which he served. Obed and Isaac's brewpub and the Conn family that operates it have a more direct and personal relationship to that history than most.

The brewhouse is located in an old coach house on property that once belonged to Obed Lewis, a family friend of Abraham Lincoln and great-great-grandfather of Court Conn. Unable to save the original Obed Lewis house, the Conns moved the Lindsay Isaac house to the property. According to legend, the Isaac house was built with a $650 loan from Lincoln. The restaurant is in another Lincoln-era mansion on an adjacent property just across the alley from the brewery.

Familial ties in the business go beyond these historical connections. Husband and wife Court and Karen Conn own the property, while their sons Casey and Adam run the restaurant and make the beer. Even the house chili comes from a fifty-year-old recipe created by Court's father. Court, Adam, and Casey shared a longtime homebrewing hobby, with Karen serving as the official "taste tester." When the decision was made to develop the property, it seemed obvious that they should take their hobby to the next level.

O'Griff's Grill and Brewhouse

ADDRESS: 415 Hampshire St.
Quincy, IL 62301
TELEPHONE: 217–224–2002
EMAIL: ogriffs@adams.net
WEB SITE: www.ogriffspub.com
MICHAEL'S PICK: Gem's India Pale Ale: While the menu description mentions the use of Noble hops, the earthy and citrus character that is the highlight of this beer suggests American and English varieties instead. The profile emphasizes hop flavor and aroma over bitterness. It is supported on a bed of lightly sweet, grainy malt. A bit more definition of flavor would be good, but it's not at all an unpleasant quaff.
TYPE: Brewpub
DATE ESTABLISHED: 2004
OWNERS: Jon Winter, John Winter, and Kim Winter
BREWMASTER: Jon Winter
BREWING SYSTEM: Ten-barrel Century brewhouse
FLAGSHIP BEERS: Gem's India Pale Ale, Old Brick Irish Amber
YEAR-ROUND BEERS: O'Griff's Lyte, Pilsner, Old Brick Irish Amber, Gem's India Pale Ale, Ivy's Blueberry Ale, Washington Park Wheat, Riverboat Porter, Haleigh's Honey Brown, Winter Street Strawberry Ale, Muddy Miss Oatmeal Stout
SEASONAL BEERS: Oktoberfest, Hefeweizen
SPECIAL RELEASES: None
TOURS: By request
BEER TO GO: Growlers
FOOD: Large assortment of pub favorites: sandwiches, salads, steaks, and ribs. Cheesecake specialties.
AMENITIES: Pool tables and darts, Mug Club, food delivery, private room available, family-friendly, Thursday-night Irish music jam session
PUB HOURS: Monday–Saturday: 11:00 A.M. to 1:00 A.M.; Sunday: 4:00 P.M. to 1:00 A.M.
NEARBY ATTRACTIONS: Gardner Museum of Architecture and Design, Dr. Richard Eell's House, Villa Kathrine, John Wood Mansion, Underground Railroad and Lincoln-Douglas Debate Sites, Lock and Dam No. 21, Indian Mounds Park, boating and fishing on the Mississippi River, Spirit Knob Winery, thirty minutes from the Mark Twain sites in Hannibal, Missouri

NOTES: Quincy, Illinois, is a historic river town that was once the third largest city in Illinois. A major riverboat and rail hub, it was a stopping-off point for the Mormons during their move west in 1838 and an important stop on the Underground Railroad. Washington Park, the city's central square, was the sight of the sixth debate between Stephen Douglas and Abraham Lincoln in 1858. Quincy's importance has waned since then, but it remains a nice place to visit and live. In 2010 *Forbes* magazine called Quincy the "eighth best small city to raise a family."

O'Griff's occupies a storefront across the street from Washington Park in the heart of the historic downtown. It's a spacious room with a long wooden bar that delineates a front and back dining area. As the name would suggest, O'Griff's is vaguely Irish-themed, although the green-painted walls are the only thing that really identify it as such. If you're there on a Thursday night, the jigs and reels from an informal Irish jam session add a welcome musical touch.

The nine or ten house beers on tap run the gamut from a light ale to an oatmeal stout. While none was outstanding, they were all pleasant enough to drink, making O'Griff's worthy of a stop if you're driving up the river roads in Missouri or Illinois.

Rhodell Brewery

ADDRESS: 619A SW Water St.
Peoria, IL 61602
TELEPHONE: 309-674-7267
EMAIL: None
WEB SITE: www.rhodells.com
MICHAEL'S PICK: Amber on Rye: Rhodell produces a few of these rye-tinged takes on classic styles. The caramel malt and moderate bitterness of an American-style amber ale is the basis for this one. Rye malt gives it a savory, spicy kick that is enhanced by spicy flavors from the hops. It's balanced, yet bold.
TYPE: Brewery
DATE ESTABLISHED: 1998
OWNER: Mark Johnstone
BREWMASTER: Mark Johnstone
BREWING SYSTEM: Half-barrel Custom Brew extract brewhouse
FLAGSHIP BEERS: None
YEAR-ROUND BEERS: The beer selection rotates constantly. You will always find a hoppy beer, a dark beer, and a wheat beer.
SEASONAL BEERS: Holiday Cheer, Winterfest, Winter Sun, Pumpkin Ale
SPECIAL RELEASES: Centennial Hop Head, Stout on Rye, Red Rye Ale, Cranberry Cream Ale, Piper's Pride Scottish Ale, Amber Bock, Golden Dragon Imperial Ale, Bees Knees Honey Lager, Double Honey IPA, Midnight Porter, Braveheart Ale, Imperial CTZ Hop Head, Hop Harvest IPA, Scottish Reserve, West Coast Stout, Cascade Pale Ale, Fiona's Scottish Farmhouse Ale, Belgian Nouvelle, Whisky Dick Imperial Stout, Midwest Amber, CTZ Hop Head, Amber on Rye, Midwest Wheat, Honey Vanilla Pils, Scottish Red, and others
TOURS: By request
BEER TO GO: Growlers
FOOD: None
AMENITIES: Free street parking, occasional cask-conditioned beers, brew-on-premises
PUB HOURS: Tuesday–Thursday: 3:00 to 10:00 P.M.; Friday: 3:00 P.M. to midnight; Saturday: 2:00 P.M. to midnight
NEARBY ATTRACTIONS: Peoria Riverfront, Peoria Civic Center events, Contemporary Art Center of Peoria, Par-a-Dice Casino, Bradley University and Illinois Central College campuses, water activities on the Illinois River, Class A baseball at O'Brien Field, Glen Oak Zoo, Luthy Botanical Garden

NOTES: There are several breweries and brewpubs in the region making beer on extract brewing systems. At most of them, the beers leave a bit to be desired. But this isn't a necessary state of affairs. Good beer can be made with malt extract. The Rhodell Brewery proves that. Crafting small batches on a half-barrel brew-on-premises system, owner/brewer Mark Johnstone produces a wide-ranging and ever-changing assortment of beers that are quite enjoyable.

The ambiance at Rhodell is also enjoyable. It maintains the aura of the old industrial/warehouse space that it inhabits, a feeling that is reinforced by the brew-on-premises kettles that occupy half of the room. It's a casual and friendly place where it is easy to strike up conversation with the other patrons seated at the bar. The service was good, too. The bartender knew the product and seemed to enjoy doling it out.

The brew-on-premises side of the business allows customers to make their own beer at the brewery. Rhodell has eight brew-your-own kettles available. Clients select a recipe and are given ingredients and instructions. Over a couple of hours they boil their wort, add hops at appropriate intervals, and sample a few Rhodell beers as they go. Two weeks later they come back to bottle the beer they made and take it home.

Rolling Meadows Brewery

ADDRESS: 3954 Central Point Rd.
Cantrall, IL 62625
TELEPHONE: 217-414-2436
EMAIL: rmbrewery@me.com
WEB SITE: www.rmbrewery.com
MICHAEL'S PICK: Lincoln's Lager: This American-style amber lager is crisp, light, and utterly drinkable. It's slightly malt forward, but only slightly. Bread crust flavors lead the way, but the hops don't let go easily. I wouldn't call it boldly bitter, but the lingering bitterness does something more than balance the malt. Spicy hop flavors and tart hints of lime citrus play over the top.
TYPE: Brewery
DATE ESTABLISHED: 2011
OWNERS: Chris Trudeau Caren Trudeau
BREWMASTER: Chris Trudeau
BREWING SYSTEM: Seven-barrel Newlands Systems brewhouse
FLAGSHIP BEER: Abe's Ale
YEAR-ROUND BEERS: Abe's Ale, Lincoln's Lager, Springfield Wheat
SEASONAL BEERS: None
SPECIAL RELEASES: Lincoln's Logger, Wet-hopped Dunkelweizen, Barrel-aged Imperial Abe's Ale
TOURS: By appointment
BEER TO GO: Growlers by appointment
FOOD: None
AMENITIES: Free parking
PUB HOURS: None

NEARBY ATTRACTIONS: Illinois State Capital, Old State Capital Historic Site, Abraham Lincoln Sites, Abraham Lincoln Presidential Library, Dana-Thomas House, Lost Bridge Bike Trail, outdoor activities on Lake Springfield

NOTES: Driving to Rolling Meadows Brewery, you might forget that you are only seven miles from downtown Springfield. As you leave town, the four-lane state highway becomes a two-lane road, and the signs of city life thin out. Leaving the main road, you follow a barely improved rural road through rolling farmland until it dead-ends at a dirt driveway. The farmstead at the end of that driveway is the home of Rolling Meadows Brewery.

The Rolling Meadows brewery on the farm near Springfield, Illinois.

Founder and Brewer Chris Trudeau is part of a small cadre of craft brewers seeking to return brewing to the land. When Trudeau decided to open a brewery, the family farm seemed a natural place to do it. Hops that have grown wild there for years are now cultivated on trellises out back. Llamas consume the spent brewing grain and in turn provide fertilizer for the hops. Vanilla, coriander, and other brewing herbs and spices are tended in a greenhouse next to the brewery. A field out back supplies wheat for the brewery's Springfield Wheat hefeweizen. Far off, there are plans for a small floor-malting operation. Trudeau dreams of one day making a 100 percent estate beer with ingredients from the farm.

Trudeau is focused on making quality beer to fit the local market. He keeps the distribution area small so that consumers are drinking the freshest possible product. His mainline beers are full-flavored and complex without being extreme. Limited Release Series beers will allow for some bolder explorations, including higher-gravity beers, bourbon-barrel aging, and perhaps even some sours.

Triptych Brewing

ADDRESS: 1703 Woodfield Dr. Savoy, IL 61874
TELEPHONE: None
EMAIL: triptychbrewing@gmail.com
WEB SITE: www.triptychbrewing.com
MICHAEL'S PICK: None available for sample
TYPE: Brewery
DATE ESTABLISHED: 2013
OWNERS: Anthony Benjamin, Joshi Fullop, and Jason Bartell
BREWMASTER: Anthony Benjamin
BREWING SYSTEM: 1.5-barrel Stout Tanks and Kettles brewhouse
FLAGSHIP BEERS: None
YEAR-ROUND BEERS: None
SEASONAL BEERS: DeLight Blonde, Dirty Hippy, Spring in Amarillo, 70 Minus, Blueberry Blonde, Pale Ale, Skajaquada, Valentine
SPECIAL RELEASES: Dinkel, Pumpkin Ale, Watermelon Wheat
TOURS: By request
BEER TO GO: Growlers and kegs
FOOD: None
AMENITIES: Parking lot, taproom
PUB HOURS: Monday–Thursday: 3:00 to 10:00 P.M.; Friday: 3:00 to 11:00 P.M.; Saturday: noon to 11:00 P.M.
NEARBY ATTRACTIONS: Destihl Brewpub, Blind Pig Brewery and Blind Pig Co. beer bar, Orpheum Children's Science Museum, performances and films at the Virginia Theatre, University of Illinois campus, Spurlock Ethnographic Museum, Krannert Art Museum

NOTES: A triptych is a work of art divided into three panels and centered on a common theme. Although each panel may stand on its own, the three together tell a complete story. And so it is with Triptych Brewing. They are three guys from different walks of life who came together to make beer.

Each partner brings something different to the business. Anthony Benjamin is a Web guy and onetime Midwest Homebrewer of the Year winner. He's got the brewing covered. Joshi Fullop brings a background in marketing and finance. Jason Bartell is a practicing attorney. He keeps them legal and tends to the business side of things. They each have overlapping skills to provide some checks and balances. Love of beer is the common theme that binds them all together.

Their brewing philosophy is to have something for everyone. They brew beers that appeal to fans of the extreme, but also reach out to neighborhood locals and students at the nearby University of Illinois campus. Session beers are an important part of their lineup. The Back-40 Series features beers with starting gravities of 1.040, coming in at about 4 percent ABV. The name pays homage to the vast rural landscape that surrounds Champaign.

SOUTHERN

Big Muddy Brewing

ADDRESS: 1430 N. 7th St.
Murphysboro, IL 62966
TELEPHONE: 618–684–8833
EMAIL: Form on Web site
WEB SITE: www.bigmuddybrewing.com
MICHAEL'S PICK: Big Muddy Monster: The brewer calls this an India brown ale, and that is just what he delivers. It's malty, but with a decidedly bitter bite. Roasted malt flavors like coffee and chocolate dominate the profile, with roasted malt bitterness adding to the bitterness of hops. Pine-resin hop flavors are layered on top. This is a beefy beer that remains balanced and drinkable.
TYPE: Brewery
DATE ESTABLISHED: 2009
OWNER: Chuck Stuhrenberg
BREWMASTER: Chuck Stuhrenberg
BREWING SYSTEM: Fifteen-barrel Global Stainless Systems brewhouse
FLAGSHIP BEER: Saluki Dunkel Dog
YEAR-ROUND BEERS: Kinkaid Wheat, Saluki Dunkel Dog, Pale Ale, Big Muddy Monster, IPA, Vanilla Stout
SEASONAL BEERS: Planned
SPECIAL RELEASES: Unfiltered Pilsner, 17th Street Smoked Amber
TOURS: Saturdays: 11:00 A.M., noon, and 1:00 P.M. Call for reservations.
BEER TO GO: Growlers, kegs, and package
FOOD: None
AMENITIES: Free parking, tasting room
PUB HOURS: During tours
NEARBY ATTRACTIONS: Shawnee Hills Wine Trail, outdoor activities in Shawnee National Forest, Garden of the Gods State Park, River to River Hiking Trail, fishing and boating on Cedar Lake, Southern Illinois University Carbondale campus, the Science Center of Southern Illinois, African American Museum of Southern Illinois

NOTES: The Saluki is an ancient Egyptian dog breed known for its intelligence and demanding disposition. Salukis are playful, but also just a bit cantankerous. Chuck Stuhrenberg thought this image was apt for the beers he produces at Big Muddy. Approaching beer with a homebrewing spirit, he enjoys playing with styles, creating flavor profiles that aren't quite this or that. Saluki Dunkel Dog, his flagship, falls somewhere between an amber ale and a Munich dunkel lager. The Big Muddy Monster is a mashup of American IPA and English brown ale. His beers are slightly experimental, but not so far out as to be unrecognizable or unpalatable to a beginner.

The Saluki also happens to be the mascot of nearby Southern Illinois University in Carbondale. The brewery has a strong following among students and alumni. According to Stuhrenberg, his Dunkel Dog has a nickname on campus: "Drunkel Dog." He once got a call from an alum in New Jersey asking where he could get Big Muddy beers. It seems an old college buddy had sent him four bottles of it. Empty bottles. That's just mean.

Stuhrenberg first started brewing in college. After graduating, he followed an entrepreneurial spirit, operating a number of businesses, including a pizza restaurant and a company that sold spray-paint booths and accessories, but he always had professional brewing in the back of his mind. When the economy crashed in 2008, so did his other businesses. In what he calls an "act of survival," he cashed out his IRAs and started buying equipment. His timing couldn't have been better. When he opened in 2009, craft-beer fever had reached southern Illinois. Now he can hardly keep up with demand.

Excel Bottling Company

ADDRESS: 488 S. Broadway
Breese, IL 62230
TELEPHONE: 618–526–7159
EMAIL: excelbrewery@gmail.com
WEB SITE: www.excelbottling.com
MICHAEL'S PICK: None available for sample
TYPE: Brewery
DATE ESTABLISHED: 1936, brewing began in 2012
OWNER: Paul Meier
BREWMASTER: Tony Toenjes
BREWING SYSTEM: Twenty-barrel Newlands Systems brewhouse
FLAGSHIP BEERS: Shoal Creek Wheat, Excel Golden Brew, Excel Citra, Carlyle Lake Lager
YEAR-ROUND BEERS: Shoal Creek Wheat, Excel Golden Brew, Excel Citra, Carlyle Lake Lager
SEASONAL BEERS: Shoal Creek Winter Ale, Oktoberfest, and others

SPECIAL RELEASES: Planned

TOURS: By request

BEER TO GO: Package

FOOD: None

AMENITIES: Parking lot, free street parking, retail store

PUB HOURS: Monday and Tuesday: 8:00 A.M. to 4:30 P.M.; Thursday and Friday: 8:00 A.M. to 4:30 P.M.; Saturday: 8:00 A.M. to noon

NEARBY ATTRACTIONS: Hidden Lake Winery, Governors Run Golf Course, water activities on Carlyle Reservoir, forty miles from St. Louis

NOTES: During the Great Depression in the 1930s, Paul Maier's father was working an ice-cream delivery route for one of three soda-bottling plants that were then operating in tiny Breese, Illinois. A bank robber's misfortune turned into his good fortune when in 1936 the elder Maier turned the criminal in and collected a reward. He invested the money in a bottling line and went into the soda business. Nearly eighty years later, Excel Bottling Company is still in the family and still making sodas the way it always has.

The expansion into making beer was largely a business decision. The family perceived that the market for soft drinks had peaked, as people were moving into other kinds of carbonated beverages. If they were going to survive, they needed to add other products to their lineup. The company also still uses old-school returnable bottles, which they have to buy in three-truckload volumes. They needed to make something besides soda to keep all of those bottles filled. They saw an opportunity in the rapidly expanding beer market.

For Excel, what's past is present. Using returnable bottles makes the brewery a bit of an odd duck in the industry. There are only about a dozen soda bottlers still using them, and perhaps only two or three beer makers. But the Maiers say that cleaning and reusing bottles is actually cost effective. They already had the bottling line from the soda operation, so there was no need to invest in new equipment to package beer. It also saves them continual expenditures on new glass. With only local distribution, they see a good rate of bottle return.

Excel isn't making challenging beers. The local market doesn't demand it. But they do plan to craft different beers for different areas—lighter beers for the accounts nearby and more flavorful brews for customers in east metro St. Louis. To keep the fermenters filled, they offer contract brewing services to St. Louis breweries that don't have bottling capability.

Kaskaskia Brewing Company

ADDRESS: 105 E. Market St. Red Bud, IL 62278

TELEPHONE: 618–282–2555

EMAIL: beer@kaskaskiabrewing.com

WEB SITE: www.kaskaskiabrewing.com

MICHAEL'S PICK: None available for sample

TYPE: Brewery

DATE ESTABLISHED: 2012

OWNERS: Derek Kueker and Jared Kueker

BREWMASTERS: Derek Kueker and Jared Kueker

BREWING SYSTEM: Three-barrel Stout Tanks and Kettles brewhouse

FLAGSHIP BEERS: Kölsch, IPA, Blond, Amber, American Wheat, Brown, Stout

YEAR-ROUND BEERS: Kölsch, IPA, Blond, Amber, American Wheat, Brown, Stout

SEASONAL BEERS: Pumpkin Beer, Winter Ale

SPECIAL RELEASES: Habenero Blonde, Imperial IPA, Hefeweizen, Raspberry Wheat, Bock, Double IPA, Porter, Chocolate Brownie Ale, Belgian Dubbel, Vanilla Cream Ale, and others

TOURS: By request

BEER TO GO: Growlers and kegs

FOOD: None

AMENITIES: Free street parking, taproom

PUB HOURS: Friday: 6:00 to 11:00 P.M.; Saturday: 2:00 to 10:00 P.M.

NEARBY ATTRACTIONS: Small downtown historic district, Kaskaskia River State Fish and Wildlife Area, Fort Kaskaskia Historic Site, Fort de Chartres State Historic Site, St. Genevieve, Missouri, thirty-five miles from St. Louis

NOTES: Not far from St. Louis, Red Bud sits squarely in what had been solid Anheuser-Busch territory. When the megabrewery was sold in 2008 to the Belgian beer giant InBev, it bred a lot of resentment in the region and sparked a renaissance of small brewing. That anger pushed Derek and Jared Kueker to start drinking better beer. Soon they were making their own beer at home and hatching plans to open a brewery. After an immersive course at Colorado Boy Pub and Brewing in Ridgeway, Colorado, they felt that the time was right to take the leap.

Although they live in St. Louis, the brothers decided to bring the brewery back to their hometown. They saw a need. When their planning began, there was only one brewery south of Springfield. They hoped that their brewery might draw outsiders to Red Bud and give locals a reason to stay there. The plan has worked. The taproom attracts visitors from

St. Louis and even Chicago. Locals have become enthusiastic supporters.

The Kuekers get a kick out of watching former Bud-drinkers take their first taste in the taproom. "It's like they are having their first beer all over again." There's a rush that comes when someone says, "I never knew light beer had so little flavor." But the brothers aren't trying to take the big breweries down. They only want to open peoples' minds to the bigger possibilities that beer presents.

The two are like yin and yang in the brewery. Jared is into classic styles, while Derek trolls the grocery store aisles for interesting ingredients and new inspirations. This balancing act fits perfectly with the brothers' taproom philosophy. They serve standard go-to brews that keep guests coming in the door, but stretch palates by offering new and unique flavors that change with every visit.

Scratch Brewing Company

ADDRESS: 264 Thompson Rd.
  Ava, IL 62907
TELEPHONE: None
EMAIL: marika@scratchbeer.com
WEB SITE: www.scratchbeer.com
MICHAEL'S PICK: None available for sample
TYPE: Brewpub
DATE ESTABLISHED: 2012
OWNERS: Marika Josephson, Aaron Kleidon, and Ryan Tockstein
BREWMASTERS: Marika Josephson, Aaron Kleidon, and Ryan Tockstein
BREWING SYSTEM: Five-barrel Stout Tanks and Kettles brewhouse
FLAGSHIP BEERS: None
YEAR-ROUND BEERS: None
SEASONAL BEERS: Basil IPA and others
SPECIAL RELEASES: Honeysuckle Blonde, Sumac Witbier, English Bitter, Black Belgian Single, Hen of the Woods Bière de Garde, Maple Sap Dubbel, Roasted Dandelion Root Stout, Bourbon-Oaked Root Beer, Stein Beer, Gotlandsdricka, Petite Saison, Cedar IPA, DoppelOct, and others
TOURS: By request
BEER TO GO: Growlers
FOOD: Small selection of sandwiches and pizzas highlighting homegrown and foraged ingredients and prepared in a wood-fired earth oven
AMENITIES: Parking lot, seasonal outdoor seating
PUB HOURS: Thursday and Friday: 3:00 to 8:00 P.M.; Saturday: noon to 10:00 P.M.; Sunday: noon to 8:00 P.M.

NEARBY ATTRACTIONS: Big Muddy Brewing Company, Von Jakob Winery and Brewery, outdoor activities in nearby preserves, state parks, and the Shawnee National Forest, River to River Trail, water activities on Kinkaid Lake, prehistoric petroglyphs on the Piney Creek Ravine Nature Reserve Trail, Historic St. Genevieve, Missouri, eighty miles from St. Louis

NOTES: Many breweries call themselves "farmhouse" breweries, but for Scratch Brewing Company the term is especially appropriate. The brewpub is located on a plot of forested land about five miles outside of the tiny rural town of Ava. It is truly a farm that has been in co-owner Aaron Kleidon's family for twenty-five years.

But "farmhouse" in this case also applies to the way they think about and brew beer. They follow an ethic that looks back to a time when beer making was carried out on every farmstead, using the ingredients at hand. They want Scratch beers to smell and taste like southern Illinois. The rustic flavors of their traditionally styled brews are enhanced by the addition of local ingredients, many of which are foraged from the property. These have included such things as nettle, elderberry, ginger, dandelion, maple sap, various roots, and cedar, among others. They grow some of their own hops and source much of the rest from Windy Hill Hops, a nearby grower.

The brewery itself is a mix of primitive and modern that reflects the different personalities of the owners. Aaron Kleidon is an expert forager who pushes a more primitive process that includes brewing in a copper kettle over an open fire. Ryan Tockstein represents the modern side of brewing, seen in the 1.5-barrel Stout Tanks brewhouse. Marika Josephson falls somewhere in between and forms a bridge between the two.

While the character of Scratch beers leans heavily on unique ingredients, don't look for them to be extreme. These brewers make beers to which modern palates will respond, but that are deeply rooted in older traditions. They look to their ingredients to complement other flavors already in the beer, not to overwhelm them.

Von Jakob Vineyard and Brewery

ADDRESS: 230 Hwy 127 N
  Alto Pass, IL 62905
TELEPHONE: 618-893-4600
EMAIL: info@vonjakobvineyard.com
WEB SITE: www.vonjakobvineyard.com
MICHAEL'S PICK: None available for sample
TYPE: Brewery

DATE ESTABLISHED: 1997, brewing began in 2010

OWNERS: Paul Jacobs and Rhoda Jacobs

BREWMASTER: Paul Jacobs

BREWING SYSTEM: Seven-barrel converted dairy-tank brewhouse

FLAGSHIP BEERS: Dark Bock, Pale Ale

YEAR-ROUND BEERS: American Pilsner, Hefeweizen, Red Ale, Nut Brown, Dark Bock, Stout, Pale Ale

SEASONAL BEERS: Roggenbier, Oktoberfest, German Pilsner

SPECIAL RELEASES: Dark Wheat, India Pale Ale, oak-aged beers

TOURS: Planned

BEER TO GO: Growlers

FOOD: Lunch menu is served daily, featuring pizzas, sandwiches, and German specialties. Dinner menu served Friday nights, featuring upscale steaks, seafood, and pasta. Reservations required for dinner.

AMENITIES: Parking lot, bed and breakfast cottages, seasonal outdoor seating with views of vineyards, winery, live music every Saturday and Sunday, catering and event space available

PUB HOURS: Monday–Friday: 10:00 A.M. to 5:00 P.M.; Saturday and Sunday: 10:00 A.M. to 7:00 P.M.

NEARBY ATTRACTIONS: Outdoor activities in the Shawnee National Forest, River to River Hiking Trail, Garden of the Gods Park, Shawnee Hills Wine Trail

NOTES: Von Jakob Vineyard and Brewery is a fermented-beverage fan's dream. In addition to beer and wine, they also make mead and apple cider. It's a working vineyard and orchard, with twelve acres of grapes and a couple acres of apples spread over two sites. The Pamona location is where wine and cider production occurs. The finished product is sold and sampled at the Alto Pass location, which is also where the brewery is housed.

Wine and beer have been a part of owner Paul Jacobs' life since childhood, when he would help his grandparents make both at home. It was a long-held dream to take this passion and turn it into a business. In 1997 he found himself with the wherewithal to do just that. He bought an orchard, established his grapes, and Von Jakob was born.

The hilltop Alto Pass site affords beautiful views of the Shawnee National Forest from the restaurant patio. In addition to being a beer and wine maker, Jacobs also has culinary training. His menu reflects his family's German roots. An assortment of traditional German specialties shares the table with German-influenced American cuisine. The beer selection is focused on classic styles, including several German lagers that are a good match to the food.

If you want to make a weekend of your visit, a pair of hundred-year-old farmhouses on the property serve as bed-and-breakfast cabins. Each cabin has several guest rooms and a common area. Von Jakob also has event facilities for weddings, parties, meetings, or retreats.

FERMENTERIES

GRAFTON WINERY AND BREWHAUS

Address: 300 W. Main St.
Grafton, IL 62037
Telephone: 618–786–3001
Email: info@thegraftonwinery.com
Web site: www.thegraftonwinery.com

GRANITE CITY FOOD AND BREWERY –EAST PEORIA

Address: 230 Conference Center Dr.
East Peoria, IL 61611
Telephone: 309–699–8080
Web site: http://www.gcfb.net/location/east-peoria

GRANITE CITY FOOD AND BREWERY– ORLAND PARK

Address: 14035 S. La Grange Rd.
Orland Park, IL 60462
Telephone: 708–364–1212
Web site: http://www.gcfb.net/location/orland-park

GRANITE CITY FOOD AND BREWERY– ROCKFORD

Address: 7140 Harrison Ave., Suite 108
Rockford, IL 61112
Telephone: 815–332–7070
Web site: http://www.gcfb.net/location/rockford

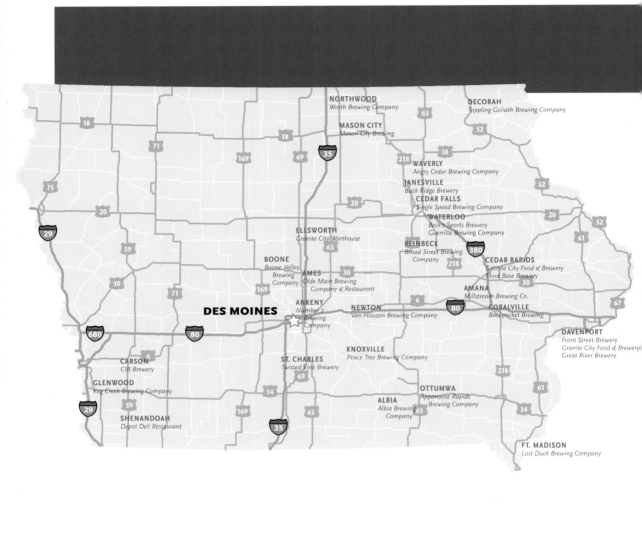

NORTHWOOD
Worth Brewing Company

DECORAH
Toppling Goliath Brewing Company

MASON CITY
Mason City Brewing

WAVERLY
Angry Cedar Brewing Company

JANESVILLE
Buck Ridge Brewery

CEDAR FALLS
Single Speed Brewing Company

WATERLOO
Beck's Sports Brewery
Guerrilla Brewing Company

ELLSWORTH
Granite City Worthouse

REINBECK
Broad Street Brewing Company

CEDAR RAPIDS
Granite City Food & Brewery
Third Base Brewery

BOONE
Boone Valley Brewing Company

AMES
Olde Main Brewing Company & Restaurant

AMANA
Millstream Brewing Co.

DES MOINES

ANKENY
Number 7 Brewing Company

NEWTON
Van Houzen Brewing Company

CORALVILLE
Backpocket Brewing

DAVENPORT
Front Street Brewery
Granite City Food & Brewery
Great River Brewery

CARSON
CIB Brewery

ST. CHARLES
Twisted Vine Brewery

KNOXVILLE
Peace Tree Brewing Company

GLENWOOD
Keg Creek Brewing Company

OTTUMWA
Appanoose Rapids Brewing Company

ALBIA
Albia Brewing Company

SHENANDOAH
Depot Deli Restaurant

FT. MADISON
Lost Duck Brewing Company

Many people perceive Iowa as the state that beer forgot. I have to admit that, before starting this book, Iowa was a blank spot on my mental beer map—the place where the great beer waterfall dropped off the edges of surrounding states and plummeted into the void. As I prepared to embark on my first weeklong tour of Iowa breweries, a common response from those who knew my destination was, "There are breweries in Iowa?" Even Iowans are unaware of what's happening in their state. A former denizen of Des Moines who had recently relocated to the Twin Cities was surprised to learn that there was a brewery in her hometown. I was happy to tell her that there were in fact four breweries in the Des Moines area at the time. There are now even more.

Iowa is hardly the state that beer forgot. Of the states covered in this guide, Iowa has the second highest number of breweries per capita. Only Wisconsin has more, and just barely. Like the region's other states, Iowa's craft-beer scene is experiencing a period of exponential growth. Between my first visit there in February 2011 and my completion of this book in March 2013, thirteen new breweries had started production. Others have likely opened since the time of this writing. And the burgeoning brewing industry is flexing some political muscle, having successfully lobbied the state legislature in 2010 to allow for the sale of beer with alcohol content above 6 percent.

Just as Iowa is the nation's archetypal representation of the Midwest, in many ways it encapsulates the beer landscape in the upper Midwest. Iowa's breweries are located throughout the state in big cities, small towns, and on farms in far-out rural places. They range in size from a microbrewery with an annual capacity of twenty-five thousand barrels all the way down to a picobrewery making beer ten gallons at a time. With old-school craft brewers like Millstream Brewing Company in Amana and Front Street Brewery in Davenport to pave the way, most of Iowa's breweries have come into existence since 2006.

The majority of beers made by Iowa brewers are representative of the region as a whole. Most ride squarely down the middle of the road, stylistically. They are balanced brews made according to classic styles, with mild flavor profiles suited to local palates, leaning more heavily on malt than hops. Midwestern IPA, the defining style of the whole region, sees perhaps its original expression in Millstream Brewing Company's Iowa Pale Ale—malty and slightly sweet, with just enough hops and bitterness to remind one that it is in fact an IPA.

But Iowans' tastes are evolving, allowing for the emergence of brewers that represent the more adventurous side of beer in the upper Midwest. Breweries like Peace Tree in Knoxville, Court Avenue and Rock Bottom in Des Moines, and Toppling Goliath in Decorah are moving beyond tradition with bold and sometimes style-bending beers. They are prodding local palates with more aggressively hopped beers and incorporating unusual but essentially Iowan ingredients like sweet corn, including the stalks. Barrel-aging is big, especially using barrels once filled with Iowa's own Templeton Rye. But even these more audacious brews maintain a midwestern moderation and balance.

The Interstate 35 and Interstate 80 corridors are a great starting point for an Iowa brewery tour. A number of breweries are easily accessible from these thoroughfares, including clusters in the urban centers of the Quad Cities and Des Moines. Heading north from Iowa City along Interstate 380 and Highway 218 through Cedar Rapids, Waterloo, and Waverly also affords easy access to a number of breweries. To reach many of the state's breweries, though, you have to get off the interstate and explore the rural back roads. This is the best way to experience Iowa. Away from the monotony of the freeway, the state offers picturesque landscapes of rolling farmland dotted with small and midsize towns. It makes for pleasant drives that are best capped off with a beer. Cheers!

The Iowa Brewing Industry at a Glance
(Based on 2012 Data)

LARGEST BREWERY: Millstream Brewing Company, Amana (4,258 barrels)*

SMALLEST BREWERY: Single Speed Brewing, Cedar Falls (10 barrels)*

LARGEST BREWPUB: Rock Bottom Restaurant and Brewery–Des Moines (1,056 barrels)*

SMALLEST BREWPUB: Lost Duck Brewing Co., Fort Madison (55 barrels)*

BREWERIES PER CAPITA: .00001, or 87,495 persons for every brewery**

*Brewers Association Data, *New Brewer* 30.3 (May/June 2013): 86–156.

**Based on 2011 population estimates from the U.S. Census Bureau (http://quickfacts.census.gov/qfd/states/19000.html) and the author's brewery list as of December 31, 2012.

Iowa Contract Breweries:

Blue Mountain Lodge, Orange City
Briar Creek Brewing Company, Janesville
Dubuque Star, Muscatine
Okoboji Brewing Company, Spirit Lake
Old Capitol Brew Works and Public House, Iowa City
Old Man River Brewing Company, McGregor

Iowa Breweries in Planning (as of March 2013):

Clear Lake Brewing Company, Clear Lake
Double Pot Brewing, Des Moines
Franklin Street Brewing, Manchester
Heartbreak Brewery, Des Moines
Heider House Brewing, Ankeny
Iowa River Brewing, Marshalltown
Joynt Brewing Company, Iowa City
Kalona Brewing Company, Kalona
Maple City Brewing Company, Osage
New American Brewing Company, Ankeny
Okoboji Brewing Company, Spirit Lake
Palindrome Brewing Company, Cedar Rapids
Slew City Brewing Company, Cedar Rapids
West Okoboji Brewing Company, West Okoboji

Iowa Beer Festivals:

Dubuque on Ice Brewfest, Dubuque, February (www.dubuquebrewfest.com)
Iowa Craft Brew Festival, Des Moines, May (www.iowabeer.org)
Lazy River Beer and Wine Festival, McGregor, June (https://www.facebook.com/pages/Lazy-River-Fest/119562451388332)
Brewfest, Des Moines, July (www.brewfestdsm.com)
Iowa City Brew Fest, Iowa City, September
Festival of Iowa Beers, Amana, September (www.millstreambrewing.com/events)
Brew Ha Ha, Davenport, September (www.wqpt.org/brew)

CENTRAL

515 Brewing Company

ADDRESS: 7700 University Ave. Clive, IA 50325

TELEPHONE: 515–661–4615

EMAIL: beer@515brewing.com

WEB SITE: www.515brewing.com

MICHAEL'S PICK: None available for sample

TYPE: Brewery

DATE ESTABLISHED: 2012

OWNERS: Bailey Forrest, Brandon Criger, Dave Ropte, and Ryan Rost

BREWMASTERS: Bailey Forrest, Brandon Criger, Dave Ropte, and Ryan Rost

BREWING SYSTEM: Three-barrel Stout Tanks and Kettles brewhouse

FLAGSHIP BEERS: None

YEAR-ROUND BEERS: Numb Nut, Dart Dodger IPA

SEASONAL BEERS: Planned

SPECIAL RELEASES: OJ IPA, Imperial Stout, Big Nuts, Kolsch, Loco Moco Stout, Mexican Spring, Milk Stout, Belgian Golden Strong Ale, Saison de Versailles, Sour Brown Cherry Ale, American Style Berliner

TOURS: By request

BEER TO GO: Growlers

FOOD: None

AMENITIES: Parking lot, taproom, special event space available

PUB HOURS: Thursday: 4:00 to 9:00 P.M.; Friday: 4:00 P.M. to midnight; Saturday: noon to midnight; Sunday: noon to 5:00 P.M.

NEARBY ATTRACTIONS: Green Belt Bike Trail, Rock Bottom Restaurant and Brewery, several Des Moines–area wineries, El Bait Shop beer bar, Iowa State Fairgrounds, Iowa State Capitol, Des Moines Botanical

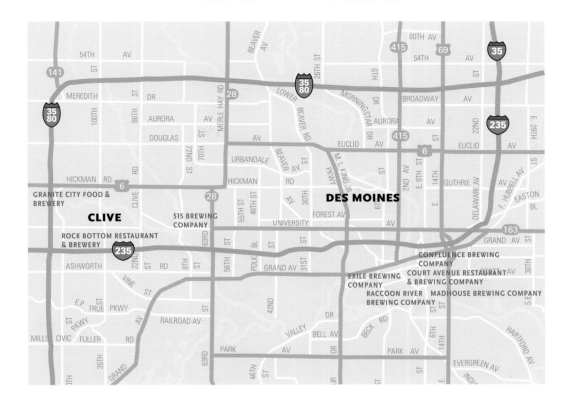

Center, Adventureland Theme Park, Blank Park Zoo, Des Moines Art Center, Iowa Cubs AAA baseball team

NOTES: The guys at 515 have a guiding motto for their business: "It's all about the beer." In their view, larger breweries sometimes get distracted by distribution issues and the quest for ever-higher sales volumes. By keeping it small and selling beer mostly from the brewery taproom, these four friends aim to keep 515 steadfastly focused on its core mission—making great beer in small batches. They strive for consistency and quality with every batch, a tall order when working on a small scale. Says co-owner Ryan Rost, "Beer is what makes our business happen. If a beer isn't good, we'll dump it. We won't serve bad beer."

Their small scale also affords them the freedom to experiment. According to Rost, their brewing philosophy involves making all different kinds of beer. "We don't want to be too well known for one thing so that we have to make a certain type of beer." They forgo a standard lineup, opting instead to brew a different beer each week. Guests to the 515 taproom will have something new to look forward to on every visit.

One thing guests can be sure of is that their beer will be served by the guys who made it. The team wants 515 to be the neighborhood "local." They strive to create the kind of place where you know the owners and the owners know you, a place where friends and neighbors can sit and socialize over a pint.

Boone Valley Brewing Company

ADDRESS: 816 7th St.
Boone, IA 50036
TELEPHONE: 515–432–1232
EMAIL: brewmaster@boonevalleybrewing.com
WEB SITE: www.boonevalleybrewing.com
MICHAEL'S PICK: None available for sample
TYPE: Brewery
DATE ESTABLISHED: 2012
OWNERS: Rick Srigley, Clare Srigley, Jon Crook, and Danielle Crook
BREWMASTER: Rick Srigley
BREWING SYSTEM: Three-barrel brewhouse, manufacturer unknown
FLAGSHIP BEERS: Roxie, Iron Horse IPA, Midnight Stout
YEAR-ROUND BEERS: Midnight Stout, Roxie, Semi-Crazy Blonde, Iron Horse IPA, Pintail Pale Ale, Backstreet Wheat
SEASONAL BEERS: Downtown Brown Ale, Vanilla Bourbon Imperial Porter, English Bitter, Hefeweizen, and others
SPECIAL RELEASES: Ol' Greg Barleywine, Rosie Irish Red, Belgian Ales, and others
TOURS: By request
BEER TO GO: 64-ounce and 32-ounce growlers
FOOD: None

AMENITIES: Parking lot across the street, free street parking, taproom, live music, available for private events

PUB HOURS: Monday and Thursday: 4:30 to 9:00 P.M.; Friday: 4:30 to 10:00 P.M.; Saturday: 1:00 to 10:00 P.M.; Sunday: 1:00 to 5:00 P.M.

NEARBY ATTRACTIONS: Olde Main Brewing Company, Boone and Scenic Valley Railroad, skiing at Seven Oaks Recreation Area, Honey Creek Golf Course, Boone Speedway, Mamie Eisenhower Birthplace, Snus Hill Winery, fifteen miles from Ames, forty miles from Des Moines

NOTES: Rick Srigley and Jon Crook started homebrewing in 2001, making simple extract batches on the kitchen stove. Brewing quickly developed into an avid hobby. Then the hobby became an obsession—or, as Crook describes it, "almost a sickness." Over the course of years they began entering their beers into competition. Crook says that while his beers occasionally medaled, Srigley's success was uncanny. In his first competition at the Iowa State Fair, he took a prize with every beer he entered. From there, his winnings continued to mount as he medaled in contests not only in Iowa but in the wider region as well. When one of his beers took best of show in a contest sponsored by the Granite City brewpub chain, they decided the time had come to go pro.

Since taking the leap, they have stayed close to their homebrewing roots. They sponsor occasional guest-brewer nights, on which they invite a local homebrewer to craft a recipe on their system. The beer is then made available for sale in the taproom.

The Boone Valley taproom is a quiet place to enjoy a pint of good American ale with friends. It's a family-friendly establishment. Children are welcome to sip on a glass of the house root beer. Crook says that much of their business comes from out-of-towners who stop in while touring the nearby wineries.

Confluence Brewing Company

ADDRESS:
1235 Thomas Beck Rd., Suite A
Des Moines, IA 50312
TELEPHONE: 515-285-9005
EMAIL: contact@confluencebrewing.com
WEB SITE: www.confluencebrewing.com
MICHAEL'S PICK: None available for sample
TYPE: Brewery
DATE ESTABLISHED: 2012
OWNERS: John Martin and Ken Broadhead
BREWMASTER: John Martin
BREWING SYSTEM: Twenty-barrel Specific Mechanical brewhouse

FLAGSHIP BEERS: Farmer John's Multi-Grain Ale, Des Moines IPA, Capital Gold

YEAR-ROUND BEERS: Farmer John's Multi-Grain Ale, Des Moines IPA, Capital Gold

SEASONAL BEERS: Gray's Lake Nessie Scottish Ale, Thomas Beck Black IPA, East Side Attitude Red Lager, Blue Corn Lager, High Water Oatmeal Stout, Bock, Mai Bock, ESB, English Pale, English Porter, and others

SPECIAL RELEASES: Scottish Farmer John's, and others

TOURS: By request

BEER TO GO: Growlers, kegs, and package

FOOD: None

AMENITIES: Parking lot, taproom, selection of Iowa guest taps, live music, seasonal outdoor seating, taproom available for private events

PUB HOURS: Wednesday and Thursday: 4:00 to 10:00 P.M.; Friday and Saturday: noon to 10:00 P.M.

NEARBY ATTRACTIONS: Des Moines–area breweries and wineries, El Bait Shop beer bar, Iowa State Fairgrounds, Iowa State Capitol, Des Moines Botanical Center, Adventureland Theme Park, Blank Park Zoo, Des Moines Art Center, Iowa Cubs AAA baseball team

NOTES: While still in high school, John Martin attempted to make beer—raisin-almond beer, to be exact. "I thought it would taste good," he says, adding, "It didn't work out so well." Martin took a hiatus from homebrewing after that misadventure, but the pause was only temporary. A few years later, on his honeymoon, he took his (fortunately, supportive) bride to the homebrew store and bought a kit. This second experiment succeeded, and he was hooked.

Martin loves to brew. He becomes noticeably animated when he talks about the brewing process, which he describes as "simple, but also miraculous." Plain malted barley yields sugary wort, which is then turned to beer through the metabolism of yeast. This love of brewing seems almost to have been with him from an early age. Growing up on a farm surrounded by grain, he says that he always had a desire to do something with it. His high-school attempt at making beer was just a manifestation of that desire.

Martin describes himself as "subtle in [his] gestures in life" and says that he works that way in beer too. He tends to brew the classic styles, but he looks for ways to add delicate creative touches. He wants the nuances of each ingredient to show through. He wants his Blue Corn Lager, for example, to taste like there are "two corn chips in every glass."

The Confluence taproom is a huge space with a sleek, industrial feel. The curved bar sports a polished concrete top that reminds me of a brewery floor. A long bank of windows offers nearly unobstructed views into the brewery. The entrance takes visitors past rows of fermenters before arriving in the taproom, creating a sense of connection to where the beer is made.

Court Avenue Restaurant and Brewing Company

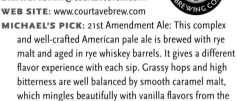

ADDRESS: 309 Court Ave.
Des Moines, IA 50309
TELEPHONE: 515-282-2739
EMAIL: kevinh@courtavebrew.com
WEB SITE: www.courtavebrew.com
MICHAEL'S PICK: 21st Amendment Ale: This complex and well-crafted American pale ale is brewed with rye malt and aged in rye whiskey barrels. It gives a different flavor experience with each sip. Grassy hops and high bitterness are well balanced by smooth caramel malt, which mingles beautifully with vanilla flavors from the barrel. Whiskey character is apparent, but pleasingly subtle and enhances the spicy bite of the rye malt.
TYPE: Brewpub
DATE ESTABLISHED: 1996
OWNER: Scott Carlson
BREWMASTER: Kevin Hall
BREWING SYSTEM: Seven-barrel Specific Mechanical brewhouse
FLAGSHIP BEER: Pointer Brown Ale
YEAR-ROUND BEERS: Two Rivers Light, Belgian White, Kaplan Hat HefeWeizen, Honest Lawyer IPA, Pointer Brown Ale, Black Hawk Stout
SEASONAL BEERS: Evie's Alt, Winter Ale, Belgian Blond, Bainbridge Street Porter, Pumpkin Ale, California Common, Oktoberfest, Sophie's Mild, Dorchester Amber, Baltic Porter
SPECIAL RELEASES: Monthly special releases such as Molé Molé Molé, Wheatmiser, Infatuation, 21st Amendment Ale, Puddledocker Double ESB, Shogun Named Marcus, and others
TOURS: By appointment
BEER TO GO: Growlers and kegs
FOOD: An eclectic mix of classic brewpub favorites and more upscale steaks and chops
AMENITIES: Metered street parking and paid parking in nearby ramps, private room available, full bar, happy-hour specials, cask beers, Sunday brunch
PUB HOURS: Monday–Thursday: 11:00 A.M. to midnight; Friday and Saturday: 11:00 A.M. to 2:00 A.M.; Sunday: 10:30 A.M. to midnight
NEARBY ATTRACTIONS: Raccoon River Brewpub, Rock Bottom Brewery, Exile Brewing Company, Several Des Moines–area wineries, El Bait Shop beer bar, Iowa State Fairgrounds, Iowa State Capitol, Des Moines Botanical Center, Adventureland Theme Park, Blank Park Zoo, Des Moines Art Center, Iowa Cubs AAA baseball team

NOTES: If you are in Des Moines, Court Avenue is a must-stop destination for some of the best made-in-Iowa brews. The standard lineup features solid interpretations of classic styles, but they're not afraid to take some risks with unusual flavor combinations such as a slightly soured raspberry Belgian Dubel.

Court Avenue is located in a historic downtown Des Moines building that has been home to a saddlery, a shoemaker, the Krispy Kone Company, and the Kaplan Hat Company, from whence the hefeweizen gets its name. When flooding decimated the ground floor in 1993, it remained vacant until Court Avenue moved in three years later.

The interior has a stately, elegant feel, with high ceilings, exposed brick, dark-stained wood, and muted color on the walls. But the elegance is not standoffish. It's an inviting space that would serve well for a business lunch, a nice dinner with family, or just hanging out in the bar enjoying a beer with friends.

Exile Brewing Company

ADDRESS: 1514 Walnut St.
Des Moines, IA 50309
TELEPHONE: 515-883-2337
EMAIL: info@exilebrewing.com
WEB SITE: www.exilebrewing.com
MICHAEL'S PICK: None available to sample
TYPE: Brewpub
DATE ESTABLISHED: 2012
OWNERS: R. J. Tursi and Bob Tursi
BREWMASTER: John Woodford
BREWING SYSTEM: Thirty-barrel Specific Mechanical brewhouse
FLAGSHIP BEERS: Hannah Weiss, Ruthie Munich Gold, Betty Blond, Gigi Munich Dunkel Lager
YEAR-ROUND BEERS: Hannah Weiss, Ruthie Munich Gold, Betty Blond, Gigi Munich Dunkel Lager
SEASONAL BEERS: Oktoberfest, Maibock, and others
SPECIAL RELEASES: Planned
TOURS: By request
BEER TO GO: None
FOOD: Gourmet bar food with a German influence
AMENITIES: Parking lot, metered street parking, full bar, seasonal outdoor seating, good selection of guest taps, private room available
PUB HOURS: Sunday–Thursday: 4:00 to 11:00 P.M.; Friday and Saturday: 4:00 P.M. to 2:00 A.M.
NEARBY ATTRACTIONS: Raccoon River Brewpub, Rock Bottom Brewery, several Des Moines–area wineries, El Bait Shop beer bar, Iowa State Fairgrounds,

Iowa State Capitol, Des Moines Botanical Center, Adventureland Theme Park, Blank Park Zoo, Des Moines Art Center, Iowa Cubs AAA baseball team

NOTES: A full-scale steel-and-copper replica of the Statue of Liberty's crown hangs near the roofline of the historic industrial building that Exile Brewing Company occupies. This homage to the "Mother of Exiles" proudly announces the origin of the brewpub's name and the inspiration behind it. Tursi family patriarch Joseph Tursi came to the United States as an immigrant from Italy. After weeks at sea, the Statue of Liberty was Joseph's first impression of his new home. To the father-and-son team of Bob and R. J. Tursi, the brewpub is a tribute to the hard work of their forbears that paved the way for them.

Exile Brewing Company is really two distinct concepts wrapped around a central brewhouse like a giant letter U. On one side is a traditional German-style beer hall set in a raw industrial space. Concrete floors, old brick, and long, communal tables provide a lively atmosphere for social imbibing. The other side, called the Annex, houses a more formal dining room. The industrial look is retained, but softened and refined with touches of sleek, modern design. It's got an air of elegance, but with a casual vibe.

The European connections that inspired the name carry over into the menu and beer selection. The food is definitely a step up from the typical pub fare. Burgers and a hot dog share the menu comfortably with pork-belly gyros and turkey-leg confit. The brewer's focus is on traditional German-style lagers and ales.

From the moment we pulled into the parking lot until we stepped back out the front door, everyone in my party said, "This place is great." Unfortunately, I visited the restaurant only a week after it opened, and they didn't yet have any house beers available.

Granite City Worthouse

ADDRESS: 1722 Detroit St. Ellsworth, IA 50075
TELEPHONE: 515–836–4060
EMAIL: brewlab@gcfb.net
WEB SITE: www.gcfb.net

MICHAEL'S PICK: Brother Benedict's Bock: This traditional bock is exemplary of what Granite City does: well-made, clean, approachable beers. It pours an appropriate dark amber color and has an aroma that is all caramel. The rich malt carries into the flavor and takes on dried, dark fruit flavors and hints of toast. Moderate bitterness and light spicy hops combine with a dry finish to make it an easy-drinking example of the style.

TYPE: Brewery
DATE ESTABLISHED: 1999
OWNER: Granite City Food and Brewery Ltd.
BREWMASTER: Cory O'Neel
BREWING SYSTEM: Twenty-five-barrel Newlands Systems brewhouse
FLAGSHIP BEER: Northern Lights Lager
YEAR-ROUND BEERS: Northern Lights Lager, Brother Benedict's Bock, Duke of Wellington, Broad Axe Stout, Wag's American Wheat
SEASONAL BEERS: Belgian Golden, Scottish Ale, Irish Red, rotating unfiltered wheat beer in the summer, Dunkelweizen, Oktoberfest, Double IPA
SPECIAL RELEASES: Blueberry Ale, Batch 1000 Double IPA
TOURS: By appointment
BEER TO GO: None
FOOD: None
AMENITIES: Parking lot
PUB HOURS: None
NEARBY ATTRACTIONS: Olde Main Brewpub, Worth Brewing, one hour from Des Moines

NOTES: One of the more interesting things about the Granite City brewpub chain is their patented "fermentas interruptus" brewing process, in which wort is brewed in a central brewhouse and then trucked to the various locations to be fermented. The heart of this unusual operation is the Worthouse in the Iowa farming hamlet of Ellsworth. Housed in a nondescript pole building on the edge of town, the Worthouse is much smaller than one would expect for a brewery that supplies twenty-six locations spread across the Midwest. Its diminutive size doesn't make what happens there any less fascinating.

The fermentas interruptus method was adopted to insure consistency of product across the chain and to spare the company the expense of maintaining twenty-six separate breweries. Wort is brewed in thirty-barrel batches and kept at near-freezing temperatures before being loaded onto tanker trucks for delivery. Each truck carries wort for several different beers, along with yeast and hops necessary for each beer. Once at the stores, wort is pumped into fermenting tanks, and the store managers take it from there, pitching yeast and nursing the fermentation to completion. Central production of wort, identical fermenter setup in the stores, and strict adherence to protocols is meant to insure a high degree of consistency across the chain.

The process does introduce possibilities for contamination that other breweries don't face. Brewmaster Cory O'Neel has a strong background in quality control and has put in place measures to reduce the risk. He has built a fully outfitted quality-control lab where product is subject to constant testing. Drivers are trained in aseptic sampling techniques, and every batch is tested before it leaves and after it is delivered. All Granite City yeast is propagated in-house and analyzed for purity.

The Granite City Worthouse was one of the most fascinating brewery visits I have ever done.

Madhouse Brewing Company

ADDRESS: 501 Scott Ave.
Des Moines, IA 50309

TELEPHONE: 641–831–3392

EMAIL: info@madhousebeer.com

WEBSITE: www.madhousebeer.com

MICHAEL'S PICK: Coffee Stout: Madhouse worked with Des Moines–based U.S. Roasterie to come up with the perfect coffee for this coffee stout, a mocha java blend. The beer leans to the sweet side, with hints of chocolate and intense coffee flavor.

TYPE: Brewery

DATE ESTABLISHED: 2010

OWNERS: Mason Groben and Allen Wells

BREWMASTER: Mason Groben

BREWING SYSTEM: Fifteen-barrel Newlands Systems brewhouse

FLAGSHIP BEER: Pastime Pale Ale

YEAR-ROUND BEERS: Honey Pilsner, Pastime Pale Ale, Coffee Stout, Hopburst, Oak Aged Imperial Red

SEASONAL BEERS: Iowa Grown IPA, Imperial IPA

SPECIAL RELEASES: Dunkelweizen, Saphire Hops Maibock, Maple Nut Brown, Barleywine, Belgian Golden Ale

TOURS: Check Web site for times

BEER TO GO: Growlers

FOOD: None

AMENITIES: Small parking lot, free street parking, taproom

PUB HOURS: Check Web site for times

NEARBY ATTRACTIONS: Des Moines–area breweries, several Des Moines–area wineries, El Bait Shop beer bar, Iowa Cubs AAA baseball, Science Center of Iowa, Iowa State Capitol, Des Moines Botanical Center, Adventureland Theme Park, Blank Park Zoo, Des Moines Art Center

NOTES: Madhouse founder and brewmaster Mason Groben is a winemaker by training and experience. He studied wine making and fermentation science at the University of California–Davis School of Viticulture. Degree in hand, he returned to Iowa to start Jasper Winery with his parents in 2003. Wine making is a highly seasonal occupation, revolving mostly around the fall grape harvest. During the rest of the year Gro-

ben found himself with plenty of spare time. He saw brewing beer as a way to fill it.

Beer making seemed like a logical extension of making wine, but Groben says that he initially confronted a steep learning curve. The differences between beer making and wine making range from the straightforward to the arcane. They can be as simple as the methods of extracting fermentable sugar from raw ingredients, or as tricky as the relative touchiness of beer yeast compared to wine yeast.

It is a learning curve that Groben admits he hasn't always negotiated successfully. His early efforts sometimes didn't live up to his own high standards. But his viticulture training gave him a sensitive palate and the ability to recognize and correct the flaws. Those less-than-stellar batches are largely behind him.

Groben is making "big-tent" beers at Madhouse. They are meant to appeal to a large audience. There's nothing extreme here. The boatloads-of-hops beers are not to be found. The classic-style beers he does make are solid and certainly easy to drink.

Number 7 Brewing Company

ADDRESS: 302 SW Maple St.
Ankeny, IA 50023

TELEPHONE: 515–964–5240

EMAIL: info@number7brewing.com

WEB SITE: www.number7brewing.com

MICHAEL'S PICK: Number 7 Amber Ale: Balanced and light, this American amber ale doesn't emphasize too much of any one thing. Caramel malt sweetness forms a base, with gentle bitterness offering a counterpoint. A touch of citrusy hops sits on top.

TYPE: Brewpub

DATE ESTABLISHED: 2012

OWNERS: Matt Sims and Jessie Alia Sims

BREWMASTER: Matt Sims

BREWING SYSTEM: Seven-barrel converted dairy-tank brewhouse

FLAGSHIP BEER: Number 7 Amber Ale

YEAR-ROUND BEERS: KB Kölsch, Number 7 Amber Ale, Coco Bessie Milk Stout, Drunken Sailor IPA

SEASONAL BEERS: Oktoberfest, Winter Ale, Pale Ale, Raspberry Wheat

SPECIAL RELEASES: Good Time Charlie Belgian Strong Dark, and others

TOURS: By request

BEER TO GO: Growlers

FOOD: A mix of new and traditional American cuisine, including barbeque, specialty pizzas, and diner food, with a focus on locally grown ingredients

AMENITIES: Parking lot, free street parking, full bar, Mug Club

PUB HOURS: Tuesday–Sunday: 11:00 A.M. to 11:00 P.M.

NEARBY ATTRACTIONS: Boating and fishing on Saylorville Lake, golf, twelve miles from Des Moines, twenty miles from Ames

NOTES: A few years ago, Matt Sims was about to be downsized from his corporate job. Faced with imminent unemployment, he and his wife Jessie started brainstorming ways to expand a catering business that they ran on the side. They made a list of every idea that popped into their heads. One idea drew them back again and again: opening a brewpub. That was idea number seven on their list.

Sims aims for drinkability in his beers. He's not trying to impress the cognoscenti with extreme flavors or off-the-wall ingredients. His goal is to lure light-lager drinkers to an appreciation of better beer. Sims is driven by what he sees as a direct attack on small brewers by the large conglomerates that are cranking out their own "craft" brands. He has a mission to show people what real small-scale brewing is all about and to coax them into keeping it local.

Sims is also maintaining his ties to the homebrewing community with Wild Card Wednesdays. He invites homebrewers to submit their creations into competitions held at the brewpub. The winning beer is brewed on his seven-barrel system and put on tap alongside the pub's regular offerings.

Number 7 is located in the Uptown section of Ankeny, the old downtown that Sims says has been somewhat forgotten as commercial activity moved toward I-35. Built in 1925, the building that houses the brewpub is the third oldest in the city. It has been a hardware store, a car dealership, and a cafe where workers from a World War II–era armaments plant would come for lunch. For the last forty years it was a family-style restaurant. The dining room retains some of that feel. Sims hopes that his brewery will serve as an anchor for the area, drawing people to rediscover the old downtown.

Olde Main Brewing Company and Restaurant

ADDRESS: 316 Main St.
Ames, IA 50010

TELEPHONE: 515–232–0553

EMAIL: info@oldemainbrewing.com

WEB SITE: www.oldemainbrewing.com

MICHAEL'S PICK: Off KILTer Scottish Ale: This Scottish ale starts with a rich caramel sweetness and creamy mouthfeel. Just the softest touch of hop bitterness serves to balance. Light, fruity ester notes flirt in the background. It finishes with a flourish of roast that cuts the sweetness and adds welcome depth.

TYPE: Brewpub

DATE ESTABLISHED: 2004

OWNER: Scott "Griff" Griffen

BREWMASTER: Jeff "Puff" Irvin

BREWING SYSTEM: Fifteen-barrel BRD brewhouse

FLAGSHIP BEER: Dinkey Wheat

YEAR-ROUND BEERS: Dinkey Wheat, Long Face Amber Ale, Off KILTer Scottish Ale, Clone American Pale Ale, Gryphonbräu American Lager, Sodbuster Stout, Red Monkey Root Beer

SEASONAL BEERS: Elkman Milk Stout, Ye Olde Shillelagh Irish Red, Lemontyme Lemon Ale, Der Festen Oktoberfest, Horseman's Revenge Pumpkin Ale, Reindeer Fuel Chocolate Porter

SPECIAL RELEASES: OA Oaked Amber, Rye Pale Ale, Double Down IPA, Rusty Crayfish, Dinkey Port Wood, Hard Pressed Cider, Bourbon Betty, Sir Plus Ale, Dark Helmet, Bourbon Aged Sodbuster, Yub Nub, Barrel-aged Pilsner in Portwood Staves, Robins Vanilla, Three Amigas, What About BOB?

TOURS: By appointment

BEER TO GO: Package

FOOD: Somewhat upscale pub fare

AMENITIES: Metered street parking, Beer Enthusiasts Union Mug Club, happy-hour specials, Sunday happy hour all day

PUB HOURS: Daily: 11:00 A.M. to 2:00 A.M.

NEARBY ATTRACTIONS: Iowa State University, Granite City Worthouse, Prairie Moon Winery, Snus Hill Vineyard, Raiman Gardens, Boone and Scenic Valley Railroad, Iowa Arboretum, thirty minutes from Des Moines

NOTES: Scott Griffen hatched the idea to open a brewpub in Ames during a ski trip in Colorado. Upon returning home, he bought a building on the city's historic Main Street, picked up a used brewery, and hired Jeff Irvin, a brewer trained at the prestigious University of California–Davis brewing school, to run it. After a long renovation that involved cutting holes in the floor to accommodate the brewhouse, Olde Main opened its doors.

The restaurant is divided into two halves, with separate entrances and different feels. The "pub" side features a long bar with the brewery visible behind it. Booth seating along one wall offers a cozy place for a burger and a beer. It feels like a neighborhood tavern, the kind of place where everyone might know each other.

The dining-room side is more open. It feels a bit more upscale, but still casual and welcoming. It's a good place for a family dinner or a get-together with friends.

I have eaten at Olde Main several times, and the food has always been delicious. Whether a simple burger, a juicy pork loin, or a homey meatloaf, I have enjoyed every bite.

If you like to dabble, the beer sampler is the way to go at Olde Main. You get sampler-size pours of every house beer on tap and the root beer for less than the cost of a pint. It's the best deal in the house.

Peace Tree Brewing Company

ADDRESS: 107 W. Main St.
Knoxville, IA 50138
TELEPHONE: 641–842–2739
EMAIL: Form on Web site
WEB SITE: www.peacetreebrewing.com
MICHAEL'S PICK: Hop Wrangler IPA: Brewer Joe Kesteloot enjoys mashing up styles. Hop Wrangler exemplifies this, combining an American IPA with Belgian yeast and English malts and hops. It's clean and crisp with a sharp bitter bite and citrusy American hop highlights. The Belgian yeast character is subtle, providing depth, but stopping short of making this a Belgian IPA. Backing malt provides the low notes in the form of sweet caramel.
TYPE: Brewery
DATE ESTABLISHED: 2009
OWNERS: Dan McKay, Scott Ziller, and Megan McKay Ziller
BREWMASTER: Joe Kesteloot
BREWING SYSTEM: Twenty-barrel JV Northwest brewhouse
FLAGSHIP BEER: Hop Wrangler IPA
YEAR-ROUND BEERS: Red Rambler Red Ale, Hop Wrangler IPA, Rye Porter
SEASONAL BEERS: Cornucopia, Black River Gumbo Stout, Double IPA
SPECIAL RELEASES: Lemon Grass Ale, Imperial Stout, and others
TOURS: By appointment
BEER TO GO: Growlers
FOOD: None
AMENITIES: Free street parking, taproom, live music twice monthly
PUB HOURS: Thursday and Friday: 4:00 to 10:00 P.M.; Saturday: 1:00 to 10:00 P.M.
NEARBY ATTRACTIONS: National Sprint Car Hall of Fame, Knoxville Raceway sprint-car track, birthplace of the Iowa state flag, Lake Red Rock, nearby hiking and biking trails, thirty minutes from Pella, Iowa, and Dutch-heritage attractions

NOTES: What happens when you combine a run-down storefront and a group of small-town Iowans with backgrounds in business, the arts, and brewing? You get one of the most interesting breweries in the

Joe Kesteloot, Scott Ziller, and Megan McKay Ziller of Peace Tree Brewing Company.

state. When the Peace Tree ownership trio bought the empty building across the street from their insurance business they considered many options for it, including a laundromat and a storage facility.

Ultimately, the idea of making beer seemed more fun. They hired Joe Kesteloot away from the Cold Spring Brewery in Minnesota and set to work converting the old car dealership into a craft brewery. In the few years it has been open, their venture has become a beer destination in southern Iowa.

From the beginning they set out to do something different from what most Iowa breweries were doing. According to Megan McKay Ziller, "Sometimes Iowans assume that people want the same old conservative stuff, but that hasn't been our experience. The community really embraces what we do."

Kesteloot is doing unique things at the brewery. His arts background shows in his combinations of disparate styles and influences. He uses unusual and homegrown ingredients like Iowa sweet corn and corn stalks to create magical zymurgic mashups. But his technical expertise is also evident. Peace Tree beers are clean, crisp, and extremely well crafted.

The arts background of many of the partners shows in the tasting room. It has the feel of a bohemian coffee shop. It's nice enough to feel special, but the industrial concrete floors and other minimalist touches keep it relaxing and casual. I could imagine sitting at my laptop or reading a book while quaffing a pint.

Raccoon River Brewing Company

ADDRESS: 200 10th St.
Des Moines, IA 50309
TELEPHONE: 515–362–5222
EMAIL: dcoy@raccoon.com
WEB SITE: www.raccoonbrew.com
MICHAEL'S PICK: Stonecrusher Imperial Stout: Big, rich, and chocolaty, Stonecrusher leans to the

sweet side with somewhat restrained hop and roast bitterness. It carries its high alcohol well, with just a touch of warming to let you know it's there. Imperial stouts tend to be too thick and charred for my palate, but I found this one to be utterly drinkable.

TYPE: Brewpub

DATE ESTABLISHED: 1997

OWNER: Jeffrey Hunter

BREWMASTER: David Coy

BREWING SYSTEM: Fifteen-barrel Specific Mechanical brewhouse

YEAR-ROUND BEERS: Tallgrass Light, Waves of Amber Grain, Bandit IPA, Vanilla Cream Ale, Rio Arriba Porter, Lakeside Wheat

SEASONAL BEERS: Renovator Doppelbock, Stonecutter Stout, Stonecrusher Imperial Stout, Cherry Wheat, Lakeside Wheat, Zustandfest Pils, Maibock

SPECIAL RELEASES: Occasional

TOURS: By appointment

BEER TO GO: Growlers and kegs

FOOD: A selection of brewpub classics and more upscale entrées, pizzas, and burgers. Unique taco selection for lunch.

AMENITIES: Metered street parking and paid parking in nearby ramps, private room available, pool tables, full bar, good selection of guest beers

PUB HOURS: Monday–Thursday: 11:00 A.M. to 11:00 P.M.; Friday and Saturday: 11:00 A.M. to 2:00 A.M.

NEARBY ATTRACTIONS: Court Avenue Brewpub, Rock Bottom Brewery, several Des Moines–area wineries, El Bait Shop beer bar, Iowa State Fairgrounds, Iowa State Capitol, Des Moines Botanical Center, Adventureland Theme Park, Blank Park Zoo, Des Moines Art Center, Iowa Cubs AAA baseball team

NOTES: Walking through the front door of Raccoon River, you enter into an open and airy space, with extra high ceilings that allow a feeling of decompression and walls of tall windows to let the sun shine in. The building, constructed in 1918, was originally a Plymouth dealership. The automobile showroom–turned–bar area sports a beautiful mosaic floor from that period, while outlines of service-department garage bays are still visible in the brick walls of the dining room. Upstairs you'll find another full bar, additional seating, and pool tables.

David Coy's beers aren't pushing any envelopes or shattering any style barriers. But that's not what he has set out to do. From the beginning, his aim has been to craft well-made beers that are suited to the local market. His lineup runs the gamut from a light, cream-ale-like creation to a robust and roasty imperial stout, with a couple of interesting-flavored

beers in between. He likes to use his Homestead Red American Amber Ale to transition light-lager drinkers into his more flavorful beers. If he can get them to drink the amber, then he has expanded their beer universe to include everything from the light beer to the stout.

Rock Bottom Restaurant and Brewery

ADDRESS: 4508 University Ave. Des Moines, IA 50266

TELEPHONE: 515–267–8900

EMAIL: desmoines@rockbottom.com

WEB SITE: www.rockbottom.com/des-moines

MICHAEL'S PICK: Vintage Dangereaux: I'm a sucker for saison, and this black saison is a beauty. Smooth chocolate notes combine with the fruitiness of the saison yeast strain to conjure up chocolate covered bananas. That's cut by peppery spice and sharp bitterness. Light coffee flavors linger into the finish.

TYPE: Brewpub

DATE ESTABLISHED: 1998

OWNER: CraftWorks Restaurants and Breweries Inc.

BREWMASTER: Eric Sorensen

BREWING SYSTEM: Twenty-barrel JV Northwest brewhouse

FLAGSHIP BEERS: Kölsch, White Ale, Red Ale, IPA

YEAR-ROUND BEERS: Kölsch, White Ale, Red Ale, IPA, Heartland Light, White Tail Pale Ale, Mud in Your Eye Red, Lumpy Dog Brown, Iron Horse Stout (rotating styles)

SEASONAL BEERS: Rotating seasonal wheat, rotating seasonal black, American Dream IPA, Pumpkin Ale, Rocktoberfest Märzen, Mary Jane Amber, Naughty Scott Wee Heavy, Liquid Sunshine, and others

SPECIAL RELEASES: Iron Horse Line of stouts, Wild Things Series of wild fermented beers, regular barrel-aged beers

TOURS: By appointment

BEER TO GO: Growlers

FOOD: Standard Rock Bottom Restaurant menu: pub food, sandwiches, and burgers, salads, chili, and a range of entrées. Good selection of steaks. Some more upscale items.

AMENITIES: Parking lot, full bar, happy-hour specials

PUB HOURS: Sunday–Thursday: 11:30 A.M. to 11:00 P.M.; Friday and Saturday: 11:30 A.M. to midnight

NEARBY ATTRACTIONS: Raccoon River Brewpub, Court Avenue Brewpub, several Des Moines–area wineries, El Bait Shop beer bar, Iowa State Fairgrounds, Iowa State Capitol, Des Moines Botanical Center, Adventureland Theme Park, Blank Park Zoo, Des Moines Art Center, Iowa Cubs AAA baseball team

NOTES: Eric Sorensen cut his brewing teeth in the early days of the microbrewery scene in Northern California. With no previous brewing experience, he was hired as assistant brewer at Lost Coast Brewery. Within six months he had moved up to the head brewer position. After a stint at the University of California–Davis brewing school and the Siebel Institute, he made the rounds of some of the seminal Humboldt County breweries like Eel River and Mad River, and even ran a winery for a time.

Sorensen has adapted the trend-setting attitude of the West Coast to his current midwestern base. He keeps his ear to the ground for the next big thing in beer but also stays grounded in the classics. As he puts it, "Beer is such a wide open thing, and it's becoming ever more so."

He keeps a wide selection of beers on tap—fourteen on my visit. There are usually three to four high-test sippers topping off a full range of tastes and strengths going all the way down to low-alcohol session beers. Styles go from funky Danish farmhouse ales to the pub-standard red ale. Two cask-conditioned beers are always available.

The ambience and menu at Rock Bottom are fairly standardized across the chain. Look for slightly upscale pub food with some nicer items tossed in. That said, the food is always delicious, and it is a comfortable place to hang out for a pint.

Twisted Vine Brewery

ADDRESS: 3021 St. Charles Rd.
St. Charles, IA 50240
TELEPHONE: 515–205–1466
EMAIL: info@twistedvinebrewery.com
WEB SITE: www.twistedvinebrewery.com
MICHAEL'S PICK: Old Crusty's Scottish Ale: The enjoyment begins when the glass hits the table. Dark amber and crystal clear, this is a pretty beer to look at. Bountiful caramel greets your palate with the first sip, accompanied by hints of roast and licorice. It's rich and creamy, but a dry finish keeps it light.
TYPE: Brewery
DATE ESTABLISHED: 2011
OWNERS: Steve Breman, Steve Becker, and Brian Sabus
BREWMASTERS: Steve Breman, Steve Becker, and Brian Sabus
BREWING SYSTEM: Three-barrel Stout Tanks and Kettles brewhouse
FLAGSHIP BEER: Twisted Blonde
YEAR-ROUND BEERS: Twisted Blonde, Amber Waves, Pirates Kettle Pale Ale, Whistling Ogre Wheat, Black Knight IPA, Parteezon Porter, RathSkelton the Red, Old Crusty's Scottish Ale

SEASONAL BEERS: LePetite Saison, Summer Blond
SPECIAL RELEASES: Tres Hombres, Rye Ale
TOURS: By request or appointment
BEER TO GO: Growlers
FOOD: Cheese platters available in tasting room
AMENITIES: Parking lot, tasting room, Madison County Winery, occasional live music
PUB HOURS:
Summer Hours: Tuesday and Wednesday: 11:00 A.M. to 6:00 P.M.; Thursday–Saturday: 11:00 A.M. to 10:00 p.m.; Sunday: noon to 5:00 P.M.
Winter Hours: Thursday–Saturday: 11:00 A.M. to 6:00 P.M.; Sunday: noon to 5:00 P.M.
NEARBY ATTRACTIONS: John Wayne's Birthplace, Covered Bridges of Madison County, Two Saints Winery, forty minutes from Des Moines

The brewhouse at Twisted Vine, behind the federally mandated fence.

NOTES: From Interstate 35, it's a scenic drive through the rolling Iowa countryside to reach the Twisted Vine Brewery. The vineyards of the Madison County Winery that hosts the brewery stretch up the hillside from the road. It's an idyllic setting, peaceful and verdant, that brings about a desire to pause, breathe, and let go.

The brewery is situated in the corner of a pole shed that it shares with the winery. It's a cozy corner, separated from the stainless-steel tanks that house fermenting wine by a low chain-link fence, an answer to federal regulations that forbid a winery and a brewery from sharing the same space. The gleaming stainless brewhouse is basically a glorified homebrewing system. Fermentation temperature is regulated by keeping the tiny tanks in coolers like those that keep beer cold in the liquor store.

Although they have some draft accounts at pubs in Des Moines, the winery taproom remains the brewery's biggest customer. It's gratifying for the brewing trio—three old homebrewing buddies whose wives have affectionately dubbed them "the Three Stooges"—to see winery patrons drinking their creations. Says Steve Bremen, "Husbands coming to the winery with their spouses are often pleasantly surprised to find beer."

Although the brewers claim "wickedly creative concoctions," the beers I sampled were fairly straightforward, albeit with an emphasis on the use of rye. I found them to be crisp, clean, and very well attenuated. They are nice beers for sipping on the tasting-room patio overlooking the vineyards.

Van Houzen Brewing Company

ADDRESS: 6602 Ginger Ave.
Newton, IA 50208
TELEPHONE: 319-594-9684
EMAIL: aren@vhbrewing.com
WEB SITE: www.vhbrewing.com
MICHAEL'S PICK: None available for sample
TYPE: Brewery
DATE ESTABLISHED: 2011
OWNER: Aren Van Houzen
BREWMASTER: Aren Van Houzen
BREWING SYSTEM: Information not available
FLAGSHIP BEERS: The Professor Double IPA, Sacrifish American Tripel, Symphony Imperial Double Chocolate Stout, Three-Toed Dog Robust Belgian White Ale
YEAR-ROUND BEERS: The Professor Double IPA, Sacrifish American Tripel, Symphony Imperial Double Chocolate Stout, Three-Toed Dog Robust Belgian White Ale
SEASONAL BEERS: Information not available
SPECIAL RELEASES: Rumplestoutskyn, Zombie Dog, Pussycat Sour
TOURS: No
BEER TO GO: None
FOOD: None
AMENITIES: Parking lot, Sugar Grove Vineyards, Sugar Grove Gatheringplace available for private events
PUB HOURS: None
NEARBY ATTRACTIONS: Madhouse Brewing Company, Peace Tree Brewing Company, Maytag Blue Cheese Factory, forty-five minutes from Des Moines, several Des Moines–area wineries

NOTES: Van Houzen Brewing Company specializes in high-alcohol beers; 8 percent ABV is as low as it goes with the brewery's mainline offerings. Double IPA, imperial stout, and strong Belgian ales are Van Houzen's stock in trade. Although the brewery isn't

open to the public, you can find Van Houzen beers on tap at several locations in Iowa City, Cedar Rapids, and Des Moines.

The brewery is located in the lower level of the Gatheringplace at Sugar Grove Vineyards. The 1870 building was originally constructed as a church and later served as the meeting place for the local Grange, a fraternal order of farmers. Today it hosts outdoor concerts, wine dinners, and private events. Visitors can take in the rolling hills of Iowa while enjoying a bottle of local wine, Iowa meats, cheeses, and bread, and, of course, Van Houzen beer. The vineyard grows eleven acres of French-American hybrid and native American grapes that are used by Iowa wineries.

Founder and brewer Aren Van Houzen is a trumpet player by trade. In addition to teaching positions at several central Iowa colleges, he performs with Orchestra Iowa and the Quincy Symphony Orchestra and frequently plays with the Quad City Symphony Orchestra and the Iowa City Chamber Orchestra. He has been a featured soloist with several Iowa performing organizations and continues to develop a modest soloing schedule.

NORTHEAST

Angry Cedar Brewing Company

ADDRESS: 730 Technology Pl.
Waverly, IA 50677
TELEPHONE: 319-961-8162
EMAIL: scott@angrycedar.com
WEB SITE: www.angrycedar.com
MICHAEL'S PICK: Angry Amber: Sweet caramel malt at the start quickly dissipates. Hop bitterness is low, and there is only the faintest citrus hop flavor. It finishes quickly, simply disappearing shortly after the swallow.
TYPE: Brewery
DATE ESTABLISHED: 2009
OWNERS: Scott Hammerlink and Amanda Hammerlink
BREWMASTER: Scott Hammerlink
BREWING SYSTEM: Seven-barrel "Frankensystem" brewhouse
FLAGSHIP BEER: Angry Amber
YEAR-ROUND BEER: Angry Amber
SEASONAL BEERS: Chocolate Porter, Maibock, Sandbagger Lager
SPECIAL RELEASES: None
TOURS: By appointment
BEER TO GO: None
FOOD: None
AMENITIES: Parking lot

PUB HOURS: None

NEARBY ATTRACTIONS: Wartburg College, Centennial Oaks Golf Club, Waverly Rail Trail

NOTES: Waverly is a small, quiet town on the banks of the Cedar River. In 2008 the rains came, and the river overflowed its banks, rushing through the home of Scott and Amanda Hammerlink. In previous floods it had been enough to bring their possessions up to the second floor for protection, but this flood was not like other floods. This flood was a record flood that destroyed everything they owned. All that survived were cases of Scott's homebrewed beer. Safely sealed, the bottles simply floated to the surface to ride out the angry waters.

Named for the swollen Cedar River, Angry Cedar Brewing Company was born out of a desire to "make lemonade" from a bad situation. Scott started out making five-gallon batches on a simple system. As he describes it, he was a "glorified homebrewer with a license." He eventually found a long-neglected, used brewhouse in New Mexico that he was able to purchase at a good price. Some alterations were made, with the help of the welder across the parking lot, and some converted dairy-processing tanks were added to the mix to create what Scott calls his "Frankensystem."

The enterprise has met with strong support from the community. Angry Cedar beers are available in several local watering holes, and thirty-two-ounce bottles are sailing off of store shelves. Scott is racing to keep up with demand. At the time of my visit he was still working out the peculiarities of his seven-barrel system. "It has been a heck of an adventure," he said. "Ratios are not one-to-one going from homebrewing to large-scale."

Angry Cedar has very limited distribution, but you can find the beer on tap in area pubs. Look for the returnable, thirty-two-ounce, swing-top bottles in local grocery stores.

Beck's Sports Brewery

ADDRESS: 3295 University Ave.
Waterloo, IA 50703
TELEPHONE: 319-234-4333
EMAIL: jesse.buck@barmuda.com
WEB SITE: www.barmuda.com/becks
MICHAEL'S PICK: Panther Pale Ale: In the Beck's lineup of beers, this one was the most solid. It is fairly balanced but leans a bit to the sweet side—an extra shot of bittering hops would serve it well. The malt exhibits hints of caramel. Spicy flavors dominate the hop character, with notes of pine and citrus Cascade hops.

TYPE: Brewpub
DATE ESTABLISHED: 2000, brewing began in 2005
OWNER: Barmuda MMC
BREWMASTER: Matt Guenther
BREWING SYSTEM: Eight-barrel Price-Schonstrom extract brewhouse
FLAGSHIP BEER: Hawkeye Golden Wheat
YEAR-ROUND BEERS: Black Hawk Braxator Bock, Cy's Clone Ale, Hawkeye Golden Wheat, Panther Pale Ale
SEASONAL BEERS: Black Hawk Pilsner, Summer Scottish Ale, Bald E's Hefeweizen, Märzen Oktoberfest, Grizzly Bock
SPECIAL RELEASES: None
TOURS: No
BEER TO GO: None
FOOD: A wide selection of sports-bar favorites: burgers, wraps, pastas, and other entrées
AMENITIES: Parking lot in front and back of building, private dining room available, food and drink specials daily and during big games, Mug Club specials
PUB HOURS: Sunday–Thursday: 11:00 A.M. to midnight; Friday and Saturday: 11:00 A.M. to 2:00 A.M.
NEARBY ATTRACTIONS: Ice House Museum, Gallagher Bluedorn Performing Arts Center, antiquing, Grout Museum of History and Science, Blackhawk Art Museum, Lake Macbride State Park, George Wyth Memorial State Park

NOTES: The upstairs dining room at Beck's has the feel of a sports bar without the noise and grunge. You are greeted by a friendly host who escorts you to your table. Television sets are omnipresent, as they should be: Beck's boasts the most screens in the Cedar Valley. The upscale furnishings are of red-tinted cherry-wood. The copper-clad brewery sits to one side behind a wood-and-glass enclosure. It's a family-friendly place for dinner with the kids. The after-church crowd makes Sunday mornings one of their busiest times.

The downstairs bar is where the action is. A more typical sports bar, it also features multiple screens showing different sporting events. The high-top seating hosts the rowdier, "whooping and hollering" crowd during big games.

General manager and brewer Matt Guenther makes the beers on an extract system using recipes supplied by Micropub Systems International, a New York company that provides turnkey systems and support to restaurants that want to become brewpubs. They supply the ingredients, and the establishment just has to boil, add hops, and ferment.

The house beers are so-so at best, but there are other selections available. If you are just looking for an easy place to take the kids and catch the game, Beck's will fit the bill.

Broad Street Brewing Company

ADDRESS: 113 Broad St.
Reinbeck, IA 50669
TELEPHONE: 319–350–0749
EMAIL: trevor@broadstreetbrewing.com
WEB SITE: www.broadstreetbrewing.com
MICHAEL'S PICK: Silver Creek Porter: Chocolate and caramel aromas set the stage for the creamy goodness that is to come. Lightly sweet, with loads of chocolate flavors, this robust porter has a hefty, satisfying body. A bit of roast and hop bitterness and faint earthy hop flavor keeps the sweetness in check.
TYPE: Brewery
DATE ESTABLISHED: 2011
OWNER: Trevor Schellhorn
BREWMASTER: Trevor Schellhorn
BREWING SYSTEM: Seven-barrel brewhouse, manufacturer unknown
FLAGSHIP BEERS: Reinbecker, Silver Creek Porter
YEAR-ROUND BEERS: Reinbecker, Silver Creek Porter, Big G Gluten Free Beer
SEASONAL BEERS: Planned
SPECIAL RELEASES: Coo Coo Cachoo ESB, Irish Red, brown ale, dry stout, oatmeal stout, American wheat, and others
TOURS: By request
BEER TO GO: Growlers and kegs
FOOD: Light snacks: cheese curds, soft pretzels, etc.
AMENITIES: Free street parking, taproom, trivia night every other Saturday
PUB HOURS: Thursday and Friday: 4:00 to 9:00 P.M.; Saturday: 1:00 to 9:00 P.M.; Sunday: 1:00 to 6:00 P.M.
NEARBY ATTRACTIONS: Canoeing and kayaking on Blackhawk Creek, nearby hiking and biking trails, twenty minutes from Waterloo–Cedar Falls

NOTES: Broad Street Brewing Company evokes thoughts of the industry as it was in the mid-1800s. It's a small brewery in a small rural town crafting small amounts of beer for consumption in a very local market. Owner and brewer Trevor Schellhorn likes it that way. A trip to Germany left him enamored of the system of local breweries that still exists there. He has visions of small breweries and wineries bringing revitalizing business back to the rural Midwest. He has even considered working with area farmers to source local barley and hops.

But brewing is a volume business. You have to make more beer to make more money. So far, Broad Street is staying afloat selling beer from the brewery's taproom and at accounts in the bigger markets of Waterloo and Cedar Falls. Schellhorn sees potential for

Broad Street brewer Trevor Schellhorn with his English brewhouse.

growth as the popularity of craft beer builds in what is still largely light-lager territory.

Schellhorn began homebrewing in the late 1990s, making larger and larger batches as he got more deeply into it. He soon became the go-to guy for the local homebrewing community. When a fellow homebrewer and Reinbeck entrepreneur suggested that he open a brewery and then backed up the suggestion with a storefront space and capital investment, Schellhorn took the leap. Although he says it has been a steeper-than-expected learning curve, he has never looked back.

Schellhorn brews his beer on a traditional English system using open fermenters. His beers are mostly brewed to traditional styles, but with little twists that make them unique. His golden ale, for instance, is made with a large percentage of rye. He also makes a gluten-free beer.

Buck Ridge Brewery

ADDRESS: 8113 Buck Ridge
Janesville, IA 50647
TELEPHONE: 319–885–4106
EMAIL: asaucke@yahoo.com
WEB SITE: www.buckridgebrewery.com
MICHAEL'S PICK: None available to sample
TYPE: Brewery
DATE ESTABLISHED: 2011
OWNER: Andrew Saucke
BREWMASTER: Andrew Saucke
BREWING SYSTEM: Fifteen-gallon Sabco Systems brewhouse
FLAGSHIP BEER: Buck Ridge IPA
YEAR-ROUND BEERS: None
SEASONAL BEERS: Buck Ridge Summer Honey Ale, Buck Ridge Scotch Ale, Buck Ridge IPA
SPECIAL RELEASES: None
TOURS: No

BEER TO GO: None

FOOD: None

AMENITIES: None

PUB HOURS: None

NEARBY ATTRACTIONS: Beck's Sports Bar and Grill, Guerilla Brewing Company, Single Speed Brewing Company, dining and shopping in downtown Cedar Falls, drag races at Cedar Falls Raceway, Hartman Reserve Nature Center and George Wyth State Park, Hearst Center for the Arts, Gallagher-Bluedorn Performing Arts Center, Ice House Museum, Grout Museum District

NOTES: Andrew Saucke's brewing career began with the chance discovery of wild hops. Driving to his job in Boulder, Colorado, he noticed the hops growing along the side of the highway. He got permission from the landowner to pick some and began making homebrewed beer with them. The beer was good. The hops gave it what he describes as a "creamy, citrusy flavor." His hobby grew. Every summer he picked more and more of the hops, which he took to calling "Boulder Wild."

When Saucke moved back to his native Iowa, he brought rhizomes of the Boulder Wild hops with him and began cultivating them on his property. He planted other hop varieties as well and continued to brew beer using only his homegrown hops. One day he took samples of his beer to the Cedar Falls Brown Bottle Restaurant, where he had held his first job as a teenager. The owner liked the beers and wanted them on tap. Buck Ridge Brewery was born.

Buck Ridge beers are still brewed with only homegrown hops, including the Boulder Wild variety. They are still only available at the Cedar Falls Brown Bottle. Saucke sometimes thinks about expanding his distribution, but he doesn't want to compromise his commitment to using his own hops. Every year he expands his hop yard just a little bit. Plans are to place the beers in Montage, another Cedar Falls restaurant operated by the owners of the Brown Bottle.

Saucke says that his beers are inspired by English styles. He makes three seasonal ales, each available only at certain times of the year.

Guerrilla Brewing Company

ADDRESS: 2401 Falls Ave.
Waterloo, IA 50701

TELEPHONE: None

EMAIL:
guerrillabrewingcompany@yahoo.com

WEB SITE: www.facebook.com/
guerrillabrewingco

MICHAEL'S PICK: None available for sample

TYPE: Brewery

DATE ESTABLISHED: 2012

OWNERS: Steve Weliver, Ty Graham, and Barry Eastman

BREWMASTER: Steve Weliver

BREWING SYSTEM: Fifteen-gallon Sabco brewhouse

FLAGSHIP BEERS: None

YEAR-ROUND BEERS: None

SEASONAL BEERS: None

SPECIAL RELEASES: DPA (Donkey Piss Ale), Sintrap, Airborn Ale v3, Hopchuey, Mudbug, Junebug, Z-Juice, Double Honey IPA, Operation Chaos, HopScotch, Booth at the Gun Show Stout, Mindbender Triple Trappist Cream Quad, 90 Minute Commando, New World Order Brew, Goof Juice, and others

TOURS: By request

BEER TO GO: None

FOOD: None

AMENITIES: Parking lot

PUB HOURS: Tuesday–Saturday: 5:00 P.M. to close

NEARBY ATTRACTIONS: Ice House Museum, Gallagher Bluedorn Performing Arts Center, antiquing, Grout Museum of History and Science, Blackhawk Art Museum, Lake MacBride State Park, George Wyth Memorial State Park

NOTES: Geode is defined by Dictonary.com as "a hollow concretionary or nodular stone often lined with crystals." The geode's ugly outside conceals the beautifully glittering formations inside. The geode is the state rock of Iowa. It's also an apt metaphor for the drinking and dining complex where Guerrilla Brewing Company makes its home.

On a nondescript road in Waterloo—a town that most people drive through on the way to somewhere else—sits an even more nondescript commercial building. It's small and drab with an unadorned functionality—nothing really to look at. But when you step through the front door the place radiates with color and kitsch.

There's the Lava Lounge bar, with its cheesy-cool 1950s vibe, and the Beer Hall, where people sip pints in midcentury-modern comfy chairs under the neon glow of vintage beer signs. At the end of the hall is Rudy's Tacos, where great Mexican food is eaten on Formica-topped, 1950s-era kitchen tables, and playful marionettes hang from the ceiling. Everywhere the walls are painted in vibrant shades of green and blue.

This is the only place that Guerilla Brewing beers are available. This seems appropriate, given the way that these guys work. Their beers are big and bold, and they bear names that are as quirky as the place where they are served. Ty Graham describes the brewery as a "beer lab" where they brew according to their mood. At the time of my interview, the Guerilla crew had never brewed a beer under 8 percent ABV. While some favorites do reappear from time to time, the lineup is mostly an ever-changing series of one-offs and specialty brews that push the boundaries of traditional styles. A new beer is released every Thursday night.

Graham summed up the Guerilla brewing philosophy in three words: unconventional, unrelenting, and unapologetic. He knows that their beers won't be for everyone, but that doesn't deter them from their quest to brew outside the box.

Mason City Brewing

ADDRESS: 28 E. State St.
Mason City, IA 50401
TELEPHONE: 641–423–1080
EMAIL: contact@masoncitybrewing.com
WEB SITE: www.masoncitybrewing.com
MICHAEL'S PICK: None available for sample
TYPE: Brewery
DATE ESTABLISHED: 2012
OWNERS: Arian Schuessler, Justin Merritt, and Jake Rajewsky
BREWMASTER: Jake Rajewsky
BREWING SYSTEM: One-barrel Blichmann Engineering brewhouse
FLAGSHIP BEERS: IPA, Saison, Porter, Belgian Ale
YEAR-ROUND BEERS: IPA, Saison, Porter, Belgian Ale
SEASONAL BEERS: Planned
SPECIAL RELEASES: Black IPA, Scotch Ale, ESB, Brown Ale, and others
TOURS: By request
BEER TO GO: Growlers
FOOD: None
AMENITIES: Free street parking, taproom, seasonal outdoor seating
PUB HOURS: Friday: 5:00 to 11:00 P.M.; Saturday: noon to 11:00 P.M.
NEARBY ATTRACTIONS: Worth Brewing Company, Frank Lloyd Wright Sites (Park Inn Hotel and Stockman House Museum), Music Man sites (Meredith Wilson's Boyhood Home and 1912 River City Streetscape), Surf Ballroom and Museum, Macnider Art Museum, Mason City Community Theatre, Cedar Lake

NOTES: There is a truism in beer making that what separates the amateurs from the pros is consistency. It's easy to make beer. It's harder to make really good beer. It's extremely difficult to make the same great beer time and time again, especially at small scales and with no formal training. For the guys at Mason City, consistency is job one. Their one-barrel brewhouse is fully automated so that every batch is brewed the same way. Their fermentation vessels, though small, are precisely temperature-controlled. The brewery bears the name of their town, and they say they want to do it proud.

Though it presents a modest first impression, Mason City is a most interesting town. It is the birthplace of Meredith Wilson, the composer of the Broadway classic *The Music Man.* His childhood home at Music Man Square is now a tourist attraction. If rock and roll is more your style, pay a visit to the Surf Ballroom in nearby Clear Lake, where Buddy Holly, Richie Valens, and the Big Bopper played their last show before perishing in a plane crash. For architecture buffs, there are two Frank Lloyd Wright buildings. The Park Inn Hotel, located just down the street from the brewery, is the only remaining Wright-designed hotel in the world.

The brewery occupies a historic 1800s building in Mason City's downtown. The long, narrow, shotgun-style space has an open floor plan that invites guests into the brewing process. A half-wall is all that separates the brewing platform from the seating area. Brewer Jake Rajewsky often brews during taproom hours, allowing curious beer fans to ask him questions about the process.

Millstream Brewing Company

ADDRESS: 835 48th Ave.
Amana, IA 52203
TELEPHONE: 319–622–3672
EMAIL: brewery@millstreambrewing.com
WEB SITE: www.millstreambrewing.com
MICHAEL'S PICK: Schild Brau Amber Lager: This traditional Vienna style is a fifteen-time national award winner, including taking the gold medal in the 2010 World Beer Cup. Its toasty, caramel profile is balanced by spicy Continental hops and moderate bitterness. Easy-drinking, clean, and crisp, it's everything a Vienna lager should be.
TYPE: Brewery
DATE ESTABLISHED: 1985
OWNERS: Chris Priebe, Tom Albert, and Teresa Albert
BREWMASTER: Chris Priebe
BREWING SYSTEM: Twenty-barrel Specific Mechanical brewhouse
FLAGSHIP BEER: Schild Brau Amber
YEAR-ROUND BEERS: Schild Brau Amber, Iowa Pale Ale, John's Generations White Ale, Windmill Wheat, Backroad Stout

SEASONAL BEERS: Hefeweissen, German Pilsner, Schokolade Bock, Oktoberfest

SPECIAL RELEASES: Brewmaster's Extreme Series release planned every three months. First release in the series was Hop² Double IPA.

TOURS: No

BEER TO GO: Growlers, kegs, and package

FOOD: None

AMENITIES: Parking lot in back and across the street, seasonal outdoor beer garden, tasting room, live music outdoors in the summer

PUB HOURS: Store and tasting room hours vary seasonally. Check the Web site for details.

NEARBY ATTRACTIONS: Third Base Brewery, Historic Amana Colonies, Iowa Beer Festival in September, five wineries in Amana, Old Creamery Theatre Company and Iowa Theatre Artists Company, thirty minutes from Cedar Rapids

NOTES: The Amana Colonies were founded in 1855 by members of the German Inspirationalist religious sect. Settlers led a communal life, sharing meals and the fruits of their labor. They supported themselves through farming and the operation of trades that included wool and calico production, clock making, wine making, and brewing. In 1932 the hardships of the Depression and the realities of the modern world led the colonists to give up their communal way of life. As many of the old trades died off, brewing in the settlement came to an end.

In 1985 Carroll F. Zuber and James and Dennis Roemig determined to revive that time-honored industry in Amana, and 130 years after the colonies' founding, Millstream Brewing Company opened its doors. The trio remained true to the settlement's heritage, brewing lagers and ales in traditional German styles.

Chris Priebe and Tom and Teresa Albert bought the brewery in 2000. They have maintained its connection to its roots while also seeking to expand beyond them. Alongside the German styles they now brew stouts, IPAs, and other nontraditional beers. Recent changes to Iowa law have allowed them to explore higher-alcohol beers with the Brewmaster's Extreme series.

But you won't find any over-hopped West Coast creations at Millstream. Brewer Chris Priebe believes in balance and in listening to what his customers want. He makes well-crafted beers that are suited to the more moderate palates of his midwestern audience. "A lot of breweries are technically spectacular," he says, "but their beers don't have any personality. Adjusting recipes to what your audience wants is one way to give them personality." The brewery's Iowa Pale

Ale is perhaps the quintessential example of what I call the "Midwestern IPA."

Single Speed Brewing Company

ADDRESS: 128 Main St.
Cedar Falls, IA 50613

TELEPHONE: 319–266–3581

EMAIL: marketing@singlespeedbrewing.com

WEB SITE: www.singlespeedbrewing.com

MICHAEL'S PICK: None available for sample

TYPE: Brewery

DATE ESTABLISHED: 2012

OWNER: Dave Morgan

BREWMASTER: Dave Morgan

BREWING SYSTEM: Three-barrel Premier Stainless brewhouse

FLAGSHIP BEERS: West Coast Amber, American Pale Ale, Black IPA, American Hefeweizen

YEAR-ROUND BEERS: West Coast Amber, American Pale Ale, Black IPA, American Hefeweizen

SEASONAL BEERS: Information not available

SPECIAL RELEASES: Belgian Wit, Imperial Coffee Stout, American IPA

TOURS: By request

BEER TO GO: Growlers and 18-ounce or 64-ounce stainless-steel Hydro Flasks

FOOD: None

AMENITIES: Parking lot, free street parking, taproom, selection of guest taps

PUB HOURS: Tuesday–Friday: 4:00 P.M. to 2:00 A.M.; Saturday: noon to 2:00 A.M.; Sunday: noon to midnight

NEARBY ATTRACTIONS: Guerilla Brewing Company, University of Northern Iowa campus, George Wyth State Park, Hartman Reserve Nature Center, Isle of Capri Casino, Hearst Center for the Arts and Sculpture Garden, Phelps Youth Pavilion, access to numerous biking and kayaking trails, several golf courses

NOTES: Cedar Falls is the smaller of the two cities in the Waterloo–Cedar Falls metropolitan area. It was founded in 1845 and was originally named Sturgis Falls after its founder, William Sturgis. The name was later changed to Cedar Falls because of the town's proximity to the Cedar River. The historic downtown has been nationally recognized as a Great American Main Street and is currently among the National Historic Trust's Dozen Distinctive Destinations. Brick sidewalks, old-fashioned lampposts, and public art make this a vibrant place for shopping, dining, and entertainment.

Single Speed Brewing Company sits in the heart of the district. The taproom merges the area's historic feel with an air of muted sophistication. High ceilings emphasize the depth of the narrow storefront space. Exposed brick walls are contrasted with whimsical hanging lights made from growlers. The brewhouse is visible through a wall of windows.

The brewery is nearby to several of the area's biking trails. A biking theme infuses the mission statement, "to brew beers built for the venturesome beer drinker, those unafraid to stray from the beaten path." The name Single Speed describes their approach to brewing: slow-paced and hand-crafted.

Third Base Brewery

ADDRESS: 500 Blairs Ferry Rd. NE
Cedar Rapids, IA 52402
TELEPHONE: 319–378–9090
EMAIL: 3bbrewer@gmail.com
WEB SITE: www.3rdbasebrewery.com
MICHAEL'S PICK: Flying Aces Pale Ale: Hop flavor and aroma are what this beer is all about. Loads of late-addition Cascade hops give it an enticing citrus punch. It's sufficiently bitter, but not over the top. There's just enough grainy malt sweetness to make it a finely balanced brew.
TYPE: Brewpub
DATE ESTABLISHED: 1996
OWNER: Joe Denny
BREWMASTER: Travis Scheidecker
BREWING SYSTEM: Eight-barrel Newlands Systems brewhouse
FLAGSHIP BEER: Bees Knees Honey Ale
YEAR-ROUND BEERS: Golden Hawk Wheat, Bees Knees Honey Ale, Red Rocket Amber Ale, Flying Aces Pale Ale, Black Cobra Oatmeal Stout
SEASONAL BEERS: Beggar Jon's Hefeweizen
SPECIAL RELEASES: Hopness Monster, Tilted Kilt, Munich-Style Summerfest, Session 70 Scottish Ale, Hopturnal Emissions Imperial IPA, and others
TOURS: By request
BEER TO GO: Growlers and kegs
FOOD: Standard pub fare: burgers, salads, wings, fish and chips
AMENITIES: Limited parking lot, full bar
PUB HOURS: Daily: 11:00 A.M. to 2:00 A.M.
NEARBY ATTRACTIONS: Cedar Greenbelt National Recreational Trail, Coralville Lake, Lake Macbride State Park, National Motorcycle Museum, Tabor Home Winery, Cedar Rapids Kernels Minor League Baseball, African American Museum of Iowa

NOTES: The first time I visited Third Base, I took one look at the unadorned entrance and darkened windows and decided not to go inside. Don't let the less-than-inviting exterior scare you away. Brewer Travis Scheidecker is crafting some of the best beers in Iowa. Whether a 3 percent ABV Scottish session ale or an 11 percent monster double IPA, each one is bright, crisp, and clean, with layers of flavor to give them depth and complexity.

Travis came to Third Base in 2001 as a bartender and bar manager. When the brewer quit suddenly in 2005, he volunteered to fill the void. Aside from occasionally helping out in the brewery, he had no brewing experience. An outside consultant was brought in for an intensive two-week training, and he devoured every book he could get his hands on. He also had a lot of help from the other Iowa brewers. All of that effort and support has paid off.

Despite what it might look like from the outside, the ambience inside is warm and inviting. The overall impression is of casual and family-friendly neighborhood bar. Upon entering, you face a large central bar with the brewery visible through windows behind it. There is table and booth seating to the left and right. It's a sports bar, so there are many television screens, but I didn't find them obtrusive or annoying.

Despite the prominent positioning of the brewery, many locals still don't realize that beer is made there. The red and green colored lights illuminating the stainless steel tanks led one customer to ask Trevor about the "hologram" behind the bar. But make no mistake, the brewery is real, and the beer coming out of it is good.

Toppling Goliath Brewing Company

ADDRESS: 310 College Dr.
Decorah, IA 52101
TELEPHONE: 563–387–6700
EMAIL: info@tgbrews.com
WEB SITE: www.tgbrews.com
MICHAEL'S PICK: Golden Nugget IPA: This is one for hop lovers. The intense tangerine and tropical-fruit aroma greets you as soon as the glass is set in front of you. That character carries right into the flavor. It's aggressively bitter, but still has enough malt to keep it balanced. A crisp, dry finish allows the hops to really shine.
TYPE: Brewery
DATE ESTABLISHED: 2009
OWNER: Clark Lewey
BREWMASTER: Mike Saboe
BREWING SYSTEM: Ten-barrel Newlands Systems brewhouse

FLAGSHIP BEERS: Dorothy's New World Lager, Tsunami Pale Ale, Golden Nugget IPA

YEAR-ROUND BEERS: Dorothy's New World Lager, Tsunami Pale Ale, Golden Nugget IPA

SEASONAL BEERS: Rush Hollow Maple Ale, Biter Double IPA, Tsunami Dark, Murph's Irish Red, Water Street Wheat, Water Street Wicked Wheat (Ws3), Naughty 90, Toasted Irish IPA, Watershed Wheat, Dark Shadow Stout, Rush Hollow Amber, TG's Honey Bee

SPECIAL RELEASES: Special releases almost daily

TOURS: No

BEER TO GO: Growlers

FOOD: None

AMENITIES: Limited parking lot, tasting room separate from production brewery, Mug Club memberships

PUB HOURS: Monday–Thursday: 2:00 to 8:00 P.M.; Friday and Saturday: noon to 11:00 P.M.; Sunday: noon to 6:00 P.M.

NEARBY ATTRACTIONS: Laura Ingalls Wilder Museum, Luther College, nearby road- and mountain-biking trails, Broadway-Phelps Park Historic District, outdoor activities on the upper Iowa River

NOTES: Toppling Goliath's beers are the result of collaboration with customers; they call it "real-life research." At the brewery's beginnings, twelve-gallon batches were brewed on a Sabco homebrewing system and presented to customers for comment. The recipes were then tweaked and the beers rebrewed until they got it right. Though recipes have now been formalized with the move to a bigger system, the collaborative spirit remains. Small-batch and experimental beers are still made on the original brewhouse and tested at the taproom.

The atmosphere at the taproom bespeaks this collaborative spirit. It's a friendly place where conversing with strangers is the norm. It's not uncommon to see the owner and brewers mingling at tables with guests. On the night of my visit, a customer brought in some home-cooked food that was shared with everyone. It is a place built on beer camaraderie.

Toppling Goliath beers are among the edgiest beers in Iowa. They are also among the best. They are clean, crisp, and flavorful, with lovely layers of complexity. Head brewer Mike Saboe isn't afraid to experiment. He goes further out on the limb than many of the more traditional Iowa brewers. Hops are prominent. One of the beers I tasted was a cranberry stout that pulled off the combination of roasted bitterness and cranberry tart with aplomb.

Worth Brewing Company

ADDRESS: 826 Central Ave. Northwood, IA 50459

TELEPHONE: 641-324-9899

EMAIL: brewer@worthbrewing.com

WEBSITE: www.worthbrewing.com

MICHAEL'S PICK: Brown Ale: Leaning to the sweet side, the Brown Ale is built on a malty bed of caramel with nice toasty and nutty flavors lying on top. Hop and roast bitterness just barely balances, and grassy English hops provide a welcome contrast to the sweetness.

TYPE: Brewpub

DATE ESTABLISHED: 2007

OWNERS: Peter Ausenhus and Margaret Bishop

BREWMASTER: Peter Ausenhus

BREWING SYSTEM: Ten-gallon Sabco Systems brewhouse

FLAGSHIP BEERS: Field Trip IPA, Brown Ale

YEAR-ROUND BEERS: Field Trip IPA, Brown Ale, Dillon Clock Stopper, Sunderland Mild, Oatmeal Stout

SEASONAL BEERS: Vienna Lager, Otis' ESB, Dunkel, Bishopweizen, 5 Seasons Cherry Elixir, Russian Imperial Stout

SPECIAL RELEASES: Belgian Dubbel, Q.P. Honey Lager, Smoked Rye Porter, Herminator Wheat Bock, Cascadian Dark, Bar Belle Blond, Mr. Chesterfield

TOURS: By appointment

BEER TO GO: Growlers and kegs

FOOD: Small menu of simple items, including hummus, ploughman's lunch, and a Mexican platter

AMENITIES: Free street parking, taproom, available for private functions, Mug Club program

TASTING ROOM HOURS: Wednesday: 5:00 to 9:00 P.M.; Friday: 5:00 to 11:00 P.M.; Saturday: noon to 11:00 P.M.

NEARBY ATTRACTIONS: Four blocks of Central Avenue in downtown Northwood are a designated historic district on the National Register of Historic Places, Diamond Jo Casino

NOTES: Situated just a few miles south of the Minnesota state line and a few miles east of the interstate, tiny Northwood is the definition of a midwestern small town. Only about six hundred people call it home. The quiet Main Street is lined with historic buildings that allude to a more vibrant past. It's an unlikely place to find a successful brewpub.

Worth's success comes mostly from locals. With only one outside draft account, the brewery sells nearly all of its beer in-house. Brewer Peter Ausenhus can barely keep up with demand, maxing out capacity crafting six batches a week on his ten-gallon Sabco brewery. He's happy to keep it small. "In America we think that bigger is always better. People ask, 'When are you going to expand?' We've looked at it, and I'm not saying that we never will, but there's no guarantee that that's going to be more lucrative or satisfying."

Ausenhus has converted the palates of the lager-drinking locals with four year-round brews and a rotating selection of seasonals. Worth's beers stay mostly within safe stylistic limits, but they do fly high with occasional specialties like 5 Seasons Cherry Elixer, an oak-aged scotch ale brewed with honey, Worth County apples, and tart cherry juice. It sounds like a train wreck, but it actually works.

Housed in a historic bank building, old wood trim and stucco walls make the brewpub cozy and welcoming. It's a nice place to hang out for a beer and conversation. Be sure to check out the bar. It's the old teller cage from the building's original occupant.

SOUTHEAST

Albia Brewing Company

ADDRESS: 11 Benton Ave. E
Albia, IA 52531
TELEPHONE: 641–932–4085
EMAIL: blindberg@iowatelecom.net
WEB SITE: www.albiabrewingcompany.blogspot.com
MICHAEL'S PICK: None available for sample
TYPE: Brewpub
DATE ESTABLISHED: 2012
OWNERS: Brian Lindberg and Barbara Lindberg
BREWMASTER: Brian Lindberg
BREWING SYSTEM: Five-barrel GW Kent brewhouse
FLAGSHIP BEER: 1889 Red Ale
YEAR-ROUND BEERS: 10 w 40 Milk Stout, Raspberry Blond, Harvester, Corn Belt, American Lager, 1889 Red Ale
SEASONAL BEERS: Pumpkin Ale, Coal Miner Bock
SPECIAL RELEASES: Planned
TOURS: By request
BEER TO GO: Growlers and kegs
FOOD: Small selection of pizzas and Italian sandwiches
AMENITIES: Street parking, seasonal outdoor seating, Iowa wines, private event space available
PUB HOURS: Wednesday–Thursday: 4:00 to 9:00 P.M.; Friday: 4:00 P.M. to midnight; Saturday: noon to midnight
NEARBY ATTRACTIONS: Peace Tree Brewing Company, Appanoose Rapids Brewing Company, Albia Community Theatre, Historic Albia town square, Rathbun Lake, Honey Creek Resort State Park and Golf Course, outdoor activities at nearby state parks and conservation areas

NOTES: Albia was founded in the 1850s during a coal-mining boom in the area. The town is centered on a painstakingly restored historic town square that is anchored by the old Madison County Courthouse. The building that houses the Albia Brewing Company is a showpiece of the district.

Skean's Block, as it is known, was built in 1889 by an early Albia merchant named Elmer Skean. It served originally as a grocery and shoe store. Over the years it has been a furniture store, undertaker's mortuary, and pool hall. One of the first buildings to be restored on the square, it had been vacant for several years before the Lindbergs purchased it.

Brian Lindberg had been homebrewing for fifteen years prior to opening the brewpub. Asked why he took the leap from homebrewer to pro, he says he was looking for a way to get his homebrew equipment out of the garage. When the opportunity arose to purchase the building, he was offered a deal that was too good to pass up. The city was anxious to have the space occupied. It had last served as a restaurant and so was basically ready to go. When they decided to pull the trigger, Barbara Lindberg pleaded, "Just promise me we won't be managing a restaurant." Now they're managing both a restaurant and a brewery.

The dining room is a warm and welcoming place, filled with references to the building's past. Exposed brick and shellacked wood give it an old-timey feel. The walls are hung with historic pictures of the building and the square, including photos of Charles Lindbergh taken by Brian Lindberg's grandmother.

Appanoose Rapids Brewing Company

ADDRESS: 332 E. Main St.
Ottumwa, IA 52501
TELEPHONE: 641–684–4008
EMAIL: tim@appanooserapidsbrewingcompany.com
WEB SITE: www.appanooserapidsbrewingcompany.com
MICHAEL'S PICK: Oak-Aged Vanilla Smoked Porter: Of the beers I tried, this one was the most intriguing and the best-made. The porter was light-bodied but full-flavored. It leaned a bit to the sweet side and could benefit from a bit more roasted malt character to give it balance. Real vanilla beans added during conditioning brought huge vanilla character. The smoke stayed well in the background.
TYPE: Brewpub
DATE ESTABLISHED: 2010
OWNER: Tim Ware
BREWMASTER: Tim Ware
BREWING SYSTEM: Fifteen-gallon Sabco Systems brewhouse

FLAGSHIP BEER: Raspberry Wheat

YEAR-ROUND BEERS: Raspberry Wheat, West Coast Pale Ale

SEASONAL BEER: Summer Weiss

SPECIAL RELEASES: Coffee Stout, Oak-Aged Vanilla Smoked Porter, Brown Ale, Centennial Blond, American Stout, American Light

TOURS: No

BEER TO GO: Growlers

FOOD: A small but varied selection of somewhat upscale entrées, sandwiches, and pastas

AMENITIES: Parking lot in back, seasonal outdoor seating, full bar, happy-hour specials, Sunday brunch

PUB HOURS: Tuesday–Sunday: 11:00 A.M. to 10:00 P.M.

NEARBY ATTRACTIONS: American Gothic House, loose-meat sandwiches at the Canteen, riverfront walking trail, Rathbun Lake and Honey Creek Resort State Park, the Beach Waterpark

NOTES: The Appanoose Rapids Brewing Company is located in a beautiful historic building in the old downtown of Ottumwa. It is part of an effort by the city to revitalize the somewhat rundown Main Street, where newer tenants still sit uneasily amid empty storefronts and crumbling buildings.

When you come inside, you enter into a different world. Built in 1875, the building originally served as a dry-goods store. Turquoise mosaics attest to its time as an Anheuser-Busch distributor in the early 1900s. The mosaics, discovered under layers of brown paint and drywall during renovation, flank the entryway, setting an appropriate tone as you enter the elegant, elongated dining room. It is a beautiful space with an old-fashioned bar, exposed brick walls, and tiny lights hanging from the ceiling. The seasonal patio in back has views of the river.

The food that I had was excellent. The Boursin stuffed chicken breast was perfectly pan-fried, juicy and tender with a crispy crust. The creamy herbed-cheese stuffing and sauce complemented each other well. Other menu items looked equally appealing, making for a difficult decision when ordering.

When I visited, the beers were still being worked out. An email shortly thereafter let me know that the brewer at the time had been replaced. I was unable to return to check out the new brews. A search of online reviews suggests that the quality may have improved.

Backpocket Brewing

ADDRESS: 903 Quarry Rd.
Coralville, IA 52241

TELEPHONE: 319–333–9565

EMAIL: info@backpocketbrewing.com

WEBSITE: www.backpocketbrewing.com

MICHAEL'S PICK: Jackknife GPA: GPA stands for "German pale ale." In keeping with their focus on German-style beers, Backpocket's IPA is brewed with a combination of German and American hops. The result is a moderately bitter beer with loads of spice and citrus hop flavors. It's a bit Midwest-sweet in your mouth, but it finishes dry and crisp with lingering licorice hops.

TYPE: Brewery

DATE ESTABLISHED: 2012

OWNERS: David Strutt and Marci Strutt

BREWMASTER: Jake Simmons

BREWING SYSTEM: Forty-hectoliter Braukon brewhouse

FLAGSHIP BEER: Slingshot Dunkel

YEAR-ROUND BEERS: Gold Coin Helles, Penny Whistle Wheat, Jackknife GPA, Wooden Nickel Scottish, Slingshot Dunkel

SEASONAL BEERS: Märzen (Oktoberfest), Winter Ale

SPECIAL RELEASES: None

TOURS: Monday–Friday: 5:30 P.M.

BEER TO GO: Growlers and kegs

FOOD: Selection of salads and wood-fired pizzas

AMENITIES: Parking lot, taproom, seasonal beer garden

PUB HOURS: Daily: 11:00 A.M. to close

NEARBY ATTRACTIONS: Iowa Children's Museum, performances at the Englert Theatre, Old Capitol Museum, University of Iowa campus, University of Iowa Natural History Museum, Antique Car Museum, Devonian Fossil Gorge, Lake McBride State Park, water sports on Coralville Lake

NOTES: Backpocket Brewing began as the Old Man River Brewpub in the tiny river town of McGregor, Iowa. Situated directly on the historic town's central square—it's actually a triangle in McGregor—the brewpub occupies a nineteenth-century building that was once the headquarters of the Diamond Joe Riverboat Company. Old Man River still serves Backpocket brews, but they are no longer brewed on premise. The ten-hectoliter brewhouse simply couldn't meet demand.

The new brewery in Coralville is designed to be a beer destination. The fifteen-thousand-square-foot, five-million-dollar facility houses a state-of-the-art German brewhouse and bottling line. The tasting room features wood-fired pizzas and has all the Backpocket beers on tap. A ten-thousand-square-foot beer garden offers seasonal outdoor seating in a traditionally German setting. You can enjoy a wood-fired pizza to accompany your pint. The plan is to support the growth of the Iowa brewing industry by leasing the old brewery in McGregor to new startups.

Backpocket's focus is on sessionable German-style lagers and ales. Jake Simmons brews his beers according to the Reinheitsgebot, the German purity law that states that beer can only be made with barley malt, hops, yeast, and water. But he isn't afraid to tweak the styles a bit. His Wooden Nickel Scottish Lager is a bock beer with a bit of peat-smoked malt to add a subtle, earthy smokiness. Jackknife GPA is an American-style IPA that emphasizes spicy Continental hop varieties over the more typical, citrusy American hops.

Front Street Brewery

ADDRESS: 421 W. River Dr.
Davenport, IA 52801
TELEPHONE: 563–322–1569
EMAIL: fsb@mchsi.com
WEB SITE: www.frontstreetbrew.com
MICHAEL'S PICK: Raging River Ale: This Americanized English pale ale is named after the great flood of 1993. It features a simple malt profile with grainy sweetness and hints of caramel. The hop bitterness is restrained, but enough to let you know it's there. Aggressive dry-hopping with American hop varieties gives it a huge citrusy nose.
TYPE: Brewpub
DATE ESTABLISHED: 1992
OWNERS: Jennie Ash and Steve Zuidema
BREWMASTER: Steve Zuidema
BREWING SYSTEM: Fifteen-barrel Crawford Company brewhouse
FLAGSHIP BEER: Raging River Ale
YEAR-ROUND BEERS: Old Davenport Gold, Hefe Weizen, Cherry Ale, Raging River Ale, Bucktown Stout
SEASONAL BEERS: Oktoberfest, Downtown Brown, Holiday Ale, Pumpkin Ale
SPECIAL RELEASES: New releases monthly
TOURS: Check Web site for days and times
BEER TO GO: Growlers and package
FOOD: Planned
AMENITIES: Parking lot, metered street parking, taproom, seasonal outdoor seating overlooking the river, farmers market in the Freight House development, banquet space available
PUB HOURS: Daily: 11:00 A.M. to midnight
NEARBY ATTRACTIONS: Great River Brewery, Blue Cat Brewpub, Bent River Brewery, Figge Art Museum, Bucktown Arts District, Fejervary Park and Zoo, Vander Veer Botanical Park, Village of East Davenport Historic District, eagle watching along the river

NOTES: Front Street was one of Iowa's pioneer breweries. It began as a brewpub just down the street from the current location, the first brewpub in the Quad Cities and only the three hundredth in the entire country.

Brewmaster Steve Zuidema says it was insanity that led him to leave his corporate job and open the brewpub with his wife, Jennie Ash. After visiting a brewpub in Arizona, he asked the fateful question, "How hard could it be to make beer?" He admits now that it was much harder than he thought. He had never homebrewed before going pro and early on didn't always get the result he was aiming for. "I wouldn't advise new startups to do it the way we did."

But their moment of insanity paid off. Demand regularly outpaced capacity at the pub, leading the couple to explore expansion options. In 2012 they moved brewing operations to the Freight House development and stepped up from a seven-barrel to a fifteen-barrel brewhouse. The new location features a lively taproom where you can enjoy a pint after shopping at the farmers market that shares the building. If you want the old-school experience, the original location still operates as a restaurant at 208 East River Drive, just a quarter mile down the road. And they still pour Front Street beers.

Don't expect boundary-bending brews. Zuidema is crafting solid, drinkable beers in classic brewpub styles—beers that are full-flavored, but with a moderate palate that will appeal to a wide range of drinkers. With the expanded capacity, plans are in place to expand on this basic lineup with some beers that are a bit more adventurous.

Great River Brewery

ADDRESS: 332 E. 2nd St.
Davenport, IA 52801
TELEPHONE: 563–323–5210
EMAIL: paul@greatriverbrewery.com
WEB SITE: www.greatriverbrewery.com
MICHAEL'S PICK: Roller Dam Red: Roller Dam Red was my pick on my first visit shortly after the brewery opened. It remains my favorite now. It's a malt-forward amber ale, with caramel malt as its centerpiece and biscuity notes to add depth. Bitterness is moderate, but enough. Peppery/spicy hop flavors balance the malt and carry through into the dry finish.
TYPE: Brewery
DATE ESTABLISHED: 2008
OWNERS: Paul Krutzfeldt and Scott Lehnert
BREWMASTERS: Paul Krutzfeldt and Scott Lehnert
BREWING SYSTEM: Twenty-five-barrel DME brewhouse
FLAGSHIP BEERS: 483 Pale Ale, Roller Dam Red

YEAR-ROUND BEERS: 483 Pale Ale, Organic Farmer Brown Ale, Straight Pipe Stout, Roller Dam Red, Redband Coffee Stout, Saison Farmhouse Ale

SEASONAL BEERS: Aaaaa BOCK, HOP*A*POTAMUS RYE PA, Dirty Blond Chocolate Ale, and others

SPECIAL RELEASES: La Jefa Lager, Dos Pistolas Negra, Golden Ale, and others

TOURS: By appointment

BEER TO GO: Growlers, kegs, and package

FOOD: None

AMENITIES: Brewer's Lounge tasting room, free street parking

PUB HOURS: Monday–Wednesday: 4:00 to 9:00 P.M.; Thursday: 4:00 to 11:00 P.M.; Friday and Saturday: noon to 11:00 P.M.; Sunday: noon to 6:00 P.M.

NEARBY ATTRACTIONS: Front Street Brewery, Blue Cat Brewpub, Bent River Brewery, Figge Art Museum, Bucktown Arts District, Fejervary Park and Zoo, Vander Veer Botanical Park, Village of East Davenport Historic District

NOTES: Great River Brewery actually began as the Old Capital Brew Works in downtown Iowa City. After a long tenure at the Abita Brewing Company in New Orleans and seven years at the Des Moines Rock Bottom Brewery, Paul Krutzfeldt was ready to go out on his own. In 2004 he teamed up with Scott Lehnert, a homebrewing buddy from college, to open Old Capital.

After four years they grew weary of the day-to-day grind of operating a brewpub. Taxes in Iowa City were high, and neither of them really wanted to be a restaurateur. They thought it would be less expensive and more fun to run a packaging brewery. In 2008 they sold the brewpub and packed up the brewery for the move to Davenport. They brewed the first beer at the new location in February 2009. Large-scale canning began in the spring of 2010. Great River's beers are still the featured house beers at the Old Capital Brew Works.

Paul and Scott like to let their beer speak for itself, choosing old-school word of mouth to promote their product instead of glitzy advertising. They tend to brew to style, but they aren't trapped by the guidelines. Their year-round lineup consists mostly of well-crafted, flavorful, and easy-to-drink session beers. As Paul explains, "We tend not to be trendy. We don't need a triple IPA because everyone else has one." With their seasonal beers they give themselves the freedom to play, producing the occasional "big bomb" beer or experimenting with wild yeast, barrel-aging, and unusual ingredients.

Lost Duck Brewing Company

ADDRESS: 723–725 Ave. H (Highway 61) Ft. Madison, IA 52627

TELEPHONE: 319-372-8255

EMAIL: brewmaster@duckbrewing.com

WEB SITE: www.duckbrewing.com

MICHAEL'S PICK: Bohemian Duck Lager: I am a fan of sessionable lagers. Bohemian Duck is a good one. Lightly sweet, graham-cracker malt leads the way. The sweetness is kept light by modest bitterness, light spicy and citrus hop flavors, and a crisp finish. It won't demand your attention or fill you up. It's a beer for the long haul.

TYPE: Brewpub

DATE ESTABLISHED: 2003

OWNER: Tim Benson

BREWMASTER: Tim Benson

BREWING SYSTEM: 3.5-barrel DME brewhouse

FLAGSHIP BEERS: Pintail Pale Ale, Pelican Porter

YEAR-ROUND BEERS: Bohemian Duck Lager, Devil Duck Ale, American Wheat, Pintail Pale Ale, Ringneck Red, Pelican Porter

SEASONAL BEERS: Long Shadow's Winter Lager, Maibock, Orange Lager, Dog Star

SPECIAL RELEASES: Premium Pilsner, Brown Ale, Oatmeal Stout

TOURS: By request

BEER TO GO: Growlers and kegs

FOOD: Small selection of pub foods featuring locally sourced elk, bison, and brats

AMENITIES: Parking lot, full bar, daily drink specials, live music, private room available

PUB HOURS: Wednesday–Saturday: 3:00 to 10:00 P.M.

NEARBY ATTRACTIONS: Old Fort Madison, Faeth Cigar Store, Sheaffer Pen Museum, Catfish Bend Casino, Heartland Harvest Winery, Quarry Creek Elk and Bison Company, Mormon sites in Nauvoo, Illinois

NOTES: Fort Madison is an old Mississippi River town. Listed on the National Register of Historic Places, the downtown retains the look and feel of a time when paddleboats plied the river. Lost Duck Brewing Company occupies two historic storefronts overlooking the river and across the highway from a replica of the 1808 fort that gave the town its name. Built in the 1860s, the buildings once housed a barber shop and tavern where riverboat workers would come for a shave, a drink, and perhaps a bit of attention from the women that are rumored to have plied their trade on the second floor.

That original tavern was called the Grand View Room because of the view out the front window.

Indeed, that view of the river and the fort was one of my favorite things about Lost Duck. A spot at the bar in the cozy dining room affords a good look, but even better would be to take a table by the window and enjoy a buffalo burger and a pint.

The brewery takes its name from the migrating ducks that fly overhead. The Mississippi River is a major flyway, and during migrations you can watch the birds circling overhead. "The river flows east/west at Fort Madison," jokes owner Tim Benson. "The ducks get confused."

Benson's beers stay true to the Iowa style. They are modest brews; no over-the-top hops or sky-high ABVs here. They lean a bit more toward malty sweetness than hoppy bitterness. But every beer is clean, full-flavored, and satisfying. Benson is partial to lagers. Four of the nine beers available on my visit were lagers.

SOUTHWEST

CIB Brewery

ADDRESS: 39036 Aspen Rd.
  Carson, IA 51549
TELEPHONE: 515–450–2981
EMAIL: CIBbreweryllc@gmail.com
WEB SITE: www.cibbrewery.com
MICHAEL'S PICK: Orange Scorpion: I don't care for chili beers, but this one was special. Trinidad Scorpion and Ghost chilies—the world's hottest—give it a tingle up front and a lingering burn on the way out. But it's not at all unpleasant. Orange provides a nice acidic balance to tone down the heat. Delicate and layered, this is a chef's beer.
TYPE: Brewery
DATE ESTABLISHED: 2011
OWNERS: Alex Carlton, Heather Carlton, and George Carlton
BREWMASTERS: Alex Carlton and George Carlton
BREWING SYSTEM: 1.5-barrel homemade brewhouse
FLAGSHIP BEERS: Yola's Artisan Ale, Morningwood Breakfast Stout, The Dethhanger Quadruple Brown Ale
YEAR-ROUND BEERS: Yola's Artisan Ale, Morningwood Breakfast Stout, The Dethhanger Quadruple Brown Ale
SEASONAL BEERS: Cheri Tart, Orange Scorpion, The Countess—Bloody Sour Ale
SPECIAL RELEASES: Sour Dethhanger, John John's Banana Porter, Umami, Bourbon Ale, ESB, and others
TOURS: No
BEER TO GO: None
FOOD: None

AMENITIES: "Official" tasting room at the 1889 saloon across the street from the brewery
PUB HOURS: None
NEARBY ATTRACTIONS: Keg Creek Brewing Company, Loess Hills Scenic Byway, Nishna Heritage Museum, Hitchcock House Underground Railroad National Historic Landmark, Breezy Hills Vineyard, forty minutes from downtown Omaha, Upstream Brewing Company, Nebraska Brewing Company, Lucky Bucket Brewing Company

NOTES: Alex Carlton and his father George come at brewing from two different directions. Alex is a trained chef and a Certified Sommelier. He likes culinary beers that hit the whole palate with complex flavor combinations—beers that require your attention. George is a homebrewer of twenty-plus years. He prefers more straightforward drinking beers that are brewed to traditional styles, albeit with slightly higher alcohol content. Together they achieve balance; the son challenges the father, and the father keeps the son grounded.

This dichotomy is reflected in their flagship beers. Yola's Artisan Ale and Breakfast Stout—an imperial amber and imperial coffee stout, respectively—are George's beers. They lean to the malty side and envelop the palate with rich but familiar flavors. Dethhanger is all Alex. Its toasty and roasty malt character is underscored by earthy flavors and slight sourness from a proprietary wild yeast culture.

This special yeast strain, cultured from Alex's kitchen, drives some of the more interesting beers the brewery produces. It is in these extra-small-batch, draft-only specialty brews that his culinary background comes through. With chef-like skill he brings together unlikely combinations of ingredients, like basmati rice and shitaki mushrooms, or Trinidad Scorpion chilies and oranges. The yeast adds earthy and acidic overtones. The resulting beers are layered, complex, and surprisingly drinkable.

The duo currently works in the basement of an old bar in tiny Carson, Iowa. The plan is to ultimately move the operation upstairs and turn the barroom into the brewery's taproom.

Depot Deli Restaurant

ADDRESS: 101 N. Railroad St.
  Shenandoah, IA 51601
TELEPHONE: 712–246–4444
EMAIL: billhillman@mchsi.com
WEB SITE: www.depotdeli.com
MICHAEL'S PICK: Red Ale: More golden than red, this easy-drinking session beer highlights mild, malty

sweetness with background bready notes. Low-level bitterness is just enough to cut the malt, and light, grassy hops add a touch of character. It may not make you jump and shout, but it's light and goes down easy.

TYPE: Brewpub

DATE ESTABLISHED: 1983

OWNER: Bill Hillman

BREWMASTER: Bill Hillman

BREWING SYSTEM: Ten-barrel homemade extract brewhouse

FLAGSHIP BEERS: Whistle Stop Wheat, IPA

YEAR-ROUND BEERS: Whistle Stop Wheat, IPA, Stout

SEASONAL BEERS: None

SPECIAL RELEASES: Pale Ale, Imperial Stout, Red Ale, Bill's Bock, and others

TOURS: By request

BEER TO GO: None

FOOD: Midwestern "family restaurant" fare, featuring sandwiches, homestyle entrees, and Mexican selections. Monday night is Italian night.

AMENITIES: Free parking, private room available, limited bar

PUB HOURS: Monday–Thursday: 6:00 A.M. to 9:00 P.M.; Friday and Saturday: 6:00 A.M. to 10:00 P.M.; Sunday: 6:00 A.M. to 8:00 P.M.

LOUNGE HOURS: Daily 6:00 A.M. to 2:00 A.M.

NEARBY ATTRACTIONS: Keg Creek Brewing Company, biking and hiking on the Wabash Trace Nature Trail, Wabash Winery, Everly Brothers' Birthplace, Shenandoah Historical Museum

NOTES: The Depot Deli is a bit of a phoenix. In 1995 the renovated rail depot and restaurant burned to the ground, leaving only walls and a floor. With minimal insurance, Bill Hillman was sure that was the end of the line. But the next day, community residents showed up with shovels and wheelbarrows. They had a roof on in ten days, and the place was open for business in a month.

That sense of community is still strong at the Depot. The busy walls are a virtual museum of Shenandoah history, covered with photographs of the people and places that have shaped the town, including native celebrities like the Everly Brothers and jazz bassist Charlie Haden, as well as the many presidential candidates that roll through town seeking support. The restaurant is a gathering spot for locals, often hosting concerts or other community events in front of the building.

Brewing at the Depot began after the fire. Hillman had homebrewed in college, but he admits that his beer wasn't all that good. Although he hadn't brewed since, he went all-in with a ten-barrel extract system

The Depot Deli in Shenandoah, Iowa

when he decided to start brewing at the restaurant. He brews beers that are suited to the local market, which he says is still mostly light-lager focused. Still, he likes to mix things up. He keeps a wheat beer, a hoppy beer, and a stout always available, but the recipes and styles are constantly changing.

Hillman is a believer in green technologies. Before opening the restaurant he had a career in solar energy. He is a strong booster of the Green Plains Renewable Energy project in Shenandoah that converts algae into biofuel. All of the cooking grease from the restaurant is recycled into biodiesel.

Keg Creek Brewing Company

ADDRESS: 111 Sharp St. Glenwood, IA 51534

TELEPHONE: 712–520–9029

EMAIL: kegcreekbrewing@mediacombb.net

WEB SITE: www.kegcreekbrewing.com

MICHAEL'S PICK: Irish Red Ale: This is a red ale that drinks like a dark American lager. It's a beer meant for long sessions of pints and conversation. Bitterness is mild and supported by light, earthy hop flavors. Caramel malt adds a touch of sweetness and makes it just interesting enough that you'll want another, but it won't demand to be the center of attention.

TYPE: Brewery

DATE ESTABLISHED: 2012

OWNERS: Randall Romens, John Bueltel, Grant Hebel, and Art Renze

BREWMASTER: Grant Hebel

BREWING SYSTEM: Three-barrel Premier Stainless brewhouse

FLAGSHIP BEERS: Wabash Wheat, Breakdown Brown Ale, Keg Creek IPA, Sharp Street Stout

YEAR-ROUND BEERS: Wabash Wheat, Breakdown Brown Ale, Keg Creek IPA, Sharp Street Stout

SEASONAL BEERS: Irish Red Ale

SPECIAL RELEASES: Black IPA, Belgo-Scottish Bourbon Barrel Ale, German Pilsner

TOURS: By request
BEER TO GO: Growlers and kegs
FOOD: None
AMENITIES: Parking lot, taproom
PUB HOURS: Wednesday–Friday: 4:00 to 10:00 P.M.;
Saturday: noon to 10:00 P.M.
NEARBY ATTRACTIONS: Vine Street Cellars Winery, Mills County Museum, Loess Hills Scenic Byway, drag races at Mid-America Motorplex, biking and hiking on the Wabash Trace Nature Trail, forty minutes from downtown Omaha

NOTES: When you walk into the Keg Creek taproom, you feel at home. It's an intimate and quiet space that's meant for conversation over a couple of pints. One of the owners is likely behind the bar manning the taps. They'll take you on an impromptu tour if you ask. The Mug Club members occupying their regular seats are likely to refer to the place as "my bar." They can probably tell you as much about the brewery as the owners can.

Keg Creek started out as a homebrew club of the same name. When a local winery approached them about selling their beer, legalities forced them to decline. But a seed was planted. They did the research, applied for licenses, found a space, bought a small brewery, and were open in a matter of months. They have received a lot of support from the beer community in nearby Omaha. For many Glenwood locals, it's a place to have a couple of beers without having to deal with sticky floors and rowdy patrons.

Keg Creek beers are solidly midwestern. Aside from an occasional experiment, like the Belgo-Scottish Bourbon Barrel Ale, you're not likely to find anything too extreme. They are solidly made brews meant for drinking, not for oohing and aahing. In true regional style, balance is central, with malt having a slight edge over hops. These are beers that will appeal to a beginner's palate but shouldn't cause tried-and-true beer geeks to turn up their noses.

FERMENTERIES

GRANITE CITY FOOD AND BREWERY– CEDAR RAPIDS
Address: 4755 1st Ave. SE
Cedar Rapids, IA 52403
Telephone: 319–395–7500
Web site: http://www.gcfb.net/location/cedar-rapids

GRANITE CITY FOOD AND BREWERY–DAVENPORT
Address: 5270 Utica Ridge Rd.
Davenport, IA 52807
Telephone: 563–344–9700
Web site: http://www.gcfb.net/location/davenport

GRANITE CITY FOOD AND BREWERY– DES MOINES
Address: 12801 University Ave.
Clive, IA 50325
Telephone: 515–224–1300
Web site: http://www.gcfb.net/location/clive

GLOSSARY OF BEER TERMS

ABV Alcohol by volume. The measurement of the alcohol content in beer expressed as a percentage of the total volume.

ABW Alcohol by weight. The measurement of the alcohol content in beer expressed as a percentage of the total weight.

ADJUNCT Any non-enzymatic fermentable sugar. Adjuncts include syrups, refined sugars, and unmalted cereals such as flaked barley or corn grits.

AERATE To mix air into solution to provide oxygen for yeast. Brewers must aerate wort prior to fermentation for healthy yeast growth.

AEROBIC A process that takes place in the presence of oxygen. Yeast fermentation begins as an aerobic process and then changes to an anaerobic one.

ALE Typically refers to beers fermented with top-fermenting yeast strains and at higher temperatures, commonly between 65 and 75 degrees Fahrenheit. Fermentation at higher temperatures promotes the formation by yeast of various flavor and aromatic compounds, including esters and phenols, that give beer fruity and spicy flavors.

ALPHA ACIDS The chemical compounds in hops that, when isomerized by boiling, give bitterness to beer.

ANAEROBIC A process that takes place in the absence of oxygen or may require its absence. Yeast fermentation begins as an aerobic process and then changes to an anaerobic one.

AROMA The fragrance that emanates from beer. Beer aroma comes from malt, hop oils, and various by-products of fermentation.

ATTENUATION The degree of conversion of sugar to alcohol and carbon dioxide through fermentation. Beers with a low degree of attenuation will be full-bodied with higher levels of residual sugar. Higher attenuated beers will be drier and lighter-bodied.

BALANCE The proportion of malt flavor and sweetness to hop flavor and bitterness in beer.

BARREL A volume measurement of beer. A U.S. barrel equals thirty-one U.S. gallons. The most common keg size is a half-barrel that contains 15.5 U.S. gallons.

BEER A fermented beverage made from cereal grains.

BEER ENGINE A hand pump that pulls cask-conditioned beer up from the cask.

BOILING The stage of the brewing process in which wort is boiled to isomerize hop alpha acids, dissolve hop essential oils, and coagulate out proteins that cause haze in the finished beer.

BOTTLE-CONDITIONED Refers to beers that have been naturally carbonated by refermentation in the bottle. Bottle-conditioned beers will usually have a thin sediment of yeast at the bottom of the bottle that should usually be left behind when pouring.

BOTTOM-FERMENTING A reference to the tendency of yeast to flocculate at the bottom of the fermenter at the end of fermentation. Usually refers to lager yeasts.

BUDDING The asexual means of reproduction by yeast in which "daughter" cells split off from the original cell.

CARAMELIZATION A chemical degradation of sugar through heat in which the sugar is converted to caramel.

CASK-CONDITIONED Refers to beer that has been refermented in the keg, usually a firkin, to create natural carbonation. Cask-conditioned beers are typically poured by gravity or pulled to the faucet with a pump rather than being pushed with carbon dioxide. They are usually served at cellar temperature and have lower levels of carbonation than draft beer. Also called "real ale."

CELLAR TEMPERATURE A temperature between 48 and 55 degrees Fahrenheit, the correct serving temperature for most ales.

CONDITIONING A period of time during which beer is allowed to mature. Conditioning imparts natural carbonation, develops flavor, and clarifies the beer by allowing suspended yeast and proteins to drop out.

CONTRACT BREWING A situation in which beer is brewed by one brewery and marketed by another. Most often the receiving entity is a "beer-marketing company" that does not own a brewery. In some cases breweries will contract some brewing to others when their own capacity is not great enough to fill demand.

CRAFT BREWER The Brewers Association, a trade group representing the brewing industry, defines a craft brewer as one that is:

SMALL: Producing less than six million barrels of beer annually.

INDEPENDENT: Less than 25 percent ownership by an entity that is itself not a craft brewer.

TRADITIONAL: Has an all-malt flagship beer or at least 50 percent of its volume in beer that is made with only malt or uses adjuncts such as corn or rice only to enhance flavor.

DECOCTION MASHING A traditional German mashing process in which a portion of the grain is removed from the mash tun, boiled, and then returned to the main mash. It is used to insure maximum starch conversion and develop rich malt character. Modern, highly modified malts have made decoction mashing less necessary.

DEGREES PLATO An alternative scale to measure the amount of sugar in wort by determining the amount of refraction of light passing through it. A specific gravity of 1.040 equals approximately 10 degrees Plato.

DIACETYL A volatile compound produced by yeast during fermentation. While in small amounts it is a desirable component of some beer styles, in most beers and at higher concentrations it is generally considered a flaw. The flavor of diacetyl is commonly compared to butter or butterscotch.

DIASTATIC POWER The amount of diastatic enzyme potential that a malt contains. Diastatic enzymes break down complex starches into simpler sugars. It is through diastatic enzyme activity that brewers convert the starches in barley to fermentable sugars during the mash step of the brewing process.

DRY HOPPING Adding hops to fermenting or conditioning beer to increase hop flavor and aroma.

ENZYMES Protein-based catalysts that effect specific biochemical reactions. Diastatic enzymes break down complex starches into simpler sugars.

ESSENTIAL OILS The volatile compounds in hops that, when dissolved into beer, provide flavors and aromas.

ESTERS Aromatic compounds formed from alcohols by yeast action. Typically fruity.

FINAL GRAVITY (FG) A measurement of the remaining sugar content of beer following fermentation that is based on the density of the fluid.

FIRKIN An English quarter-barrel keg. A firkin contains nine imperial gallons. Commonly used for cask-conditioned beer.

FLOCCULATION The state of being clumped together. For yeast, the clumping and settling out of solution after fermentation has completed.

GELATINIZATION The process of rendering starches soluble in water by heat or a combination of heat and enzyme action. For making beer, the starches in grains must be gelatinized for the enzymatic conversion to fermentable sugars to occur.

GERMINATION The stage of plant growth during which the seed puts forth a sprout. Germination is the first step in the malting process.

GRAIN BILL The list of grains used in a beer recipe.

GRIST Milled grain prior to the mashing step of the brewing process.

GROWLER A large jar or jug, usually a half gallon, for taking home beer from a brewery or brewpub.

GRUIT A beer that is flavored and made bitter with a mixture of herbs and spices. Also refers to the spice mix itself.

HOP BACK A vessel filled with hops that acts as a filter, removing coagulated proteins from wort on the way to the chiller. As hot wort flows through the hop back, it dissolves aromatic essential oils from the hops.

HOPS The conelike flower of the perennial vine Humulus lupulus. Used in beer, hops provide bitterness, flavor, and aroma. They also have preservative properties that can help extend the shelf-life of beer.

INFUSION MASHING The process in which grains are soaked in water of a certain temperature for a certain period of time to activate enzymes that convert starches to sugars. In infusion mashing, the grains are not boiled. For a single infusion mash, all of the water is added at one time, and the grains are allowed to soak at a constant temperature. In a stepped-infusion mash, a portion of the water is held back and heated to a higher temperature. When added to the mash tun, it raises the temperature of the grains by carefully controlled degrees.

INTERNATIONAL BITTERING UNITS (IBU) A chemical measurement of the actual bitterness in beer. An IBU is defined as one milligram of isomerized alpha acid per liter of beer. May be different from perceived bitterness.

IPA India Pale Ale. A beer style developed in England in the eighteenth century for export to India. It is characterized by higher alcoholic strength and higher levels of hop bitterness, flavor, and aroma than standard pale ale. IPA has become one of the most popular styles among American craft-beer drinkers.

ISOMERIZATION A chemical process in which a compound is changed into another form with the same chemical composition but a different structure. Alpha acids in hops must be isomerized to impart bitterness in beer.

KREUSEN Foamy head of yeast, proteins, and hop resins that forms on beer during peak fermentation.

KREUSENING The practice of adding a small amount of fermenting wort to conditioning beer. The intent is to create natural carbonation through secondary fermentation.

LAGER Typically refers to beers that are fermented with bottom-fermenting yeast strains at cooler temperatures, commonly between 48 and 55 degrees Fahrenheit. Fermentation at colder temperatures inhibits the production by yeast of various flavor and aromatic compounds, resulting in beers with a crisp, clean flavor profile. Lagers are typically conditioned at temperatures near freezing for periods lasting from weeks to months.

LOVIBOND A unit of malt-color measurement based on

standardized colored solutions. Malt color is measured in degrees lovibond. Lower numbers are lighter-colored, and higher numbers are darker.

LUPULIN GLANDS Small, bright yellow nodes at the base of each hop petal that contain the alpha acids and essential oils utilized by brewers.

MAILLARD REACTION A browning reaction caused by external heat wherein a sugar and an amino acid form a complex. Maillard reactions occurring during the kilning stage of the malting process yield grains that impart amber to brown color and toasty, caramel flavor compounds called melanoidins in the finished beer.

MALT A cereal grain, usually barley, that has gone through the malting process to begin the breakdown of starches into simpler sugars. The malting process includes germination, drying, and kilning to various degrees of color and flavor intensity. Other malted grains commonly used in beer include wheat, oats, and rye.

MALT EXTRACT Wort that has been dehydrated into a concentrated powder or syrup form; it is rehydrated by dissolving into water during brewing.

MASHING The stage of the brewing process in which cereal grains are steeped in water to activate enzymes that break down the complex starches into simple sugars that are fermentable by yeast. Mashing occurs in a vessel called a mash tun.

MODIFICATION The degree to which the starches in grain are enzymatically degraded and simplified during the germination step of the malting process. Brewers desire highly modified malt to achieve maximum efficiency in the conversion of starches to sugar during the mash step of brewing. But modification must be stopped by heating before all of the starch has been degraded.

MOUTHFEEL A description of how beer feels in the mouth. Mouthfeel includes such things as body, texture, alcoholic warmth, and carbonation.

ORIGINAL GRAVITY (OG) A measurement of the sugar content of wort prior to fermentation based on the density of the fluid.

OXIDATION Exposure of beer to oxygen. May cause stale or cardboard flavors. In some stronger beers the effects of oxidation can be favorable, giving sherry-like character.

PHENOLS A class of aromatic compounds formed by yeast during fermentation. Typically spicy or smoky, but can also be medicinal or like Band-Aids. Phenols are often considered a flaw, but in some beers a bit of clove-like phenolic character is an essential part of the style.

PITCHING Adding yeast to wort.

RACKING Moving beer/wort from one brewing vessel to another.

RANDALL A hop-filled vessel that is placed in the draft line between the keg and the faucet to impart enhanced hop flavor and aroma.

REAL ALE Beer that has been refermented in the keg, usually a firkin, to create natural carbonation. Cask-conditioned beer is typically poured by gravity or pulled to the faucet with a pump rather than being pushed with carbon dioxide. They are usually served at cellar temperature and have lower levels of carbonation than draft beer. Also called "cask-conditioned."

REINHEITSGEBOT The Bavarian purity law of 1516 that permitted only three ingredients in the making of beer: barley malt, hops, and water.

SESSION BEER A beer, usually with a low alcohol content, that allows one to drink several in one sitting without becoming inebriated or full.

SPARGING The process of spraying spent grains with water at the end of the mash in order to rinse out any sugars that remain when the wort is drained from the mash tun.

SPECIFIC GRAVITY (SG) A measure of the malt-sugar concentration of wort or beer based on the density of the fluid. The specific gravity of water is 1.000 at 59 degrees Fahrenheit. Typical original gravities for beer fall between 1.035 and 1.060.

STANDARD REFERENCE METHOD (SRM) A method for measuring color in beer. Lower numbers represent lighter color, and higher numbers darker.

TOP-FERMENTING A reference to the tendency of yeast to flocculate at the top of the fermenter at the end of fermentation. Usually refers to ale yeasts.

TRUB The sediment at the bottom of a fermenter. Pronounced "Troob."

WORT Unfermented beer. Pronounced "Wert."

YEAST A class of unicellular fungi. During fermentation, yeast metabolizes sugar and converts it into alcohol, carbon dioxide, and an assortment of other aromatic and flavor compounds that include esters and phenols. Brewing yeasts fall into the family *Saccharomyces*. Top-fermenting ale yeasts are of the species *Saccharomyces cerevisiae*. Bottom-fermenting lager yeast is *Saccharomyces pastorianus*.

BIBLIOGRAPHY

Anfinson, John O. *River of History: A Historic Resources Study of the Mississippi National River and Recreation Area.* St. Paul: National Park Service and U.S. Army Corps of Engineers, 2003.

Cochran, Thomas C. *The Pabst Brewing Company: The History of an American Business.* New York: New York University Press, 1948.

DeWitte, Dave. "Underground Tunnels in Iowa City Brew Dreams of Historical Attraction." *Iowa City Gazette,* January 10, 2011; accessed September 2, 2013, http://thegazette.com/2011/01/10/underground-tunnels-in-iowa-city-brew-dreams-of-historical-attraction/.

Dutcher, John F. *The History of the Breweries of Galena, Illinois.* Fort Gratiot, Mich.: American Breweriana Association, n.d.

"Grain Belt Brewery." Placeography, Minnesota Historical Society, December 6, 2009; accessed September 2, 2013, http://www.placeography.org/index.php/Grain_Belt_Brewery%2C_1215%2C_1220_Marshall_Street_Northeast%2C_Minneapolis%2C_Minnesota.

"Grain Belt History." August Schell Brewing Company, accessed April 28, 2012, http://www.grainbelt.com/history.php.

"History of Craft Beer." Brewers Association, accessed April 28, 2012, http://www.brewersassociation.org/pages/about-us/history-of-craft-brewing.

Hoverson, Doug. *Land of Amber Waters: The History of Brewing in Minnesota.* Minneapolis: University of Minnesota Press, 2007.

Ingalls, Marlin R. *A Phase II Historic Architectural Evaluation of the Law Brewery Cave, Site 31-0008 Primary Roads Project STP-32-1(1)—2C-32 a.k.a. PIN 95-31080-1, Dubuque County, Iowa.* Iowa City: Highway Archeology Program of the University of Iowa, 1999.

Ingalls, Marlin R. Interview by the author, February 2012.

Jacobson, Don. "Hot Property: Grain Belt Terrace." *Minneapolis Star Tribune,* February 8, 2013; accessed January 9, 2014, http://www.startribune.com/housing/commercial/190366111.html.

"The Jazz Age: The American 1920s—Prohibition." Digital History, accessed April 28, 2012, http://www.digitalhistory.uh.edu/disp_textbook.cfm?smtID=2&psid=3383.

John, Tim. *The Miller Beer Barons: The Frederick J. Miller Family and Its Brewery.* Oregon, Wisc.: Badger Books Inc., 2005.

Kaas Wilson Architects. "Grain Belt Terrace." Accessed January 9, 2014, http://www.kaaswilson.com/project_1205/.

McGahan, A. M. "The Emergence of the National Brewing Oligopoly: Competition in the American Market, 1933–1958." *Business History Review* 65.2 (Summer 1991): 229–84.

Oliver, Garrett, ed. *The Oxford Companion to Beer.* New York: Oxford University Press, 2011.

Reilly, Mark. "Long-planned Grain Belt Terrace project begins in NE Minneapolis." *Minneapolis/St. Paul Business Journal,* November 14, 2013; accessed January 9, 2014, http://www.bizjournals.com/twincities/morning_roundup/2013/11/long-planned-grain-belt-terrace.html.

"Revolutions of 1848 in the German States," Wikipedia, accessed April 19, 2012, http://en.wikipedia.org/wiki/Revolutions_of_1848_in_the_German_states.

Ryan Companies U.S. Inc. "Grain Belt Brewhouse." Accessed April 28, 2012, http://www.ryancompanies.com/projects/grain-belt-brewhouse/.

Stack, Martin H. "A Concise History of America's Brewing Industry." EH.net, February 1, 2010, http://eh.net/encyclopedia/article/stack.brewing.industry.history.us.

Von Skal, Georg. *History of German Immigration in the United States and Successful German-Americans and Their Descendants.* New York: F. T. and J. C. Smiley, 1908.

Zimmerman, Mark. Interview by Teri Tenseth. "The Old Bub's Brewery Building." *Don't Cha Know.* KQAL, December 30, 2010; accessed October 28, 2013, https://www.prx.org/pieces/57379-the-old-bub-s-brewery-building.

INDEX OF BREWERIES BY LOCATION

INDEX

MICHAEL AGNEW writes about beer for the *Minneapolis Star Tribune, Beer Connoisseur,* and other publications. He is the author of the home-brew recipe book *Craft Beer for the Homebrewer.* He blogs at A Perfect Pint, www.aperfectpint.net.

HEARTLAND FOODWAYS

The University of Illinois Press
is a founding member of the
Association of American University Presses.

Designed by Kelly Gray
Composed in 8.5/11 Arnhem Pro
with Scala Sans Pro and Old Letterpress type display
by Kelly Gray
at the University of Illinois Press
Manufactured by Versa Press, Inc.
University of Illinois Press
1325 South Oak Street
Champaign, IL 61820–6903
www.press.uillinois.edu